CIVIL RIGHTS

Civil Rights and Beyond

African American and Latino/a Activism in the Twentieth-Century United States

EDITED BY BRIAN D. BEHNKEN

The University of Georgia Press
Athens

Athens, Georgia 30602
www.ugapress.org

Set in Minion Pro and Futura by Graphic Composition, Inc., Athens, GA
Printed and bound by Sheridan Books
The paper in this book meets the guidelines for permanence and durability of the Committee on Production Guidelines for Book Longevity of the Council on Library Resources.

Most University of Georgia Press titles are available from popular e-book vendors.

Printed in the United States of America
20 19 18 17 16 P 5 4 3 2 1

Library of Congress Control Number: 2016930747
ISBNs: 9780820349169 (hardcover : alk. paper) | 9780820349176 (paperback : alk. paper) | 9780820349152 (ebook)

CONTENTS

CIVIL RIGHTS AND BEYOND

CHAPTER 1

African American and Latino/a Activism(s) and Relations

An Introduction

BRIAN D. BEHNKEN

In June 1968 José "Cha-Cha" Jiménez founded the first chapter of the Young Lords Organization (YLO) in Chicago. One of the most vibrant Puerto Rican civil rights organizations in American history, the YLO quickly spread to New York City, Philadelphia, and other locales.[1] Jiménez, a confidant of Fred Hampton, the leader of the Chicago branch of the Black Panther Party (BPP), modeled the YLO in part on the Panthers. The Young Lords fought against police brutality and "slum" clearance programs and for medical service for the poor, among other things. The group also pioneered alliances with other activist groups of the period, including the BPP and the Chicano Brown Berets. These alliances, however, proved tentative and ultimately short lived. As Jiménez recalled, government infiltration and oppression caused people in these groups to start "turning on each other. . . . There were splits everywhere, splits between the student groups, the Black Panther Party, and a split between the Young Lords Party [in New York City] and the Young Lords in Chicago." Harassment by the Chicago police and the Federal Bureau of Investigation (FBI), and especially the murder of Panther leader Fred Hampton, decimated coalition building at this time.[2]

Jiménez and black-Latino/a coalition building reemerged only a few years later, however, in a rebuilt political alliance. Tapping into the activist networks of the late 1960s and early 1970s, Jiménez ran for a seat on the Chicago City Council and, though he lost, garnered significant support from Latinos and African Americans. A few years later he was still coalition building, this time uniting behind the 1983 mayoral candidacy of Harold Washington, who also built on the coalitions of the 1960s and 1970s. Latino/as and African Americans propelled Washington to victory.[3] Chicago, therefore, is a good example of how black and Latino/a activism and relations worked in the civil rights and post–civil rights era. While coalitions foundered in the early 1970s—unsurprising, given the general climate of the time and the harassment activist groups experienced—the networks built in the earlier period reformed to produce an activist politics that once again united blacks and browns in the 1980s and after.

Civil Rights and Beyond examines the dynamic relationships and activist moments shared by African Americans and Latino/as in the United States from the 1940s to the present day. While a growing body of scholarship has begun to elucidate the nature of black-Latino relations in the United States, this research has tended to focus on the civil rights era of the 1960s and 1970s and on distinct groups, primarily African Americans and Mexican Americans in the Southwest.[4] These studies have also been inclined to see the civil rights struggles and race relations of blacks and Mexican Americans, and Latinos more broadly, through the prism of concepts such as cooperation or conflict. This book shifts the focus to the activism(s) and race relations of blacks and a variety of Latino groups and pushes the time frame beyond the standard chronology of the civil rights era. Moreover, the authors in this book utilize activism as the guiding theme by which to view black-Latino civil rights efforts and relations. We thus move the analytical framework of black-brown scholarship away from conflict and cooperation, shift the historical discussion on black-Latino activism(s) beyond African Americans and Mexican Americans, and move beyond the paradigm of *the* civil rights movement.

Civil Rights and Beyond looks at a host of black and Latino/a community histories—each with different historical experiences and activisms—to explore group dynamics, differing racial geographies around the country, areas of coalition building and their successes and failures, the often divergent paths people followed in the pursuit of group power, an d the broader quests of these communities for civil rights and social justice. The book examines African American and Cuban American relations; interactions between blacks and Puerto Ricans; Mexican American and African American activisms; and more contemporary interactions between blacks and recent Latino immigrants in new gateway destinations, such as North Carolina. This wider focus allows the authors, and the book as a whole, to reframe our understanding of the "civil rights movement," pushing that concept beyond standard regional, temporal, and ethnoracial boundaries. We also explore the often collaborative, and simultaneously divergent, nature of black-Latino activism in the twentieth-century United States.

The book is framed around the concept of activism. In each chapter, activism is analyzed as a trope that illuminates the multiple ideas, concepts, strategies, and ideologies that African Americans and Latino/as have used to guide, organize, and direct civil rights and social justice struggles. Activism in this sense includes efforts aimed at political, economic, social, legal, and racial change, most often utilizing direct action tactics: boycotts, political campaigns, marches, pickets, and other forms of protest. This framing is, in part, what makes the book unique.

The broad geographical coverage of this volume is also important. To fully understand the historical experiences of Latino/a and African American people, it is important to examine those groups in a variety of places and spaces. There are a number of chapters that focus on black-Latino activism across the United States and several that explore specific—and largely unexamined—locales, such as Camden, New Jersey; Philadelphia, Pennsylvania; and Bakersfield, California. When the authors do explore more well-known areas, such as Los Angeles or Chicago, they do so in new ways. Our hope is not simply to cover new ground, but also to revise our understanding of established areas of scholarship.

Academic research on comparative civil rights and black-brown relations has exploded in the twenty-first century. A number of historians and social scientists have written important accounts of African American and Latino interactions. A growing body of literature on Mexican American and African American relations, especially in California and Texas, has offered important analysis of cross-racial civil rights efforts.[5] Explorations of black and Puerto Rican relations have complicated our understanding of the African American–Mexican American dynamic.[6] Scholarship on Cuban/Cuban American relations with African Americans remains in its infancy, although important work is emerging.[7] While a number of publications have focused on Latinos and blacks in recent years, most of those texts are sociological studies of the South that focus on the contemporary era.[8] There is, in short, a critical need to look at black-brown relations and civil rights activism in a geographically broad, but also a methodologically wide, fashion.

Many of the authors in this collection are at the forefront of this developing scholarship. My own work on African American and Mexican American relations in Texas during the civil rights era fits into this pattern. Jakobi Williams has done much to explain Black Power, Chicano Power, and Puerto Rican Power in Chicago. Gordon Mantler has detailed the broad history of interethnic relations during the antipoverty campaigns of the 1960s in his excellent book on the Poor People's Campaign. Chanelle Rose was one of the first scholars to discuss tensions between African American and Cuban/Cuban American people.[9] Other authors in this volume are part of a new and developing cohort of black-brown scholars. Alyssa Ribeiro, Oliver Rosales, and Laurie Lahey are all exploring black-Latino civil rights struggles in parts of the United States where few scholars have yet to tread.[10] Dan Berger, Hannah Gill, Mark Malisa, and Kevin Leonard are all established scholars with a host of publications to their credit who are venturing into the field of comparative race scholarship. In other words, the contributors in this book are many of the pioneers of the discipline.[11]

In the midst of this explosion in comparative or relational scholarship on African Americans and Latino/as, it seems that two distinct camps are developing in this literature. One camp, I would speculate, tends to see Latino/as and blacks as inherently conflicted, while the other side views the two groups as naturally cooperative. In my first edited collection, *The Struggle in Black and Brown*, I attempted to warn against this trend, writing that scholars who adhere to either viewpoint "make the mistake of seeing black-brown relations as a zero sum game, as either all good or all bad. . . . While cooperation and conflict existed . . . these terms were certainly not mutually exclusive and they unfortunately flatten a varied and exciting history."[12]

So preoccupied have scholars become with the issues of conflict and cooperation that Laura Pulido and Josh Kun subtitled their excellent collection on Los Angeles "Beyond Conflict and Coalition," and Rodney Hero and Robert Preuhs subtitled their book on black-Latino politics "Beyond Conflict or Cooperation."[13] Some scholars acknowledge conflict while simultaneously dismissing it. For instance, in her pathbreaking book on Puerto Rican and African American civil rights in New York City, Sonia Song-Ha Lee notes that coalitions between blacks and Puerto Ricans were "uneasy," but goes on to reprove other works that have "tended to see blacks and Latinos as either naturally unified as 'people of color' or irreconcilably at odds as two competing minorities."[14] John Márquez in his fine book *Black-Brown Solidarity* admits that tensions between these two communities existed, but he largely rejects conflict. Márquez seems to read the cooperation of the post–civil rights present back into the past, unmooring the broader history of African American and Mexican American relations from their earlier, and often more tense, Jim Crow origins.[15]

Certainly the criticisms of some of the works on black-brown relations make sense, and I encourage scholars to read these critiques carefully. They have merit because, indeed, some scholars seem to see relations between blacks and Latinos as too conflicted. For example, in his book *The Presumed Alliance*, legal scholar Nicolás Vaca describes black-brown relations negatively as "troubled," "conflicted," and "divided."[16] He also blames African Americans and Latinos for their inability to unite, noting that "the ostensible moral and philosophical bases for coalition politics have largely fallen apart because of competing self-interests."[17] For him, the concept of black-brown unity is largely a fiction—"the presumed ideological alliance" between blacks and browns.[18] Similarly, historian Neil Foley's book *Quest for Equality* has a provocative subtitle: "The Failed Promise of Black-Brown Solidarity." While Foley deals with some coalition building and offers important and well-conceived analysis of black-Latino relations, it remains unclear in his book where the "promise" of black-brown solidarity was made and why, if coalitions did exist, black-brown solidarity was such a failure.[19]

While it is important to understand black-Latino civil rights efforts and relations beyond the concept of conflict, it is equally important to remember that African Americans and Latino/as were not always united. It has become something of a cliché, for example, to think that a common experience of oppression has somehow given these groups a natural affinity and an innate sense of cooperation. That thinking is inaccurate. And many of the books on black-Latino civil rights efforts that focus on coalition building, from Mantler to Lee and a host of others—books that are frequently held up as models of the cooperative efforts of these groups—are far more nuanced than that, showing the building of coalitions but simultaneously the tenuousness and tepidness of some collaborative efforts. These issues have even begun to appear in published book reviews. For instance, in her review of Mantler's *Power to the Poor*, historian Shana Bernstein offers a critique of conflict while she praises cooperation. "In contrast to the many scholars and commentators who contend that identity politics undermined the possibility for cross-race class coalitions," Bernstein writes, Mantler "shows how they complemented each other. In this way, he rehabilitates the late 1960s and early 1970s as an era significant to both coalitional politics and community empowerment."[20] But Mantler's book does much more than that and should be held up not as a model that emphasizes coalition over conflict, but rather as an excellent account of coalition building *and* intergroup tension and conflict.

To argue that blacks and browns experienced only conflict or cooperation is, of course, simplistic and even silly. In many instances, a lack of cooperation did not mean that conflict existed. If blacks and Latinos had different ideas and differences of opinion—and they did—that does not necessarily imply that conflict existed. Similarly, we should strive to remember that conflict does not mean combat, and tension does not mean hostility. It is also the case that different communities and different civil rights struggles borrowed strategies, tactics, and ideas from one another, but did that mean they were united? Coalitions sometimes proved short lived, but often a variety of factors caused their demise, not just conflict. In my research on Texas I have found numerous examples in which African Americans and Mexican Americans chose not to join forces because of perceptions of ethnic and cultural difference or variances in leadership style or organizational strength, and not because of some inherent disdain or conflict between the two groups. In the South, historian Julie Weise has shown that in the early twentieth century black and Latino/a workers frequently bonded together in labor alliances, which were on occasion fragile but nevertheless real.[21] Gordon Mantler beautifully illustrates these complexities when he states that in the Poor People's Campaign blacks and Mexican Americans "constructed their poverties differently because of distinct historical trajectories. . . . moments of cooperation should be viewed for what they were: unique instances worthy of study but not to be held up automatically as the natural and desired outcome or goal of the era's black and brown activists."[22] Perhaps historian Mark Brilliant puts it best when he notes that in California's civil rights campaign—one of the most multiethnic civil rights movements to have occurred in the United States—most activism "took place in the large space between the poles of civil rights making that was either coalition based or conflict ridden. Through this wide terrain flowed the separate streams of California's civil rights history that never came together for long enough to form a river."[23] Brilliant demonstrates that California had no singular civil rights struggle and that distance, be it geographical, ideological, metaphorical, or otherwise, did not mean "conflict."

Many activist-participants in various civil rights struggles have themselves pointed to the complexity and the difficulties of black-Latino coalitions and activist moments. Cha-Cha Jiménez certainly underscored some of the tensions between African Americans and Puerto Ricans in Chicago, while also noting, of course, that the challenges of the period and local and federal repression were just as much the culprits in any black-brown conflict as long-standing community differences or racial acrimony. Mickey Melendez, a Young Lords activist in New York City, admitted that there were relatively few blacks who openly joined with the Young Lords. He also had to travel to Florida to witness the racism that African Americans experienced on a daily basis.[24]

Community differences or other disconnects certainly contributed to intergroup tensions. In Texas, Mexican American activist José Angel Gutiérrez noted that blacks and Mexican Americans did not really know each other, and before they could work together they had to learn about one another.[25] Perhaps nothing demonstrated this learning curve better than the planning sessions Martin Luther King Jr. called to organize the Poor People's Campaign. At one of the major gatherings during the campaign, the Minority Group Conference, the leadership of the black civil rights movement was confronted with a variety of ethnic leaders, many from Latino organizations, whom they did not know. Staffers had to frequently remind King about the difference between people of Mexican origin and Puerto Ricans. This lack of knowledge would seem to indicate an unfamiliarity that would not lead to comfortable coalitions.[26]

And yet, steep learning curves can be overcome, as they ultimately were in many ways during the Poor People's Campaign. Jiménez commented on the fragmentation of the Black Power and Puerto Rican Power activists, but of course for a coalition to fragment there had to be a coalition in the first place. Melendez's, Gutiérrez's, and King's lack of knowledge of each other's struggles did not ultimately impede them from working with members of other ethnic communities. Similarly, by looking at the black civil rights movement as something African Americans did, at the Mexican American civil rights struggle as solely populated by Mexican Americans, or at the Puerto Rican civil rights effort as something distinctly Puerto Rican, we miss the numerous examples of members of other ethnic communities joining these struggles.

While I believe that focusing on conflict or cooperation may yet be good tools for comparatively examining black-brown civil rights efforts, if we are to get beyond conflict and cooperation, focusing on activism may be one way to do it. By looking at activism we can begin to see the many connections, similarities, and examples of coalitions that clearly were a part of many, if not all, of the civil rights movements that took place during the twentieth century. At the same time, not all activisms worked, and the efforts of one group may have worked against the aims of another. Thus, activism may well help us also to understand some of the reasons for black-brown disunity and the limits of interethnic cooperation.

Part of the goal of *Civil Rights and Beyond* is to shed light on the past in order to understand the present. In numerous recent instances, black-Latino cooperation and strife have seemed to befuddle contemporary Americans, especially political pundits and the media. I want to stress here that there are what I would call "real" conflicts and those that are media created. Take, for instance, the self-described homeless advocate Ted Hayes. He was one of only a few African Americans to join the Minuteman Project in the mid-2000s. Hayes opposed the massive 2006 pro-immigration rallies and stated, "We are saying to them today, 'yes, civil rights, for the illegal aliens, yes, civil rights for them, but in Mexico.' . . . We are Americans and we are here to fight for freedom for our country and for the world!"[27] Jim Gilchrist, the co-founder of the Minutemen, called Hayes the "icon of the African American segment" of the Minuteman Project.[28] In an interview with the Southern Poverty Law Center, Hayes explained his support of the Minutemen: "This illegal invasion, in my opinion, is the greatest threat to American black citizens since chattel slavery itself." Hayes went on to compare African American history to Latino history, airing familiar sentiments of competitive victimization and declaring that "everything they did was based upon what we already laid down."[29] Hayes's viewpoints are not the norm for most black people. He is, nonetheless, a very public African American face who gives hope and comfort to the enemies of Latin American immigration. Hayes's numerous appearances on local television in places such as Los Angeles and Phoenix, in many cases with prominent local black leaders, has given credence to the viewpoint that some blacks dislike Latino immigrant activism. He is a visible example of black-Latino discord.

There are also conflicts that have been the result of gang violence. In California, for instance, Latino gangs have specifically targeted and killed African Americans in a campaign that political pundits and scholars have labeled "ethnic cleansing." Such murders seem to be the result of the increased numbers of Latino/as who have moved into formerly all-black areas such as Compton. Aside from the territorial issues, long-standing economic and political competition in LA has exacerbated racial tensions. And some black gangs have responded in kind, killing Latinos indiscriminately in retaliation for the deaths of African Americans.[30] The violence has also spread to other parts of the United States.[31]

These are real conflicts that paint a dire picture of black-Latino relations, but there are just as often media-created conflicts that do not jibe with reality. While Ted Hayes and gang violence are real, the attention given by the media to individuals like Hayes and events like gang killings overemphasize their importance and impact. Certainly there have been conflicts and violence between black and Latino gangs, and that violence has often led to intercommunity tension and animosity. But in some ways, the gang issues are media-created conflicts too. To my knowledge, no gang members described their efforts as "ethnic cleansing." Rather, political pundits and journalists applied that term. Perhaps that language does black-brown gang violence justice, but perhaps it is an incredibly hyperbolic and jaded way of envisioning tension—one that almost automatically evokes vile and negative images in the minds of many Americans.

Similarly, take the media's approach to the 2008 presidential primaries and election. Many political observers and pundits wondered aloud if Latinos would vote for a black candidate. "Will Latinos vote for Obama?," journalists asked.[32] They should probably have avoided such a loaded question because it contained inherent contradictions and factual inaccuracies that were clearly visible while the primaries, and later the election, were still ongoing. For instance, in the Democratic primary contests in Texas and California, which Senator Hillary Clinton won, Senator Barack Obama secured 32 percent and 43 percent of the Hispanic vote, respectively. Exit polling done in California showed that 55 percent of Latino voters had a favorable opinion of Obama. And the Pew Research Center found that 74 percent of Hispanics held favorable opinions of Obama during the primaries. Instead of waiting for these facts, the media instead jumped to the conclusion that Latinos would probably not vote for a black candidate.[33]

Given the outcome of the 2008 and 2012 presidential elections, in which Latino/as voted for Obama at the rate of 67 percent and 71 percent, respectively, the media's "will Latinos vote for Obama?" question seems stupid. Such a question and the assumptions it encapsulated thus were revealed as nothing more than media hype once the votes were tallied. And even a casual observer of Latino political leanings and black-Latino political coalitions could have seen the final results coming based on one simple fact: Obama's opponent. The only instance I could find in 2008 of a reporter speaking against this media-created conflict was from *Time* magazine's Gregory Rodriguez, who noted that when discussing perceptions of Latino/a voters' attitudes toward Obama, "the only problem with this new conventional wisdom is that it's wrong." The 2008 and 2012 presidential contests in the United States certainly proved this point.[34]

There have also been some similar issues in relation to cooperation in civil rights battles. Some journalists seem to view the civil rights era as a halcyon period when everyone got along and worked together, and only now in the present are divisions beginning to surface. In noting black-Latino tensions, for instance, *Time*'s Alex Prud'homme commented that "bitter divisions are breaking out between the nation's two largest minorities. Once solidly united in the drive for equality, blacks and Hispanics are now often at odds over such issues as jobs, immigration and political empowerment."[35] I would argue that what happened in the past is more important than how we choose to remember it, and there are two points to make regarding how this quotation is wrong. The first error is the claim that divisions are "breaking out." The second is the notion that the two communities were "once solidly united." These are two rather casual statements that fly in the face of a large and growing body of literature that has demonstrated just how difficult cooperation and coalition building could be in the period before the passage of the Civil Rights Act. With Jim Crow segregation the norm and the black and Latino communities frequently segregated from one another, collaboration often proved difficult and coalitions were hard to maintain. If anything, in the aftermath of the formal, legal dismantling of Jim Crow segregation there has been a rise of interethnic coalition building, not its erosion. Prud'homme's statement, then, is an example of media-created "knowledge" that posits conflict as new and unification as something that characterized the black-brown past, both of which are inaccurate.

Perhaps nothing demonstrates this media-created sense of black-brown conflict better than the killing of Trayvon Martin by George Zimmerman. The media had a difficult time understanding Zimmerman's ethnoracial heritage, first describing him as a white man, then as a Hispanic, then as a white Hispanic. By finally settling on Hispanic, the media seemed to suggest that Latinos kill African Americans, a sure sign of black-brown conflict. This media-created hype was even visible in African American news organizations. The *Grio*, for example, ran a piece titled "Trayvon Martin Case: Will It Deepen the Black vs. Brown Divide?"[36] Journalists and pundits wondered if Martin's murder had anything to do with Latinos' dislike of black people. Such thoughts struck many Latinos as not only odd, but patently untrue. While many Latino civic groups, such as the venerable League of United Latin American Citizens, were silent on the case, others, such as the National Council of La

Raza, got active. Latinos also formed new groups, including Latinos for Trayvon, which supported the prosecution of Zimmerman. The group, founded in New York City by community activists, college professors, and everyday people, in addition to calling for justice for Trayvon Martin wrote, "We also speak out because we are troubled by the specter that some in the media have chosen to focus on the irrelevant issue of Zimmerman being Latino because of his Peruvian mother. We are also very disturbed by what we perceive as an effort to divide Black and Latino communities by implying that Latinos have remained 'silent' on Trayvon's killing."[37]

Whether real or media created, the examples mentioned above point to our fundamental and superficial understanding of black-Latino relations in the present day. Not all community relations fall under the rubric of "civil rights," and we must be careful not to conflate civil rights struggles with everyday interactions, communications, and intergroup contacts. Those conflations matter because they help to set a tone concerning ethnic relations and interactions that many people absorb. *Civil Rights and Beyond* attempts to paint a different picture of black-Latino/a relations, one that moves us past dichotomies such as conflict and cooperation and binaries such as black and white. In taking up the topic of activism(s) the chapters in this volume seek to complicate our understanding of black-Latino civil rights organizing and race relations. To move beyond the rather static categories of conflict and collaboration, we utilize a thematic approach that systematically emphasizes the analytical and methodological category of activism. All of the chapters in this book examine black-Latino activism in new and important ways. We begin with examinations of African American and Mexican American historical experiences. From there, Cuban/Cuban American and African American activism and relations are explored. Several chapters examine black and Puerto Rican civil rights battles. Finally, the last few chapters focus on more recent African American and Latino/a activisms that are not exclusively connected to any specific ethnonational Latino/a community.

In the second chapter, "From the 'Next Best Thing to One of Us' to 'One of Us,'" Kevin Allen Leonard examines in a new light the political activism of city council members Edward Roybal and Gilbert Lindsay in Los Angeles. For many years scholars have understood Roybal as the quintessential coalition-building politician, someone who worked carefully to create a successful Mexican American and African American political machine. Such a rosy portrayal of Roybal, Leonard notes, downplays or omits serious African American criticism of Roybal. Many African Americans came to see Roybal as rather spineless in confronting racism, and they believed he did not represent their interests. When Roybal decided to run for Congress, a bitter protracted battle began, as Mexican Americans and African Americans struggled over who should replace Roybal. Gilbert Lindsay, Roybal's eventual successor, encountered fairly stiff resistance from Mexican American leaders who wanted to see another Mexican American in Roybal's seat. But Lindsay won and did a great deal to incorporate people of Mexican origin into his administration. Leonard concludes by noting that political activism and coalition building helped propel both Roybal and Lindsay into office, but that activism and those coalitions proved hard to maintain between elections.

In chapter 3, "Civil Rights 'beyond the Fields,'" Oliver Rosales explores Mexican American and African American civil rights activity in Bakersfield, California. While Bakersfield is primarily known as a site of farmworker labor activism, Rosales shows that protest activism was much more diverse and involved many issues unrelated to agriculture. In particular, an antiracist civic unity movement developed by white liberals served to bring Mexican Americans and African Americans into the city government with the goal of correcting civil rights inequities. This movement lasted for some time, and activists eventually went beyond government civic unity groups to push for a stronger vision of civil rights, demanding a more open local government, battling against housing discrimination, and developing a strong opposition to a local chapter of the racist White Citizens' Council.

While African Americans and Mexican Americans found common cause in southern California, that was not always the case in southern Florida. In the fourth chapter, "Beyond 1959," Chanelle Rose examines Cuban exiles and African Americans in Miami's black freedom struggle. She contends that the broader U.S. Cold War agenda not only created antagonisms between blacks and Cubans, but also it directly impacted the course of the black civil rights movement at the local level. With government aid programs that benefited Cubans, coupled with divisive urban renewal and economic injustices that hurt black people, many African Americans found themselves further marginalized and neglected. The civil rights movement in Miami, therefore, not only fought against Jim Crow, but also was forced to develop an activism that pushed back against a burgeoning—and largely conservative—Cuban elite bolstered by federal patronage.

In chapter 5, Mark Malisa shifts our perspective on African American–Cuban interactions and activisms by detailing the participation of Afro-Cubans in Malcolm X's Organization of Afro-American Unity (OAAU).

Aptly titled "Internationalizing Civil Rights," Malisa's chapter demonstrates that many Latin American immigrants, especially some black Cuban émigrés, found common cause with the OAAU as well as with the broader anti-apartheid movement. In particular, Carlos Moore ("Carlos the Cuban") and A. Peter Bailey, an activist who helped Malcolm X found the OAAU, were drawn to Malcolm X because of his internationalist, pan-Africanist vision. They joined protests against the assassination of Patrice Lumumba and opposed the apartheid South African government; while they generally supported the Cuban Revolution, they were also often critical of Fidel Castro. Malisa reminds us that African American–Cuban relations were not always discordant and, especially when Afro-Cubans were involved, could be quite collaborative.

In "'We Need to Unite with as Many People as Possible,'" the sixth chapter, Jakobi Williams sets his sights on Chicago and the coalition building of the Black Panther Party's Fred Hampton and the Young Lords Organization's José "Cha-Cha" Jiménez. These activist leaders developed the original Rainbow Coalition, an alliance that worked to oppose police brutality and urban renewal, among other things, and pushed for an inclusive politics that would give a voice to all underrepresented groups in the city. The BPP and YLO, which operated both independently and cooperatively, provide a useful example of how to develop a racial coalition in a major city with deep-seated residential segregation.

In chapter 7, "'A Common Citizenship of Freedom,'" Dan Berger picks up where Williams leaves off. Berger paints a vivid picture of police repression and activist coalition building in Chicago. Black Power and Puerto Rican Power groups developed a deeply analytical, discursive critique of U.S. imperialism via a Third World internationalism that worked at the local level to support multiethnic activism and against the development of the carceral state. Berger aims to understand the ideological, tactical, and strategic borrowings that occurred among black and Puerto Rican activists. In particular, he investigates how Black Power concepts underpinned Puerto Rican nationalism, and how the Puerto Rican independence movement then morphed into an anti-carceral struggle designed to free activists imprisoned for their political beliefs. Puerto Rican activists, borrowing from blacks, actively opposed mass incarceration, in some ways more successfully than the African Americans who taught them how to fight the system.

Laurie Lahey continues the focus on African American and Puerto Rican activism in chapter 8, "'Justice Now! ¡Justicia Ahora!'" She examines civil rights efforts in a relatively understudied area, Camden, New Jersey. Lahey's exploration is centered on the case of Rafael Rodriguez Gonzales, a Puerto Rican man brutally beaten by two white Camden police officers in 1971. He died three weeks later. Camden had no connection to a national civil rights organization: there was no chapter of the National Association for the Advancement of Colored People, no BPP or YLO. Instead, grassroots activists such as Charles "Poppy" Sharp, the brothers Joseph and Mario Rodriguez, and Gualberto "Gil" Medina joined forces to demand changes in how the police treated minority suspects. They organized a massive rally to convince Mayor Joseph Nardi to alter police procedures. The mayor's lackadaisical response ultimately led to a riot in Camden, a multiethnic upheaval that violently demanded the rights denied to local communities of color.

In the ninth chapter, "Forgotten Residents Fighting Back," Alyssa Ribeiro shifts the focus to African American and Puerto Rican activism in Philadelphia. Black and Puerto Rican residents of North Philadelphia's Ludlow neighborhood had for many years fought for their rights and for better neighborhood conditions, but in the late 1960s and early 1970s they became more confrontational when dealing with the city government. Members of both ethnic communities, especially a cadre of female activists, founded the Ludlow Community Association (LCA) to push for local recreation centers and housing. The LCA brought black and Puerto Rican residents together in a shared organization and around the rallying cry of community improvement and uplift. Ribeiro demonstrates that where a shared space and shared concerns are present, a shared and unified activism can easily develop.

In chapter 10, "The Next Struggle," Brian Behnken picks up this theme of shared grievances leading to a shared, united movement. He explores Latino/a and African American activism and coalition building in the late 1970s and 1980s. In particular, he highlights three instances of coalition development: the work of blacks and Latinos to come together in political organizations such as Jesse Jackson's National Rainbow Coalition, activism aimed at curbing police brutality, and African American–Latino efforts to stop the Ku Klux Klan in the 1980s. Behnken avers that the end of formal Jim Crow segregation facilitated the growth of coalitions. Thus, later struggles involved blacks and Latinos attempting to find ways, in many cases successfully, to join forces.

In chapter 11, "Rainbow Reformers," Gordon Mantler investigates Latino and black interactions and activism in the mayoral race of Chicago's Harold Washington. Mantler shows how African American and Latino/a activists and voters organized under the banner of a Rainbow Coalition, which had its roots in 1960s–1970s community organizing that had experienced considerable support and vibrancy. While Washington's victory suggested nascent black political strength, and many commentators saw it solely in this light, Mantler shows that it was the result of a broad, multiethnic political activism. Washington was supported by numerous Latino/a groups and made numerous Latino/a political appointments. While the relationships between blacks and Latino/as in the campaign and later in the administration were not always smooth, they represent a type of political activism that has become more common in the late twentieth and early twenty-first centuries.

Civil Rights and Beyond concludes with "Southern Solidarities," Hannah Gill's chapter. Gill highlights many of the important issues that have impacted black and Latino/a relations and activism in the twenty-first-century South, especially in North Carolina. The Tar Heel State has become one of the new immigrant gateways. When Latino/as challenged retrograde immigration policy reforms and local forms of racism, they fused the more recent history of anti-Latino/a racism with a broader African American history of southern forms of discrimination. Thus new Latino/a civil and human rights organizations such as the Association of Mexicans in North Carolina have joined with traditional African American groups like the NAACP to fight for immigrant rights and social justice. These groups have also formed several successful black-Latino/a coalitions. Leaders from immigrant communities of color and the African American community have articulated a vision of shared issues, they have exchanged strategies and tactics to advance their work, and they have built coalitions.

Taken together, the chapters in *Civil Rights and Beyond* expand our understanding of black-Latino activism and relations. This book builds on the new wave of studies on black-brown relations and also offers new interpretations of black-Latino interactions. By comparing African American activism to a variety of Latino/a groups' activism, and vice versa, this book breaks new scholarly ground on how different communities of color in different parts of the United States came together to fight similar battles for civil rights. By examining these communities through the lens of activism, by exploring new, understudied areas of cooperation, and by focusing on well-established areas of scholarship but viewing them in a new light, this book complicates our understanding of minority rights activism and the nature of Latino/a and African American relations. In the final analysis, we hope to draw attention to the multiplicity of civil rights histories as we offer close readings of activisms, coalitions, politics, and the occasional conflicts and tensions of these groups beyond the Southwest, beyond the 1960s and 1970s, and beyond the traditional view of civil rights struggles.

NOTES

1. In this introduction, I use the terms "black" and "African American" to denote people of African heritage. For persons of Latin American ancestry, I use "Latino," "Latino/a," and occasionally "Hispanic." Individuals from the Latino/a community are also differentiated by their ethnonational heritage: for people of Mexican origin, "Mexican American" and "Chicano/a"; for members of the Puerto Rican community, "Puerto Rican"; for members of the Cuban community, "Cuban" and "Cuban American." Additionally, I occasionally refer to Latino/as from various ethnonational communities as "brown" or as "browns," a common, albeit largely academic, way to describe them. For those of European heritage I use "white." The authors of the chapters in this book chose the ethnic/racial designations they preferred for African Americans, Latino/as, and European Americans.

2. "The Young Lords, Puerto Rican Liberation, and the Black Freedom Struggle," interview with José "Cha Cha" Jiménez, *OAH Magazine of History* 26, no. 1 (January 2012), http://maghis.oxfordjournals.org/content/26/1/61.full?X (accessed January 19, 2014). For a fuller history of these events, see Jakobi Williams, *From the Bullet to the Ballot: The Illinois Chapter of the Black Panther Party and Racial Coalition Politics in Chicago* (Chapel Hill: University of North Carolina Press, 2013).

3. See Gary Rivlin, *Fire on the Prairie: Harold Washington, Chicago Politics, and the Roots of the Obama Presidency* (Philadelphia: Temple University Press, 2013); and Mantler, this volume.

4. See, for example, Laura Pulido, *Black, Brown, Yellow, and Left: Radical Activism in Los Angeles* (Berkeley: University of California Press, 2006); Mark Brilliant, *The Color of America Has Changed: How Racial Diversity Shaped Civil Rights Reform in California, 1941–1978* (New York: Oxford University Press, 2010); Brian D. Behnken, *Fighting Their Own Battles: Mexican Americans, African Americans, and the Struggle for Civil Rights in Texas* (Chapel Hill: University of North Carolina Press, 2011); Lauren Araiza, *To March for Others: The Black Freedom Struggle and the United Farm Workers* (Philadelphia: University of Pennsylvania Press, 2013); Shana Bernstein, *Bridges of Reform: Interracial Civil Rights Activism in Twentieth-Century Los Angeles* (New York: Oxford University Press, 2011); Max Krochmal, "Labor, Civil Rights, and the Struggle for Democracy in Texas, 1935–1965" (PhD diss., Duke University, 2011).

5. See Brilliant, *The Color of America Has Changed*; Bernstein, *Bridges of Reform*; Behnken, *Fighting Their Own Battles*; John D. Márquez, *Black-Brown Solidarity: Racial Politics in the New Gulf South* (Austin: University of Texas Press, 2014).

6. See Sonia Song-Ha Lee, *Building a Latino Civil Rights Movement: Puerto Ricans,*

African Americans, and the Pursuit of Racial Justice in New York City (Chapel Hill: University of North Carolina Press, 2014).

7. See Chanelle N. Rose, *The Struggle for Black Freedom in Miami: Civil Rights and America's Tourist Paradise 1896–1968* (Baton Rouge: Louisiana State University Press, 2015); Ruth Reitan, *The Rise and Decline of an Alliance: Cuba and African American Leaders in the 1960s* (East Lansing: Michigan State University Press, 1999); Frank Andre Guridy, *Forging Diaspora: Afro-Cubans and African Americans in a World of Empire and Jim Crow* (Chapel Hill: University of North Carolina Press, 2010).

8. José María Mantero, *Latinos and the U.S. South* (Santa Barbara, Calif.: Praeger, 2008); Mary E. Odem and Elaine Lacy, eds., *Latino Immigrants and the Transformation of the U.S. South* (Athens: University of Georgia Press, 2009); Helen Marrow, *New Destination Dreaming: Immigration, Race, and Legal Status in the Rural American South* (Stanford, Calif.: Stanford University Press, 2011).

9. Behnken, *Fighting Their Own Battles*; Brian D. Behnken, ed., *The Struggle in Black and Brown: African American and Mexican American Relations during the Civil Rights Era* (Lincoln: University of Nebraska Press, 2012); Williams, *From the Bullet to the Ballot*; Gordon K. Mantler, *Power to the Poor: Black-Brown Coalition and the Fight for Economic Justice, 1960–1974* (Chapel Hill: University of North Carolina Press, 2013); Chanelle Nyree Rose, "Neither Southern nor Northern: Miami, Florida, and the Black Freedom Struggle in America's Tourist Paradise, 1896–1968" (PhD diss., University of Miami, 2007).

10. Oliver Rosales, "'Mississippi West': Race, Politics, and Civil Rights in California's Central Valley, 1947–1984" (PhD diss., University of California, Santa Barbara, 2012); Alyssa Ribeiro, "'The Battle for Harmony': Intergroup Relations between Blacks and Latinos in Philadelphia, 1950s to 1980s" (PhD diss., University of Pittsburgh, 2013); Laurie Lahey, "'The Grassy Battleground': Race, Religion, and Activism in Camden's 'Wide' Civil Rights Movement" (PhD diss., George Washington University, 2013).

11. Dan Berger, *Outlaws of America: The Weather Underground and the Politics of Solidarity* (Oakland, Calif.: AK Press, 2006); Dan Berger, ed., *The Hidden 1970s: Histories of Radicalism* (New Brunswick, N.J.: Rutgers University Press, 2010); Kevin Allen Leonard, *The Battle for Los Angeles: Racial Ideology and World War II* (Albuquerque: University of New Mexico Press, 2006); Hannah Gill, *The Latino Migration Experience in North Carolina: New Roots in the Old North State* (Chapel Hill, University of North Carolina Press, 2010); Mark Malisa, *Out of These Ashes: The Quest for Utopia in Critical Theory, Critical Pedagogy, and Ubuntu* (Saarbrücken, Germany: VDM, 2009); Mark Malisa, *(Anti)Narcissisms and (Anti)Capitalisms: Human Nature and Education in the Works of Mahatma Gandhi, Malcolm X, Nelson Mandela and Jurgen Habermas* (Boston: Sense, 2010).

12. Behnken, "Introduction," *Struggle in Black and Brown*, 6, 16.

13. Josh Kun and Laura Pulido, *Black and Brown in Los Angeles: Beyond Conflict and Coalition* (Los Angeles: University of California Press, 2014); Rodney E. Hero and

Robert R. Preuhs, *Black-Latino Relations in U.S. National Politics: Beyond Conflict or Cooperation* (New York: Cambridge University Press, 2013). These are both wonderful books (as are Lee's and Márquez's), and my discussion of them is not meant to impugn the authors' scholarship but rather to emphasize this volume's focus on moving past the binary of conflict and cooperation.

14. Lee, *Building a Latino Civil Rights Movement*, book description.

15. Márquez, *Black-Brown Solidarity*, chap. 1. Some scholars, such as Márquez and Mantler, see my work as part of the "conflict" camp. Mantler, for example, criticizes *Fighting Their Own Battles* and writes that scholars such as myself seem to think "rather simplistically, that little more than unvarnished racism is at play [in black-brown relations]." See Mantler, *Power to the Poor*, 7. I certainly deal with racism and the causes of tension, but I also detail the attempts of blacks and Mexican Americans to build coalitions in Texas. For examples, see Behnken, *Fighting Their Own Battles*, 10–11, 55–56, 58–60, 95–97, 100, 108, 118, 123, 124–26, 164, 174–75, 185–87, 124–26, 191, 200, 220–24, 236–37, and chap. 5.

16. Nicolás C. Vaca, *The Presumed Alliance: The Unspoken Conflict between Latinos and Blacks and What It Means for America* (New York: Rayo, 2004), 4, 8.

17. Ibid., 188.

18. Ibid., 2.

19. Neil Foley, *Quest for Equality: The Failed Promise of Black-Brown Solidarity* (Cambridge, Mass.: Harvard University Press, 2010).

20. See Shana Bernstein, review of Mantler, *Power to the Poor*, in *American Historical Review* 19, no. 1 (February 2014): 209–10.

21. Julie Weise, *Corazon de Dixie: Mexico and Mexicans in the U.S. South since 1910* (Chapel Hill: University of North Carolina Press, forthcoming).

22. Mantler, *Power to the Poor*, 7.

23. Brilliant, *The Color of America Has Changed*, 264.

24. Miguel "Mickey" Melendez, *We Took the Streets: Fighting for Latino Rights with the Young Lords* (New Brunswick, N.J.: Rutgers University Press, 2005), 49–53.

25. Behnken, *Fighting Their Own Battles*, 230.

26. Jorge Mariscal, "Cesar and Martin, March '68," in Behnken, *Struggle in Black and Brown*, 158–59.

27. "Ted Hayes and the Minutemen March through Los Angeles," *Metacafe*, http://www.metacafe.com/watch/475453/ted_hayes_and_the_minutemen_march_through_los_angeles_part_1/ (accessed January 12, 2012).

28. "The Federation for American Immigration Reform Creates Black Front Group," *Southern Poverty Law Center Intelligence Report* 123 (Fall 2006), http://www.splcenter.org/get-informed/intelligence-report/browse-all-issues/2006/fall/the-stalking-horses?page=0,0 (accessed January 12, 2012).

29. Ibid.

30. See "Race Relations: Browns vs. Blacks," *Time*, July 29, 1991; "The Rift," *Southern*

Poverty Law Center Intelligence Report 118 (Summer 2005); "L.A. Blackout," *Southern Poverty Law Center Intelligence Report* 124 (Winter 2006); "Roots of Latino/Black Anger," *Los Angeles Times*, January 7, 2007; "Gang Mayhem Grips LA," *Observer*, March 18, 2007; "Simple as Black vs. Brown," *Los Angeles CityBeat*, March 19, 2008; "The Rainbow Coalition Evaporates," *City Journal* 18, no. 1 (Winter 2008); "Fear of a Black-Brown Race War in Los Angeles," *Final Call*, April 3, 2008, http://www.finalcall.com/artman/publish/article_4526.shtml (accessed May 13, 2008).

31. "The Rift," *Southern Poverty Law Center Intelligence Report* 118 (Summer 2005); "Blacks, Latinos in the South: Cooperation or Confrontation?," *USA Today*, November 4, 2006.

32. See, for example, "Hispanics' Reluctance on Obama Highlights Black-Brown Divide," *New York Sun*, February 11, 2008; "The Black-Brown Divide," *Esquire*, May 21, 2008.

33. "Hispanics Give Clinton Crucial Win," Pew Hispanic Center, March 7, 2008, http://pewresearch.org/pubs/759/hispanics-give-clinton-crucial-wins (accessed March 13, 2008); "The Latino Vote Is Pro-Clinton, Not Anti-Obama," *Los Angeles Times*, February 7, 2008; "Can Obama Connect with Hispanic Voters?," *Houston Chronicle*, February 10, 2008; "Latinas Held Key to Clinton's Texas Victory," *Womens eNews*, March 4, 2008, http://www.womensenews.org/article.cfm?aid=3515 (accessed March 13, 2008).

34. Gregory Rodriguez, "The Black-Brown Divide: Hillary Clinton Has Done Well with Latino Voters in the Early-Primary States. Is That Because Her Opponent Is African American?," *Time*, January 26, 2008, http://content.time.com/time/magazine/article/0,9171,1707221,00.html (accessed February 27, 2014).

35. Alex Prud'homme, "Race Relations: Browns vs. Blacks," *Time*, July 29, 1991, http://content.time.com/time/magazine/article/0,9171,973496,00.html (accessed February 27, 2014).

36. James H. Burnett III, "Trayvon Martin Case: Will It Deepen the Black vs. Brown Divide?," *Grio*, April 3, 2012, http://thegrio.com/2012/04/03/trayvon-martin-case-will-it-deepen-the-black-vs-brown-divide (accessed May 14, 2015).

37. "Latinos for Trayvon Martin," *LatiNegr@s Project*, April 5, 2012, http://lati-negros.tumblr.com/post/20800664579/latinos-for-trayvon-martin (accessed February 28, 2014).

CHAPTER 2

From the "Next Best Thing to One of Us" to "One of Us"

Edward Roybal, Gilbert Lindsay, and Racial Politics in Los Angeles in the 1950s and 1960s

KEVIN ALLEN LEONARD

In his March 8, 1962, column, the *Los Angeles Sentinel*'s publisher, Leon H. Washington Jr., criticized Edward Roybal, the representative of the Ninth District on the Los Angeles City Council. Washington reported that he was "constantly getting complaints from citizens that they are not getting the action they believe they are entitled to from Councilman Edward Roybal." Washington mentioned flooding along South Central Avenue during recent rains and a group of residents who had been "trying for a long time to get an alley paved, but, despite their persistent pleas, no improvement has been made." He also noted the existence of a sinking sidewalk that "should have been corrected some time ago," when nearby residents first complained, adding, "there are many, many unimproved and even improved alleys in the Eastside area where weeds and rubble are accumulating without attention by the city's department of public works." Washington further held Roybal responsible for the fact that a poultry slaughterhouse at Vernon Avenue and Ascot Avenue had "been a health menace and a nuisance to the neighborhood" for nearly two years. Washington acknowledged that Roybal was in part responsible for the filing of a criminal complaint against the slaughterhouse operator, "but, up until now, the case has been marked by postponements and continuances." Washington indicated that residents of Roybal's district could see improvements being made in other parts of the city and had come to the conclusion that "the 9th District is apparently one of the most neglected areas in the entire metropolitan area." He insisted that "the voters in this area tell me they are tired of promises of improvements and corrections of these defects. What they are demanding now, is ACTION."[1]

Washington's criticism infuriated Roybal. In an angry response, Roybal pointed out that he was responsible for taking the owner of the poultry slaughterhouse to court and that "it is not my fault this case was continued." Roybal also explained that he was not responsible for unpaved alleys. Under city laws, residents had to agree to pay for improvements to alleys. Roybal noted that an insufficient number of residents were willing to sign petitions expressing their willingness to pay to pave the alleys.[2]

The council member and the newspaper publisher accused each other of acting on their racial prejudices. In dismissing Roybal's explanation for the conditions in the district, Washington insisted that Roybal had neglected the part of his district in which most African Americans lived. He criticized Roybal's "lax stand in bringing about betterment of these conditions, in a district which is populated heavily by Negro citizens." Although the record of what Roybal said or wrote to Washington is incomplete, the publisher's words suggest that Roybal had charged him with anti-Mexican bias. "And for Mr. Roybal's information," Washington retorted, "many of my best friends are Mexicans."[3]

Washington's criticism of Roybal and Roybal's angry response brought into public view some of the underlying tensions in the relationships between African Americans and Mexican Americans in Los Angeles in the 1950s and early 1960s. On the surface, there appeared to be few points of conflict between these communities. Many African Americans, Mexican Americans, and Asian Americans acknowledged that all of them experienced similar difficulties due to racial prejudice and discrimination, even though some believed that "the discrimination against persons of Mexican descent is not as extreme as that faced by Negroes and Orientals."[4] A number of scholars have noted the significance of multicultural coalitions to Roybal's election and later to Tom Bradley's election to the city council, and some have even suggested that these coalitions made Los Angeles unique among large U.S. cities.[5]

By carefully examining the relationship between Edward Roybal and his African American constituents, this chapter seeks to add complexity to narratives that emphasize the degree to which harmony prevailed in relationships between African Americans and Mexican Americans in midcentury Los Angeles. Even though many Los Angeles residents, and later scholars, believed that interracial cooperation should grow naturally out of shared experiences of racial discrimination, it is clear that the political needs and interests of African Americans and Mexican Americans differed. As a result, their political activism was not characterized by deep or lasting cooperative efforts. Drawing upon a careful reading of articles in African American newspapers and Roybal's records, I conclude that Roybal was a skillful politician and elected official who was able to use his office to meet many of the needs of his constituents and who courted leaders in the African American community, which helped him to retain his council seat in the 1951, 1953, 1957, and 1961 elections. However, these records also show that African Americans remained largely outside the on-the-ground coalitions that were forged in Boyle Heights, where most of the Ninth District's Jewish and Mexican Americans lived. Even after large numbers of Jews left Boyle Heights for westside or suburban areas, many retained ties to the neighborhood: relatives or friends remained, and many continued to operate businesses in the eastside district.

But with each council election, African Americans grew increasingly frustrated by the fact that the growing number of blacks in the city remained unrepresented by one of their own on the council. By 1958, some African Americans had begun to criticize Roybal. Most African Americans, however, waited until Roybal announced his candidacy for a seat in the U.S. House of Representatives before they began to express their dissatisfaction with him. Criticism of Roybal was not persistent or sustained, but it did coincide with efforts on the part of a number of activists and community leaders to encourage African Americans to unite behind a single African American candidate, who would then have the best chance of winning the election to succeed Roybal on the city council.

ROYBAL AND MULTICULTURAL LOS ANGELES

Since the 1990s scholars have acknowledged the significance of Edward Roybal's election to and service on the Los Angeles City Council. Roybal, the first individual of Mexican ancestry elected to the city council in the twentieth century, was a powerful political figure for more than forty years. In a 1992 doctoral dissertation and a 1997 article, political scientist Katherine Underwood demonstrated that Roybal's actions as a member of the city council were limited by the fact that he was always part of a liberal minority on the city's governing body. Despite this limitation, Roybal won reelection four times by demonstrating to his constituents that he could represent residents from all sections of the district. This political acumen allowed him to provide and take credit for some material benefits to his constituents.[6]

In his 2009 Whitsett Lecture at California State University, Northridge, which was published the following year in the *Southern California Quarterly*,

George J. Sánchez encouraged scholars of multiracial California to acknowledge more fully "the critical role of Edward Roybal in setting the standard for politicians who actively sought to represent a multiracial constituency."[7] Although most of Sánchez's lecture focused on Roybal's effort to protect the residents of Boyle Heights from freeway construction and redevelopment, he did observe that Roybal was the most vocal supporter on the city council of African Americans' efforts to desegregate the fire department. But Sánchez concluded, "In the transition from one coalition to another in the mid-1960s . . . the future of a progressive multiracialism was torn asunder and replaced with the lesser goal of simple racial representation."[8] Following Sánchez, historian Shana Bernstein offered the most detailed analysis of the emergence of interracial coalitions in Los Angeles during the 1940s and 1950s in her 2011 book, *Bridges of Reform*. Although Bernstein mentioned Roybal's electoral success in her introduction, Roybal is not central to her study. Instead, she painstakingly sifted through the records of groups such as the Community Service Organization (CSO) and the Jewish Community Relations Committee. While she referred occasionally to the National Association for the Advancement of Colored People (NAACP), her analysis suggests that African Americans were not intimately involved in the activities of the CSO, despite the fact that some African Americans were members.[9]

Although these scholars argue that interracial coalitions were responsible for Roybal's electoral success, my analysis of articles and editorials in African American weekly newspapers and Roybal's records leads me to conclude that African Americans in Los Angeles were not fully integrated into a multicultural electoral coalition in the late 1940s, 1950s, or early 1960s. Roybal's skillful responses to the needs and concerns of Mexican American, black, Jewish, and Anglo constituents discouraged members of these communities from challenging the incumbent when he sought reelection. African American activists instead worked to elect black candidates in the adjacent Eighth and Tenth Districts. The failure of these efforts led black activists to mobilize to make certain that an African American succeeded Roybal in the Ninth District, in which African Americans had come to outnumber Mexican Americans. Not only were African Americans largely absent from any sustained coalition that supported Roybal, but also some blacks questioned Roybal's commitment to progressive legislation, such as a fair employment practices ordinance.

The earliest analysts of Roybal's 1949 election acknowledged that the votes of African Americans were important to his victory. Beatrice W. Griffith, the author of *American Me*, reported that Roybal had courted African American voters by telling them, "Our skin is also brown—our battle is the same. Our victory cannot but be a victory for you, too."[10] Griffith also noted that the campaign of Roybal's opponent, Parley Parker Christensen, tried to rouse Anglo voters with telephone callers who asked, "We don't want Mexicans in the city hall, do we?" The caller would then point out that "Roybal is a Mexican." According to Griffith, "These telephone enthusiasts, however, made one big mistake. They forgot that Negroes have Anglo names also, and when the Negroes were called and given the 'Roybal is a Mexican' line, they blew up in wrath."[11] Underwood's examination of the election results showed that Roybal saw a dramatic increase in votes from the largely African American South Central Avenue district. In the primary election, Roybal received only 889 of the 3,404 votes cast in the thirty-three precincts of the South Central area. The incumbent, Christensen, received 1,009 votes; Julia Sheehan received 247 votes; Daniel Sullivan received 238 votes; and 1,021 voters did not mark their ballot in this contest.[12] In the general election, however, there was a decisive shift toward Roybal. In that contest, 1,991 voters in the thirty-three South Central precincts cast their votes for Roybal, and 1,317 voters cast their votes for Christensen.[13] Although African American voters did not constitute the margin of victory in the election, since Roybal outpolled Christensen by more than 8,000 votes overall, the vote totals show that a solid majority of African Americans were persuaded that Roybal would better represent them than would the incumbent.

A close examination of African American newspapers reveals that black support for Roybal in the 1949 election was seen as natural. The publishers of at least two weekly newspapers often wrote about African Americans and Mexican Americans as if these two groups faced nearly identical discrimination and should be allies. In a March 1948 article, for example, the *Sentinel* mentioned "the laudable fight to get better transportation means for the more than 55,000 Negro[es] and Mexicans" in Watts.[14] An April 1, 1948, article noted that "the Sentinel was informed that day after day Negroes and Mexicans, some of whom had many years' automotive experience," were not being considered for employment at a new Ford Motor Company factory in Maywood.[15] These papers clearly endorsed cooperative political activism.

Even though black journalists acknowledged the similarities between the experiences of African Americans and those of Mexican Americans, the publishers of two black newspapers did not mention Roybal's ethnicity when they urged their readers to support him. The *Los Angeles Tribune* simply listed all of the city council candidates it endorsed. This list included Roybal.[16] The author of the *California Eagle* editorial that endorsed Roybal in a runoff election described the candidate as "a true son of the District" and as "the real Voice of the working people." The editorialist predicted that Roybal would "be the exponent of a better life for the struggling masses whose children are suffering from malnutrition because parents are not able to pay the high prices for food." The author insisted that such issues were "the things Edward R. Roybal knows from the ground up. . . . And these are the things he will fight with all his heart and soul, to make the Ninth District as a part of Los Angeles, one of the beauty spots and home-like spots of this City of the Angels."[17] Neither of these newspapers suggested that Roybal's experiences as a Mexican American would make him a good representative for the African Americans who lived in the Ninth District. In contrast, the author of a three-sentence endorsement in the *Los Angeles Sentinel*, published before the primary election, did mention that Roybal was a Mexican American who "deserves the nod because of his long interest in minority group affairs."[18]

In the years following Roybal's election, the city's African American newspapers occasionally included articles that presented the council member's actions in a positive light. These articles gave Roybal credit for sponsoring ordinances that were supported by most African Americans, such as a fair employment practices measure, which Roybal co-sponsored in August 1949, but many people wanted him to do more than just co-sponsor legislation.[19] Both the *Los Angeles Tribune* and the *California Eagle* later gave Roybal credit for saving Pilgrim House, a settlement house providing services for the residents of Little Tokyo that was scheduled for demolition.[20] In September 1950, the author of an editorial in the *California Eagle* praised Roybal for opposing an ordinance that required all members of the Communist Party to register with law enforcement. The editorialist suggested that the Communist registration ordinance would have the effect of silencing African American proponents of racial equality. The author stated, "We are humbled by the performance of this man for we know at what cost he dared to cast his lot with the partially disenfranchised Negro people who have no voice in the City Council if that voice is not his own."[21] Three years later, Roybal lent his support to a campaign against the fire department's policy of assigning African American firefighters only to stations in black neighborhoods, promising, "I will do whatever I can to help bring to an end the segregation in the Fire Department."[22]

Despite the fact that African American newspapers infrequently published

Los Angeles City Council member Edward R. Roybal meets with the Reverend H. H. Collins in Los Angeles in 1953. Collins, the president of the Bakersfield branch of the National Association for the Advancement of Colored People, was elected to the Bakersfield City Council in April 1953. Roybal's willingness to meet with African American leaders earned him praise and electoral support from his black constituents. Los Angeles Daily News Collection, Library Special Collections, Charles E. Young Research Library, UCLA.

articles about Roybal's activities in his first two terms on the city council, both the *Tribune* and the *Sentinel* published glowing endorsements of Roybal's candidacy for the office of lieutenant governor in 1954. In February of that year, *Tribune* editor Almena Lomax deemed Roybal the "next best thing to one of us." Lomax noted "the special bond he has with us, being of a minority group" and declared that Roybal's nomination "serves to encourage the flagging trust of liberals and wistful minorities who are turned hopefully toward the Democratic party for the realization of their dreams and aspirations, for complete equity and the cherished anonymity of full citizenship."[23] In August 1954 the *Sentinel* published a column that praised Roybal's record on the city council. The column's author, William E. Pollard, wrote, "If there was ever a political candidate who is in accord with the aims and aspirations of our community, it is Edward R. Roybal, Democratic candidate for Lieutenant Governor." Pollard described Roybal as a "tireless champion of the people" and pointed out that the council member had led battles for public housing, rent control, and fair employment practices and against racial segregation, disease, and smog.[24] Although Roybal lost, the results of the election indicated that he was popular among African Americans. The *Eagle* reported that Roybal earned more votes in thirty Los Angeles precincts with large African American populations than any other candidate for statewide office.[25]

After Roybal failed in his bid for election as lieutenant governor, and with his district now including a greater number of African Americans as a result of redistricting in 1952, the *Sentinel* at least seemed to devote more attention to his actions. Most of the articles about Roybal in the *Sentinel* prior to 1962 depicted the council member positively and emphasized his effectiveness in providing municipal services to his constituents. Perhaps because he honored his promises to residents of his district, many black community leaders agreed to serve on a fifty-member reelection campaign committee in 1957. Even though Roybal was running unopposed, his campaign manager explained, "a number of his supporters decided to band together in order to urge the voters of his district to give him a big vote of confidence as a tribute to his outstanding record." The African Americans who joined this campaign committee included a California Assembly member, Augustus F. Hawkins; the *California Eagle*'s publisher, Loren Miller; the *Los Angeles Sentinel*'s publisher, Leon H. Washington Jr.; the *Los Angeles Tribune*'s editor, Almena Lomax; a dentist who was an NAACP leader, H. Claude Hudson; and a Women's Political Study Club past president, Betty Hill.[26] Roybal easily won reelection in 1957; the *Eagle* did not even publicize the election.

FROM POLITICAL COOPERATION TO CONFLICT: AFRICAN AMERICAN CRITICISM OF ROYBAL

While Roybal received praise from some African Americans, other black leaders began to express disappointment with him. A March 1955 article in the *Eagle* suggests that some African Americans believed that Roybal should have been more assertive in the pursuit of a fair employment practices ordinance.[27] His actions in 1955 seem to have played a significant role in Almena Lomax's decision to oppose Roybal's bid for a seat on the Los Angeles County Board of Supervisors in 1958—even though Lomax supported Roybal's reelection to the city council in 1957. Lomax offered a long explanation of her opposition to Roybal in 1958, describing him as "an over-ambitious, over-expedient, political fop, who will do anything to raise himself to higher office." She accused Roybal of being a "gutless wonder" who took orders from labor leaders who professed to support fair employment practices legislation but in reality "have done more to defeat FEPC in the City, County, and State than all the chambers of commerce of California, which are publicly committed against it." Lomax identified Roybal as "the man who refused to report FEP [*sic*] out of his committee in 1955 when we had the necessary grass roots support for it, and had Councilman [Charles] Navarro, with two Negroes running against him, where he would have to have voted for it."[28] Without explaining why he did not support Roybal's bid for a supervisor seat in 1958, Loren Miller, the publisher of the *Eagle*, endorsed Roybal's opponent, city council member Ernest Debs. The editorial that announced the endorsement stated that Debs's "consistent support of fair employment legislation, his skillful work in securing a non-discriminatory clause in the Bunker Hill re-development project, and his devotion to progressive causes stamp him as the man we need on the Board of Supervisors."[29]

Others continued to look for African American politicians to serve on the city council. Black candidates had begun seeking seats on the Los Angeles City Council as early as the 1930s. As the city's African American population grew dramatically in the 1940s and 1950s, many African Americans anticipated the election of a member of their community. Some people may even have believed that the redrawing of district boundaries, which the council was required to do every four years, would increase the likelihood of an African American's election to the city council. However, redistricting proposals in the 1950s and in 1960 increased the frustration of African Americans who believed that representation on the city council would lead to laws against racial discrimination and to improved conditions in their neighborhoods. Miller pointed out that, under the 1952 plan, "the Seventh District will stretch from Alameda Street on the east to Baldwin Hills on the West and will include a large number of voters with widely different interests." Miller insisted that "no councilman can properly represent people with such conflicting interests." The *Eagle* publisher attacked the redistricting plan as part of the "same old scheme of keeping the Negro vote chopped up in various districts in order to forestall the possibility of electing a Negro councilman."[30] The author of a related editorial in the *Eagle* insisted that "somebody is going to be neglected and our experience tells us that the victims of lack of representation are far more apt to be Negro voters than the more powerful and articulate white voters." The editorialist concluded, "We've been without direct representation in the City Council long enough."[31]

African American leaders did not simply criticize the city council for its redistricting schemes. They also urged members of their community to work together in coordinated and unified campaigns in order to increase the chance of electoral success. In the January 20, 1955, issue of the *Eagle*, for example, Miller expressed the hope that two of the three African Americans who had announced their intent to seek election to the Tenth District council seat would withdraw, leaving one candidate behind whom the entire black community could unite.[32] After the primary election in 1955, the author of an editorial in the *Eagle*, insisting that "the need for Negro representation in the City Council is as great as ever," criticized "haphazard campaigns" and "candidacies of unknowns who lack the experience and the funds to put their case before the people." This editorialist cautioned African Americans against entering contests "where the incumbent has a good record of his own; race is an important factor with the Negro voter but it is not the only consideration."[33] This editorial seems to indicate that some black leaders understood that it would be very difficult for an African American candidate to defeat an incumbent such as Roybal.

Five years later, as the city council considered another redistricting plan, Roybal expressed his support for a plan to assure the election of an African American to the council. Roybal proposed adding two additional districts—one in the San Fernando Valley and the other in the southern part of the city—to the current fifteen. He suggested that the boundaries of the second new district should be drawn to assure that the council member from that district would "be a Negro—man or woman—to adequately represent the Negro community."[34] Even though the council rejected Roybal's proposal, the author of an editorial in the *Eagle* praised Roybal for having "the courage to speak out against" the successful redistricting proposal, which continued "to divide the Negro population and keep a Negro out of [the] City Council."[35] In endorsing Roybal's reelection bid in 1961, the author of another editorial in the *Eagle* reminded readers that "Mr. Roybal has waged a long fight in [the] City Council to protect his constituents and to extend their rights. He was the only member of the Council to protest against this year's gerrymander which deprives Negroes of a seat in the Council. No person in California has done more than he to further civil rights. His defeat would be a calamity."[36]

After the Tenth District's council member, Charles Navarro, was elected city controller and resigned his council seat, Roybal spoke in favor of the appointment of an African American to the vacant position. Roybal told the *Eagle* that three African American applicants—J. Edward Atkinson, Tom Bradley, and George Thomas—"are highly qualified. In fact, their qualifications are better than those of any of the white applicants." Roybal added, "Personally, I feel a Negro should be considered seriously. There is a definite need for one in the Council, and our city would suffer in human relations with the Negro community if a Negro was bypassed."[37] In the end, however, a majority of the council members voted to appoint Joe E. Hollingsworth, a white Baldwin Halls real estate agent.[38] Hollingsworth's appointment prompted angry African Americans to take action. Shortly after the council's decision, community leaders began exploring the possibility of recalling Hollingsworth.[39] The author of an editorial in the *Eagle* argued that "Negroes constitute about 14 per cent of the city's population and on that basis should be able to elect Two Negroes to the Council. They can't do so because they are gerrymandered in a number of districts." The editorialist insisted that "Los Angeles, and the people who put the unsavory Hollingsworth deal across, should be thoroughly ashamed."[40]

In the April 4, 1961, primary election, Edward Roybal was elected for the last time to the seat on the city council he had occupied since 1949.[41] Roybal's outspoken support for African American representation on the city council and his continued efforts to address the concerns of his constituents earned him accolades in his final years on the council. Black activists continued to praise Roybal's service on the city council, and many enthusiastically supported his campaign for the U.S. House.[42] Some of these activists undoubtedly recognized that an African American had a good chance to win election to Roybal's council seat if he were elected to Congress.

Even before the November 1962 election, in which Roybal won a seat in the

House of Representatives, black community leaders began encouraging African Americans to unite behind a single candidate in the Ninth District. In his August 16, 1962, column in the *Sentinel*, William E. Pollard pointed out, "in November of this year, the odds are that Councilman Roybal will be Congressman Roybal." Pollard expressed the opinion that "a 'broad' cross-section of citizens and organizations should be meeting weekly to jell, if possible, a united front behind a single candidate, in order for Los Angeles to have its first Negro city councilman." Pollard insisted that "a Negro can be elected in the 9th Councilmanic Dist. when we recognize that we cannot afford, at this time, the luxury of multiple candidates in a district with a low voter registration."[43]

Shortly after Roybal won election to Congress, a number of Mexican Americans expressed their interest in filling the council seat he would soon vacate. The November 29, 1962, issue of the *Eastside Sun* reported that Felix Ontiveros had filed as a candidate to replace Roybal on the city council. Ontiveros was a business owner who had served on the Los Angeles Commission on Human Relations.[44] Four nights later, leaders of the Mexican American community gathered at a meeting called by Juan Acevedo, the vice president of the Mexican American Political Association. According to the *Eastside Sun*'s publisher, Joseph Eli Kovner, a liberal Jewish activist with strong ties to the Mexican American community, the purpose of this meeting was "to select a candidate for the 9th Councilmanic District to replace Congressman-elect Edward R. Roybal." Kovner reported that Roybal had expressed his opposition to a "mock election" designed to select a candidate. But Roybal's opposition did not prevent the vote, which Kovner dismissed as "nothing but a popularity contest." Richard Tafoya, Roybal's cousin and an aide to Mayor Samuel Yorty, won this mock election. Josefa Sánchez, a leader in the Mexican American Political Association, finished second. Ontiveros and the other candidates present received only a few votes each. Kovner expressed his fear that the vote at the meeting would perpetuate divisions among liberals in Boyle Heights. He concluded his column by stating, "I myself will never forgive myself if the great, progressive liberalism of Ed Roybal will be shot to blazes by the election of a candidate who does not share his views. Every citizen of the ninth district will be the loser. Let us have care!"[45]

GILBERT LINDSAY AND BLACK-BROWN POLITICS

Shortly after Roybal's election to Congress, it became clear that both African Americans and Mexican Americans saw the contest to fill the Ninth District's council seat as a struggle between the two communities. Sánchez, Ontiveros, and other Mexican American candidates refused to withdraw, and Mexican American political activists did not unify behind a single candidate. African Americans had hoped Roybal's departure would open his seat for a black politician, and they quickly united behind the candidacy of Gilbert Lindsay, who had served for a decade as a deputy to Los Angeles County supervisor Kenneth Hahn. Nearly every issue of each newspaper in November and December 1962 and January 1963 featured articles about Lindsay. On November 15, 1962, for example, the *Sentinel* published an article that indicated that Lindsay was likely to end up occupying the Ninth District seat.[46] The following week the *Sentinel* reported that most African American community leaders had endorsed Lindsay's candidacy.[47] An editorial in the *Eagle* and a statement by Lindsay both pointed out that African Americans outnumbered Mexican Americans in the district.[48] Lindsay portrayed himself as the representative of the African American community, but he also insisted that he would not neglect the concerns of the district's Mexican American, Asian American, and Anglo American residents, pointing out that "the majority of registered voters in the 9th are Negroes. And the majority of residents of the 9th are Negroes, contrary to what has become a popular misconception. However, I am not totally dependent upon the Negro vote." Lindsay elaborated, stating that "many of the top leaders in the Mexican community are supporting me. They consider me the best qualified from experience in municipal government and political service."[49] In a statement published later in the *Eastside Sun*, Lindsay further promised that his office "will include members of all racial groups in the area composing the 9th Councilmanic District. . . . I state categorically that I will select a Mexican-American as my field secretary."[50]

By December 1962, the *Sentinel*'s Washington began treating Lindsay as if he were already the council member for the Ninth District.[51] Articles in both the *Eagle* and the *Sentinel* also hinted at potential divisions between the African American and Mexican American communities. The publishers of both newspapers paid little attention to Mexican American candidates as they continued to urge African Americans to unite behind Lindsay. The author of one editorial in the *Sentinel*, for example, declared that "Lindsay must put on a hard-hitting and intensive campaign for solidarity in our community, because the Mexican-Americans might get together before the spring elections. To help Lindsay win, we must unite our efforts in the ninth."[52]

The city council's late January 1963 appointment of Gilbert Lindsay to fill the seat left vacant by Roybal's election to the U.S. House surprised many

African Americans, Mexican Americans, and Anglos,[53] but black activists expressed tremendous satisfaction with Lindsay's appointment. The author of an editorial in the *Sentinel*, for example, declared, "Lindsay's appointment represents the most important milestone of progress for Negroes in Los Angeles in two decades and the most significant achievement in this century in our constant fight for fair representation in city government." Even as this editorial celebrated the significance of Lindsay's appointment, it also looked toward the coming election. The author encouraged *Sentinel* readers to help "keep for our community this council post when election time rolls around . . . by giving him your loyal support." The editorialist cast Lindsay's election campaign as a struggle between African Americans and Mexican Americans. "Because he will obviously have some opposition from the Mexican community," the author wrote, "he will need our unstinted support to keep his seat after election day."[54] For his part, Lindsay continued to say that he would not simply serve his African American constituents. Instead, he insisted, his job as a council member was to represent "people of all colors and faiths in this city's Ninth District."[55]

African Americans were pleasantly surprised by the council's vote to appoint Lindsay, but Mexican American activists were enraged. Roybal's cousin and would-be successor, Richard Tafoya, invoked Roybal in criticizing the council's action, decrying the appointment as "the most undemocratic thing that has ever happened in the history of the City of Los Angeles. . . . Powerful interests are smothering out the voice of the people. This is in direct contradiction of the wishes of Congressman Edward Roybal who asked that no appointment be made." Tafoya insisted that "the people of the district are entitled to have a Councilman elected by free choice rather than being shackled by the dictates of the City Council."[56] Josefa Sánchez, who also sought to succeed Roybal, argued that the council members who appointed Lindsay and Mayor Sam Yorty, who supported Tafoya, had put their political interests ahead of the needs of Ninth District residents. Sánchez insisted that the appointment of Lindsay was another example of politicians' acting as if the Ninth District were "the expendable district." Sánchez accused politicians in City Hall of thinking that because the district was "populated largely by Negro[es] and Mexican Americans," "the people are too poor and too ignorant . . . to protest when they are used as pawns in the various political and power schemes."[57]

Less than two weeks after his appointment to the council, Lindsay honored his promise to appoint a Mexican American chief deputy. He selected

Felix Ontiveros, who had been one of the first people to announce his candidacy for the Ninth District's council seat. In announcing the appointment, the *Sentinel* identified Ontiveros as a founder and former president of the Mexican Chamber of Commerce, the president of the Arrow Fence Company, and a member of the Los Angeles County Commission on Human Relations and the Council on Mexican-American Affairs. Meanwhile, Lindsay reinforced his message that he would represent all residents of the district. He declared, "Mr. Ontiveros' door, as well as mine, will be open to the citizens of the Ninth District, irrespective of social, or financial status, or of race, nationality or creed."[58] Although few Mexican American community leaders publicly endorsed Lindsay, Ontiveros helped to make Mexican Americans more visible at Lindsay's campaign events.[59]

In the weeks between Lindsay's appointment of Ontiveros and the April 2 primary election, African Americans continued to unite behind Lindsay.[60] The author of an editorial published in the *Eagle* five days before the primary declared, "There is no sound reason why Mr. Lindsay should be replaced. He has had long experience in government and his voice will be invaluable in [the] City Council. He holds a job he deserves and he should be retained by the voters of his district, both for their own good and for that of the city at large."[61] Both the *Sentinel* and the *Eastside Sun* published articles that emphasized Lindsay's effectiveness as a council member.[62] While African Americans united behind Lindsay, Mexican Americans remained divided. Three Mexican American candidates—Tafoya, Sánchez, and Tony Serrato—appeared on the primary ballot. In the campaign, Sánchez continued to attack both Lindsay and Tafoya, suggesting that they would owe allegiance not to the people of the Ninth District but to their political patrons. Sánchez frequently invoked Roybal's name and indicated that she would follow in Roybal's progressive footsteps. She solicited African American votes by promising to "give my support to the election of a Negro councilman in the 8th and 10th Council districts."[63]

After the April 2 primary, in which Lindsay led all candidates but fell short of a majority, both Leon Washington and Loren Miller urged their readers to continue to work for Lindsay's election in the May 28 runoff. In his April 4, 1963, column, for example, Washington insisted that "now is the time for all loyal Negroes to rally to the support of Lindsay."[64] Some African American leaders feared that Roybal would campaign for Tafoya and prevent Lindsay's election. In an effort to discourage the U.S. representative from exerting influence in the election, the Interdenominational Ministers' Alliance sent Roybal a telegram urging him not to campaign against Lindsay. The telegram warned that "your future support from Negro constituents will certainly be affected by any action you take, and we sincerely urge you to continue to represent us well in Congress and let the people decide the councilmanic issue without your personal intervention."[65] Despite this warning, Roybal endorsed Tafoya, stating that Tafoya's election "will bring about equal minority group representation, maintaining the council seat it took our community a century to acquire." In an almost classic depiction of ethnic political competition, Roybal insisted, "in keeping with the tradition and culture of Los Angeles, a qualified Spanish-speaking person must serve on this legislative body."[66]

In the runoff election, 16,440 voters cast their ballots for Lindsay, and 13,109 cast their ballots for Tafoya.[67] Eighty percent of voters in Boyle Heights and 65 percent of downtown voters supported Tafoya, but 85 percent of the mostly black voters in the South Central Avenue district supported Lindsay.[68] African Americans voted overwhelmingly for Lindsay because they wanted to be represented by a black official. Black voters could also justify their support for Lindsay by pointing to Roybal. Since Roybal had represented African Americans in the Ninth District for more than thirteen years, black voters argued that Lindsay could adequately represent the interests and concerns of his Mexican American constituents, particularly since he had already appointed Felix Ontiveros as his chief deputy. It is also important to recognize that some Mexican Americans voted for Lindsay. After the runoff election, Kovner offered the opinion that Lindsay's appointment of Ontiveros "contributed a great deal to the Lindsay victory."[69] Not all of the Mexican Americans who supported Lindsay, however, did so simply because he had appointed Ontiveros. John Serrato, the brother of Tony Serrato, one of Lindsay's opponents in the April primary, endorsed Lindsay because Lindsay "has shown he has the welfare of the people at heart." Serrato also indicated that Lindsay would be independent; he would not have to check with the mayor before making a decision.[70]

CONCLUSION

Scholars familiar with the latter years of Lindsay's twenty-seven-year tenure on the city council might be tempted to dismiss his election as a symbol of retreat from Edward Roybal's progressivism. However, Lindsay's performance in his early years on the council bears a remarkable resemblance to Roybal's performance in 1949 and the early 1950s, before some African Americans began questioning Roybal's commitment to antidiscrimination legislation.

Lindsay stood up for the rights of his constituents against the more powerful conservative interests in the city. In the fall of 1963, for example, he opposed the merger of the city and county health departments, calling it a "'give-away' of one of the country's best health agencies."[71] Lindsay and Billy Mills, the council member for the Eighth District, introduced a motion to "revoke registration certificates of all real estate brokers who engage in discrimination in the sale, leasing or rental of real property."[72] In May 1964, Lindsay argued for a pay increase for municipal employees and moved to address the concerns of African American and Mexican American homeowners whose houses had been condemned by city officials.[73] His actions also helped to improve wages for the lowest-paid city employees: elevator operators, janitors, and security guards.[74] Even before Lindsay had proved that he would work to protect the interests of his working-class constituents, he had earned the respect of a number of prominent Roybal supporters. Some people recognized in Lindsay some of the qualities they admired in Roybal. After Lindsay won the runoff election, for example, Joseph Eli Kovner declared that "Councilman Lindsay will serve the Ninth District well. He is a man of courage, determination and above all . . . he believes in ethical conduct."[75]

Between 1949 and 1963, then, black and Mexican American activists in Los Angeles occasionally worked together to gain and maintain minority group representation on the city council. They also cooperated in their efforts to improve city services and conditions in the Ninth District. However, neither Mexican American nor African American activists worked with Councilman Edward Roybal to establish a coalition that would persist between elections and exert sustained pressure on city officials. The conflict that surfaced when Roybal ran for and was elected to a seat in Congress reflected the divergent interests of black and Mexican American activists. On the one hand, many African American community leaders supported Roybal in all of his electoral campaigns, but most of these activists also grew to believe that the large number of black voters in the Ninth District should be represented by an African American. On the other hand, Mexican American activists feared that the needs and interests of their community would be neglected if an African American succeeded Roybal on the council.

It can be tempting for historians and other scholars to emphasize discontinuity. For example, to some historians, Roybal's departure from the city council might seem to mark the end of a golden age of interracial cooperation. Such an interpretation might suggest that the political conflicts that erupted over War on Poverty programs would not have occurred if Roybal had not sought a seat in Congress.[76] My interpretation, by contrast, emphasizes both continuity and the complexity of black-brown relations. I have argued that the words and actions of Mexican American and black political activists in Los Angeles in the 1950s and early 1960s indicate that these years should not be viewed as a golden age of interracial cooperation. Knowledge of the conflicts over representation on the city council in these years can lead to a more complete comprehension of the conflicts during the War on Poverty. Even though both African American and Mexican American activists, including Edward Roybal, insisted that they recognized that members of both communities experienced racial discrimination, activists from both communities were unable to overcome their differences and forge a united course of action that would have satisfied the needs and interests of both Mexican Americans and African Americans.

NOTES

1. Leon H. Washington Jr., "Wash's Wash," *Los Angeles Sentinel*, March 8, 1962, A6.

2. Leon H. Washington Jr., "Wash's Wash," *Los Angeles Sentinel*, March 15, 1962, A6.

3. Ibid.

4. "The Right to a Decent Home," *Los Angeles Sentinel*, September 15, 1949, A7. Between 1949, when Roybal was elected to the city council, and 1963, when Gilbert W. Lindsay was elected to fill the seat long occupied by Roybal, the *Sentinel* published more than thirty articles, editorials, and columns that emphasized the similarities between the discrimination faced by African Americans and by Mexican Americans. See, for example, "Faithless Public Officials," October 20, 1959, A8; "Neither Slums nor Ghettos," December 29, 1949, A8; "An Ounce of Prevention," June 1, 1950, A10; "New Chief," August 10, 1950, A8; "Public Housing Problem," August 31, 1950; A8; "Civil Rights Proposals," January 27, 1955, A9; "The Plight of Dr. Lee," August 25, 1955, A9; "Something Has to Give," May 30, 1957, A6; "Everything's Not Kosher Here," January 28, 1960, A6; "Chief Parker," July 13, 1961, A6; "Orals Hearing," November 16, 1961, A6; and Edmund Bradley, "L.A. School System Charged with Underrating Minorities," November 23, 1961, A8.

5. See, for example, Shana Bernstein, *Bridges of Reform: Interracial Civil Rights Activism in Twentieth-Century Los Angeles* (New York: Oxford University Press, 2011), 3–5.

6. Katherine Underwood, "Process and Politics: Multiracial Electoral Coalition Building and Representation in Los Angeles' Ninth District, 1949–1962" (PhD diss., University of California, San Diego, 1992), 95, 115, 143, 149. Underwood's 1997 article presents

many of the conclusions from her dissertation. See Katherine Underwood, "Pioneering Minority Representation: Edward Roybal and the Los Angeles City Council, 1949–1962," *Pacific Historical Review* 66, no. 3 (August 1997): 399–425.

7. George J. Sánchez, "Edward R. Roybal and the Politics of Multiracialism," *Southern California Quarterly* 92, no. 1 (Spring 2010): 55.

8. Ibid., 56. In a 1996 article Kenneth C. Burt interpreted Roybal's 1949 electoral success as an indicator of "Latino empowerment in Los Angeles." Although he mentioned a cohort of Jewish donors, labor activists from several ethnic communities, and endorsements from the *California Eagle* and the *Los Angeles Sentinel*, the city's most important black newspapers, Burt's focus was on the political activism of Mexican Americans instead of on the development or maintenance of a multicultural political coalition. See Kenneth C. Burt, "Latino Empowerment in Los Angeles: Postwar Dreams and Cold War Fears, 1948–1952," *Labor's Heritage* 8, no. 1 (Summer 1996): 7–25. In a 2003 article Burt placed a bit more emphasis on the importance of African Americans to Roybal's election. Because Mexican Americans were a minority in the district, Burt observed, Roybal could only win election as a result of coalition politics. See Burt, "The Power of a Mobilized Citizenry and Coalition Politics: The 1949 Election of Edward R. Roybal to the Los Angeles City Council," *Southern California Quarterly* 85, no. 4 (December 2003): 421–23, 428–29.

9. According to sources examined by Shana Bernstein, approximately 12 percent of the CSO's members in 1949 were not Mexican American. This percentage increased to 15 percent by the mid-1950s. However, Bernstein does not break down this small percentage by race, ethnicity, or culture. It seems likely, considering the connections that Burt and Bernstein have explored between the Community Relations Committee and the CSO, that many were Jewish, and some were undoubtedly Anglo Americans. See Bernstein, *Bridges of Reform*, 144.

10. Beatrice W. Griffith, *American Me* (Boston: Houghton Mifflin, 1948); Griffith, "Viva Roybal—Viva America," *Common Ground* 10, no. 1 (Autumn 1949): 66.

11. Griffith, "Viva Roybal," 68.

12. Underwood, "Process and Politics," 106.

13. Ibid., 111.

14. "Watts Transit Fight Ends in Smashing Victory for People," *Los Angeles Sentinel*, March 18, 1948, 9.

15. Grace Simons, "New Ford Plant at Maywood Hiring without Jim-Crow Bias," *Los Angeles Sentinel*, April 1, 1948, 4.

16. "Tribune Slate: City Primary, Tuesday, April 5," *Los Angeles Tribune*, April 2, 1949, 3.

17. "Roybal for Council," *California Eagle*, May 26, 1969, 6. The *Eagle* also published articles about other groups that supported Roybal's candidacy; see "IPP Works for Election of Ed Roybal, City Council," May 19, 1949, 3, and "Roybal Endorsed by Dems. And Reps. For City Council," May 26, 1949, 2.

18. "Candidates['] Qualifications Reviewed; Voters Urged to Cast Ballots Tuesday," *Los Angeles Sentinel*, March 31, 1949, C7.

19. "City Council Considering FEPC with Different Name," *Los Angeles Tribune*, August 13, 1949, 2. See also "Racial Bigotry Flared at City Hall to Defeat FEPC," *California Eagle*, September 29, 1949, 1, 2.

20. "Pilgrim House Saved on Motion of Roybal," *Los Angeles Tribune*, October 8, 1949, 3; "Roybal Praised for Service to Pilgrim House," *California Eagle*, October 20, 1949, 4.

21. "He Stands Alone," *California Eagle*, September 21, 1950, 6.

22. "City Councilmen Lash Fire Dept.," *California Eagle*, December 24, 1953, 1.

23. "Roybal Next Best Thing to One of Us," *Los Angeles Tribune*, February 12, 1954, 10.

24. William E. Pollard, "Labor's Side," *Los Angeles Sentinel*, August 5, 1954, A9. The *Eagle* also endorsed Roybal, although it did not offer a detailed explanation as to why he deserved the votes of African Americans. See "Eagle Tells Choices in Tuesday Election," *California Eagle*, October 28, 1954, 1.

25. "The Negroes Win Congress Seats; Lomax, Lundy Defeated," *California Eagle*, November 4, 1954, 1.

26. John Q. Observer, "Political Digest," *Los Angeles Sentinel*, March 21, 1957, A5. In this article, Lomax is incorrectly identified as the *Tribune*'s publisher.

27. "Hopes Dim for FEPC at Local Los Angeles Level," *California Eagle*, March 17, 1955, 1.

28. "Why the Tribune Didn't Endorse Ed Roybal," *Los Angeles Tribune*, June 6, 1958, 8.

29. "Debs for Supervisor," *California Eagle*, May 22, 1958, 4.

30. "Council Re-District Plan Would Split Negro Vote," *California Eagle*, October 23, 1952, 2. See also "Gerrymandering Us Again," *California Eagle*, October 16, 1952, 4.

31. "Gerrymandering Us Again," *California Eagle*, October 16, 1952, 4.

32. "Too Many Candidates," *California Eagle*, January 20, 1955, 4. See also "Make the Best of It," *California Eagle*, February 3, 1955, 4.

33. "Election Lessons," *California Eagle*, April 14, 1955, 4.

34. "Seat Negro Councilman, Roybal Urges; Favors 2 New Districts," *Los Angeles Sentinel*, October 27, 1960, A3. See also "Council Votes to Keep Jim Crow District Plan," *California Eagle*, October 27, 1960, 1.

35. "City Council Gerrymander," *California Eagle*, November 10, 1960, 4.

36. "Vote for Richardson, Tinglof, Roybal," *California Eagle*, March 23, 1961, 4.

37. "Negroes Best Fitted, Say Wyman, Roybal," *California Eagle*, August 10, 1961, 1, 4.

38. Grace E. Simons, "City Council Rejects Negro in 10th District," *California Eagle*, August 31, 1961, 1, 4.

39. "Groups United for Redress in 10th Dist.," *California Eagle*, August 31, 1961, 1.

40. "Hollingsworth Chosen by Race," *California Eagle*, August 31, 1961, 4.

41. See "Kickoff Campaign for Roybal," February 2, 1961, B1; Joseph Eli Kovner, un-

titled column, March 5, 1961, A1; and Kovner, untitled column, April 2, 1961, A2, all in *Eastside Sun.*

42. "Businessmen Back Roybal for Congress," *California Eagle*, April 19, 1962, 2.

43. William E. Pollard, "Labor's Side," *Los Angeles Sentinel*, August 16, 1962, A15.

44. "Felix Ontiveros Files for 9th D. Council Seat," *Eastside Sun*, November 29, 1962.

45. Joseph Eli Kovner, untitled column, *Eastside Sun*, December 6, 1962, A1, A3. Although scholars frequently note that Richard Tafoya was Roybal's cousin, newspaper articles from late 1962 did not mention this relationship. In addition to Kovner's December 6, 1962, column, see "Tafoya Files for Council," *Eastside Sun*, December 6, 1962, 1.

46. "Consider Gilbert Lindsay Major Choice for Council," *Los Angeles Sentinel*, November 15, 1962, A1.

47. "Community Unites in Lindsay-for-Council Drive," *Los Angeles Sentinel*, November 22, 1962, A1. See also the following articles, all in the *Los Angeles Sentinel*: "Lindsay for Council Drive Gains Support," November 29, 1962, A1; Leon H. Washington Jr., "Wash's Wash," November 29, 1962, A6; "Ministers Endorse Lindsay," December 6, 1962, A1; "GOP Group Backs Lindsay for Council," December 13, 1962, A1.

48. "Vacancy in 9th District," *California Eagle*, November 22, 1962, 4.

49. "Lindsay Files for Ninth Race," *Los Angeles Sentinel*, January 10, 1963, A2.

50. "Gilbert Lindsey [*sic*] Files to Fill 9th CD Vacancy," *Eastside Sun*, January 10, 1963.

51. "Lindsay Cleanup Bid Hailed in 9th District," *Los Angeles Sentinel*, December 20, 1962, A1, and "We Need Lindsay," ibid.

52. "Council Race," *Los Angeles Sentinel*, January 10, 1963, A6.

53. "Naming of Lindsay Called Double-Cross," *California Eagle*, January 31, 1963, 1, 4; "Lindsay in Middle, Mayor Yells 'Foul!'" *California Eagle*, January 31, 1963, 1, 4; "Councilman Lindsay Vows Civic Action," *Los Angeles Sentinel*, January 31, 1963, A1.

54. "At Long Last," *Los Angeles Sentinel*, January 31, 1963, A6. See also Leon H. Washington Jr., "Wash's Wash," *Los Angeles Sentinel*, January 31, 1963, A6.

55. "Councilman Lindsay Vows Civic Action," A1, A4.

56. "Statement by Dick Tafoya on Appointment," *Eastside Sun*, January 31, 1963.

57. "Josefa Sanchez Makes Statement," *Eastside Sun*, February 14, 1963, A1, A2.

58. "Lindsay Selects Top Deputy," *Los Angeles Sentinel*, February 14, 1963, A1.

59. For example, the *Eagle* published a photograph of a campaign brunch whose guests included "Mrs. Rose Lopez, Ricardo Gonzales, Esther Avila, Ruth Avila, . . . Felix Ontiveros (deputy to Councilman Lindsay, [and] Mrs. Sally Ontiveros." *California Eagle*, March 7, 1963, 2. See also "Women Host Brunch for Gil Lindsay," *Los Angeles Sentinel*, March 14, 1963, C5.

60. "Pastors Group Endorses Lindsay, Bradley, Mills," *Los Angeles Sentinel*, March 14, 1963, A1; "Plan Massive Parade in 9th for Lindsay," ibid.; "Motorcade for Lindsay Rolls Sunday," ibid., March 21, 1963, A1; "Lindsay Pledges Support to Elderly," ibid., A12.

61. "Bradley, Lindsay, Mills," *California Eagle*, March 28, 1963, 4.

62. "Lindsay Urges Regular Street Cleaning in Area," *Los Angeles Sentinel*, March 14,

1963, A3; "Eastside Streets to Be Swept at Regular Intervals Is Program Requested by Lindsay," *Eastside Sun*, March 21, 1963, A1.

63. "Mrs. Sanchez Aids Negroes in 8th, 10th," *California Eagle*, March 7, 1963, 14.

64. Leon H. Washington Jr., "Wash's Wash," *Los Angeles Sentinel*, April 4, 1963, A6. See also "Task Ahead," ibid., April 11, 1963, A6; and "Let's Finish the Job," *California Eagle*, April 11, 1963, 4.

65. "Ministers Tell Roybal to Shun 9th Dist. Campaign," *California Eagle*, April 18, 1963, 1, 4. See also Leon H. Washington Jr., "Wash's Wash," *Los Angeles Sentinel*, April 18, 1963, A6.

66. "Tafoya-for-Council Gets Roybal Support," *Los Angeles Sentinel*, May 16, 1963, A5. Paid advertisements in the *Eagle* quoted extensively from Roybal's telegram to Tafoya. See, for example, *California Eagle*, May 16, 1963, 8.

67. Joseph Eli Kovner, untitled column, *Eastside Sun*, May 30, 1963, A1.

68. Underwood, "Process and Politics," 290.

69. Kovner, untitled column, May 30, 1963.

70. "Urge All-Out Vote for Lindsay," *Los Angeles Sentinel*, May 23, 1963, A1, A5.

71. "Lindsay Checks County-City Health Merger," *Los Angeles Sentinel*, November 14, 1963, B3.

72. "Mills, Lindsay Seek to Curb Biased Licensees," *Los Angeles Sentinel*, March 5, 1964, A1.

73. "Lindsay Plugs Pay Hike for City Workers," *Los Angeles Sentinel*, May 14, 1964, A1; "Lindsay Cites Concern on Homes Condemnation," ibid., A10; "Condemnation of Homes Hit by Councilman," ibid., June 4, 1964, A4.

74. "Lindsay Wins Hike for Low-Pay Group," *Los Angeles Sentinel*, May 21, 1964, A1.

75. Kovner, untitled column, May 30, 1963.

76. Robert Bauman, *Race and the War on Poverty: From Watts to East L.A.* (Norman: University of Oklahoma Press, 2008), 52–68.

CHAPTER 3

Civil Rights "beyond the Fields"

African American and Mexican American Civil Rights Activism in Bakersfield, California, 1947–1964

OLIVER A. ROSALES

Between World War II and the mid-1960s, urban multiracial coalitions championed civil rights reform in Bakersfield, California. Mexican Americans, African Americans, and white liberals forged coalitions rooted in farm labor, fair housing, and the struggle to establish a Fair Employment Practices Commission (FEPC). White liberal activists worked as cultural brokers between black and brown communities in confronting an institutional conservatism complicit in the city's long-standing history of racial segregation. Without white liberal involvement in the early Bakersfield civil rights struggle, black-brown civil rights coalitions may have remained culturally and politically segregated in the southeastern corridor of Bakersfield. The Bakersfield branch of the National Association for the Advancement of Colored People (NAACP) and the predominantly Mexican American Community Service Organization (CSO) worked in concert with the Kern Council for Civic Unity (KCCU) to address civil rights issues in the racially divided city. These coalitions battled anti-statist and racially conservative politics, which were hostile toward civil rights reform initiatives and enforcement at both the city and county levels.

Known as the breadbasket of the United States, the Bakersfield region is rich in social and political history. Bakersfield was home to the Yokuts people, white gold-seekers, mestizos, and generations of immigrant groups, including southern whites and blacks, Basques and Chinese, and European hopefuls. This multiracial infusion created some interesting experiences in the nation's last continental frontier—in terms of both political development and the influence of a southern cultural diaspora.

The dusty, oil-well-dotted fields and back roads of Bakersfield and Kern County meander through the heart of California's interior. Located in the southern San Joaquin Valley of California's Central Valley, Bakersfield has long been the home of Far West American conservatism. The legacy of the "Okie" migration of the 1930s and 1940s shaped significantly the political and cultural history of Bakersfield during the latter half of the twentieth century.[1] The particular brand of Bakersfield conservatism, notes historian Thomas Wellock, has been anti-statist in its orientation toward localism and hostility toward the state and federal governments.[2] This conservatism shaped in part the activism of the city's black and brown residents both before and after Kern County became the center of a labor and civil rights struggle after September 1965, when Filipino and Mexican farmworkers organized a strike against local growers. Within the context of the farm labor struggle, black and brown activism flourished in the urban sector.[3]

To propel the goals of racial integration and civil rights, progressive community leaders formed the Intergroup Relations Board (IRB) in 1963, charged with advising the city government on civil rights and race relations. Local activists believed the formation of the IRB marked a triumph of racial liberalism. The IRB's mandate to work collaboratively with local government, however, proved difficult to implement. The resistance of local officials to this community body ultimately prevented the board from becoming an effective civil rights body. Multiracial collaboration with local government proved to be unfeasible in Bakersfield and Kern County.[4]

Although organized conservative resistance toward political, social, and economic reform stymied civil rights enforcement, the emergence of the KCCU in the immediate post–World War II years and its subsequent resurgence through the later fair housing and FEPC movements were significant in Bakersfield's urban grassroots civil rights history. The civic unity movement in Bakersfield drew on the larger efforts of the California Federation for Civic Unity (CFCU), an important, albeit short-lived, multiethnic civil rights organization founded in the immediate postwar years. Although the CFCU ultimately suffered disarray as a statewide organization, due in part to what historian Mark Brilliant calls California's "multiple streams" of civil rights efforts, multiracial civic unity activists were key in sustaining Bakersfield's urban civil rights movement.[5] Unfortunately, the early Bakersfield movement suffered a leadership vacuum when its founder, Rabbi Sanford Rosen, migrated north to San Mateo, California. Bakersfield's civic unity movement nevertheless survived the anticommunist politics of the 1950s and reemerged to champion civil rights reform a decade later.

The course of this civic unity movement highlights the successes and limits of multiracial coalition building in Bakersfield, as well as the racial liberalism that defined multiracial coalition efforts in California's interior during this time. When the civic unity movement rematerialized in 1963, it did so in direct opposition to the politics of the IRB and that group's ineffectiveness in pressing civil rights enforcement and reform. Black and brown civic unity activists, brought together in part by their white liberal allies, posited and practiced a more direct form of civil rights protest. These efforts, while not always successful, are important examples of black and brown unity during the civil rights era. Black organizations and activists especially drove urban civil rights reform efforts in the late 1950s and early 1960s in Bakersfield. Mexican American organizations also joined these causes. Organizational conflicts between the IRB, the KCCU, and the Bakersfield City Council, however, as well as an ideological challenge mounted by the Black and Chicana/o Power movements regarding the tenets of racial liberalism, altered the course of civil rights reform in Kern County after 1965.[6]

EARLY ACTIVISM

Improving the living conditions of farmworkers was the agenda of civil rights reformers following the end of the failed farm labor strike in the late 1940s, which had been led by Ernesto Galarza and the National Farm Labor Union (NFLU) against Kern County's most influential grower, Joseph DiGiorgio.[7] The three-year strike nevertheless put the San Joaquin Valley on the radar for national civil rights organizations. Writing to the national NAACP offices in New York City in 1950, the West Coast regional director, Franklin Williams, commented, "in all of my experience as an NAACP worker throughout the deep South I have never seen conditions as dreadful, unsanitary and depressing as those under which thousands of Negro migrant workers have to live on the outskirts of Bakersfield."[8] But the Kern County farmworker population in the late 1940s was multiracial and included African American migrants from Texas, Arkansas, and Oklahoma as well as whites, Mexican Americans, and Mexican nationals. The area's poverty had been the subject of Dorothea Lange's photography a decade earlier, when she documented the conditions faced by migrant families, including black and brown families, when they came to California in search of agricultural work.[9] Assessing the segregated communities outside Bakersfield's city limits, Williams continued, "there are hundreds of ramshackle temporary dwellings without light or sanitation in which approximately 10,000 Negroes reside. . . . There are no sanitary facilities whatsoever, the people having to use pit toilets, the odors from which are readily recognizable for miles away."[10] Such poor living conditions were synonymous with migrant labor camps and settlements. In August and September 1950, state inspectors from the Division of Housing (Department of Industrial Relations) surveyed housing conditions for agricultural workers in the San Joaquin Valley. Of the seven counties surveyed in California's Central Valley, Kern County had the highest number of estimated labor camps (375) and ranked near the bottom in number of annual inspections (85).[11]

In light of the national attention brought to the alarming conditions of rural poverty and migration faced in Kern County, Bakersfield's civic unity movement articulated a multiracial approach as a means of solving the social and economic problems among the region's poor. The first target area for reform was the old Mayflower District census tract. Originally a rural black colony, the Sunset-Mayflower district developed at the dawn of the twentieth century as a space for black farmworker families.[12] During the first half of the twentieth century migrant farmworkers continued to settle in and around this unincorporated section of southeastern Bakersfield. What united the black and brown communities and, for a time, the white residents was rural poverty. Efforts to improve relations between the more affluent residents in the urban core with these rural poor residents met resistance, however. In a January 1950 CFCU board of directors meeting, Rabbi Rosen highlighted the difficulties of organizing a Bakersfield Council for Civic Unity, as well as "the serious cases of segregation and discrimination in Bakersfield . . . [and the] organized opposition the Council [had] to meet" in becoming an effective unity branch in Bakersfield.[13] While Rosen was central in creating a civic unity movement in Bakersfield and serving as a liaison to the statewide CFCU, his departure in the early 1950s created a leadership vacuum. Assessing the legacy of the CFCU as a statewide organization, Mark Brilliant writes, "The CFCU floundered from its founding. Its fate reflected in microcosm the challenge that racial diversity posed for racial liberals throughout California's civil rights era to forge a multiracial civil rights movement."[14] Nevertheless, civil rights reform efforts were by no means absent in Bakersfield. The renewed efforts after the failed DiGiorgio farm labor strike, the success of the local NAACP in forcing the city to remove local Jim Crow racial segregation signs, and the establishment of the Community Service Organization in Bakersfield all signaled a politically engaged citizenry of color.

In early 1950, the Greater Bakersfield Ministerial Association pressured the Bakersfield City Council to adopt an antidiscrimination ordinance, making it a misdemeanor crime to "display discriminatory signs in restaurants and businesses."[15] The city council's law, known officially as Ordinance 860, was approved on February 14, 1950. It stated that places of public accommodation in Bakersfield known to have signs excluding racial groups from such accommodations had to remove those signs.[16] Led by the Reverends Lynn Wood and John Whiteneck Jr. and the Bakersfield NAACP's secretary, Clara Howard, the ministerial alliance and the NAACP then successfully lobbied the Kern County Board of Supervisors to follow the city council's lead in early March 1950 and remove racially discriminatory signs. Despite the efforts of civil rights leaders to force municipal and countywide anti-segregation measures, the legacy of "sundown" towns persisted in the county outside the city of Bakersfield, particularly in Taft just south of Bakersfield and Oildale directly north of the city limits. While the idea of opening places of public accommodation to all persons regardless of race gained the approval of municipal government and generally was viewed favorably as an indicator of social difference from the Jim Crow South, other matters of racial integration proved much more divisive.

The contentious issue of expanded public housing in southeastern Bakersfield mobilized urban civil rights reform groups. In March 1953, a heated local political battle surfaced over the issue of subsidized public housing in the Sunset-Mayflower district—the predominantly African American and Mexican American area of the city that earlier in the year had been annexed into the city's metropolitan limits. The contest centered around a local initiative known as Measure 4, which expanded city services into the racialized southeastern area of the city. This rezoning ordinance was designed to expedite a contract between the city of Bakersfield and the Kern Housing Authority involving the construction of a public housing project at Owens Street and East California Avenue, just east of California Avenue Park (later renamed Martin Luther King Jr. Park).[17] A "citizens committee" emerged to challenge Measure 4 in early 1953. In newspaper advertisements, the "citizens committee" urged taxpayers to vote against Measure 4, arguing that its passage would ultimately cost more money for "ALL KINDS OF PUBLIC SERVICES FOR THEM . . . schools, police, and fire protection, etc."[18] Such public denunciations against the initiative clearly indicated to Bakersfield voters the connection between the allocation of local tax dollars and racially segregated spaces.

The Sunset-Mayflower Improvement Committee sponsored Measure 4 in an appeal to pragmatic concerns and a sense of civic duty to assist the poor. On March 24, 1953, however, Measure 4 for the Oro Vista Housing Project was defeated,[19] but the referendum's failure did not sever the legal mandate of the contract between the city of Bakersfield and the Kern Housing Authority. Construction of the Oro Vista Housing Project therefore pressed forward. Opposition to Measure 4 would not be the last time Bakersfield's conservative base utilized the ballot box to oppose state-subsidized efforts to improve living and working conditions for Bakersfield's poor residents of color.[20]

In mid-1950s Bakersfield, opposition to subsidized housing projects was rooted in anticommunist politics and hostility toward migrant labor. Anticommunism, moreover, provided local politicians with useful language for appealing to Cold War conservatives and some civil rights reformers, particularly Mexican Americans. In Bakersfield, many Mexican American groups, such as the CSO, were clearly anticommunist and promoted the virtues of U.S. citizenship. Established in Los Angeles in the late 1940s as "an offshoot of Saul Alinsky's Back of the Yards Neighborhood Council," writes historian Zaragosa Vargas, the CSO organized active chapters throughout California.[21] The Bakersfield chapter was established by Cesar Chavez and other key Mexican American activists. The Bakersfield CSO, like many branches, was a family affair. The Govea family, including Juan, Margaret, and their young daughter Jessica (who later became a key organizer in the United Farm Workers), was particularly significant. Margaret Govea, following the death of her daughter from breast cancer in 2005, recalled, "My daughter Jessica was at one time president of the junior CSO. . . . They had . . . quite a few projects . . . [including] voter registration. . . . They were bird dogs" (activists too young to legally register voters).[22] Later the UFW used similar techniques of door-to-door organizing in the Central Valley. The CSO's tactics thus proved influential in community organizing in the following decade in the farmworker movement.

The Bakersfield CSO worked closely with Democratic congressman Harlan Hagen, whose anticommunist credentials reflected the political sentiments of his Central Valley constituents. In March 1954 Hagen proposed legislation in Congress to outlaw the Communist Party in the United States.[23] Hagen's alliance with the Bakersfield CSO was evident in matters concerning immigration. The congressman worked diligently to prevent the Immigration and Naturalization Service (INS) from closing its Bakersfield office during the first six months of 1955. The office was scheduled to be closed in July of that year because of budget cuts. Hagen's effort to keep the branch open was in response to local support, including members of the city and county government, and an especially effective letter-writing campaign from the CSO. The letter writers argued that "many laws will be violated and enforcement of immigration laws will be down. The cost of return transportation of aliens will be imposed on the local law enforcement agencies and . . . paid by the taxpayers."[24] As labor and civil rights scholars have noted, the "alien" or "wetback" labor problem of the 1950s became a rallying cry for Mexican American civil rights leaders. Ernesto Galarza, who spent a significant amount of time as a labor organizer in California's Central Valley, pressed for the deportation of "wetback" labor. Such positions, however, "reflected . . . pro-union rather than anti-immigrant politics."[25] The tension between Mexican American citizens and undocumented laborers, illustrated by the conflict over the closure of the INS center, continued well into the Delano grape strike (1965–1970) and the subsequent activism of the United Farm Workers.[26]

CIVIC UNITY REDUX

While African American and Mexican American coalitions had begun to form around farmworkers' rights and housing, the municipal FEPC movement in Bakersfield aroused the most important cross-ethnic activism of the period. California cities began adopting municipal FEPC ordinances following World War II. The Earl Warren gubernatorial administration, however, resisted signing a state FEPC civil rights law. In May 1949, the Richmond City Council passed the first fair employment practices ordinance. Over the next decade, other cities followed suit until 1959 when California finally adopted a statewide FEPC law under Democratic governor Pat Brown.[27]

In 1957, Bakersfield had attempted to model its ordinance on what other California cities were doing. Bakersfield mayor Frank Sullivan visited Oakland with Bakersfield city councilman Henry Collins, an African American, to study job laws in preparation for the creation of Bakersfield's municipal FEPC law.[28] The struggle to implement a municipal FEPC ordinance in Los Angeles also influenced the strategies adopted by Bakersfield civil rights leaders.[29] Despite the failure of the Los Angeles civil rights coalition to pass a municipal FEPC in the late 1940s, Bakersfield civil rights leaders adopted a version of the Los Angeles plan. The multiracial and organizational diversity of the FEPC movement between 1949 and 1959 illustrates the dynamics of multiracial coalition building and multiethnic civil rights activism in California.

Despite these cooperative efforts, the FEPC movement initially provoked a good deal of controversy. The West Coast office of the NAACP had pressed FEPC legislation as the organization's most "paramount concern" in light of potential job losses in postwar California.[30] But other civil rights groups pushing for reforms chafed under the leadership and attitudes of the statewide NAACP officers.[31] Moreover, while a municipal FEPC ordinance was enacted in Bakersfield in September 1957, implementing the reform proved problematic. Specifically, an "enforced gag rule" for complaints registered with the local commission was controversial. Section 6 of Ordinance No. 1146, as Bakersfield's municipal FEPC was known, described the duties of the commission: "it shall constitute malfeasance . . . for any Commissioner to divulge or reveal to any person . . . evidence obtained in any proceedings."[32] The *Bakersfield Californian* came out publicly against the FEPC ordinance because of this "secrecy clause." "The ordinance includes provisions for secrecy that would damage seriously the public welfare," noted one editorial.[33] While the *Californian*'s editorial staff sympathized with the goal of preventing discrimination and promoting equal employment opportunities, the secrecy clause obscured issues that the local press deemed public information. Defenders of the FEPC ordinance countered, noting that the law "provides for open court hearings in the event [closed] arbitration was unsuccessful."[34]

Local civil rights leaders lauded the passage of the Bakersfield FEPC, despite controversy over the gag rule. Assessing the legacy of the FEPC movement, Vargas remarks, "FEPC laws in the southwestern states were defeated or narrowly passed, [but] were put on the agenda by a labor and civil rights coalition that mobilized community support on an enormous scale, anticipating the mass action efforts of the 1960s civil rights movements."[35] In Bakersfield, such a carryover effect was evident. The fair housing and antipoverty movements of the mid- to late 1960s were rooted in coalitions formed to create a meaningful municipal FEPC in Bakersfield during the 1950s.

Racial integration in Bakersfield's housing market became a reality in the late 1950s and early 1960s. On August 9, 1960, for example, an African American family moved into the Hillcrest area of northeastern Bakersfield, a white and affluent community near the Bakersfield Country Club. But the family was not welcomed. They kept a journal of the events and subsequently published their account anonymously in the city's only liberal periodical,

California Crossroads. Among other things, repeated racist telephone calls forced the family to disconnect their phone service the first week in their new home. Airing their grievances to the *Crossroads* readership, the black couple wrote, "We have not enjoyed one single moment in the beautiful house we bought. It is no pleasure to leave work tired at the end of the day and be called names and be looked down on by people who judge themselves to be better than you because they belong to a different ethnic group."[36]

The struggle over fair housing in the early 1960s led to the second coming of the civic unity movement in Bakersfield. In the fall of 1960, Bakersfield's racially progressive religious community struck an alliance with their southern California neighbors, borrowing some of the progressive strategies used by Los Angeles–based activists. On October 11, 1960, George Thomas of the Los Angeles Human Relations Council attended a large meeting at the Bakersfield Police Department auditorium sponsored by the Bakersfield Council of Churches. Thomas discussed the potential of implementing a strategic plan used in Pasadena to promote open housing in Bakersfield.[37]

The rebirth of the civic unity movement was central to interethnic activism. One of the early attempts at 1960s multiracial civic unity was the Intergroup Relations Board, an advisory group formed in July 1963 by the Bakersfield City Council. The IRB's mandate was to advise the city council in all matters related to "promoting harmonious racial relations" within the city limits of Bakersfield.[38] Resolution 47-63 noted that as of that year there was "no organization [in Bakersfield] enjoying official status nor representative of the entire community, having the promotion of inter-racial, religious, and ethnic harmony and progress as its primary purpose."[39] Although the IRB may have been the city council's effort to temper and control civil rights protesting, African American and Mexican American civil rights leaders expressed faith that the IRB could become a meaningful civil rights body. After the struggle to establish a municipal FEPC ordinance in Bakersfield, the IRB seemed a logical step for black, brown, and white civil rights activists. And while some activists were skeptical of working with the local government on civil rights matters, the vast majority of black and brown residents were enthusiastic and hopeful about the IRB. In a 1963 field report, however, an NAACP West Coast officer criticized the fact that civil rights efforts in Bakersfield were being carried out under the banner of the IRB and not the local NAACP. "Some of the things that are being done, are not being done in the name of the NAACP. The local NAACP branch and the black churches organized about 1,200–1,400 people to attend a city council meeting where the human relations board was formed. It was apparently never included into the community dialogue that the NAACP branch was instrumental in this achievement."[40]

The most important aspect of the IRB was that it had both official city sanction and grassroots support from African Americans and Mexican Americans. Two key African American leaders who helped form the IRB were a prominent local attorney, Gabriel Solomon, and the Reverend Julius Brooks. Solomon served as the legal representative for the Bakersfield NAACP, and Brooks was the pastor of Cain AME Church in East Bakersfield, one of the area's oldest and largest black churches. Brooks was appointed to be the IRB chair. Unfortunately, the original IRB resolution was vague, particularly regarding the group's exact functions. Brooks expressed confusion in August 1964, petitioning the city council to "write a resolution stating the purpose, powers, and functions of the board."[41] This political dilemma led to the eventual collapse of the IRB and to the development of the Kern Council for Civic Unity.

KCCU ACTIVISM

The fundamental difference between the IRB and the KCCU was the inclination of civic unity activists toward direct action. The IRB had been perpetually stymied by conservative resistance on the city council and by a lack of organizational clarity. Integrating Bakersfield's housing market would require direct action, according to civic unity activists.

The passage of the Rumford Fair Housing Act in 1963 brought hope to civil rights activists that California's segregated cities might finally be liberated from the racial covenants that had prohibited people of color from moving into all-white neighborhoods for decades. But one year later, the passage of Proposition 14 overturned Rumford, halting efforts to end the legality of racial covenants in the California housing market until 1967, when the state supreme court ruled Proposition 14 unconstitutional. In Bakersfield, civil rights leaders had mobilized against Prop 14 during the 1964 campaign season. According to an early KCCU recruitment flyer, the ad hoc "No on 14" committee "developed a great sense of *espirit* [*sic*] and despite the overturning of the Rumford Act, decided to hold the committee together by forming the KCCU."[42] Founding KCCU members included a Bakersfield College faculty member, Duane Belcher; the local NAACP chair, Art Shaw; and a War on Poverty activist and teacher, Mel Brown. A consortium of urban civil rights organizations (including the NAACP, the CSO, the National Farm Workers Association, and antipoverty workers), the KCCU emphasized civic unity and racial liberalism rather than endorsing a narrow civil rights agenda defined by an alliance with a national civil rights organization or a particular racial group.

The KCCU had a broad agenda. Beyond housing, the KCCU worked to improve "education, employment, and [cross-racial] communication."[43] After 1965 the group worked diligently to publicize and assist African Americans and Mexican Americans in social, political, and economic issues. One early KCCU effort included a photo publicity project of Bakersfield's southeastern ghettos and barrios since Bakersfield's white residents seldom approached these communities. A handful of housing tracts in southeastern Bakersfield the previous year had become the proposed site for implementing antipoverty programs, and KCCU chair Duane Belcher held public forums to highlight the poverty in the area.[44] Despite the legal limbo of the Rumford Act's mandate to partially end racial discrimination in the housing market, KCCU members implemented a voluntary, good-neighbor fair-housing program, requesting that homeowners and realtors sign nondiscrimination pacts for sales and property rentals.[45] This program foreshadowed later efforts when KCCU members attempted to force fair housing among resistant local realtors after Prop 14 was overturned in 1967.[46]

In March 1965, the KCCU organized a large peaceful protest in the name of civic unity and racial harmony in Bakersfield. Like many other civil rights groups throughout the United States, the organizers were influenced by events occurring in the South. The protest was described as "a combined civil rights demonstration and memorial for the Unitarian clergyman James Reeb slain in Selma, Alabama."[47] A multiracial crowd of nearly three thousand people marched from Cain AME Church to the Kern Civic Center in downtown Bakersfield. The speaking roster indicated a connection between the southern civil rights movement and Bakersfield. The Reverend Ralph Click of the Church of the Brethren spoke passionately about what the day's march meant and its connection to Selma: "The freedom of both black and white is at stake. This is true of areas outside the South. I know there were people afraid to join us today; they were afraid to be seen here. They might lose their job, or their status in the community or their friends. . . . We are met here today for freedom for Selma and Bakersfield."[48]

Other community leaders in attendance included IRB members and antipoverty activists. Sylvia Ganz, who was appointed a member of the IRB in

1965, addressed the crowd: "Our destiny and the destiny of the children [are] inseparably bound up with the people [and] will determine the meaning of democracy for all of us."[49] For Ganz, this notion rang especially true. Her son, Marshall, was at the time a Harvard senior on academic leave working with the Student Nonviolent Coordinating Committee (SNCC) in Mississippi. Soon, Marshall Ganz returned home to Bakersfield "with Mississippi eyes" and joined the struggle in the agricultural fields, working full time as an organizer for the newly founded National Farm Workers Association (NFWA) under the leadership of Cesar Chavez.[50] An ethos of civic unity and racial harmony characterized the speeches made that day at the KCCU rally, and racial liberalism was at the core of civil rights leadership in Bakersfield through 1965.

The beginning of 1966, however, tested the limits of racial liberalism in Bakersfield. In January, the White Citizens' Council initiated a public campaign to develop its local chapter in order to counter civil rights activism occurring in both the agricultural fields of Kern County and the city of Bakersfield. White supremacy had a long history in the county. In 1922, the Kern County grand jury returned its first partial report on an investigation of the local Ku Klux Klan. This was the first such investigation in the United States, and the grand jury found that over four hundred Klan members resided in the county.[51] As the decades wore on, white supremacy manifested itself in somewhat more discreet and subtler organizations, like the John Birch Society and White Citizens' Councils. Founded in Mississippi following the *Brown* decision in 1954, Citizens' Councils spread rapidly throughout the southern states, espousing a rhetoric of "states rights and racial integrity."[52] The effectiveness of the IRB and the KCCU was tested when the White Citizens' Council made public inroads in establishing a grassroots challenge to racial liberalism in Bakersfield.

Cooperative activism between black, brown, and white liberal activists was clearly seen in the opposition to the White Citizens' Council. On January 18, 1966, the White Citizens' Council held a meeting in downtown Bakersfield to publicize the group's activities and distribute racist literature. African American, Mexican American, and white civil rights activists protested the meeting. About thirty to forty community demonstrators disrupted the Citizens' Council meeting at the El Tejon Hotel, after a "broken water pipe" forced the Citizens' Council to relocate from a previously booked downtown conference center. After the demonstrators had delayed the meeting for two hours, the Los Angeles White Citizens' Council field director, Frank Bain, phoned the Bakersfield city police, informing them that the protesters were disrupting a private meeting. The protesters in turn claimed that the Citizens' Council had invited any interested community members to attend the meeting and that the demonstrators had become upset when they were not welcomed.[53]

As local folks protested the Citizens' Council gathering, the demonstrators called the newspapers to document what was happening. Speaking to reporters, Bain said, "Kern County was in need of a group that could speak for the majority white citizens. . . . The White Citizens' Council . . . opposed . . . federal intervention in local affairs, especially education."[54] The civil rights protesters were blunter. Marshall Ganz, who was working with the NFWA and was fresh from his work in Mississippi with SNCC, told reporters that the "Citizens Council was a secret Deep South organization made up of racists."[55] Direct action against the expansion of the White Citizens' Council was the type of activism KCCU members embraced, especially compared to the more passive responses offered by the overly bureaucratic human relations commission.

On January 21, 1966, the IRB reported to the city council that the board should officially investigate what had happened between the civil rights protesters and the White Citizens' Council just days prior. Julius Brooks, the IRB chair, was one of two board members especially concerned with the presence of the Citizens' Council in the city. According to his testimony and others, the White Citizens' Council had confronted the Community Action Program Committee earlier that year and sought out information about antipoverty programs and black members who had initiated the antipoverty movement two years earlier.[56] Art Shaw reported at the city council meeting that the White Citizens' Council was very "selective" at the El Tejon Hotel and did not give any of the group's literature to African American or Mexican American civil rights activists, who sought the information in the hotel lobby. Shaw reported that the principal view of the White Citizens' Council "promote[d] separation of the races, . . . [and] school segregation . . . [was its] primary target."[57] Vice Mayor Richard Stiern interrogated Shaw, questioning whether or not the IRB was investigating other segregationist groups, such as the Black Muslims.[58] Stiern's thinking epitomized the larger Bakersfield community of voters. James Armstrong of the Bakersfield Forum for American Opinion publicly accused antipoverty activist Mel Brown, the Reverend Julius Brooks, and other civil rights "agitators" of being "behind the White Citizens' Council and the Muslims [*sic*] . . . attempt[s] to trigger another Watts in Bakersfield."[59]

Hyperbolic claims by conservatives regarding left-wing minority conspiracies surfaced noticeably during these years, especially as the Delano grape strike garnered national attention.

Brooks urged the city council members to send an official letter condemning the presence of the White Citizens' Council and its disruptive and mean-spirited activities in Bakersfield. But after a heated debate, the council members decided not to issue a letter condemning the Citizens' Council.[60] They instead agreed to send the group a copy of Resolution 47-63, the resolution that had produced the Intergroup Relations Board and articulated the goals of the IRB. The only city council member to support the IRB's position to publicly condemn the Citizens' Council was African American councilman Del Rucker, a longtime funeral home proprietor and the only racial minority member of the city council. Representing Ward 1 in southeastern Bakersfield, Rucker made a motion to have the city council officially take a stand and go on record condemning the White Citizens' Council, reiterating that the group was "disturbing racial harmony." Rucker's motion died for lack of a second.[61] Other city councilmen, particularly Bill Park and Dennis Hosking, disagreed with the Citizens' Council's message, but stressed that it was not within the legal right of the city council to condemn the presence of any group.

African Americans and Mexican Americans nevertheless continued to bombard the city council in protest over the White Citizens' Council. On January 31, 1966, Reverend Brooks again addressed the city council, this time speaking for forty-five minutes. He addressed the city council's failure to directly rebuke the comments made the previous week by a White Citizens' Council field representative. Brooks declared that the Citizens' Council preached "hate and segregation" and that as the IRB chair and a concerned citizen and taxpayer, he felt it was the moral duty of the city council to officially condemn their presence in Bakersfield. Responding to Brooks, Park stated that he agreed but was not sure "why all the minority people were there" that night in the city council chambers. Once again, the chamber was filled to capacity with Bakersfield's African American and Mexican American residents. Park told Brooks and the audience that the "city council had taken a stand against the White Citizens' Council" by sending the group a copy of Resolution 47-63, which stated the official goals of the IRB.[62] Park did not understand why the "minority people" were in attendance since action had already been taken.

Park's confusion about the large racial minority presence that night in the chamber illustrates the ideological division in Bakersfield over the politics of civil rights. Civil rights activists and community leaders expressed an ethos of racial liberalism, petitioning the city council for redress given the actions and presence of the White Citizens' Council in Bakersfield. African Americans and Mexican Americans hoped that if they demonstrated how the ideas and presence of the Citizens' Council promoted racial disharmony and racial segregation, the city council would respond favorably. The majority of the city council countered, however, that as the city's official governing body, it had done everything within its legal authority to remedy the community disturbance by sending the letter reiterating the goals of the IRB to the Citizens' Council. City council members asserted that the city government had no legal right to tell the Citizens' Council that the organization could not assemble peacefully in Bakersfield.

The city council's unwillingness to condemn the Citizens' Council ultimately helped to sever the limited alliance between multiracial civil rights groups and the local government. Indeed, the anti-statist logic the city council demonstrated in the debate over the White Citizens' Council coupled with the city's simultaneous rationale to legislatively oppose the funding of antipoverty programs with local tax dollars indicated the city's inaction to end poverty and segregation. The city council's willingness to use the power of the government to oppose civil rights was contingent rather than being based on political principles. In brief, the city council discriminatingly used the powers of local government to champion conservatism and would continue to do so specifically to stymie the liberal, federally funded War on Poverty.[63]

The conflict between the IRB and the city council over the White Citizens' Council also encouraged reforms to limit city council meetings as a forum for civil rights protest. The city council voted to limit the public forum aspect of the meetings shortly after it sent the Citizens' Council a copy of Resolution 47-63. The large presence of "minority people" at the city council meetings had become a source of contention between the city council and minority residents, and the city council passed a resolution to "regulate the procedure by which citizens could address the council."[64] The state attorney general approved. According to the attorney general's office, the Bakersfield City Council was perfectly within its legal rights and the proper use of police power to regulate the manner in which the public addressed the body.[65] This new procedural rule for public meetings further strained the relationship between the city council and the city's African American and Mexican American citizens, silencing what had been the principal forum for urban civil rights protest in Bakersfield.

CONCLUSION

The civil rights mobilization engendered by the civic unity, FEPC, and human relations commission movements encapsulated racial liberalism in Bakersfield. Nondiscrimination and equal opportunity were core tenets of racial liberal thinking in California.[66] Racial liberals opposed both de jure and de facto racial segregation and the economic, political, and social disparities between the city's and county's white population and their black and brown neighbors. Although well intended, the racial liberalism that defined these multiracial coalition movements waned with the rise of ethnic power movements. Following the national attention brought to SNCC and the Black Power movement in Los Angeles and Oakland, civic unity coalitions struggled to come to terms with the implications of Black and Brown Power. With even greater local impact, the United Farm Workers built a strong coalition of civil rights activists, especially among African American leaders in Oakland, concerning the union's boycott against grapes.[67]

Encouraged by the farmworker movement's challenge to Bakersfield racial conservatism, urban Chicana/o activists would soon take on a primary role in the KCCU, eventually eclipsing the well-intentioned white activists who had defined the earlier years of the civic unity movement and brokered organizational relations between black and brown activists. Ethnic power movements subsequently alienated many white racial liberals, as well as some black and brown civil rights activists of earlier generations. The older generations' efforts to build multiracial coalitions in southeastern Bakersfield seemed contrary to the idea of ethnic separatism authored by Chicana/o and Black Power activists. Last and perhaps most important, increased Mexican migration to Kern County bolstered Chicana/o civil rights leaders, who moved to the center of an ideological battle over race relations and the future of civil rights reform in the lower San Joaquin Valley.[68]

The various black and brown civil rights activisms, demonstrated by efforts to work both cooperatively and outside the bounds of local government, were significant in establishing Bakersfield's urban civil rights movement. Black and brown activists, traditionally segregated, although de facto in both labor and housing markets, found common ground in these movements. While known more broadly for its brand of anti-statist conservatism in the second half of the twentieth century, Bakersfield witnessed a vibrant and multiracial challenge to both political marginalization and racial segregation. As we commemorate the fifty-year anniversary of the United Farm

Workers' epic struggle in the agricultural fields of Kern County, the multiracial activism of Bakersfield's urban core should not be ignored nor minimized. Such activism played a critical and foundational role in extending the scope and impact of both labor and civil rights reform in the American Far West.

NOTES

1. James Gregory, *American Exodus: The Dust Bowl Migration and Okie Culture in California* (New York: Oxford University Press, 1989).

2. Thomas J. Wellock, "Stick It in L.A.! Community Control and Nuclear Power in California's Central Valley," *Journal of American History* 84, no. 3 (December 1997): 942–78.

3. On Bakersfield's multiracial civil rights history, see Oliver Rosales "'Mississippi West': Race, Politics, and Civil Rights in California's Central Valley, 1947–1984" (PhD diss., University of California, Santa Barbara, 2012). For other scholarship on the United Farm Workers, see Miriam Pawel, *The Union of Their Dreams: Power, Hope, and Struggle in Cesar Chavez's Farm Worker Movement* (New York: Bloomsbury, 2009); Randy Shaw, *Beyond the Fields: Cesar Chavez, the UFW, and the Struggle for Social Justice in the 21st Century* (Berkeley: University of California Press, 2008); Frank Bardacke, *Trampling Out the Vintage: Cesar Chavez and the Two Souls of the United Farm Workers* (London: Verso 2011); Todd Holmes, "The Economic Roots of Reaganism: Corporate Conservatives, Political Economy, and the United Farm Workers Movement, 1965–1970," *Western Historical Quarterly* 41, no. 1 (Spring 2010): 55–80; Matt Garcia, *From the Jaws of Victory: The Triumph and the Tragedy of Cesar Chavez and the Farm Worker Movement* (Berkeley: University of California Press, 2012); Lauren Araiza, *To March for Others: The Black Freedom Struggle and the United Farm Workers* (Philadelphia: University of Pennsylvania Press, 2013).

4. On the long civil rights movement in Bakersfield, see Rosales, "Mississippi West."

5. Mark Brilliant, *The Color of America Has Changed: How Racial Diversity Shaped Civil Rights Reform in California, 1947–1978* (New York: Oxford University Press, 2010), 9.

6. In this chapter, I use the term "Mexican American" to refer to U.S. citizens of Mexican descent; the term "Mexican national" to refer to noncitizen U.S. residents of Mexican descent; and the term "Chicana/o" to refer to youth activists in the late 1960s and early 1970s who self-identified using this term.

7. On the DiGiorgio strike, see Ernesto Galarza, *Spiders in the House and Workers in the Field* (Notre Dame, Ind.: University of Notre Dame Press, 1970); Richard Steven Street, "Poverty in the Valley of Plenty: The National Farm Labor Union, DiGiorgio Farms, and Suppression of Documentary Photography in California, 1947–66," *Labor History* 48, no. 1 (February 2007): 25–48.

8. Franklin Williams to Walter White, November 17, 1950, carton 77, folder 2, National Association for the Advancement of Colored People, Region 1, Records, BANC MSS 78/180 c, Bancroft Library, University of California, Berkeley (hereafter NAACP-WC).

9. Linda Gordon, *Dorothea Lange: A Life beyond Limits* (New York: Norton, 2009); Jan Goggans, *California on the Breadlines: Dorothea Lange, Paul Taylor and the Making of a New Deal Narrative* (Berkeley: University of California Press, 2010).

10. Franklin Williams to Walter White, November 17, 1950, carton 77, folder 2, NAACP-WC.

11. "A Report on Housing in the San Joaquin Valley to the San Joaquin Valley Agricultural Labor Resources Committee," Governor's Committee to Survey the Agricultural Resources of the San Joaquin Valley Records, F3845, California State Archives, Sacramento. The migrant camp inspections by county in 1950 were as follows:

County	*Estimated Number*	*Inspections of Labor Camps (12 months)*
Fresno	350	290
Kern	375	85
Kings	150	102
Madera	100	33
Merced	150	87
Stanislaus	300	46
Tulare	300	200

12. Michael Eissinger, "African Americans in the Rural San Joaquin Valley, California: Colonization Efforts and Townships" (master's thesis, California State University, Fresno, 2008).

13. Board of Directors meeting, January 28, 1950, box 7, folder 13, California Federation for Civic Unity Records, Bancroft Library, University of California, Berkeley (hereafter CFCU).

14. Brilliant, *The Color of America Has Changed*, 16–17.

15. "Discriminatory Signs Hit by Minister Group," *Bakersfield Californian*, March 7, 1950.

16. "Ordinance 860," Ordinances of the Bakersfield City Council, http://www.bakersfieldcity.us/administration/citymanager/cityclerk/city_records.htm/ (accessed February 10, 2011; hereafter BCC).

17. "Annexed District Wants Sewers, Better Streets," *Bakersfield Californian*, March 29, 1953.

18. Measure 4 advertisement, *Bakersfield Californian*, March 23, 1953.

19. Election results, *Bakersfield Californian*, March 25, 1953.

20. For an account of how voter propositions at the state level racialized California politics, see Daniel Martinez HoSang, *Racial Propositions, Ballot Initiatives and the Making of Postwar California* (Berkeley: University of California Press, 2010).

21. Zaragosa Vargas, *Crucible of Struggle: A History of Mexican Americans from Co-*

lonial Times to the Present Era (New York: Oxford University Press, 2011), 282. On CSO activities in California, see Juan Gómez-Quiñones, *Chicano Politics: Reality and Promise, 1940–1990* (Albuquerque: University of New Mexico Press, 1990), 53–56; Fred Ross, *Conquering Goliath: Cesar Chavez at the Beginning* (Keene, N.H.: El Taller Grafico, 1989); Katherine Underwood, "Pioneering Minority Representation: Edward Roybal and the Los Angeles City Council, 1949–1962," *Pacific Historical Review* 66 (August 1997): 399–425; Shana Bernstein, *Bridges of Reform: Interracial Civil Rights Activism in Twentieth-Century Los Angeles* (New York: Oxford University Press, 2011), 138–84.

22. Interview with Margaret Govea, CSO Project, University of California, San Diego.

23. "Statement of Congressman Harlan Hagen before House Judiciary Committee—a Bill to Outlaw the Communist Party," Harlan Hagen Papers, Misc. Correspondence 1954–1964, 11.8.25–11.8.30, 11.8.25, Communism (Inactive), 1954–1961, Harlan Hagen Collection, Walter Stiern Library Special Collections, California State University, Bakersfield (hereafter HHC).

24. Justina and Daniel Arias to Harlen Hagen, n.d., Immigration 1953–1956, 1957, 11.25.08–11.25.16, 11.25.14, Immigration & Naturalization Off. Bakersfield 1956 #1, HHC.

25. Brilliant, *The Color of America Has Changed*, 151.

26. See, for example, Bardacke, *Trampling Out the Vintage*.

27. Brilliant, *The Color of America Has Changed*, 122.

28. "Collins, Sullivan Visit Oakland to Study Job Laws," *Bakersfield Californian*, April 23, 1957.

29. On the civic unity of Los Angeles, see Zaragosa Vargas, *Labor Rights Are Civil Rights: Mexican Workers in Twentieth-Century America* (Princeton, N.J.: Princeton University Press, 2005), 258–60.

30. Brilliant, *The Color of America Has Changed*, 90.

31. Ibid., 126.

32. "Ordinance No. 1146," BCC.

33. "Secrecy Is Dangerous," *Bakersfield Californian*, August 26, 1957.

34. Ibid.

35. Vargas, *Labor Rights Are Civil Rights*, 258.

36. "A Negro Moves into a White Neighborhood," *California Crossroads* 2, no. 10 (October 1960), Jack McGuire Local History Room, Beale Memorial Library, Bakersfield, California (hereafter CC-BL).

37. Rabbi Arthur J. Kolatch, "Human Relations Commission," *California Crossroads* 3, no. 7 (July 1961), CC-BL.

38. "Resolution 47-63," Resolutions of the Bakersfield City Council, BCC.

39. Ibid.

40. West Coast regional NAACP field report, October 17–21, 1963, carton 77, folder 3, NAACP-WC.

41. Minutes of the Bakersfield City Council, August 3, 1964, BCC.

42. Kern Council for Civic Unity Newsletter, 1965, Jack Brigham Collection (hereafter JBC), in author's possession.

43. Membership pamphlet, KCCU, JBC.

44. KCCU pamphlet, n.d., JBC.

45. Ibid.

46. Ray Gonzales interview by author, May 11, 2009. Gonzales, Kern County's first elected Latino assemblyman in 1972, epitomized the multiracial origins of Chicano activism in Bakersfield. See Oliver Rosales, "'Hoo-ray Gonzales!': Civil Rights Protest and Chicano Politics in Bakersfield, 1968–1974," in *The Chicano Movement: Perspectives from the Twenty-First Century*, ed. Mario T. Garcia (New York: Routledge, 2014).

47. For an overview of the march, see "1000 Join Bakersfield Procession," *Bakersfield Californian*, March 15, 1965; Johnnie Mae Parker, *How Long? Not Long! The Battle to End Poverty in Bakersfield* (Bakersfield, Calif.: Johnnie Mae Parker, 1987), 20.

48. "1000 Join Bakersfield Procession"; Parker, *How Long? Not Long!*, 20.

49. See "1000 Join Bakersfield Procession"; Marshall Ganz, email to author, February 28, 2009.

50. For an overview of Marshall Ganz's work in the UFW, see Ganz, *Why David Sometimes Wins: Leadership, Organization, and Strategy in the California Farm Worker Movement* (New York: Oxford University Press), 2009.

51. "Grand Jury Files Report on KKK," *Bakersfield Californian*, May 19, 1922. On the activities of the Ku Klux Klan in Bakersfield, Kern County, and surrounding areas, see Kenneth E. Farmer, "The Invisible Empire in Kern County, 1922" (thesis, California Polytechnic State University, 1972); Edward Humes, *Mean Justice* (New York: Simon and Schuster, 1999); David Mark Chalmers, *Hooded Americanism: The History of the Ku Klux Klan* (Durham, N.C.: Duke University Press, 1987), 125. On the connection between the Klan and the Kern County Board of Supervisors, see Rick Wartzman, *Obscene in the Extreme: The Burning and Banning of John Steinbeck's "The Grapes of Wrath"* (New York: Public Affairs, 2008).

52. Neil R. McMillen, *The Citizen's Council: Organized Resistance to the Second Reconstruction, 1954–64* (Urbana: University of Illinois Press, 1971), xii.

53. "Huelga, Citizens Council, the NAACP," *California Crossroads* 8, no. 2 (February 1966), CC-BL.

54. "Segregationists Stalled by Sit-In," *Bakersfield Californian*, January 19, 1966.

55. Ibid.

56. On the creation of and controversy surrounding Kern County's Community Action Program, see Rosales, "Mississippi West," 52–121. On the antipoverty programs, see "Segregationist More Viewed by IGR [Inter-Group Relations] Board," *Bakersfield Californian*, January 21, 1966.

57. Ibid.

58. "City Urged to Denounce Segregationist," *Bakersfield Californian*, January 26,

1966; "Segregationist Controversy Sparks City Council Meeting," *Bakersfield Press*, January 26, 1966.

59. Minutes of the Bakersfield City Council, January 31, 1966, BCC.

60. Ibid.

61. "Cannot Outlaw Group—Says Council," *Bakersfield Californian*, February 2, 1966.

62. Minutes of the Bakersfield City Council, January 31, 1966, BCC.

63. See Rosales, "Mississippi West," 52–121.

64. Minutes of the Bakersfield City Council, March 7, 1966, BCC.

65. Ibid.

66. Brilliant, *The Color of America Has Changed*, 7.

67. Lauren Araiza, *To March for Others: The Black Freedom Struggle and the United Farm Workers* (Philadelphia: University of Pennsylvania Press, 2013).

68. On the evolution of Bakersfield's long civil rights movement, see Rosales, "Mississippi West."

CHAPTER 4

Beyond 1959

Cuban Exiles, Race, and Miami's Black Freedom Struggle

CHANELLE NYREE ROSE

In 1974 an anonymous writer made the following statement in direct response to African American radical activist Cecil Rolle's impassioned editorial about Miami's Cuban refugee problem and its detrimental impact on native-born blacks: "Cubans have brought no defects to this country that have not always been here." Moreover, the writer argued, "The Cubans are a blessing to the Blacks. They have made many dumb 'negroes' see that they cannot depend on [a] 'white boss' for jobs but have to get off their behinds and do for self." Finally, he asserted that "Cubans have as much right to want to liberate Cuba from communism as you do to liberate this country from racism . . . or do you want to do that?"[1] His comments reflected the popular perception of black Miamians as lazy, dependent, and apathetic. This image was often contrasted with the portrayal of hard-working and self-sufficient refugees pulling themselves up by their bootstraps to establish a vibrant community. But such divergent viewpoints present a distorted picture of both groups' experiences in Miami, particularly those of African Americans.

Two competing narratives have dominated the popular and historical discourses on black-Cuban relations in Miami since the 1960s. On the one hand, the "exile model" in much of the scholarship has universally portrayed Cuban refugees as staunchly anticommunist, white, and well educated. This characterization of all exiles is closely tied to their social status, strong work ethic, and ingenuity, which have become the standard markers of the Cuban "success" story.[2] In this model, the individual efforts and distinct culture of these refugees take center stage while other mitigating factors that aided their progress remain largely overlooked or devalued. On the other hand, a "job displacement" debate fostered vitriolic rants from both sides as increasing numbers of African Americans blamed the exile community for exacerbating their economic woes while many Cubans decried the exploitation of their people as scapegoats for the deep-seated racial inequities that existed long before they arrived. In addition, the urban riots that beset the city between the late 1960s and the 1980s have been partially attributed to the increasing black discontent with economic injustice and police brutality, compounded by the ascendancy of many Cubans in all areas of society.[3] Moreover, since the Cuban influx coincided with civil rights legislation, blacks may have lost potential jobs in department stores, banks, and service companies to refugees.[4]

Focusing on the unique experience of Cuban exiles or on the ethnic discord over competition for jobs has obscured the extensive ramifications of U.S. Cold War policy and the federal government's comprehensive refugee assistance program, the most far-reaching in the nation's history. A few historians have documented how government support aided Cubans' progress while negatively impacting African Americans in housing and other critical areas.[5] But there remains a need for scholarship that details how this aid and the subsequent progress of Cubans helped to lay the foundation for some of the structural inequalities and black-Cuban tensions that exist today. This chapter examines how the post-1959 influx of Cuban refugees critically influenced the course of the black freedom struggle in greater Miami during the 1960s and 1970s. Like other large cities undergoing rapid changes at that time, the city witnessed the rise of Black Power activism among black youths who were increasingly dissatisfied with the pace of the civil rights movement. In the face of rampant economic injustice and urban renewal programs that crippled black communities, African American leaders staunchly criticized the white power structure for failing to adequately address the glaring inequalities in housing and employment. In contrast to various other cities, however, the historic mass migration of Cuban émigrés significantly altered the local racial discourse and national civil rights leaders' view of the fight for racial equality in Miami. I argue that the profound impact of the first two waves of predominantly white Cuban exiles (1959–1962, 1965–1973) not only dimmed the spotlight on local civil rights activities, but also accelerated the Latinization of the city, relegating native-born blacks to the bottom of a complex racial hierarchy that extended some of the privileges of whiteness to Spanish speakers while denying those opportunities to non-Hispanic blacks.[6]

RACE AND U.S. COLD WAR POLICY

The Cuban Revolution of 1959 has become the transnational marker of the migration of Caribbean Spanish speakers to the city of Miami. However, this ethnic group has had a long and complex history in the southern metropolis. Long before the revolution, the city welcomed a small influx of Cuban exiles who had escaped the dictatorial regime of Gerardo Machado. Additionally, working-class Cuban and Puerto Rican women increased the ranks of the local garment industry as it began to expand in the mid-1950s and over the following decades. These Spanish-speaking migrants from the Northeast, particularly New York City and New Jersey, contributed to the early Latinization of Miami. Like their counterparts in other urban areas, they suffered gender and ethnic discrimination that thwarted unionization efforts and interracial alliances. While their experiences often paralleled the ascribed in-between racial identity of Hispanics in other cities, the rising number of Latin American migrants and Caribbean Spanish-speaking tourists during the early postwar period began to alter Miami's racial terrain as the Anglo business community sought ways to accommodate this relatively new group of foreign consumers. White Cuban exiles settled within this racial milieu, and they would become an integral part of U.S. efforts to bolster the global fight against communism.[7]

Early Cuban exiles—particularly the refugees who arrived in Miami between 1959 and 1973—stood at the crux of U.S. government efforts to defeat its closest enemy in the Cold War: Cuba. A significant number of these émigrés shared a strong anticommunist zeal because of their political and economic persecution in Cuba. The Cuban Refugee Committee (CRC), a local group of civic and community leaders established in August 1960, underscored U.S. national interests in its appeals for funds from the federal government. After discussing the rising number of Cuban exiles arriving daily and the potential problems in a city already experiencing a mild economic recession, the chair of the CRC, former city manager Ira F. Willard, addressed the "unique and critical situation" in Dade County. In a letter to President Dwight D. Eisenhower, Willard pointed out that Miami "has become a 'front-line' in the cold war tactics of the Communist world and a point of first asylum for those Cubans who find their present regime intolerable."[8] Eisenhower allocated $1 million under the Mutual Security Act to help facilitate the resettlement of Cuban refugees by partially funding the Cuban Refugee Emergency Employment Center, which opened on November 21, 1960.[9] However, the Kennedy administration would ultimately take the lead in directing U.S.–Cuban relations.

Shortly after his inauguration in January 1961, President John F. Kennedy set the tone for an administration that prioritized foreign policy over civil rights. He clearly stated his position on the Cuban refugee crisis in a letter to Abraham Alexander Ribicoff, the U.S. secretary of Health, Education, and Welfare (HEW). After extolling America's role as a "humanitarian sanctuary" and "protector of those individuals as well as nations who cast with us their personal liberty and hopes for the future," Kennedy declared: "Immediate action should be taken to assure no interruption in present services for the refugees."[10] He requested that Ribicoff consider "the use of surplus U.S. foods if needed for them, and possible utilization of the many qualified physicians and other professionally or technically qualified refugees." In support of this agenda, Ribicoff characterized the exiles' decision to seek refuge from Fidel Castro as a "stirring testimony to their faith in the determination of the Americas to preserve freedom and justice."[11]

Such lofty claims about the nation rang hollow for African Americans confronting white terrorism throughout much of the South. As many historians have noted, nonviolent black protests and the Freedom Rides ultimately forced the president to take a much stronger stand on civil rights toward the end of his term in office.[12] Kennedy's willingness to put Cold War interests and the concerns of southern congressmen before the civil rights of black citizens not only discredited his early reputation among native-born blacks in places like Jackson, Mississippi, but also undermined the image of the federal government among African Americans living in less volatile, yet racially oppressive, southern cities like Miami. Moreover, the support bestowed on Cuban exiles arriving in the city exacerbated African Americans' deep-rooted tensions with federal, state, and local white power structures that had instituted policies that left black citizens economically and politically disempowered.

During the 1960s, black Miamians were still locked in the less-skilled and lowest-paying jobs because of limited educational opportunities and job discrimination. The median family income for blacks in 1960 was 38 percent less than that of white households.[13] At that time, African Americans constituted an estimated 17 percent of Miami's population. Despite the existence of a small, prosperous black professional class, black men were grossly overrepresented in Dade County's service industry, and almost 31 percent worked as day laborers. Black women comprised 67 percent of the service occupations, particularly domestic work.[14] In 1962, the Florida Council on Human

Relations (FCHR) found serious black underrepresentation in unions, transportation service jobs, apprenticeship training programs, construction, and other areas of employment. During the same year, the FCHR reported that despite the growth of Miami's tourist economy, the overall unemployment rate of 5.1 percent outpaced the national average of 4.5 percent. According to the Hotel Employees Union, "The employment situation in this town is so bad that many whites are now taking menial jobs who never did so before." The average weekly earnings of local residents paled in comparison to their counterparts in other southern cities like Atlanta, Houston, and Nashville.[15]

The relatively peaceful desegregation of public accommodations in Miami alongside its perceived racially moderate tourist image had overshadowed the economic plight of blacks. Commenting on the glaring racial disparities still afflicting the city's African American population, *Miami News* editor Bill Baggs observed, "Education and jobs and housing are the extremely complicated challenges ahead of Miami in trying to make complete the end of racial injustice."[16] To make matters worse, the national and local governments' unwillingness to adequately address such racial injustices contrasted with their concerted efforts to provide employment, housing, and educational opportunities for the rising influx of Cuban exiles.

Although many Miamians sympathized with the plight of Cuban exiles, the federal government's decision to offer them services that many local residents did not receive fostered resentment. Even though the early Cuban refugees were professional and business elites, most of them came with very little and were in dire need of food, clothing, and jobs. Tensions escalated as the burden of assisting more refugees began to weigh heavily on public officials, despite the extensive assistance from state and local voluntary organizations, which carried much of the financial responsibility. In response, Kennedy authorized the establishment of the Cuban Refugee Program (CRP) under HEW in 1961 to offset the financial strain on the city. The CRP provided aid in different ways, including food, clothing, job training, and monthly relief checks. Between 1961 and 1966, Cuban refugees received an unprecedented estimated $158 million in aid.[17]

In an effort to convey the importance of supporting Cuban exiles in the anticommunist struggle, U.S. government officials pointed out their distinction from other immigrants who had previously received political asylum, such as Hungarian refugees. In 1961, J. Arthur Lazell, the deputy director of the CRP, asserted that "the displaced Cuban population in Miami is not just another refugee group when considered in the light of United States Latin

American policy." After explaining some of the similarities between Cuban exiles and other refugee groups, he declared, "How the Cubans are treated is, in the minds of many Latin Americans, indicative of the extent of the United States' determination and effectiveness in combatting Communism in the Western Hemisphere. To Americans, this may be illogical, but the emotional values implicit in the Cuban political situation are dominating factors." In this Cold War climate, the refugee status of the Cubans made them a national responsibility, and the federal government portrayed them as a model of U.S. freedom and democracy for Latin American countries. Yet the mounting financial burden on Miami compounded by the frustration of the city's residents still presented serious problems. The national government decided to accelerate the relocation focus of the CRP in order to mitigate what the Miami Cuban Refugee Committee had envisioned as a "potentially explosive social and economic problem" if exiles continued to arrive in the city.[18]

Despite the efforts of the CRP, most Miamians adopted nativist views toward Cuban exiles that indirectly undermined U.S. foreign policy. In 1962, the *Miami Herald* published a letter from a local resident who posed the questions, "Is Miami going to be maintained as Miami? Or will it become a relocated Havana[?]"[19] Such statements revealed an ignorance of the history of the Cuban community in Miami.[20] Even though the prerevolutionary Cuban population of Miami never surpassed thirty thousand, approximately fifty thousand wealthy Cuban tourists came during the summer months to shop and vacation. By the mid-1950s, these Cubans, primarily white, made annual trips and had access to the local beaches, hotels, and restaurants. Most white Miamians continued to hold racially prejudiced views toward Hispanics, regardless of their social status, but the tourist dollars of the wealthy Cubans distinguished them from most other groups, who were not recognized as fully white in other ethnically diverse southern communities. Similarly, the representation of émigrés as "model immigrants" allowed them to receive certain opportunities available to neither native-born blacks nor Hispanics living outside of Dade County.[21]

Historian Antonio Lopez has noted that "Miami is the capital of Cuban Whiteness." This comment provides insight into the complex socioeconomic and political history of the exiles following the revolution. Lopez asserts that "it was overwhelmingly White criollos who settled in Miami after 1959" and wielded a power that "naturalized Cuban Whiteness and White privilege in its everyday practice of Cold War antirevolutionary politics."[22] The first wave of upper- and middle-class Cubans was composed of doctors, lawyers, and educators who had greatly contributed to the social and economic development of their homeland. In addition to circumventing the established immigration policies by attaining special status, the first two waves of Cuban exiles were not subjected to the same racialization as other Hispanic groups in the United States. Indeed, the socioeconomic class and racial classification of these affluent white refugees enhanced their social status; government officials and CRP administrators heavily advertised the success stories of resettled Cuban exiles to demonstrate how their perceived white American attributes distinguished them from other émigrés. For example, in response to criticism about assisting Cuban refugees, Secretary Ribicoff of the HEW pointed out that Americans should not view them as a charity case because "they are proud and resourceful people" who only sought help under extreme conditions.[23] Such depictions of Cuban exiles were intended to counter the negative stereotypes commonly associated with other Latin American immigrants, especially Mexicans.

The U.S. government expanded the boundaries of whiteness for early Cuban refugees in order to bolster national and local support.[24] This allowed the federal government to wield the refugees as a weapon in the broader ideological Cold War rhetorical battles. According to Cheris Brewer Current, "Whiteness and an anticommunist stance became indispensable traits needed to garner public support for any refugee group, as the U.S. provided refugee policies only to groups that reflected the U.S.'s dominant understanding of desirable racialized and ideological identities."[25] In effect, the markers of whiteness not only included physical attributes, but also entailed agreed-upon presumed values and actions. Not surprisingly, this more inclusive definition of whiteness opened opportunities for Spanish speakers while simultaneously garnering increased resentment from the larger Miami community, particularly African Americans. As the privileges of whiteness spilled over into state and local educational policies that benefited the children of early Cuban exiles, the local chapter of the National Association for the Advancement of Colored People (NAACP) engaged in a fierce battle against the segregation of public schools in Dade County.[26]

EDUCATION AND ACCESS IN THE TRIETHNIC CITY OF MIAMI

Early Cuban exiles attained various citizenship rights that were denied to black Miamians, especially in regard to education. Four years after the landmark 1954 *Brown* decision, public schools in Dade County remained segregated. The protracted fight of Miami NAACP leaders to have four black plaintiffs admitted at the Orchard Villa Elementary School resulted in the state's first integrated school in September 1959, despite a "school closing" bill orchestrated by Florida legislators. Notwithstanding the valiant efforts of the local NAACP branch, in less than a year Orchard Villa had become an all-black school as white families moved out of the neighborhood. At the same time, the school desegregation struggle prompted vicious anticommunist attacks from the Florida Legislative Investigation Committee against the NAACP.[27] Yet, within this hostile environment, the state legislature and the Dade County School Board (DCSB) admitted exiled Cuban children to local schools, and CRP officials worked closely with the district to ensure the acclimatization of refugee children to the American system.

In 1962, the HEW helped finance the continuation of Dade County schools' "accelerated English program." Recommendations to improve the education of Cuban children included translating American textbooks into Spanish and establishing tutoring classes to train former Cuban teachers.[28] Commenting on the treatment of Cuban children by the white power structure, a black minister facetiously, yet accurately, wrote that "the American Negro could solve the school integration problem by teaching his children to speak only Spanish."[29] His statement gives insight into the increasingly debased value of black children in a city that had made the definition of whiteness more inclusive for Spanish speakers, particularly Cuban exiles and their children.

Both Puerto Rican and Mexican children in South Florida were often subjected to acts of racial injustice that native-born black children also commonly faced. During the same year as the *Brown* ruling, white parents at Redland Elementary School in Homestead, a suburb of Miami in southern Dade's agricultural region, organized a three-day boycott against the enrollment of Puerto Rican and Mexican children. According to the *St. Petersburg Times*, a group of parents submitted a resolution to the DCSB stating that "the children of migrant workers constituted a health menace to the children of permanent residents." The prolonged absence of over four hundred white children convinced the school board to order the temporary relocation of the Hispanic children to the grounds of the John W. Campbell Labor Camp.[30]

At the same time, the influx of Cuban exiles and growing Latinization of the city allowed middle-class Puerto Ricans to transcend conventional race boundaries in Miami. Middle-class Puerto Rican children did receive some of the same opportunities as their Cuban counterparts. The buddy system became one of the most successful practices, pairing Cuban and Puerto

Rican children with English-speaking peers. Commenting on the program, a Cuban-born teacher observed that "most of the youngsters are doing well in English by the time they come back from the Christmas Holidays." The parents of Puerto Rican children also took advantage of night classes in English offered at the Lindsey Hopkins vocational school, which had an enrollment of over two hundred Spanish-speaking adults in these classes in 1956.[31]

Local colleges and universities also benefited Latinos in Miami. The University of Miami (UM) gave a significant number of Cuban refugees special advantages, underscoring the school's long history of recruiting Spanish-speaking students. Its historical ties to Latin America, coupled with Miami's emergence as a frontline city of the Cold War, significantly influenced UM's policy toward Cuban exile students. Meanwhile, UM, like other postsecondary schools in the state, refused to enroll African Americans except for a few tokens.[32] With the partial support of federal funds, the university administration offered Cuban émigrés a variety of educational opportunities, including special English courses for professionals, a creative writing program, and at least 300 loans for those students who no longer received adequate support from their parents in Cuba. By 1961, the foreign student population of the school had increased to 7.4 percent, and Cuban exiles constituted the majority of these new enrollments. During the same year, the UM Law School provided a free tuition program in Spanish and English to over 400 exiled Cuban lawyers to qualify them for job opportunities in the United States and Latin America. In April, the institution's student newspaper, the *Miami Hurricane*, reported that 154 Cuban physicians had graduated from a three-month postgraduate medical course directed by Ralph Jones, the chair of the Medical Department. Apparently, no course similar to this one had ever been taught in an American institution.[33] In the summer of 1965, the UM School of Education offered a similar program for Cuban refugee teachers. This form of aid for refugees contributed to the progress of a Cuban middle class, while African Americans continued to face racial discrimination that prohibited them from attaining higher education.[34]

The University of Miami had denied the admittance of native-born blacks since its inception. In 1960, the *Miami Hurricane*'s editor, Bernie Weiner, had addressed the economic dangers of continuing segregation at the university if the federal government decided to deny funding to colleges that defied its mandate for eliminating racism in higher education. He also raised moral and pragmatic questions about upholding Jim Crow at an institution that professed progressivism and ethnic diversity. According to Weiner, opposing integration no longer seemed tenable at a school that had historically admitted "so-called 'yellow' Orientals" and Latin American students of "mixed parentage." He posed a perennial question: "Can the University of Miami remain in the eyes of the world—particularly, Latin America, Asia and Africa—a segregated institution and still hold their respect as a progressive dynamic school?"[35] The rising social cost of segregation at a school that touted cultural tolerance, alongside the mounting pressure of local civil rights activism, ultimately led to a token desegregation of UM in 1961.

LOCAL BLACK AGITATION AND NATIONAL ATTENTION

Various black leaders from the professional, religious, and business communities bemoaned the detrimental impact of Cuban émigrés on the city's already stagnant economy. Even though the *Miami Times* was very sympathetic to the challenges confronting Cuban exiles, some editorials reflected the mounting resentment of some of their black readers. Daniel H. Lang, the executive director of the Greater Miami Urban League (GMUL), told the Senate Subcommittee on Refugees and Escapees that he had received numerous complaints from blacks who claimed they were being "systematically pushed out of jobs to make room for Cubans."[36] In March 1963, three members of the Greater African Methodist Episcopal Ministerial Alliance wrote a letter to President Kennedy requesting assistance in resolving the escalating ethnic hostilities. After briefly explaining their Christian duty to welcome Cuban exiles in need, they focused on the problems facing the city's black population and pointed out that "certain hostilities have developed because native Americans are left jobless, some with large families, having been replaced in their jobs by refugees."[37]

Those hostilities were clearly elucidated in a *Jet* magazine article written by John Britton that featured a black family of ten with an unemployed father and a mother who had recently lost her job at a Miami hotel. Britton quoted the mayor of Miami as saying that "he couldn't point to many specific instances, but he was sure some Negroes had been 'retired' from their jobs and replaced by Cuban refugees."[38] In a letter to the editor of the *Miami Times* a local black resident blamed the small number of African American employees in positions that had traditionally barred native-born blacks on the influx of exiles. She observed that the increasing percentage of Cuban exiles hired as sales clerks and office workers had compelled the business community to employ a few "token Negroes" as a perfunctory measure to placate black Miamians.[39] While Cuban exiles seemingly were the main target, the litany of complaints from blacks ultimately held white officials accountable for scapegoating exiles to avoid dealing with the city's culpability in the socioeconomic plight of African Americans.

Even though accusations of job displacement animated public discourse in black communities, African American leaders primarily directed their grievances toward the federal and local governments. This made sense to black leaders because of the willingness of these institutions to provide support for Cuban exiles. In many different ways, blacks called on the president and municipal leaders to provide native-born blacks with the same treatment and opportunities as Cuban exiles received. Talmadge Willard Fair, who replaced Daniel Lang as the executive director of the GMUL in 1963, praised the refugees for their rising economic success in Miami, but he remained highly critical of a white power structure that "treats Cuban immigrants better than it treats its black citizens." In response to reports of rising ethnic tensions, Fair observed, "the hostility among blacks toward Cubans is small. We're not angry at the Cubans, but at a system that will do more for outsiders than for its own citizens."[40] In light of the federal, state, and local governments' neglect in regard to the economic plight of African Americans, most native-born blacks viewed the financial support awarded Cubans as hypocritical and an act of betrayal.

Miami's black leaders intensified their demand for economic justice as national civil rights activists, grassroots organizations, and liberal whites prepared for the 1963 March on Washington for Jobs and Freedom. Under the Reverend Edward Graham's direction, the Greater Miami Ministerial Alliance petitioned the Kennedy administration about Jim Crow hiring practices in the city's two largest public utilities: the Southern Bell Telephone Company and Florida Power and Light. Commenting on the Cuban refugee situation, Graham commended black Miamians for remaining tolerant "while many around them were losing their heads." At the same time, he strongly criticized members of the white establishment who were benefiting from exploiting ethnic tensions between the groups: "We resent those who would cover up the basic issue of the Negroes' denial to [an] equal share of his country's resources with the cry of Cuban encroachment."[41] In June 1963, the chair of the Congress of Racial Equality (CORE), A. D. Moore, threatened one of the city's largest demonstrations at Shell's City unless the supermarket hired black store clerks. After a three-year economic boycott against the store's Jim Crow policy, Moore expressed the growing dissatisfaction of black Miamians with gradualism and delay. Like Graham, he drew attention to the privileged status of Cuban refugees to embolden his demands. Moore declared that "we have seen the Cubans come into this community and receive equal treatment immediately. . . . why should we wait?"[42]

Other black leaders pushing for economic empowerment adopted a more radical approach in their demand for substantive change. Cecil Gaylord Rolle, the militant African American editor of the *Liberty News*, became one of the most outspoken leaders on civil rights issues and the Cuban situation in Miami. As the black freedom struggle in the United States adopted a more nationalistic and radical tone, he infused his rhetoric with more Black Power fervor. Shortly after the establishment of his newspaper in 1961, Rolle began to address the unrelenting anger of many of his readers in his fiery biweekly column, "Seize the Time." He observed, "The Black American so-called citizen with all kinds of Supreme Court decisions" continued to confront racial discrimination in the areas of housing, employment, and police brutality. In contrast to the enduring racial plight of African Americans in the city, he pointed out that "the white Cuban exile or refugee doesn't need a Civil Rights Bill, or a School Desegregation Supreme Court decision, or an 'open Housing Bill' out of Congress."[43] He heavily criticized the federal government, which provided ample opportunities for recently arrived exiles while steadfastly resisting the fight for racial equality of African Americans with a long history in the United States. Emerging black leaders like Rolle accelerated the fight for economic empowerment in the 1960s, but he adopted a black nationalist agenda that deemphasized integration and focused more broadly on community control over resources. Various members of the established black leadership, particularly Rev. Graham and Father Theodore Gibson, did try to reduce ethnic tensions by seeking redress for racial discrimination from the white civic and business communities. But Rolle's efforts seemingly fueled the fire because he advanced a more hostile attitude toward Cuban refugees.

Rolle made a concerted effort to organize a contingent of black Miamians around the August 1963 March on Washington to protest black job displacement by Cubans. With the aid of a group of disgruntled African American businessmen, he distributed approximately five thousand circulars and subsequently received support from unemployed black workers. In regard to the purpose of making such a public display of protest against high black unemployment, Rolle reportedly stated: "We're sitting down here without keys and trying to get in some of the local doors. Since we do have the keys to local doors in Washington, as U.S. citizens, we'll take our protests there to get something done." However, his efforts yielded few results since his campaign did not garner enough support. Rolle maintained that the Cuban influx had compounded the unemployment crisis confronting blacks, yet he also pointed out that "social injustice existed before the Cuban migration began."[44]

Frustrations over the problems confronting black Miamians soon attracted national attention, particularly from the African American press. Allan Morrison of *Ebony* magazine reported on the stark contrast between Florida's insufficient welfare checks and the local relief payments awarded to refugees. He pointed to the racially biased welfare policies in the state and the absence of a minimum wage as the real sources of economic injustice.[45] For Cuban exiles classified as temporary visitors in 1959, a single person received $72 a month and a married couple collected $100, irrespective of children.[46] To avert a potential explosion, by 1963 Mayor Robert King High advocated for the acceleration of relocation efforts, the modification of rigid welfare qualifications for black Miamians, and the increase of federal projects located in the city to boost employment.[47]

The post-1959 Cuban migration animated the broader civil rights discourse as some African American leaders highlighted the exiles' ability to reap the fruits of democracy while native-born blacks continued to struggle for racial equality. On the one hand, the Cuban Revolution became a symbol of black liberation and Third World solidarity for radical African American activists who lauded Castro's defiance against the U.S. government and his professed policies of racial reform.[48] In effect, the revolution carried a national significance that inspired black nationalist leaders in North America who advanced a global black freedom struggle. On the other hand, the ascendancy of the exile community in Miami illuminated the second-class status of African Americans, and civil rights leaders railed against the U.S. government for treating refugees better than American citizens. After visiting Miami during a southern tour organized to celebrate a hundred years of African American emancipation, Wiley Branton, an attorney and the director of the Voter Education Project in the South, sarcastically noted that the only way for black Miamians "to share the same fruits of American democracy now extended to Cuban refugees would be for them to renounce American citizenship, go to Castro's Cuba—and then return as Cuban refugees."[49] His caustic but astute remarks shed light on the unequal status of native-born blacks in a city that privileged Cuban exiles over other groups.

During one of his several visits to the city of Miami, Martin Luther King Jr. challenged the Cuban "success" model and stressed the disadvantaged position of all minority groups in a country that had failed to adequately address the ills of its underprivileged populations. During a mass meeting of over 1,500 people at the Reverend Edward Graham's Mount Zion Baptist Church, organized in celebration of the newly established Miami chapter of the Southern Christian Leadership Conference, King told the congregation, "The Negro does not get a square deal in Mississippi, but he doesn't get a square deal in Miami either." He further explained, "In Chicago and New York, Atlanta and Jackson, and Miami, the Negro is freer in 1966, but not yet free."[50] King's words reflected the views of local African American leaders, who argued that the exploitation of both Cubans and native-born blacks ultimately served the Anglo business community. But his remarks failed to recognize how the changing definition of whiteness in Miami had complicated the racialized experiences of its black residents.

AN UNEASY ALLIANCE BETWEEN ANTICOMMUNISM, RACISM, AND CONSERVATIVE EXILE POLITICS

After the 1959 revolution a symbiotic relationship developed between the racism of a segment of the white Cuban population on the island and their counterparts in exile, particularly in South Florida. Very few Afro-Cubans were part of the first and second waves of exiles who settled in Miami. Nonetheless, the personal accounts of some of these individuals, who either passed through the city seeking refuge elsewhere or chose to reside permanently in the area, help to illuminate the racism underpinning the ideology of some staunchly conservative white Cuban exiles in the 1960s. For example, in 1961, the *Crisis*, the official organ of the national NAACP, published an important article by Juan Betancourt, a prominent Afro-Cuban attorney appointed to the National Federation of Negro Societies by the newly established Cuban government. He had left the island one year after the revolution. While Betancourt seemingly supported various advancements for the Afro-Cuban population in the areas of employment and schools (despite his opposition to their use as a form of revolutionary propaganda to mask continued racial inequality in the Cuban political leadership and other areas), he assailed the government for closing the Afro-Cuban mutual aid societies that had served the interests of this group for over a century. He also heavily criticized the monolithic, elitist, and racially conservative nature of Cuban exile communities. With the exception of the Christian Democratic Party, he asserted, all of the political parties "are controlled by white Cubans, members of the upper or middle class, who have refused to accept Castro's pattern of subhuman living. Yet they do not exhibit the slightest interest in the fate of the Cuban Negro."[51] Similarly, a black salsa musician who had left Cuba in 1966 had lived in New York City, Detroit, and Los Angeles. He recalled that, after relocating to South Florida, "I was never rejected on racial grounds until I came to Miami." "Here there is a separation because Cubans in Miami act more like white Americans than Latins," he added.[52]

In the ensuing decades, Afro-Cuban Enrique Patterson noticed similar issues. Patterson, the son of a Cuban father who proudly embraced his black identity, recalled that in his Cuban hometown "everyone was conscious of the color line" despite the nonexistence of legal segregation. After enduring much hardship in Cuba, partially because of his independent and assertive Afro-Cuban identity, he joined a counterrevolutionary group and later moved to Miami in the early 1990s. He argued that many of the early white Cuban exiles adopted an ideology that denied the long history of racism on the island:

> The White Cuban exile community in south Florida continues to perpetuate the codes and ways of thinking about race relations that were already present on the island before the revolution. . . . In a word White Cuban exiles have constructed a racial myth that virtually erases all traces of the racial discrimination. As a result, prerevolutionary Cuba is often depicted as a lost paradise characterized by prosperity and racial harmony, a notion that is frequently evidenced in the Miami press. According to this myth, Castro invented racism (of course Fidel blames the exiles for racism in Cuba). This idealized version of Cuba before Castro exempts the Cuban exile community from taking any responsibility for the current racial tensions present in south Florida.[53]

In part, his account resembles the experiences of Afro-Cuban Carlos Moore, who is considered a persona non grata in Miami's Cuban exile community. During his formative years in Cuba, Moore also learned that his color carried a negative connotation. In his autobiography he recalled: "As early as the age of six I was aware that whites did not approve of my dark skin color. By the time I was a teenager, I had had enough of the penury into which I was born and the contempt attached to my blackness." He further explained that his "town proper was made up of a racially segregated park, a racially segregated movie house, and three social clubs that operated on strict color line[s]."[54]

Since employing the rhetoric of racial equality constituted a critical part of Castro's propaganda campaign, a particular strain of exile politics perpetuated the idea of prerevolutionary harmonious race relations in attempts to undermine his leadership. And even though supporting an anticommunist movement to overthrow Castro dominated the political activity of those refugees engaged in local resistance, they perceived any critique of U.S. race relations as a weapon that could be wielded by the Cuban president. On the contrary, Afro-Cubans like Moore spoke out against racial discrimination in the United States and later assailed the Castro government and white Cuban exiles. For example, in the detailed account of his personal journey, Moore chronicled his thirty-four years in exile, including his activism in Harlem's diverse black community during the height of the civil rights–Black Power era. Before he became completely disillusioned with Castro and the revolution's unfulfilled promises of racial equality, Moore had been a staunch supporter of the 26th of July Movement. After rather reluctantly taking a teaching position at Florida International University in 1986, Moore came under serious fire from various members of the Cuban exile community, who accused him of spreading pro-Castro propaganda in his courses. Coverage of this story in the *Miami Herald* revealed that these charges were unfounded. However, Moore later concluded, "I could only be a Communist provocateur and a Castro undercover agent since I only talked about the racial oppression and segregation that prevailed in Cuba long before Castro took power."[55]

Betancourt's, Patterson's, and Moore's critiques of white Cuban refugees shed light on the conflation of communism and civil rights activism within an important part of the exile community in Miami. It is true that Left-leaning organizations, which sometimes included communist sympathizers, had historically played an important role in antiracist causes and civil rights activism in the United States. But segregationists also waged communist smear campaigns against civil rights organizations like the NAACP to thwart their desegregation efforts. The high profile of the Miami chapter of the NAACP, coupled with the city's early "red scare," heightened suspicions about communist-inspired racial agitation in the civil rights organization, and the early Cuban influx to Miami coincided with the local branch's spirited defense against mounting attacks from the Florida Legislative Investigation Committee. According to Gene Strul, the news director of Biscayne Television Corporation, the American-born communist Jacob Rosen had attended the Socialist Youth Congress in Havana and subsequently infiltrated racial minority groups in Miami. Strul noted, "From these the Congress of Racial Equality which has a branch in Miami has been selected to spearhead the spreading communist propaganda. WCKT News had learned that CORE's mailing list has been given to a communist sponsor organization called 'Spanish Refugee Aid.'"[56] While this report offered no proof that the CORE chapter in Miami was a communist front, it reinforced the assumed relationship between civil rights and communism. As María de los Angeles Torres, an exiled Cuban living outside Miami, recalled, "Those of us raised outside of the enclave, and therefore more exposed to racism, were ostracized in Miami when we tried to discuss racism or raise our voices in support of the civil rights movement."[57]

CONCLUSION

The U.S. Cold War policies in concert with the leadership of Miami's white civic elite had a profound impact on the trajectory of racial politics in the city. Cuban exiles brought a variety of skills and entrepreneurial ideas that aided their progress, but government aid and local support greatly contributed to their economic and political success. The ascribed whiteness of the first wave of Cuban émigrés helped to facilitate this process. After the Cuban migration, African Americans continued to wage an uphill battle against an Anglo leadership that had weakened their political power by supporting at-large elections while failing to adequately address the pervasive economic inequalities. Their struggles mirrored those of African Americans in other southern metropolises. But unlike in other southern cities, blacks in Miami confronted an emerging white Cuban leadership with a politically conservative ideology that discouraged the efforts of civil rights and Black Power activists. Social ills in the black community today cannot be understood outside the context of long-term U.S. policies and structural changes in Miami.

One unintended consequence of the large Cuban influx has been the comparatively meager share of local, state, and federal support for African Americans, which has thwarted their progress in the areas of education, housing, and economic growth. Not surprisingly, the ramifications of Miami's unique Cuban migration fanned the flames of unattended urban problems. Police brutality, deindustrialization, economic discrimination, urban renewal, and interstate highway construction, which often ripped through historically black neighborhoods, served to fuel Miami's first major race riot in 1968. While the National Advisory Commission on Civil Disorders cited the job displacement of blacks by Cuban refugees as a source of frustration peculiar to this urban protest, the report also revealed that the origins of the social unrest primarily stemmed from the white business community's unfulfilled promises to provide jobs for black people and from ongoing police brutality.[58]

The U.S. Cold War policies and the racialization of Cuban refugees as white not only strained black-Cuban relations, but also presaged the emergence of a Cuban American leadership with a staunchly politically conservative ideology that discouraged the efforts of civil rights and Black Power activists pushing for socioeconomic justice. Miami's blacks found themselves enmeshed in a contentious struggle against a burgeoning Cuban political establishment that did not have the racial consciousness of the Latin American immigrants with a long history of racial oppression in the United States. In addition, the support for Cuban exiles bolstered the Latinization of Miami and helped to lay the foundation for an economic and political system that showed partiality toward Spanish speakers. Despite local resistance toward the Latinization of the city, vividly expressed through the homegrown English-only backlash against the 1970s trend toward bilingualism in the state, the unprecedented support from government officials interested in discrediting Castro's communist regime coupled with city leaders' concerted efforts to revitalize the economy helped to secure Cuban refugees' success. In 1985, the election of a Cuban mayor, Xavier Suarez, signified a definite shift from the historically Anglo-dominated leadership in the local government and foreshadowed the development of what many non-Latino blacks perceived as the hegemony of Cubans.

To be sure, African Americans, particularly members of the middle class, made significant gains from Miami's civil rights struggle. Since the appointment of Athalie Range as the first black city commissioner in 1966, there has been continued black representation in the city commission and the state legislature. Members of the black elite benefited from desegregation as they escaped the confines of the inner city and entered new arenas that previously had denied them access. Miami's black working class did not fare as well. Undeniably, the historical roots of the city's impoverished black communities are multilayered and complex. However, their current problems need to be understood in the context of long-term U.S. policy decisions and structural choices in the city that had a disproportionate negative impact on native-born blacks.

NOTES

1. "Concerned Citizens," *Liberty News*, January 20, 1974.

2. Scholarly works abound that detail how hardworking Cuban immigrants transformed Miami from a declining tourist and retirement center into the capital of the Caribbean and Latin economies, despite the new burden placed on the city. These studies

show how refugees boosted the city's economy, established a viable ethnic enclave, revitalized various blighted communities, and provided the impetus for millions of federal dollars to be pumped into the local government. See Guillermo J. Grenier and Alex Stepick, eds., *Miami Now! Immigration, Ethnicity, and Social Change* (Gainesville: University Press of Florida, 1992); Alejandro Portes and Alex Stepick, eds., *City on the Edge: The Transformation of Miami* (Berkeley: University of California Press, 1993); Alex Stepick, Guillermo Grenier, Max Castro, and Marvin Dunn, eds., *This Land Is Our Land: Immigrants and Power in Miami* (Berkeley: University of California Press, 2003); Joel Garreau *The Nine Nations of North America* (New York: Houghton Mifflin, 1981); Joan Didion, *Miami* (New York: Simon and Schuster, 1987); Thomas D. Boswell, *The Cubanization and Hispanization of Miami* (Miami, Fla.: Cuban American National Council, 1994); Sheila Croucher, *Imagining Miami: Ethnic Politics in a Postmodern World* (Charlottesville: University Press of Virginia, 1997). See also Damian J. Fernandez, ed., *Cuban Studies since the Revolution* (Gainesville: University Press of Florida, 1992); Rafael Prohías and Lourdes Casal, *The Cuban Minority in the U.S.: Preliminary Report on Need Identification and Program Evaluation* (Boca Raton: Florida Atlantic University, 1973); Alejandro Portes and Robert Bach, *Latin Journey: Cuban and Mexican Immigrants in the United States* (Berkeley: University of California Press, 1985); Alex Stepick III and Guillermo Grenier, "Cubans in Miami," in *In the Barrios: Latinos and the Underclass Debate*, ed. Joan W. Moore and Raquel Pinderhughes (New York: Russell Sage Foundation, 1993), 79–100.

Stepick and Grenier list the "Cuban welfare benefits," but they also provide a detailed analysis of other social, economic, and political factors that have contributed to the success of Cuban exiles in Miami. I employ the racial category of "white Cuban" to refer to the first wave of Cuban exiles in Miami, who attained whiteness because of their complexion, socioeconomic situation, and political status. In many ways, this construction of Cuban whiteness did not develop in other American cities. See also Grenier and Stepick, *Miami Now! Immigration, Ethnicity, and Social Change.*

3. See Marvin Dunn and Bruce Porter, *The Miami Riot of 1980: Crossing the Bounds* (Lexington, Mass.: Lexington Books, 1984); Darryl B. Harris, *The Logic of Black Urban Rebellions: Challenging the Dynamics of White Dominion in Miami* (Westport, Conn.: Praeger, 1999). Some twenty-first-century scholarship has challenged the Cuban exceptionalism model by examining the heterogeneity of this ethnic group alongside exile politics while highlighting the U.S. government's critical role in helping to construct the success story for political gain during the height of the Cold War. See Cheris Brewer Current, *Questioning the Cuban Exile Model: Race, Gender, and Resettlement, 1959–1979* (El Paso, Tex.: LFB, 2010); Nancy Raquel Mirabal, "'Ser de Aquí': Beyond the Cuban Exile Model," *Latino Studies* 1 (2003): 366–82; María de los Angeles Torres, *In the Land of Mirrors: Cuban Exile Politics in the United States* (Ann Arbor: University of Michigan Press, 1999); Silvia Pedraza-Bailey, *Political and Economic Migrants in America: Cubans and Mexicans* (Austin: University of Texas Press, 1985).

4. Edward S. Cooke and Sheila Croucher, *Imagining Miami: Ethnic Politics in a Postmodern World* (Charlottesville: University Press of Virginia, 1997), 173.

5. See Raymond Mohl, "Miami: The Ethnic Cauldron," in *Sunbelt Cities: Politics and Growth since WWII*, ed. Richard M. Bernard and Bradley R. Rice (Austin: University of Texas Press, 1983); Mohl, "On the Edge: Blacks and Hispanics in Metropolitan Miami since 1959," *Florida Historical Quarterly* 69, no. 1 (Summer 1990): 37–56; Mohl, "Shadows and the Sunshine: Race and Ethnicity in Miami," *Tequesta* 49 (1989): 63–80. Mohl argues that the socioeconomic progress of Cuban exiles did have a deleterious impact on the black community, particularly in the areas of housing and politics.

6. For a detailed look at the early Latinization of Miami, see Chanelle Rose, "Tourism and the Hispanicization of Race in Miami, 1945–1965," *Journal of Social History* 45, no. 3 (Spring 2012): 735–56.

7. Louis A. Pérez Jr., *On Becoming Cuban: Identity, Nationality, and Culture* (Chapel Hill: University of North Carolina Press, 1999); Melanie Shell-Weiss, *Coming to Miami: A Social History* (Gainesville: University Press of Florida, 2009).

8. Ira F. Willard to Dwight D. Eisenhower, October 17, 1960, Dante B. Fascell Committee: Inter-American Affairs and International Organizations and Movements, 1960–1963, box 1937, folder 7, Dante B. Fascell Congressional Papers, Special Collections, Otto Richter Library, University of Miami, Miami, Fla.

9. Several months before the formation of the CRC, Eisenhower had authorized the Central Intelligence Agency to train a Cuban exile brigade to topple the Castro government. See Lars Schoultz, *That Infernal Little Cuban Republic: The United States and the Cuban Revolution* (Chapel Hill: University of North Carolina Press, 2009); Stephen G. Rabe, *Eisenhower and Latin America: The Foreign Policy of Anticommunism* (Chapel Hill: University of North Carolina Press, 1988).

10. "Text of President John F. Kennedy's Letter to Secretary Ribicoff," ca. February 1961, Cuban Refugee Center Records (General Correspondence and Documents), box 1, folder 2, Cuban Heritage Collection, Otto G. Richter Library, University of Miami, Miami, Fla. (hereafter CHC).

11. "Report of Secretary Abraham A. Ribicoff on the Cuban Refugee Problem," February 2, 1961, 1, box 1, folder 2, Cuban Refugee Center Records, CHC.

12. For one of the most compelling and meticulously researched accounts of President Kennedy's tepid support for the civil rights movement, see Nick Bryant, *The Bystander: John F. Kennedy and the Struggle for Black Equality* (New York: Basic, 2006).

13. James W. Morrison, *The Negro in Greater Miami—Fact Sheet: An Analysis of Population, Housing, Family Characteristics, Occupation, Income Distribution, and Education* (Miami, Fla.: Greater Miami Urban League, 1962), 20; Raymond Mohl, "Changing Economic Patterns in the Miami Metropolitan Area, 1940–1980," *Tequesta* 42 (1982): 63–73.

14. Morrison, *The Negro in Greater Miami*, 17.

15. Harold M. Rose, "Metropolitan Miami's Changing Negro Population, 1950–1960," *Economic Geography* 40 (July 1964): 2.

16. "A Special and Private Report to Miss Rebecca Pierce for William C. Baggs," 1958?, box 19, folder 519, 3–4, Bill Baggs Collection, Special Collections, University of Miami, Miami, Fla. In 1959 the Dade County grand jury's preliminary investigative report described Miami's slum clearance program as a failure and declared that the heart of downtown was "in danger of becoming an over-crowded, disease-spawning jungle." See Juanita Greene, "Miami's Slum Clearance Plans Face Intensive Investigation," *Miami Herald*, November 15, 1959.

17. John Egerton, *Cubans in Miami: A Third Dimension in Racial and Cultural Relations* (Nashville, Tenn.: Race Relations Information Center, 1969), 3.

18. J. Arthur Lazell to Marshall Wise, June 27, 1961, box 1, folder 3, Cuban Refugee Center Records, CHC.

19. Ibid.

20. Pérez, *On Becoming Cuban*, 423–33.

21. See Chanelle Rose, "Neither Southern nor Northern: Miami, Florida, and the Black Freedom Struggle in America's Tourist Paradise, 1896–1968" (PhD diss., University of Miami, 2007), chap. 8.

22. Antonio Lopez, "Enrique Patterson: Black Cuban Intellectual in Cuban Miami," in *Afro-Latin@ Reader: History and Culture in the United States*, ed. Miriam Jimenez Roman and Juan Flores (Durham, N.C.: Duke University Press, 2010), 439.

23. "Report of Secretary Abraham A. Ribicoff on the Cuban Refugee Problem," February 2, 1961, 3, box 1, folder 2, Cuban Refugee Center Records, CHC.

24. Ibid.

25. Cheris Brewer Current, "Expanding the 'Exile Model': Race, Gender, Resettlement, and Cuban-American Identity, 1959–1979" (PhD diss., Washington State University, 2007), 24; Current, *Questioning the Cuban Exile Model: Race, Gender, and Resettlement, 1959–1979* (El Paso, Tex.: LFB, 2010).

26. "Miami Welcomes Cubans, Boots Haitian[s]: Cubans? SI? Haitians? NO?," *Miami Times*, September 21, 1963.

27. This movement was led by a state organization better known as the Johns Committee, named for its ultrasegregationist chair, Charley E. Johns. For works that examine the Miami chapter of the NAACP's fierce battle against the Florida Legislative Investigation Committee, see Clarence Taylor, *Black Religious Intellectuals: The Fight for Equality from Jim Crow to the Twenty-First Century* (New York: Routledge, 2002); Steven Lawson, *Civil Rights Crossroads: Nation, Community and the Black Freedom Struggle* (Lexington: University Press of Kentucky, 2003), 196–216. See also Michael J. Klarman, *From Jim Crow to Civil Rights: The Supreme Court and the Struggle for Racial Equality* (New York: Oxford University Press, 2004); Kisha King Williams, "The Civil Rights Movement in Miami" (MA thesis, Florida International University, 1999); Bonnie Stark, "McCarthyism in Miami: Charley Johns and the Florida Legislative Investigation Committee, July 1956–July 1965" (MA thesis, University of Florida, 1985).

28. A. A. Micocci to Hermina Cantero Guim, June 12, 1962, and Robert M. Ball to

Dante Fascell, ca. June 1962, both in Cuban Refugees—Miami—Aid, 1961–1962, Dante Fascell Congressional Papers, Special Collections, Otto G. Richter Library, University of Miami, Miami, Fla.

29. María Cristina García, *Havana USA: Cuban Exiles and Cuban Americans in South Florida, 1959–1994* (Los Angeles: University of California Press, 1997), 49.

30. "Migrant Youths Ordered Out of Dade School," *St. Petersburg Times*, March 25, 1954.

31. "Education Helping to Solve Problems of Big Islander Population Here," *Miami News*, April 25, 1957.

32. As early as 1937 the president and secretary of UM met with Cuban officials and faculty from the University of Havana to discuss plans for a pan-American institute. In addition, the administration worked closely with local organizations to recruit Hispanic/Latin American students and fund their education through scholarships. See Rose, "Tourism and the Hispanicization of Race," 750–56.

33. "Creative Writing Offered for Cubans," *Miami Hurricane*, February 17, 1961. This program was designed to help Cubans write for English-language publications. See also "Cubans Up Foreign Enrollment," *Miami Hurricane*, April 14, 1961; "Exiled Cubans Graduate Here," ibid., both in University Archives, Otto G. Richter Library, University of Miami, Miami, Fla.

34. The Office of Education made loans totaling $100,000 and awarded UM $75,000 for a program designed to train teachers. In 1965 the administration partnered with the U.S. Office of Education to award $73,000 for the training of Cuban exiles with two or more years of college education. As a result of this program, over 121 émigrés graduated from UM with professional certification as Spanish or elementary school teachers. "Cubans Trained to Teach School," *Miami Hurricane*, October 19, 1965; "Summer Program Offered for Cuban Teachers," ibid., February 24, 1967.

35. Bernie Weiner, "We Can't Wait Much Longer," *Miami Hurricane*, December 9, 1960.

36. "Urban League Official Says Negroes Losing Jobs to Cuban Refugees," *Miami Times*, December 16, 1961.

37. "A Letter to Pres. Kennedy," *Miami Times*, April 6, 1963.

38. John Britton, "March on Washington to Dramatize Big Job Freeze," *Jet*, March 21, 1963, 16.

39. Letter to the editor, "Cuban Exiles Treated Better than Negroes," *Miami Times*, September 27, 1968.

40. Egerton, *Cubans in Miami*, 4–5, 11.

41. "Jim Crow Hiring Practices," *Miami Times*, April 6, 1963.

42. "Local Head Outlays Demonstration Plans," *Miami Herald*, June 1, 1963.

43. "Concerned Citizens," *Liberty News*, January 20, 1974, in National Council for Negro Women Collection, Black Archives History and Research Foundation of South Florida, Miami.

44. "Rolle Marches on Miami and Metro," *Miami Times*, August 31, 1963; "March on Washington," 16.

45. Allan Morrison, "Miami Cuban Refugee Influx," *Ebony* 18 (June 1963): 96–104.

46. García, *Havana USA*, 47.

47. "March on Washington," 16.

48. See Cynthia Ann Young, *Soul Power: Culture, Radicalism, and the Making of a U.S. Third World Left* (Durham, N.C.: Duke University Press, 2006); Cedric Johnson, *Revolutionaries to Race Leaders: Black Power and the Making of African American Politics* (Minneapolis: University of Minnesota Press, 2007); Peniel Joseph, *Waiting 'til the Midnight Hour: A Narrative History of Black Power in America* (New York: Holt, 2006); Van Gosse, *Rethinking the New Left: An Interpretive History* (New York: Palgrave Macmillan, 2005). Several of these works address the activities of the Fair Play for Cuba Committee, a grassroots organization of radical black activists, artists, and intellectuals that was established in New York City in 1960 and was sympathetic to the Castro government and building postrevolutionary support in the United States.

49. "March on Washington," 16.

50. "King Warns Miami about Complacency," *Miami Times*, April 22, 1966; "Dr. Martin Luther King Speaks Here Wednesday Night," ibid., April 8, 1966.

51. Juan Betancourt, "Castro and the Cuban Negro," *Crisis* 68, no. 5 (May 1961): 270–74.

52. Jon Nordheimer, "Black Cubans: Apart in Two Worlds," *New York Times*, December 2, 1987.

53. Andrea O'Reilly Herrera, "An Interview with Enrique Patterson," in her *Remembering Cuba: A Legacy of Diaspora* (Austin: University of Texas Press, 2001), 41.

54. Carlos Moore, *Pichón, a Memoir: Race and Revolution in Castro's Cuba* (Chicago: Lawrence Hill, 2008), xvi, 1.

55. Ibid., 301.

56. Gene Strul to Dante Fascell, ca. December 1960, box 1937, folder 7, Dante B. Fascell Committee: Inter-American Affairs and International Organizations and Movements, 1960–1963, Dante B. Fascell Congressional Papers, Special Collections, University of Miami, Miami, Fla.

57. Torres, *In the Land of Mirrors*, 197.

58. National Commission on the Causes and Prevention of Violence, *Miami Report: The Report of the Miami Study Team on Civil Disturbances in Miami, Florida during the Week of August 5, 1968* (Washington, D.C.: Government Printing Office, 1969).

CHAPTER 5

Internationalizing Civil Rights

Afro-Cubans, African Americans, and the Problem of Global Apartheid

MARK MALISA

In September 2013, I attended a conference commemorating the fiftieth anniversary of the 1963 March on Washington. Many presenters spoke about the progress (or lack thereof) since the march and the passage of the Civil Rights Act. Some of the panelists took time to highlight the global reach and legacy of both the March on Washington and the civil rights movement. It was there that I met A. Peter Bailey, one of the founding members of the Organization of Afro-American Unity (OAAU). Bailey introduced me to the work of "Carlos the Cuban" (Carlos Moore) and his role in the civil rights movement in the United States and in the Lumumba protests at the United Nations, which were staged to demand the realization of civil and human rights in the Republic of the Congo. There, Afro-Cubans, African Americans, and Africans spoke with one voice and acted as one people in protesting global apartheid. It became apparent that the civil rights struggle was simultaneously local and international.

This chapter focuses on the relationship between Cuban Americans and African Americans in the struggle for civil rights in the United States and the ways they tried to internationalize that effort. I also explore how these groups extended that struggle to colonized countries in Africa. I draw on the works of Malcolm X, Bailey (a student of Malcolm X), and Moore, a Cuban American who briefly worked as a translator for an Angolan organization in Los Angeles, California, and also taught at Florida International University before working as a consultant for the Organization of African Unity (OAU).[1] I build on the work of Malcolm X with regard to internationalizing civil and human rights, especially in Africa and through his group the Organization of Afro-American Unity.[2] Like A. Peter Bailey, Carlos Moore was connected to Malcolm X and came to Malcolm X's rescue when the latter was denied entry into France. Unlike Bailey, Moore was critical and cautious about the achievements of the Cuban Revolution with regard to advancing the civil rights of people of African descent. Both men were members of the OAAU, both worked at universities in the United States, and both contributed to a new civil rights discourse and activism that called into question the hegemony of a Eurocentric curriculum in which the achievements of Africans, African Americans, and Latinos were made invisible. This chapter also highlights universities as sites of struggle for civil rights, and African American and Afro-Cuban professors as politically engaged intellectuals.[3]

I begin with a brief overview of the internationalization of civil rights struggles in the work of Malcolm X, Bailey, and Moore, while acknowledging the importance of locating the genesis of their work in the United States. Next, I discuss the solidarity of African Americans, Africans, and Afro-Cubans; the revitalization of pan-Africanism; and the triple consciousness within which black Cubans and African Americans functioned, especially in their desire to place civil and human rights within an African ethic or world view. Perhaps what was unique in the vision of Malcolm X and those who came after him was the role of international organizing in ending racism in the United States.[4] The Organization of Afro-American Unity was modeled after the Organization of African Unity and had the goal of bringing a concerted effort by black people against the white power structure in the United States. As such, institutions like the OAAU and the OAU became part of the conduit for internationalizing civil rights. I also address the transformation of the academy into a place of struggle for civil rights. Prior to the passage of the Civil Rights Act there were few, if any, black intellectuals employed in most white-dominated institutions of higher learning. Both Bailey and Moore became professors and utilized their scholarship and the academy to further civil rights.

In focusing on the work of Malcolm X's heirs, this chapter also addresses a possible revisionist reading of the civil rights struggle in relation to Cuba, the United States, and Africa. Toward the end of the twentieth century and in the first decades of the twenty-first century, the United States painted itself as a champion of human rights across the globe. Yet, when it came to ending racism, promoting civil rights, and ending colonialism, the United States has been largely silent on the suppression of people of African descent at home and abroad. The U.S. government even provided the apartheid regime in South Africa with military, logistical, and ideological support.[5] It was only the achievements of various independence movements in Africa, Asia, and South America that forced the U.S. government to address even minimally the problems of legal racism.[6] For these reasons, among others, Malcolm X and Malcolmites (Malcolm X's heirs) saw the Organization of African Unity as a good vehicle for pressuring the United Nations to pass a resolution on rights for African Americans.

The belief in the mid-twentieth century was that the international community had a lot to teach the United States about civil and human rights and the eradication of racism. In 1957, Paul Robeson observed that "American Negroes can no longer lead the colored peoples of the world because they far better than us understand what is happening in the world today."[7] As Malcolm X was quick to point out, the problem of racism/apartheid was global and not confined to the United States, and those struggling for civil rights in the United States should work in solidarity with others across the globe. Malcolmites followed in this path. Just like Robeson, Malcolm X was also aware of the leadership role played by other countries in advancing civil and human rights: "Now the black revolution has been taking place in Africa and Asia and Latin America; when I say black, I mean non-white—black, brown, red or yellow. Our brothers and sisters in Asia . . . Africa . . . and Latin America . . . who were colonized by Europeans have been involved in the struggle since 1945 to get the colonialists . . . the Europeans off their land."[8] What was important was for African Americans to work for their own freedom in solidarity with international struggles for ending racism, which were going on in Asia, Africa, and Latin America. The struggles in other parts of the world informed those occurring in the United States. For Malcolm X, it was also important to move beyond civil rights to full human rights.

MALCOLM X AND THE INTERNATIONALIZATION OF RIGHTS

Malcolm X observed that when it came to the practice of racism, Anglo Americans and their institutions did not take the time to identify the nationalities of black people. Consequently, black Cubans living in the United States often found themselves victims of the racism visited on African Americans. The same was true for Africans. The shared brutalization by virtue of race formed the basis of unity. In addition, black Cubans who moved to the

United States were already familiar with racism in Cuba, and as their international awareness grew, so too did their realization that racism was a global problem. That recognition also created solidarity between black Cubans living in the United States and African Americans.[9]

The civil rights movement was an attempt to redress the problems caused by racism and capitalism.[10] Indeed, Malcolm X often conflated the two, pointing out that it was impossible to have capitalism without simultaneously having racism. For Afro-Cubans, this connection made perfect sense. It is important to note that while many Americans may see the terms "Cuban American" and "Latino" as synonymous, they are not, especially for Cubans of color, who are phenotypically erased by both of these terms. White Cubans, who also came to the United States, did not actively support policies of racial justice and civil rights either in the United States or abroad. According to Nancy Raquel Mirabal, white Cuban Americans generally tended to be counterrevolutionary and aligned themselves with the Republican Party in the United States. Mirabal also contends that at times white Cubans became foot soldiers who actually engaged in counterinsurgency wars on behalf of the United States in Latin America and Africa. Afro-Cubans, on the other hand, generally aligned themselves with Cuban policies that advanced the rights of nonwhites, both locally and globally.[11]

For Malcolm X the issue of civil rights was clearly global. His work in New York had exposed him to the struggles waged by other countries. His famous meeting with Cuban president Fidel Castro in New York City had an impact on Malcolm X's views regarding civil rights in general and global racism in particular. Later, the Cuban American Carlos Moore became an important member of the Organization of Afro-American Unity and helped set up its office in Paris, France.[12] Malcolm X was convinced that events in other parts of the world had a bearing on the course of civil rights in the United States. His reading of the 1955 Bandung Conference gives an indication of the link between the local and the international: "And once you study what happened at the Bandung conference . . . it actually serves as a model for the same procedure you and I can use to get our problems solved. At Bandung . . . there were dark nations from Africa and Asia. . . . [but] despite their economic and political differences they came together. All of them were black, brown, red, or yellow."[13] In addition, Malcolm X stressed the importance of civil rights in the United States to individual African leaders and within the context of the Organization of African Unity. He met with either heads of state or their representatives from Egypt, Ethiopia, Ghana, Nigeria, and Kenya. He spoke on the plight of African Americans at the OAU's 1964 meeting, where he was instrumental in the drafting of a resolution condemning human rights abuses in the United States.[14] The civil rights struggle, from the perspective of Malcolm X and his followers, was inherently international and internationalist.

Toward the end of his life Malcolm X realized the challenges that capitalism poses for a world without racial justice. Reflecting on the relationship between racism and the global political scene, he observed that "the American political, economic, and social atmosphere . . . automatically nourishes a racist psychology in the white man."[15] This contrasts with his pre-Mecca equating of biological race with ideological identity. Although Malcolm X had for the most part taken pride in his African heritage, it was during his travels in Africa that he realized the potential of a global solidarity that could challenge the injustices associated with advanced capitalism: "I reflected many, many times to myself upon how the American Negro has been entirely brainwashed from ever seeing himself as part of the non-white peoples of the world. The American Negro has no conception of the hundreds of millions of other non-whites' concern for him: he has no conception of their feeling of brotherhood for and with him."[16] In many respects, Malcolm X realized not only the predicaments facing blacks in the United States, but the untapped global solidarity that could undo racism. Without internationalizing the struggle against both capitalism and racism, Malcolm X believed, the struggle by black Americans was bound to flounder. It was in this context that the Organization of Afro-American Unity was formed. He also gained a lot of insights from his meetings with African American exiles in Ghana and Nigeria, many of whom were engaged in anticolonial struggles in Africa.[17]

SOLIDARITY BETWEEN AFRICAN AMERICANS, AFRO-CUBANS, AND AFRICANS

The history of civil rights struggle in the United States has to be understood in the context of racism and the problems posed by capitalism. For example, while many white Cubans enjoyed the privileges that came with whiteness in the United States, black Cubans faced a different proposition by virtue of being black. Miguel Gonzalez-Pando observes that the U.S. media "contributed to glamourizing the Cuban exiles as model emigres: white, well-educated and enterprising."[18] But he is also aware that, for the most part, Afro-Cubans identified with African Americans. For example, when Nelson Mandela visited Miami in April 1990, shortly after he was released from prison, many white Cubans protested, whereas Afro-Cubans and African Americans expressed their solidarity with Mandela because he had been a victim of South African apartheid/racism.[19] For white Cubans, it was relatively easy to assimilate, and there were tensions between African Americans and white Cuban Americans around discrimination.

The roots of the solidarity between African Americans and Afro-Cubans began long before the civil rights movement of the 1960s. Historian Frank Guridy points out that even in the era of Jim Crow, there was mutual assistance and collaboration between the two groups. Marcus Garvey's pan-Africanist movement and organization had several offices in Cuba and the United States, and sometimes the delegates from the two countries conferred. Cuba's struggles for freedom and civil rights had a strong hold on the African American imagination, to the extent that in the early part of the twentieth century the Afro-American Cuban Emigration Society explored avenues for funding migration to Cuba.[20] At the same time, many African Americans saw the oppression of blacks in Cuba as no different from the racism faced by African Americans in the United States.

For African Americans and Afro-Cubans, New York City offered many opportunities for political activism and engagement. Afro-Cubans could, if they so desired, use the Spanish language as a marker of their being "foreigners" and therefore not African American. However, many chose political activism and welcomed African Americans in their organizations. El Club Cubano InterAmericano, for example, opened its membership to black people, even those who were not from Cuba. Nancy Mirabal notes that the civil rights movement "inspired many, especially second-generation Afro Cubans to organize across culture and create a fused political agenda that emphasized shared African roots, slavery, colonialism, and disenfranchisement at the hands of European populations."[21] Over time, newly arrived immigrants from Africa joined El Club. Even in the cultural and entertainment spheres, Afro-Cubans and African Americans began to identify with Africa. And as the liberation struggles continued working to end colonialism in Africa, Afro-Cubans and African Americans took an active interest.

New York was a cosmopolitan city that made it possible for activists to meet to discuss issues affecting them. For Carlos Moore, it was where he met and worked with Malcolm X, Jomo the Kenyan, and Maya Angelou, among others. Afro-Cubans connected their struggles to those of African Americans and Africans. For all these groups, the stumbling block to the acquisition of full civil and human rights was global apartheid or racism. They protested racism in the United States, in Africa, and in Latin America. Local problems were also global problems. When LeRoi Jones (Amiri Baraka) visited Cuba, it was with the help of black Cuban Americans based in New York City.[22] It was also in New York City that Moore, together with African Americans, met Cuban leader Fidel Castro. To most African Americans, Moore became known as "Brother Carlos" or "Carlos the Cuban."[23]

Perhaps one of the events that showed the solidarity among Malcolm X, Moore, and Bailey was the demonstration at the United Nations in 1961 to protest the assassination of Patrice Lumumba. Maya Angelou, other African and African American women, and Carlos the Cuban organized a march that was initially designed to begin in Harlem and end at the United Nations.[24] After successfully demonstrating at UN headquarters, they marched to the Belgian embassy. When Carlos Moore and an African protester found themselves outnumbered by the police, they pretended to be African students and escaped the threat of physical and possibly fatal harm. It was immediately after that demonstration that Moore deemed himself "to be earnestly at war with the United States on several fronts: Cuba, the Congo, the civil rights struggle of black Americans."[25] Later, he worked temporarily in Egypt and then in Paris, mostly with the intention of helping the peoples of Congo attain their full human and civil rights. In New York Moore got to meet many Africans (some of them diplomats) and African Americans who were active in the civil rights struggle. As an Afro-Cuban immigrant he actively sought communities and organizations that were working toward the realization of civil rights. In such organizations he met, among others, Malcolm X, Angelou, and activist and historian John Henrik Clarke.

But it was not only in New York City that Afro-Cubans and African Americans worked together to advance civil rights in the United States. Miguel Torres observes that Afro-Cubans played a role in creating coalitions of minorities in the electoral campaigns of Harold Washington for the Illinois House (served 1965–1976), the Illinois Senate (1977–1980), the U.S. House (1981–1983), and mayor of Chicago (1983–1987). In his positions, Washington worked to advance the civil rights of African Americans, Afro-Cubans, Latinos, and other marginalized ethnic groups. Torres argues that an overwhelming majority of Afro-Cubans voted for Washington, seeing in him an advocate for civil and human rights. This solidarity endured for many years.[26]

TRIPLE HERITAGE, MULTIPLE LOYALTIES: AFRO-CUBANS, AFRICAN AMERICANS, AND PAN-AFRICANISM

Afro-Cubans and African Americans operated in an environment that demanded multiple loyalties. Afro-Cubans had a relationship with Cuba that informed their struggles in the United States. Torres notes that multiple experiences and identities are part of what it means to be Cuban. Revolutionary African Americans were also cognizant of the place of both Africa and Cuba in their quest for a world free of apartheid/racism. The struggle for civil rights was thus informed by local ideologies, as well as those that originated in Cuba and newly independent African nations.[27] According to Malcolm X, it was important for all to realize that the common enemy that people of African descent faced was racism. Pan-Africanism provided the ideological tool for forging a collective response to the problem of racism. What many African Americans and Afro-Cubans discovered was that they were oppressed by virtue of being black, rather than because they belonged to a specific nation. That is, racism was international and occurred all over the globe where people of European descent encountered people of African descent.

Antonio Lopez contends that Afro-Cubans generally formed identities that transcended the nation or state. In negotiating how to live sanely in the United States, they had to balance their Hispanic heritage with their being identified with African Americans by virtue of their color. For some Afro-Cubans, their identity could not be tied to either the United States or Cuba; neither could their understanding of human and civil rights. In addition to alliances with African Americans, they also had *afrolatinidad*, that is, ties with Latinos of African descent. In many respects, the ideology of pan-Africanism offered a way for African Americans and Afro-Cubans to realize their civil and human rights.[28] As a concept and an ideology, pan-Africanism made it possible for Afro-Cubans to view themselves as part of the African diaspora. Displaced from Cuba, sometimes yearning to return to Cuba, and not fully at home in the United States, some Afro-Cubans embraced pan-Africanism, and some, like Carlos Moore, worked to promote civil and human rights in Africa. In the diaspora, Afro-Cubans understood their blackness in relation to other displaced blacks. For Moore, "Africa was everything to me, and the Cuban Revolution was but an extension of Africa, and Fidel an extension of Lumumba. . . . because of him [Lumumba] I discovered my links to Africa."[29]

Because of white racism, for Malcolm X and Malcolmites the source of human and civil rights, of what it means to be human, had to come from non-Western values. Pan-Africanism, and sometimes Islam, offered a viable way to understand civil and human rights. For Malcolm X, this meant a reconnection with Africa, as well as a cultural and psychological migration to an African world view. He argued that the U.S. system as it existed could not bring about civil rights or freedom for black people: "A chicken just doesn't have it within its nature to produce a duck egg. It can't do it. It can only produce according to what the particular system was constructed to produce. The system in this country cannot produce freedom for an Afro-American. It is impossible for this economic system, this political system, this social system, as it stands, to produce freedom right now for the black man in this country."[30] Blacks had a deep mistrust of the United States, and as a result Malcolm X sought a source for civil and human rights outside the legal framework of the United States, including in the United Nations, the Organization of African Unity, and Islam.

Prior to his conversion to Sunni Islam, Malcolm X branded the white man as the devil, mainly because of the history of racism in the United States. The material and psychological burden of slavery was readily evident, as was the nation's reluctance to welcome blacks into the human family. The legal system, disguised as a reflection of civilization and progress, was a hindrance to attaining liberation, especially for blacks. For blacks, history and precedent revealed America's unwillingness to grant liberty for all its citizens. Malcolm X observed: "[The black man] sees not an iota of progress because, number one, if the Civil War had freed him, he wouldn't need civil-rights legislation today. If the Emancipation Proclamation, issued by that great shining liberal called Lincoln, had freed him, he wouldn't be singing 'We Shall Overcome' today."[31]

Obeying the law had not yielded any meaningful rights for blacks. However, Malcolm X was explicit that he valued the law. On many occasions he reminded his audience of the importance of the legal system by telling them that he was "not against the law." He saw the law as an integral part of a just society. Malcolm X was fully aware that the legal system in the United States was always to the disadvantage of black people, but he also believed in the potential of transforming the system through the legal mechanisms available to America's citizens. His "Ballot or Bullet" speech in Ohio revealed not only the urgency of the need to attain human rights, but the possibility of using the voting system to change conditions and undo racism. It appeared as if the ballot was an answer to the challenges blacks faced in America, and

Malcolm X encouraged his audience to use it to effect changes in all spheres of life. Of course, his reference to the bullet was not just a rhetorical device but a reminder of the importance of attaining freedom at any cost.[32]

The loftiness of the Constitution and most of the laws that are the foundation of the American republic places the United States in an ideal position to create a better society, perhaps unrivaled in the history of humankind. However, for Malcolm X, this idea was a farce: "There is no system more corrupt than a system that represents itself as the example of freedom, the example of democracy, and can go all over this earth telling other people how to straighten out their house."[33] The availability of the best laws, according to Malcolm X, positioned the United States as one of the few countries in the world that could have a peaceful revolution: "America today is at a time or in a day or at an hour where she is the first country on this earth that can actually have a bloodless revolution. . . . But America is not morally equipped to do so." He saw America's reluctance to recognize the humanity of blacks as a stumbling block to attaining that ideal. Regarding the few concessions that the U.S. government had made to acknowledge the humanity of blacks, Malcolm X was convinced that such goodwill did not come from the government's own volition: "It was no sudden awakening of their moral consciousness. It was Hitler. It was Tojo. It was Stalin."[34] Most of the changes had been made in an attempt to appear morally better than the Nazis and communists.

After his travels outside the United States, Malcolm X began to link the problems of racism in the United States with those in other parts of the world, notably Asia, Africa, and Latin America. He began to see that racism was "not a Negro problem or an American problem. It's part of the world problem. It's a human problem." What he had initially thought to be unique to the United States, he realized, was a phenomenon associated with the European conquest of nonwhites. Aware that the United Nations was in the process of making and enforcing resolutions against apartheid in South Africa, Malcolm X was quick to make a comparison and asserted that "America is worse than South Africa, because not only is America racist, but she is also deceitful and hypocritical. . . . She preaches one thing and practices another."[35] Malcolm X was aware of the work of Nelson Mandela and others involved in the worldwide struggle to end racism. Instead of limiting the U.S. struggle to civil rights, Malcolm X saw this internationalism as an important way to expand the struggle to attain full human rights. He thus sought to bring the plight of blacks in the United States before the United Nations and the Organization of African Unity.

THE LUMUMBA PROTEST AT THE UNITED NATIONS

The mainstream media, and perhaps the United States itself, could not allow the protest against the assassination of Patrice Lumumba to be attributed to activism and organization among African Americans, Afro-Cubans, and Africans. In fact, the U.S. government needed to give the impression that the protest was the work of communists, and it used the media to spread false propaganda, ascribing the demonstration to communist agitators. For the United States, it was unacceptable that an assassination that had taken place in Congo could bring such militant activism to the attention of the world, especially the United Nations General Assembly.

However, for the protesters, the assassination of Lumumba reignited the passion and realities of pan-Africanism that were already present in the thought and activities of Carlos Moore, Malcolm X, John Henrik Clarke, and Maya Angelou, among others. And for them, there was no connection at all to communism. Instead, the problem was global apartheid, whose collective force could be seen in the Western powers represented at the United Nations. It is important to note that the protest was international in nature, and present at the march were blacks of many nationalities: "Africans and oppressed people from all over the world were making New York the arena where they could fight for justice."[36] Angelou credited Moore, who "moved through Harlem's political sky like a luminous meteor," with organizing and leading the march.[37]

To a great extent, the Lumumba protest was evidence of a long and active collaboration among African Americans, Afro-Cubans, and Africans in New York City. By the time Congo gained independence in 1960, Moore had become intimately involved in African affairs, as well as issues affecting African Americans. At one time he worked as a translator for the Congo delegation at the United Nations and even met Ambassador Thomas Kanza.[38] At times he was mistaken for one of the African delegates, partly because of his involvement with issues related to Africa at the United Nations. Like many black people in New York City, he took a great interest in Lumumba and Congo, which were his introduction to Africa. When Lumumba was assassinated, Moore, Angelou, Malcolm X, and Clarke were heavily invested in the well-being of that newly independent African nation. Because of his work with the Congo delegation, Moore was able to gain passes to the UN Security Council meeting, which he used to get the demonstrators into the building.

According to Moore, the Lumumba protest had a huge impact with regard to internationalizing the struggle for human and civil rights and the role of the United Nations: "Our demonstration at the UN was unprecedented. It was unheard-of for protesters to disrupt the proceedings of the Security Council. Radio and television stations the world over flashed the news, for the first time since its founding in 1945, the United Nations was under what the media described as [a] 'terrorist' attack."[39] The demonstration was both an act of solidarity with the Congolese people and an acknowledgment that the struggles in Africa were linked to those in the United States. For Angelou, part of the motivation was to "let the Congolese people and all the other Africans know that we are with them. Whether we come from New York, or the South or from the West Indies, . . . black people are a people and we are equally oppressed."[40] The language or discourse of civil and human rights, as well as the struggle for those rights, was beginning to be understood and articulated in relation to events outside the United States in ways that made the United States akin to the practitioners of apartheid. Although the U.S. media gave the impression that most of the demonstrators were African American, the reality was that the participants were international.

Some of the protesters connected local events related to the denial of civil rights to African Americans with the assassination of the Congolese president. For John Henrik Clarke, "The demonstrators in the United Nations gallery interpreted the murder of Lumumba as the international lynching of a Black man on the altar of colonialism and white supremacy. Suddenly, to them at least, Patrice Lumumba became Emmett Till and all other black victims of lynch law and the mob."[41] He appropriated the language of oppression associated with the black experience in the United States to mirror the denial of human rights in Congo. Likewise, for James Meriwether, "the slain Lumumba symbolized for broader black America the struggle of African nationalism and freedom against continued white exploitation and oppression."[42] The struggles were intertwined and global in nature, as were the protesters. What became apparent, even if not verbalized, was that the attainment of civil rights in the United States was closely tied to decolonization in Africa in general, and Congo in particular. For Carlos Moore, the struggles in the United States, Africa, and Latin America were inseparable. Reflecting on the death of civilians in Congo and the indifference of the UN, the Guinea foreign minister asked the UN: "Was it because the thousands of Congolese killed had black skins, like the black Americans in . . . Mississippi?"[43]

Although the possibility of freedom seemed palpable with the independence of Congo, and human rights seemed within sight with the *Brown v.*

Board of Education decision in the United States, the assassination of Lumumba and continued segregation were actually evidence of the absence of both globally. Clarke observed: "The plight of Africans still fighting to throw off the yoke of colonialism, and the plight of Afro-Americans, still waiting for a rich, strong and boastful nation to fulfill the promise of freedom and citizenship became one and the same. Through their action, the UN demonstrators announced their awareness that they were far from being free and a long fight lay ahead."[44] Although some of the demonstrators still believed in the United Nations, many were also aware of the complicity of the UN in the assassination of Lumumba, dismissing it as the "united white nations."

But it was not only the UN that was complicit in the assassination of Lumumba. Some of the protesters were aware of U.S. involvement, together with Belgium and France. In thinking about a possible response to the question of who killed Lumumba, Angelou said, "When asked who killed Lumumba—I will not say the Belgians, the French, the Americans. The whites killed a black man. Another black man."[45] Apartheid knew no national boundaries and did not respect any. For Angelou, it could have easily been any black man in any part of the world dying at the hands of any white man. But the fact that the United States was involved in the assassination of Lumumba at a time when blacks were struggling for their civil and human rights made it impossible to ignore, in the words of John Henrik Clarke, that "the United States has never had an official complete policy on the granting of complete citizenship to Afro-Americans, nor has the United States ever had a complete policy based on the complete elimination of, or approving of the complete elimination of, colonialism in Africa."[46] Moore, Angelou, Malcolm X, and Clarke worked tirelessly to advance the realization of freedom and human rights in the United States, Africa, and Cuba. They were aware of the extent to which the struggle for civil rights in the United States was tied to undoing global apartheid. For Carlos Moore, the success of the protest and the unity among the African diplomats, Afro-Cubans, and African Americans could be ascribed to the work of Malcolm X.[47]

THE UNIVERSITY AND POST–CIVIL RIGHTS STRUGGLES: KNOWLEDGE MATTERS

Prior to the passage of the Civil Rights Act there were few African American or Latino students or scholars in higher education in the United States. As with many institutions, segregation was the norm, and there was a significant amount of resistance when African American and Latino students sought admission to state-funded, but white-dominated, universities and colleges. Malcolm X realized the importance of institutions of higher learning with regard to promoting civil rights both nationally and internationally. His speeches and debates at Harvard and Oxford Universities, for example, brought the urgency of civil rights to a younger international generation. Indeed, university students played a leading role in the voter registration initiatives of the civil rights movement. Likewise, Malcolm X spoke to university students in Africa and the Middle East, which helped internationalize civil rights discourses.

The segregation that barred African Americans and Latinos from institutions of higher education was supported by an Anglo American curriculum that emphasized the value of white people in the United States and stressed the inferiority of nonwhites. Jamie Wilson has observed that almost every academic discipline, prior to the passage of the Civil Rights Act, was devoted to scientifically proving the superiority of whites over nonwhites. For the most part, European and European American scholars presented nonwhites as not deserving to be part of the human community. Since education and institutions of higher learning were central to understanding what constituted human civilization, the heirs of Malcolm X took it upon themselves to contest the hegemony of the Eurocentric curriculum. To a great extent, this meant rethinking and researching the place of Africa and African culture in global human history and their implications for civil and human rights.[48]

By the late 1970s and early 1980s, many previously segregated universities in the United States had begun offering African American and Latino studies. This new development led to universities recruiting students and professors of African American and Latino ancestry. But integration was not the goal of post–civil rights African American and Latino student and faculty activism. Many took the opportunity to conduct specific research on African American and Latino histories and cultures. For Afro-Cubans and African Americans, Africa retained a special place, which is evident in the work of Afro-Cuban scholar Carlos Moore and African American scholars Peter Bailey and John Henrik Clarke—all members of the Organization of Afro-American Unity. In conducting this research, Latino and African American scholars contributed to a new discourse on black-Latino activism and multiculturalism.[49]

Inasmuch as Africa became the locus for recapturing human and civil rights in the work of Malcolm X, for most Malcolmites the immediate task was researching and producing knowledge about Africa's history and its contributions to human civilization. Additionally, these scholars wanted to understand the African presence in the Americas. Moore and others highlighted the residues of African cultures among people of African descent in the Americas.[50] For intellectuals like Clarke, this meant researching more about Africa's history and cultures before the encounter with European modernity, as well as the changes subsequent to that encounter. The recovery and realization of civil and human rights lay within a world view characterized by African values. It seemed to most African American and Afro-Cuban Malcolmite researchers that white professors had been committed to erasing African history from the global cultural and historical memory. These scholar-activists saw it as their duty to insert the positive contributions of Africans into academic disciplines such as history as a way of correcting the distortions of Eurocentric versions of history and culture. Research became a form of activism and the university a place where Afro-Cuban and African American scholars could be intellectuals whose scholarship was tied to their political beliefs. These researchers critiqued and rejected European and Anglo American definitions of human and civil rights that were steeped in racism.

Universities, in many ways, became a place for collaboration and activism, especially when blackness was not defined or limited by nationality. The examples of Peter Bailey and Carlos Moore reflect the way Afro-Cuban and African American scholar-activists were also deeply connected to communities outside the academy in ways that harmonized academic pursuits with the pursuit of civil and human rights. Malcolmite, Afro-Cuban, and African American students and academics did not shy away from pointing out the racism and imperialism inherent in American practices at home and abroad and thus tied the issue of civil rights at home to civil and human rights internationally. Black student unions, at that time, were not based on nation of origin. Rather, they were deliberately international. In addition, because most universities in the United States had made it almost impossible for African Americans to study for doctorates prior to 1964, many universities recruited faculty of color from abroad. Those from colonies quickly realized that, to a great extent, the condition of blacks in the United States was similar to that of a colonized people. Such faculty helped to internationalize civil and human rights without neglecting the production of knowledge related to Africans, African Americans, and Latinos.[51]

CONCLUSION

The collaboration between Afro-Cubans and African Americans during and after the civil rights movement in the United States changed the discourse and nature of civil and human rights. Although they were concerned with the racism that existed in the United States, these activists were quick to realize the global nature of apartheid. As a result, they internationalized the struggle for human and civil rights by tying it to the liberation of peoples of African descent worldwide. Even though for them the civil rights struggle was informed primarily by the events happening in the United States, they sought answers outside the European and Anglo American cultural, legal, political, and economic framework. There was marked skepticism about the capabilities of the U.S. Constitution and voting processes to fully protect and affirm the civil and human rights of people of African descent in the United States, as evidenced by Malcolm X's critiques of the two. Although Malcolm X had tried to bring about civil and human rights through Islam, by the time he formed the Organization of Afro-American Unity, he had realized that religion on its own (including Christianity) could not bring about human rights for blacks. Although his meeting with Fidel Castro in New York City generated a lot of interest, the surviving members of the OAAU rejected the idea that socialism or any ideology concocted in Europe would be of use in solving the problem of racism. This was especially clear in the work of Carlos Moore. As activists began participating in research and scholarship, it became apparent that it would be well-nigh impossible for people of African descent to create and realize civil rights based on this false consciousness.

The university became a place where the struggle for civil rights took a new turn, especially after the passage of the Civil Rights Act. African American, Afro-Cuban, and African scholars working in different universities researched and disseminated scholarship related to Africa and began articulating civil and human rights from an African, rather than a Eurocentric, perspective and history. In the period immediately after the Civil Rights Act, when universities in the United States began hiring and admitting African American faculty and students, Afro-Cuban, African American, and African students and faculty collaborated, and this led to the creation of African American, Africana, and Latino studies. In many ways, these collaborative ethnic studies and disciplines contributed to the birth of what later became known as multiculturalism in the United States. Activists changed the discourse and nature of civil rights in multiple ways, but what was common among them was a rejection of racism and a refusal to accept white supremacy as the norm. Scholar-activists like Carlos Moore and Peter Bailey—and of course Malcolm X—created a powerful, vibrant, and cooperative platform for the worldwide liberation of people of African descent.

NOTES

1. Malcolm X was one of the key figures in the struggle for civil rights in the United States. See Britta Nelson, *Dreams and Nightmares: Martin Luther King, Jr., Malcolm X, and the Struggle for Black Equality in America* (Gainesville: University Press of Florida, 2012); Lewis V. Baldwin and Amiri YaSin Hadid, *Between Cross and Crescent: Christian and Muslim Perspectives on Malcolm and Martin* (Gainesville: University Press of Florida, 2002). Peter Bailey has written a number of books on Malcolm X and is currently working on issues related to education. See Bailey, *Witnessing Brother Malcolm X: The Master Teacher* (Plantation, Fla.: Illumination, 2013). See also Carlos Moore, *Castro, the Blacks, and Africa* (Los Angeles: Center for Afro-American Studies, 1988); Moore, *Pichón, a Memoir: Race and Revolution in Castro's Cuba* (Chicago: Lawrence Hill, 2008).

2. Modeled after the Organization of African Unity, the OAAU was formed with the intention of bringing together all groups interested in advancing the rights of the oppressed. See Bailey, *Witnessing Brother Malcolm*.

3. Craig Collisson, "The Fight to Legitimize Blackness: How Black Students Changed the University" (PhD diss., University of Washington, 2008).

4. In 1963 Malcolm X was given observer status at the annual meeting of the Organization of African Unity, and at that meeting he urged African heads of state to use their voting powers in the United Nations to advocate for the rights of African Americans. Bailey, *Witnessing Brother Malcolm*.

5. Among such policies is "constructive engagement." See Christopher Coker, *The United States and South Africa, 1968–1985: Constructive Engagement and Its Critics* (Durham, N.C.: Duke University Press, 1986).

6. Bailey. *Witnessing Brother Malcolm*.

7. Quoted in Besenia Rodriguez, "Long Live Third World Unity! Long Live Internationalism: Huey P. Newton's Revolutionary Intercommunalism," *Souls* 8, no. 3 (2006): 126.

8. See Malcolm X, "Message to the Grassroots" (1964), in Malcolm X and George Breitman, *Malcolm X Speaks: Selected Speeches and Statements* (New York: Grove, 1990).

9. In this chapter I use the terms "black Cubans" and "Afro-Cubans" interchangeably.

10. Malcolm X, *The Autobiography of Malcolm X as Told to Alex Hailey* (New York: Ballantine, 1987).

11. Nancy Raquel Mirabal, "Scripting Race, Finding Place: African Americans, Afro-Cubans, and the Diasporic Imaginary in the United States," in *Neither Friends nor Ene-*

mies: Latinos, Blacks, and Afro-Latinos, ed. Suzanne Oboler and Anani Dzidzienyo (New York: Palgrave, 1986).

12. Peter Bailey, *Witnessing Brother Malcolm*; Moore, *Pichón*.

13. Malcolm X, "Message to the Grassroots."

14. See Malcolm X and Breitman, *Malcolm X Speaks*; Louis Decaro, *On the Side of My People: A Religious Life of Malcolm X* (New York: New York University Press, 1996); James Tyner, *The Geography of Malcolm X: Black Radicalism and the Remaking of American Space* (Hoboken, N.J.: Taylor and Francis, 2013); J. Marah, *African People in a Global Village: An Introduction to Pan-African Studies* (Lanham, Md.: University Press of America, 1998).

15. E. Victor Wolfenstein, *The Victims of Democracy: Malcolm X and the Black Revolution* (Berkeley: University of California Press, 1981), 10.

16. See Candice Mancini, *Racism in the Autobiography of Malcolm X* (New York: Greenhaven, 2008), 120.

17. Bailey, *Witnessing Brother Malcolm*.

18. Miguel Gonzalez-Pando, *The Cuban Americans* (Westport, Conn.: Greenwood, 1998), x.

19. For an overview, see James Stewart Olson and Judith E. Olson, *Cuban Americans: From Trauma to Triumph* (New York: Twayne, 1995).

20. Frank Guridy, *Forging Diaspora: Afro-Cubans and African Americans in a World of Empire and Jim Crow* (Chapel Hill: University of North Carolina Press, 2010); see also Mirabal, "Scripting Race, Finding Place."

21. Mirabal, "Scripting Race, Finding Place," 202.

22. LeRoi Jones, later known as Amiri Baraka, traveled to Cuba in the early 1960s. Many other African Americans visited Cuba for a variety of reasons, including a search for possible solutions to the problem of racism. LeRoi Jones, *Home: Social Essays* (New York: William and Morrow, 1968). See also Ruth Reitan, *The Rise and Decline of an Alliance: Cuba and African American Leaders in the 1960s* (East Lansing: Michigan State University Press, 1999).

23. Moore, *Pichón*, 144.

24. Maya Angelou, *The Heart of a Woman* (New York: Random House, 1981), gives a detailed account of the protest and the role played by Carlos the Cuban. After the demonstration/protest, she and other activists met Malcolm X to talk about strategies for advancing civil and human rights.

25. Moore, *Pichón*, 158.

26. Miguel Torres, *From Exiles to Minorities: The Politics of the Cuban Community in the United States* (Ann Arbor, Mich.: UMI Dissertation Services, 1988). See also María de los Angeles Torres, *In the Land of Mirrors: Cuban Exile Politics in the United States* (1999; Ann Arbor: University of Michigan Press, 2001); Antonio Lopez, *Unbecoming Blackness: The Diaspora Cultures of Afro-Cuban America* (New York: New York University Press, 2012).

27. Torres, *In the Land of Mirrors*, 201.

28. Lopez, *Unbecoming Blackness*, 189.

29. Moore, *Pichón*, 147.

30. Quoted in Wolfenstein, *Victims of Democracy*, 10.

31. Malcolm X and Breitman, *Malcolm X Speaks*, 52.

32. Ibid., 23–44.

33. Ibid., 50.

34. Ibid., 57.

35. Ibid., 70.

36. Angelou, *Heart of a Woman*, 155.

37. Ibid., 155.

38. Moore, *Pichón*, 136

39. Ibid., 154.

40. Angelou, *Heart of a Woman*, 147.

41. Quoted in Onishi Yuichiro, *Transpacific Antiracism: Afro-Asian Solidarity in 20th Century Black America, Japan, and Okinawa* (New York: New York University Press, 2013), 127.

42. James H. Meriwether, *Proudly We Can Be Africans: Black Americans and Africa, 1935–1961* (Chapel Hill: University of North Carolina Press, 2002), 232.

43. Quoted in Bailey, *Witnessing Brother Malcolm*, 90.

44. Quoted in Nico Slate, *Black Power beyond Borders: The Global Dimensions of the Black Power Movement* (New York: Palgrave Macmillan, 2012), 151.

45. Angelou, *Heart of a Woman*, 151.

46. Quoted in Slate, *Black Power beyond Borders*, 152.

47. Bailey, *Witnessing Brother Malcolm*, 91.

48. Jamie J. Wilson, *Civil Rights Movement* (Santa Barbara, Calif.: Greenwood, 2013); Collisson, "Fight to Legitimize Blackness," 115.

49. Collisson, "Fight to Legitimize Blackness," 165.

50. Carlos Moore, *African Presence in the Americas* (Trenton, N.J.: Africa World Press, 1995), contains works produced at a conference on the same theme in 1987, which has been aptly described as the first conference of African communities in the Americas, organized by Moore at Florida International University.

51. See Collisson, "Fight to Legitimize Blackness," 177.

CHAPTER 6

"We Need to Unite with as Many People as Possible"

The Illinois Chapter of the Black Panther Party and the Young Lords Organization in Chicago

JAKOBI WILLIAMS

> We're not gonna fight fire with fire, we're gonna fight fire with water. We're not gonna fight racism with racism, we're gonna fight racism with solidarity. We're not gonna fight capitalism with Black capitalism, we're gonna fight capitalism with socialism.
>
> Fred Hampton, "The People Have to Have the Power"

By 1968 the Black Panther Party (BPP) was popular not only because it defied law enforcement but also because its socialist ideology resonated with African American youth. The *Black Panther* newspaper and members' speaking tours communicated the party's message and purpose to African American communities and helped the party establish branches in numerous cities. On November 1, 1968, the Illinois Chapter of the Black Panther Party (ILBPP) was established. Led by Deputy Chairman Fred Hampton and Deputy Minister of Defense Bobby Rush, the unit's immediate target was Mayor Richard J. Daley's Democratic machine, which the ILBPP believed controlled various mechanisms of oppression. The ILBPP began reaching out to other groups that were engaged in campaigns against the Daley Democratic machine. This effort resulted in the creation of the ILBPP's Rainbow Coalition, "a political coalition that respected ethnic communities of all kinds" and was "led by poor, black youth." It later became famous when Harold Washington used it as a base for his successful bid for mayor of Chicago in 1983.[1]

The key factor that bonded this multiracial coalition together was opposition to the Daley Democratic machine's perceived political corruption and to police brutality, urban renewal, and gentrification. The long history of political activism and coalition politics in Chicago notwithstanding, the Rainbow Coalition was the first of its kind, not only because it was established and led by teenagers and young adults but also because poor ethnic groups led by (indeed, for the first time, *including*) African Americans organized as one entity to fight for political power that was denied to them all. These young people used the positive aspects of their age cohort to significantly reduce the rigid racial and ethnic tensions between these groups, which had persisted since the nineteenth century. It was Hampton who coined the term "Rainbow Coalition," and in Chicago the name became code for class struggle.[2] The groups that joined the ILBPP to form the original Rainbow Coalition were the Young Lords Organization (YLO), a socially conscious Puerto Rican group from Lincoln Park; the Young Patriots, a group of Appalachian white migrants located in Uptown; and Rising Up Angry, a club of young "greasers" from Logan Square.[3]

By focusing on the relationship between the Illinois Chapter of the Black Panther Party and the Young Lords Organization, this chapter highlights the nuanced connections of the themes of resistance, racial coalitions, local studies, and liberation movements. The ILBPP and the YLO solidified African American and Latino coalition activism in Chicago. The activist campaigns of both communities against dilapidated housing, urban renewal, and police brutality (waged against organizations and residents alike) had tremendous mass appeal and eventually led to the reform of city social services. The ILBPP and YLO alliance established a different form of racial coalition politics by including the politicization of gangs, which in turn revolutionized Chicago politics. The activism of both the African American–led and Puerto Rican–led revolutionary groups was grounded in socialist principles. Together the ILBPP and the YLO provide a model of how to conduct effective multiracial coalition campaigns in a large city with a high concentration of racially residentially segregated communities.

URBAN RENEWAL, PUERTO RICAN INDEPENDENCE, AND BLACK-BROWN UNITY

Immediately following the establishment of the Illinois Chapter of the Black Panther Party, the group targeted two of the many socioeconomic problems that plagued much of black Chicago during this period: urban renewal and the political and economic exploitation by and corruption of the Daley Democratic machine. The Puerto Rican community in the 1960s was located in Lincoln Park on the Near Northwest Side of Chicago along Division Street.

A mass migration of Puerto Ricans had settled in the Lincoln Park neighborhood beginning in the 1950s. From 1955 through 1960, construction of the Carl Sandburg Village and the University of Illinois Circle Campus eliminated the homes of tens of thousands of Lincoln Park's Puerto Rican residents.[4] In 1960 Mayor Daley's urban renewal projects aimed to keep the area predominantly white and wealthy; there were already over eighty-four thousand white ethnic inhabitants.[5]

The Young Lords, formed by José "Cha-Cha" Jiménez, Orlando Davila, Santos Guzman, Joe Vicente, Benny Perez, Angel Del Rivero, and Fermin Perez in 1959, offered Puerto Rican youths protection from white ethnic gangs in the Lincoln Park area. The group saw how the Black Panther Party worked in the African American community and how the Students for a Democratic Society worked with students and decided to organize their community in a similar fashion. At the same time, Lincoln Park was in the middle of a transformation. Puerto Ricans were being displaced by urban renewal.[6] Developers renovated properties in Lincoln Park and severely increased rents to force out poor and Latino people. Latino residents argued that only young "white professionals could pay the $250-a-month rents that were necessary after the developers' renovations."[7]

After the Young Lords became a community organization, the composition of the membership also changed. The YLO expanded from an exclusive Puerto Rican group to include African Americans, whites, and other Latinos.[8] At least one-fifth of the organization was Mexican American or Chicano, since the YLO saw a need to work together with other Latinos to build a unified political base for the community.[9] The YLO had broad ties since members hailed from every Latino gang and community in Chicago and from numerous factories in the city.[10] In addition to Latino unity, "Jiménez envisioned a Puerto Rican revolutionary organization to realize [the] liberation of Puerto Ricans on the island and in the mainland."[11]

From the very beginning, Cha-Cha Jiménez and the Young Lords were staunch advocates for Puerto Rican independence and liberation. The members identified themselves as revolutionary nationalists, and many of them had strong ties with revolutionary leaders on the island. Before migrating to Chicago, the YLO communications deputy, Tony Baez, was very active in the liberation struggle on the island. He fled to Chicago to avoid imprisonment. "The Lords see their roles as one of making Americans realize that the U.S. government has its own resort colony in just the same manner as the 19th century European empires."[12] As one Young Lord explained, "Why the stress on a nationalistic feeling for an island so far away? For a Puerto Rican living in Chicago who was forced to come here as a cheap laborer, that rallying point gives a sense of pride and identity. All were brought here because of the systematic destruction of the Puerto Rican economy and the death of jobs and promise."[13]

The YLO's ideology shifted to reflect the growth of political awareness in minority and community youth groups citywide. Even before the Young Lords Organization joined the Panthers' Rainbow Coalition, it was very politically active. Its community campaigns secured the support of Lincoln Park's residents. Members became the social workers of their community by sponsoring picnics and a drug education program and giving food baskets to needy families. The group held dances and toy drives for Lincoln Park's children. The YLO initiated a dialogue with the largest street gang in the country, the Black Stone Rangers, to form an alliance. According to scholar Jeffrey O. G. Ogbar, "The efforts of the Lords and Rangers indicated a political transformation that could make them into agents of liberation and harbingers of freedom, justice, and power for the people."[14] On February 14–16, 1969, the YLO joined with Black, Active and Determined, a political organization located in the Cabrini Green housing project, in the Third World Unity Conference in Chicago.[15] The Young Lords also took the initiative to build coalitions with other groups. Members met with all Latino organizations and organizers in the city to form a chain of unity.

In December 1968 the YLO had challenged three realty companies, Bissell, Crown, and Romano, which were attempting to force Puerto Ricans out of Lincoln Park.[16] According to one community report, "Larry from Bissell Realty says he has nothing against Puerto Ricans. Moving them out is just good business. . . . He can make a lot more money renting to rich whites. . . . Many working class families happen to be living 'over a goldmine,' as a realtor recently called the land in Lincoln Park at a meeting of the Wrightwood Neighbors."[17] Jiménez argued that Bissell Realty was a front for organized crime, which also "had political connections to the Daley Democratic machine. Alderman George McCutcheon had mafia ties. . . . Lincoln Park, the 43rd Ward had mafia ties dating back to the 1930s. . . . Personally, I knew there were mafia ties because my father used to run numbers when I was younger and he used to turn in his money to the Bissell Realty office."[18] Puerto Ricans saw the Bissell company as crooks who used real estate to exploit the Latino community. Thus, organized crime was also a player in gentrification and urban renewal. The YLO accused the companies of trying to buy most of the properties in the area to drive up rents, thereby forcing poor people to relocate. Residents responded by breaking the real estate companies' windows and destroying furnaces in buildings owned by those accused of being slumlords. The YLO led this campaign, which won the support of the community.

In January 1969 the group confronted the Community Conservation Council over the issue of urban renewal. The contingent forced the CCC to include Latinos, blacks, and working-class whites from Lincoln Park in the decision-making process.[19] In May 1969 the YLO occupied the McCormick Theological Seminary's administration building to protest the forced removal of Lincoln Park's poor residents as a result of gentrification and urban renewal.[20] The group wanted to negotiate with the seminary to have it invest money in low-income housing in the area. McCormick Theological Seminary had purchased a number of properties in Lincoln Park and was viewed by residents as a participant in the forced removal of its poor neighbors. Jiménez recalled, "We went into the place, barricaded the doors and set up security with walkie-talkies. At first there were only 40 people. We had a press conference and by morning the place was full of poor people and guilty middle class people."[21] The next morning, people from the community brought food to the youth to demonstrate their support for their effort. "They came in with the kids . . . so they wouldn't shoot at us," Jiménez explained. "So it was a community effort that kept the police away from probably annihilating us at that time."[22]

The YLO occupation forced the clergy to invest over half a million dollars in housing for poor and working-class people in Lincoln Park.[23] Arthur McKay, the president of McCormick Theological Seminary, agreed to the demands of the coalition's leaders, Jiménez of the YLO and Obed Lopez of the Latin American Defense Organization, to provide the community with "low income housing, welfare organizing, the Puerto Rican cultural center and a legal defense fund."[24] McKay also agreed that the seminary's "financial records be open [to the public], that McCormick join to help community groups, that it publicly oppose the racist policies of Urban Renewal, and that it open its facilities to the use of the community."[25]

Such YLO actions caught the attention of the Illinois Chapter of the Black Panther Party. In 1969 Fred Hampton personally approached the YLO to encourage them to join the Rainbow Coalition. A day before their encounter, about fifty or sixty YLO members had made headlines by using nonviolent direct action to take over the Chicago Avenue police station. The group had forcefully occupied the facility to protest a police propaganda campaign in Lincoln Park that painted the group as criminals in an effort to destroy community support for the youth organization and its campaign against urban renewal. The YLO had been in contact with the Black Panthers in Oakland prior to the event and were unaware that there was a chapter of the Black Panther Party in Illinois. So Hampton met with the group and offered guidance. He told the YLO that it had to study what was taking place at the international level and relate those larger events to the movement happening in Chicago. Soon after, the YLO joined the party's Rainbow Coalition.[26] Hampton helped the YLO to realize that the group's function as social workers for their community only addressed the symptoms and not the causes of social ills.[27]

According to scholar Laura Pulido, one major reason that the BPP appealed to organizations like the YLO was because of its internationalist framework: "Despite its base in the black community, a close examination of BPP texts reveals that the Party called for freedom and liberation of *all* poor and oppressed people, not just African Americans."[28] The YLO was not only influenced by the BPP but also emulated the Panthers' ideology and methodology. For instance, to join the YLO, a potential member had to take political education classes and karate instruction, as well as participate in community service. Similar to the Panthers, the YLO advertised itself as a propaganda and armed self-defense unit:

> [The] YLO is a propaganda machine that is committed to educating the masses of people. Our primary task is informing and showing the people why they are being exploited and oppressed, who is responsible, and how they can eventually eradicate the many injustices committed against them.
>
> We are also an armed group prepared to protect our communities from the brutal assaults by the power structure that are committed every day. As the people become aware of what has been happening, they will turn their guns away from each other and aim them at the pig power structure that has been messing with us for so long.[29]

The *Y.L.O.*, the organization's newspaper, was modeled after the Panthers' newspaper, the *Black Panther*. The YLO also adopted an organizational structure similar to that of the Panthers, "which included ministers of information, defense, education and a central committee with field marshals."[30] While the Panthers advocated a Ten Point Platform and Program, the YLO promoted a Thirteen Point Platform and Program. In addition to the founding points of the BPP's platform, the YLO also advocated the liberation of the island of Puerto Rico and all Third World people and equality for women.

Like the Panthers, the YLO offered a free breakfast program for children, set up the Puerto Rican Cultural Center, and opened a medical center in Lincoln Park.[31] The YLO's free breakfast program, modeled after the Panthers' project, received support from many local shopowners and businesspeople: "Most of the food for the breakfasts is given freely by local grocers. One record store owner, a staunch supporter of the Puerto Rican Independence Movement, has given recordings of the Puerto Rican national anthem to be played each morning at the breakfast program."[32] The YLO medical center was located inside the People's Church at 834 W. Armitage, and the center's immediate target was children. The YLO advertised that its medical program was intended to improve the medical and dental health of children because the Puerto Rican community had a high infant mortality rate and too many children had decayed teeth. The YLO declared, like the Panthers:

> We are opening these health programs because profit-making doctors refuse to take care of poor people and always open offices only in neighborhoods where they can make money . . . because all hospitals in the area do not think it is important to provide decent health care for poor people . . . because hospitals in the area don't hire enough doctors and nurses to meet the health needs of the poor . . . because we are tired of seeing young brothers and sisters die because the people who control health services are more interested in making money than in providing health care for all people. We are tired of seeing children with decayed teeth because they can't get dental care.[33]

Not only did their programs attend to children who were sick, they also offered preventive measures that included prenatal programs for women.

Although there were numerous parallels between the Panthers and the Lords that can be attributed to the Panthers' ideological influence, there were some areas in which the YLO demonstrated foresight and principle where the Panthers came up short. One such aspect related to gender and patriarchy. According to Jiménez, in 1969 the YLO created "the first community daycare center in the city so that women could join us in our movement. We had women in our organization from the very beginning."[34] The ILBPP would not open a community daycare center until 1972. Unlike the Panthers, the YLO included "gender equality as a goal worthy of their political platforms."[35] The YLO platform's item 10 noted:

> WE WANT EQUALITY FOR WOMEN. MACHISMO MUST BE REVOLUTIONARY . . . NOT OPPRESSIVE.
> Under capitalism, our women have been oppressed by both the society and our own men. The doctrine of machismo has been used by our men to take out their frustrations against their wives, sisters, mothers, and children. Our men must support their women in their fight for economic and social equality, and must recognize that our women are equals in every way within the revolutionary ranks.[36]

The Young Lords, as Laura Pulido points out, "took a significant step in acknowledging the problems of *machismo*, male supremacy in Latin American cultures, and in condemning male terror and domination."[37]

The YLO was also a leader in dealing with gangs. One of the first requests of the ILBPP was that the YLO build alliances with gangs in Lincoln Park with the aim of politicizing these groups. The party believed that gang members made good potential community organizers because the gangs were made up of disaffected youth from poor neighborhoods experiencing transition as a result of urban renewal.[38] What these youth required, the Chicago Panthers believed, was guidance toward politicization as a response to their communities' plight. The Panthers made numerous attempts to politicize Chicago-area gangs by appealing to what all of the gangs had in common with the Panthers: opposition to the Daley machine's urban renewal policies, which were destroying the neighborhoods in which the gang members lived, and to the police brutality and mistreatment that were common in their neighborhoods. These efforts were remarkably successful, leading to both formal organizational affiliation through the Rainbow Coalition and to unofficial alliances between the Panthers and the Conservative Vice Lords and Disciples.[39]

On two occasions, the YLO established citywide truces among the gangs. At that time, there were at least seven different gangs in Lincoln Park alone: the Hudsons, the North Parks, the Mohawks, the Paragons, the Latin Eagles, the Black Eagles, and a Puerto Rican biker gang called the Horsemen. The Young Lords Organization actually had people from all the different gangs in the group, and these members were dispatched to work within the gangs. The purpose was to organize the gangs and get them involved in the main issue at that time, which was the removal of inner-city poor people. As a result, the YLO and the gangs "became friends" and perceived "a common enemy" in those who attempted to evict the poor. Jiménez recalled that during the late 1960s "Lincoln Park had a very large concentration of Puerto Ricans . . .

but it was also a mixed community . . . a working class community."[40] Thus, it was possible for the YLO to find common cause with gangs on issues that affected the poor.

One such issue was the elimination of drugs and drug dealers from the community. During early 1974, the corner of Wilton and Grace near the YLO office was a prime drug sales area until the YLO allied with the Latin Eagles gang to end such practices. There were tensions between Chicago Police commander Tom Hanley of the Nineteenth Police District and the Latin Eagles because Hanley believed the Eagles were muscle for the YLO. Jiménez "disagrees—and credits the Eagles with helping to push dope dealers from the area. 'The Latin Eagles are part of the community. A little respect is all that was necessary in dealing with them. [The YLO members] weren't always in favor of their tactics, but they did put pressure on the dealers.'"[41] Also influenced by the YLO, Chicago's largest Puerto Rican gang, the Latin Kings, "organized themselves politically and . . . started their own breakfast-for-children program."[42] Such community control efforts led by the YLO challenged police authority, which did not sit well with law enforcement.

REPRESSION AND POLICE BRUTALITY

Similar to the Panthers and its relationship to the African American community, many Puerto Rican community members supported the efforts of the YLO without joining the organization. Sometimes, these supportive residents were subjected to increased police repression and brutality. One example was a widow, Ceil Keegan, whose husband died after he was turned away from a local hospital because he did not have health insurance. She and her two small children were beaten by six white men from Cicero, and she was harassed by Chicago police because she volunteered in several YLO community service programs. The six white men who assaulted her told her to give the YLO leader Jiménez a message: he was "not as smart as he thinks he is." Three weeks prior to this incident, three plainclothes police also beat Ceil Keegan and forced her into a police car to scare her to prevent her from continuing her "'activities' inside the People's Church," where she worked "with the YLO and the poor people in the community."[43] The three policemen "slapped" Keegan around and beat her "for three hours." "Later they dumped her back at home, nearly dead."[44] Sympathy and anger regarding Keegan's treatment only caused more Puerto Rican residents to get involved in the movement.

The Young Lords made attempts to curtail such police brutality. In February 1969, the YLO led three hundred residents to the Police Community Relations Workshop to protest police brutality and harassment, the police department's defense of slumlords, and a police shooting that had resulted in the death of a fifteen-year-old black youth.[45] These efforts intensified after the death of YLO member Manuel Ramos, who was shot and killed on May 4, 1969, by off-duty policeman James Lamb from the Bridgeport district (Mayor Daley's community). When he was shot, Ramos was standing outside of a birthday party for Orlando Davila, who was the president of the Young Lords. Lamb claimed that he was threatened with a gun, but the weapon was never found.[46] The Young Lords arrested Lamb and turned him over to the police. According to Jiménez, this action did not have the desired result: "We went to court and instead of them arresting the police[man], they arrested four Young Lords, we called them the Quatro Lords at that time. We went through trials and again nothing was done about it. . . . During that time there was a lot of police brutality going on. . . . there were no Latinos on the police force at that time and very few African Americans. . . . It was a way to educate the people about police brutality."[47] A coroner's jury decided that Ramos's death was a justifiable homicide. "I think it was at that point that I became a real revolutionary," Jiménez says, referring to Ramos's murder. "Instead of going out and killing a pig, I saw the need to sit down and analyze the ways of getting even. Not with a gun. It wasn't the right time. . . . We have to educate the people before we think about guns."[48] Jiménez and the YLO would organize their community and form alliances with other city residents and organizations that had experienced similar oppression by the city's police and officials.

The Rainbow Coalition responded with a series of marches to protest what it classified as state murder. Led by the YLO, the Young Patriots, Students for a Democratic Society, and the Panthers, two thousand Chicagoans first marched on the Bridgeport police station. Days later, Cook County state's attorney Edward Hanrahan announced that he would be at the Eighteenth District police station on Chicago Avenue. The Rainbow Coalition, along with several thousand supporters, marched to the station to confront Hanrahan, but he did not appear. The next day, several thousand people attended Ramos's funeral. The large turnout for the marches and the funeral brought publicity and support to the Rainbow Coalition. Membership in the affiliated organizations spiked as a result.[49]

The marches related to Ramos's death were the first in a series. The Albizu Campos march started on Halstead and Armitage and went to Humboldt

Park, with the goal of teaching the Puerto Rican community about the concept of self-determination.[50] "We were the first organization in this country to have a massive rally for the independence of Puerto Rico," Jiménez claimed.[51] Marchers chanted, "The streets belong to the people," "Free Puerto Rico now," "Viva Don Pedro," and "Que viva los Young Lords."[52] The march started with only about a thousand people, but by the time participants reached Humboldt Park there were about ten thousand people in the audience. Jiménez said: "We had no one supporting self-determination for Puerto Rico in our area. No one, everyone was afraid to go against old Mayor Daley at that time. And so we were the ones who created and developed that movement, the Young Lords, Rising Up Angry and other groups like ourselves."[53] The YLO speakers included Hilda Ignatin and Cha-Cha Jiménez of Chicago and David Perez and Pablo "Yoruba" Guzman from the New York Young Lords, who came to Chicago along with other Puerto Ricans from New York and other cities that had chapters of the Young Lords Organization.[54]

On September 10, 1969, the Young Lords and the Chicago Panthers held a memorial service for Larry Roberson and Ho Chi Minh at the Armitage Methodist Church. Chicago Panther Roberson had been killed earlier that month during a shootout with police after he tried to intervene in the arrest of several African American residents on West Madison Street. Ho Chi Minh, the president of the Democratic Republic of Vietnam (communist North Vietnam), had died on September 2, 1969. Fred Hampton was the main speaker at the event, which also featured several members of the Young Lords. The memorial service was a further effort to express the Rainbow Coalition's solidarity with and dedication to the struggle of working-class Chicagoans.[55]

RACIAL COALITION POLITICS: BLACK AND BROWN ACTIVISTS AND CHICAGO'S POLITICAL ARENA

The Illinois Chapter of the Black Panther Party's deputy chair, Fred Hampton, and Peoria, Illinois, branch member Mark Clark were assassinated by the FBI and Chicago police on December 4, 1969, during a police raid at Hampton's apartment. This heinous act was the beginning of the eventual end of the ILBPP in 1974. Meanwhile José "Cha-Cha" Jiménez kept the movement and the Rainbow Coalition alive. Probably the most underappreciated legacy of the Illinois Panthers is their creation of the original Rainbow Coalition: this idealism continued to inspire the relationship between African Americans and Puerto Ricans in Chicago and in particular inspired Jiménez to continue to honor the life and death of Fred Hampton.

The original Rainbow Coalition and its popularization of the concepts of socialism and class solidarity changed the political landscape of Chicago by helping to severely weaken the city's Democratic machine. The role of the state's attorney's office and the FBI in the assassination of Fred Hampton galvanized the city.[56] Hampton became a martyr for the movement, and Jiménez and Rainbow Coalition members stepped up efforts to organize against the Daley machine. The state's attorney, Edward Hanrahan, once heralded as Chicago mayor Richard J. Daley's successor, was voted out of office in the early 1970s primarily as a result of the Daley administration's role in the cover-up of Hampton's murder.[57] For the first time in more than two decades, "a majority of black voters rejected the Democratic machine and voted for a Republican."[58] Hanrahan's defeat as a result of his involvement in Hampton's murder and the subsequent cover-up ended his political career.[59] In 1976, Mayor Daley died in office, and Republican, Democratic, and independent politicians who had lacked any real political influence under the weight of the Daley machine intensified their challenges to Democrat-held seats in almost every political office.

Jiménez believed that he had a duty to Fred Hampton and the movement to keep the fight for revolution and the implementation of socialist policies alive. On the same night that Hampton and Clark were assassinated, the YLO reported, "an attempt was made to burn the National Headquarters of the Young Lords Organization," probably by local police or provocateurs.[60] "The political murders of brothers Fred Hampton and Mark Clark . . . the murder of Manuel Ramos on May 4, 1969," advocated the YLO, are "the reason why the Young Lords Organization has been informing the community and stressing the importance of the struggle that is being waged by the Black, Brown, and poor whites for self-determination and the need to bring all struggle[s] of the poor to one united front."[61] Jiménez explained, "The work of the Black Panther Party on the West Side and South Side of Chicago built a strong movement that clarified the issues. . . . Fred [Hampton] clarified the issues—[that] these are our friends and these are our enemies . . . and that we need to unite with as many people as possible."[62]

On June 20, 1974 (the year the ILBPP officially ended), Jiménez held a press conference to announce to a coalition of blacks, whites, Latinos, Asians, and Native Americans that he would run for the North Side's Forty-Sixth Ward alderman seat, openly advertising that he had once supported Hampton and he still believed in the Rainbow Coalition.[63] His campaign kept the Rainbow Coalition movement alive as "fragments of the old SDS crowd, the old Black Panther crowd, and the old sympathetic media crowd" provided their services for his campaign; like Jiménez, they believed in the continuation of a "people's movement."[64] More important, Jiménez had studied "Bobby Seale's efforts at elective office in Oakland and . . . [Saul] Alinsky's techniques at organizing the poor. He [was] determined to use the Lords to organize Latinos and seek a political power base."[65] After all, Chicago in the early 1970s was the country's fourth largest Latino community with nearly 250,000 Latino residents; only New York, Los Angeles, and San Antonio had larger numbers. Despite Chicago's large Latino numbers, which ranked second to African Americans, there had never been a Latino alderman elected in Chicago, and there were only three Latino elected officials in the city's history: "One is a circuit court judge, another is a county commissioner, and the third is a University of Illinois trustee."[66] Urban renewal, gentrification, and police brutality were still unwanted realities in the Latino community. In October 1974 Jiménez and the Young Lords Organization orchestrated a unity rally that drew 1,500 people to demonstrate their organizing ability to constituents. Thus, Jiménez's campaign for political office continued the ILBPP Rainbow Coalition's platform of community control and self-determination: "Cha-Cha talks of 'stabilizing' the community. He endorses Dick Simpson's community zoning board ordinance that would give zoning power to citizens of the ward. He supports a landlord security deposit. For each apartment, building owners would have to ante up $100 to be used for emergency repairs."[67]

The Panthers had white allies in the Midwest under the leadership of Walter "Slim" Coleman, the coordinator for the Campaign for Community Control, a group active since 1971 in setting up legal and medical assistance programs primarily for southern whites in Uptown, which had then moved to Chicago to continue racial coalition organizing under the rubric of the Intercommunal Survival Committee. Coleman later set up the Uptown Coalition, which included progressive whites who had supported the Rainbow Coalition before Hampton's assassination and former members of the Young Patriots, and he established chapters throughout white communities in Chicago. Coleman was also one of Jiménez's closest advisors. Along with the Panthers, these groups organized support for Jiménez's city alderman campaign. Coleman explained that the coalition "is seeking support from what Coleman called the powerless masses. If we can bury our differences to elect an alderman, I'd say the revolution is not dead."[68] Coleman discussed why he adamantly supported Jiménez for alderman: "Cha-Cha woke a lot of us [up] to what urban renewal was doing. And all along, he has shown a good ability to build coalitions. . . . We *had* to be practical. In looking around, it seemed to us that Cha-Cha had the best chance. He'll get the Latino vote. We have to see that he gets half of the remainder of the east side."[69]

Jiménez was the first Puerto Rican to run for office in Chicago against the Daley Democratic machine, and his candidacy, though unsuccessful, revealed the Latino community as a viable voting group. Others also had the audacity to challenge the machine following Hampton's death. Bobby Rush, described by the *Chicago Reader* as the "magnetic former Black Panther leader," also ran for alderman.[70] The Independent Voters of Illinois, a group of progressive whites, ran William Singer for mayor of Chicago against Daley; the group also supported Jiménez's campaign.[71] Fred Hampton's political assassination thus helped to unite African American, Latino, and progressive white groups and activists in a political movement against the Daley machine. Though the multiracial coalition's candidates failed to gain a significant political office between 1970 and 1977, the groups and activists continued to organize in their respective communities. Jiménez recalls that many activists burned out from the struggle against the Democratic machine, but when Harold Washington announced his campaign for mayor of Chicago, the movement was reignited.[72]

Washington, an Illinois state senator, had become a Panther supporter following Hampton's death. After he "toured the bullet-ravaged apartment" where Fred Hampton and Mark Clark were assassinated, he found himself shaken and "outraged" by the Daley administration's wanton use of force, and he began to work politically with members of the original Rainbow Coalition.[73] The height of his political alliance with ILBPP-influenced activists and grassroots organizations was his mayoral campaign. In 1983, Washington, a Democratic candidate, ran on a Rainbow Coalition platform—"a policy of racial justice and equality for working people and the poor"—and was elected as Chicago's first African American mayor.[74] Congressman Bobby Rush, the former deputy minister of defense of the Illinois Panthers, later declared that Washington's election was "directly linked to the 'assassination' of Mr. [Fred] Hampton, and the outcry and change that it prompted."[75] According to Illinois Panther and Rainbow Coalition co-founder Bob Lee, "It was not until the election of Harold Washington that organizers realized the actual strength of the Rainbow Coalition, which also helped members to understand the local power structure's commitment to eliminating the group, as it was a real political threat to machine politics in Chicago."[76]

Robin D. G. Kelley pointed out that in order for Washington to win Chicago's mayoral election, "he [had] to appeal to a significant proportion of white and Latino voters, and convince hundreds of thousands of complacent, frustrated black adults to register and come out to the polls."[77] The Rainbow Coalition in Chicago had already paved the road of multiracial coalitions and class solidarity in Chicago by 1983, and its members continued their work in Washington's mayoral campaign. Numerous individuals and organizations also participated in an African American voter registration drive on behalf of Washington.[78] Many leaders of the organizations that made up the original Rainbow Coalition were key community organizers for Washington's campaign. They included Mike James of Rising Up Angry, Jiménez of the Young Lords, Bobby Rush of the Illinois Black Panther Party, and several other former Panthers, such as Yvonne King, who provided community-sensitive legal guidance for the Task Force for Black Political Empowerment, a group organized outside of the formal campaign structure to "advance the struggle for political reform (symbolized by Washington's campaign) in a manner consistent with the broader goals of the movement."[79] Washington stated, "Since 1955, women, Latinos, Blacks, youth, and progressive whites have been left out of the Chicago government. . . . We have a school system which does not educate. . . . We no longer have dependable housing in this city. . . . I see a Chicago of compassion; a city where no one has to live with rats, where the sick can be cured. . . . As mayor of this city, I would open the doors of City Hall. I would dig into that untapped reservoir of talented whites, Latinos, women and Blacks and unleash that ability for the benefit of this city."[80]

Original Rainbow Coalition members organized and ran the Washington campaign's voter registration and turnout projects, and they used the strengths of their communities as a base, which they then extended to other areas of the city. For example, Jiménez served as Washington's North Side precinct coordinator and introduced the candidate to voters in Lincoln Park and bordering districts (mostly Puerto Rican and other Latino communities), and many former Panthers got involved in the campaign, predominantly in African American communities. In 1983, more than one hundred thousand people participated in a march from Lincoln Park to Humboldt Park to unite the community behind Washington. Thirty thousand of the marchers wore Young Lords buttons; the group "was the first Latino organization to support Harold Washington for Mayor."[81]

CONCLUSION

By 1967 the Young Lords Organization was popularly recognized as "the most potent revolutionary organization of Puerto Rican youth in the United States."[82] In 1969 members of the Young Lords Organization traveled to other American cities to establish branches of the political group in Puerto Rican communities. Its largest and most successful affiliate was the New York branch, primarily because that city had the highest concentration of Puerto Ricans in the United States. As in Chicago, the YLO in New York allied with the Black Panther Party. The Lords and the Panthers worked together in a Bronx housing coalition to establish tenants' right to confront their landlords. Together, the organizations addressed police brutality, deplorable housing, poor hospital care, insufficient food, and inadequate education.[83]

The Black Panther Party was the most popular Black Power revolutionary group of the period, primarily as a result of its coalition-building reputation. Coalitions formed by groups like the ILBPP and the YLO in Chicago are vivid examples of the parallels of the activism of black and Puerto Rican people in post–World War II America. Both communities were plagued by the critical issues of urban renewal, police brutality, gangs, poverty, and political and economic exploitation. The Panthers provided a model of self-determination and self-empowerment founded in socialist principles to address these critical issues. The YLO utilized this model to address its community's local concerns while simultaneously leading the struggle in the United States for the independence of the island of Puerto Rico.

The ILBPP and the YLO activist campaigns were remarkably successful due in large part to the two groups' charismatic leaders and their ability to connect to and provide voices for their communities. The only pitfall of the unity of the ILBPP and the YLO was their underestimation of the extremes of state repression—which led to the assassinations of Hampton and Clark and forced Jiménez underground to avoid a prison sentence. Fortunately, he was eventually able to rebound and rejoin the movement. The friendship between Hampton and Jiménez was genuine, and their relationship carried over to their respective communities, which helped to solidify the coalition bonds between blacks and Puerto Ricans in the city. After Hampton's death, Jiménez picked up the baton as the de facto leader of the racial coalition movement in Chicago. Washington's election as Chicago's first African American mayor is the most recognized success and legacy of black and Puerto Rican activism and coalition efforts.

Original Rainbow Coalition members such as Jiménez supported Washington because his platform addressed the coalition's tenets, such as prioritizing neighborhoods over the needs of City Hall, opposing gentrification and urban renewal, and advocating for Puerto Rican liberation. Ironically, the strength of the Rainbow Coalition was Chicago's staunch segregation. The city's various racial/ethnic neighborhoods were extremely territorial. The original Rainbow Coalition members understood that their coalition succeeded—despite failing to eradicate the deeply ingrained patterns of residential segregation—because of the organization's advocacy for neighborhoods to control the political, economic, and social dimensions of their own communities. For example, Latinos in Lincoln Park and Humboldt Park accepted the guidance of the African American ILBPP in the late 1960s primarily because the Panthers made it clear that the group did not want to lead or control Latino communities. The ILBPP's method was to train communities in how to be self-sufficient and develop empowerment, and then the Panthers would leave the area, allowing the Latino residents to evolve on their own, although they understood that the Panthers would return to assist the residents if and when the Latino communities needed their input and support. This approach was reflected in one of the primary tenets of Washington's platform: *neighborhoods first*. Washington's political grassroots organizers, many of whom were original members of the Rainbow Coalition, spread this message throughout the city.

The ILBPP and the YLO in Chicago provide two key lessons about African American and Latino activism. The most important lesson is that relationships matter in racially residentially segregated cities. Relationships among leaders of grassroots radical organizations, such as the friendship between Fred Hampton and José "Cha-Cha" Jiménez, not only are inspiring but also highlight how the idealism of identity politics and racial coalition politics can result in cross-class and interracial solidarity rather than fragmentation of the Left.[84] The second lesson is that grassroots organizing is the most effective element of a racial coalition movement because it helps to maintain and sustain the protracted struggle for political and social change in a large city like Chicago. These two lessons are best exemplified by the original Rainbow Coalition—a strong grassroots movement that clarified the issues, chose its own leaders, and united with as many people as possible. Hampton served as the de facto leader of the grassroots organization, and then Jiménez picked up the mantle after Hampton's assassination to keep the movement alive. Both revolutionaries helped people in their communities to build bridges with other Chicago residents in spite of their differences, and they both helped people of different races/ethnicities to actually see their commonalities and shared humanity. Such efforts led to the election of Chicago's first African American mayor; former Panther Bobby Rush was first elected to the U.S. Congress in 1992 and has represented his district ever since; and the Latino community was opened up as a viable political force that has gone on to elect several city council members, state representatives and senators, and members of the U.S. Congress.

NOTES

This chapter is adapted from *From the Bullet to the Ballot: The Illinois Chapter of the Black Panther Party and Racial Coalition Politics in Chicago* by Jakobi Williams. Copyright © 2013 by the University of North Carolina Press. Used by permission of the publisher. www.uncpress.unc.edu.

1. Jon Rice, "The World of the Illinois Panthers," in *Freedom North: Black Freedom Struggles outside the South, 1940–1980*, ed. Jeanne Theoharis and Komozi Woodard (New York: Palgrave Macmillan, 2003), 55–56.

2. Henry "Poison" Gaddis, interview by author, May 17, 2008; James Tracy, "The (Original) Rainbow Coalition," *Solidarities*, September 30, 2006.

3. Rice, "World of the Illinois Panthers," 54; "Young Lords Running Log, 1968–1970: Misc. File Rainbow Coalition, Item 37, Pages 1–2," box 386, folder 15, item 1, 22, Chicago Police Department–Red Squad, Bureau of Investigative Services, Intelligence Section, Surveillance Unit, Chicago History Museum (hereafter Red Squad Papers); "Young Lords Running Log, 1968–1970: Black Panther Party Vol. 11, Item 448, Page 1," box 386, folder 15, item 1, 23, Red Squad Papers. A "greaser" was a young white male usually of working-class background who participated in the countercultural trend of using grease to slick back their hair.

4. National Young Lords timeline, http://nationalyounglords.com/YoungLordsTimeline.html (accessed January 25, 2009); José Jiménez, interview by author, September 14, 2009.

5. Amanda Seligman, "Lincoln Park," in *The Encyclopedia of Chicago*, ed. James R. Grossman, Ann Durkin Keating, and Janice L. Reiff (Chicago: University of Chicago Press, 2004), 746.

6. José "Cha-Cha" Jiménez, interview by Michael James, "Live from the Heartland: Young Lords Radio Interview," WLUW Chicago, November 2005; Jiménez, interview by author; Les Bridges, "Cha-Cha Jiménez," *Chicago Reader* 4, no. 18 (February 7, 1975): 1.

7. Bridges, "Cha-Cha Jiménez," 1.

8. "Young Lords," *Rising Up Angry* 1, no. 1 (July 1969): 14.

9. Jiménez, interview by James; Jiménez, interview by author.

10. "YLO in Revolution," *Y.L.O.* 4, no. 1 (October 1969): 6.

11. Jeffrey O. G. Ogbar, *Black Power: Radical Politics and African American Identity* (Baltimore, Md.: Johns Hopkins University Press, 2004), 178.

12. Frank Browning, "From Rumble to Revolution: The Young Lords," *Ramparts* 9, no. 4 (October 1970): 23.

13. Ibid.

14. Ogbar, *Black Power*, 177–78.

15. "Information Report: Attention—Third World Unity Conference, Blacks and Latins Unite," February 12, 1969, box 304, folder 10, item 5-6, Red Squad Papers; "Interview Report: Young Lords," February 7, 1969, box 304, folder 10, item 2, Red Squad Papers; "Young Lords."

16. "Police Harassment of Young Lords Reported," Young Lords Organization Newsletter, n.d., box 304, folder 10, item 10, Red Squad Papers.

17. Richard Vission, "Class War in Lincoln Park," *Lincoln Park Press* 2, no. 2 (March 1969): 2.

18. Jiménez, interview by author.

19. Ibid.; "Jose (Cha Cha) Jimenez," *National Young Lords*, http://nationalyounglords.com/?page_id=15 (accessed April 15, 2015).

20. "McCormick Take Over," *Y.L.O.* 1, no. 2 (May 1969): 4; "Young Lords"; Jiménez, interview by author. McCormick Theological Seminary was located at Halsted and Belden Streets. It was a Presbyterian divinity school that had about 250 students. Later, it was purchased by DePaul University.

21. Browning, "From Rumble to Revolution," 20.

22. Jiménez, interview by James; "Jose (Cha Cha) Jimenez"; Jiménez, interview by author.

23. "McCormick Take Over," 4; "Young Lords"; Jiménez, interview by author.

24. "McCormick Revisited," *Y.L.O.* 1, no. 5 (January 1970): 11.

25. Browning, "From Rumble to Revolution," 20.

26. Jiménez, interview by James; National Young Lords timeline; Jiménez, interview by author.

27. Ogbar, *Black Power*, 178.

28. Laura Pulido, *Black, Brown, Yellow, and Left: Radical Activism in Los Angeles* (Berkeley, University of California Press, 2006), 167.

29. "YLO in Revolution," 6.

30. Ogbar, *Black Power*, 179.

31. "Young Lords."

32. Browning, "From Rumble to Revolution," 22–23.

33. "Health Care Is a Human Right," *Y.L.O.* 1, no. 5 (January 1970): 12.

34. Jiménez, interview by James; Jiménez, interview by author.

35. Pulido, *Black, Brown, Yellow, and Left*, 185.

36. Philip S. Foner, ed., *The Black Panthers Speak* (Cambridge, Mass.: Da Capo, 1970), 237.

37. Pulido, *Black, Brown, Yellow, and Left*, 185–86.

38. Jiménez, interview by James.

39. Gaddis, interview by author; Yvonne King, "Presentation on Illinois Black Panther Party," Fortieth Reunion of the Black Panther Party, Oakland, Calif., October 13, 2007, audio and video files in possession of author.

40. "Jose (Cha Cha) Jimenez"; Jiménez, interview by author.

41. Bridges, "Cha-Cha Jiménez," 6.

42. Browning, "From Rumble to Revolution," 19.

43. "And the People," *Y.L.O.* 1, no. 5 (January 1970): 15.

44. Browning, "From Rumble to Revolution," 19.

45. "Information Report: Police Harassment—Political Repression," Young Lords Organization Newsletter, February 12, 1969, box 304, folder 10, items 5-4 and 5-5, Red Squad Papers.

46. *Y.L.O.* 1, no. 2 (May 1969): 3, 8; Jiménez, interview by author.

47. *Y.L.O.* 1, no. 2 (May 1969): 3, 8; Jiménez, interview by James; Jiménez, interview by author.

48. Browning, "From Rumble to Revolution," 20.

49. *Y.L.O.* 1, no. 2 (May 1969): 3, 8; "Young Lords"; National Young Lords timeline; Jiménez, interview by author.

50. Jiménez, interview by James; National Young Lords timeline; Jiménez, interview by author. Dr. Pedro Albizu Campos was a Puerto Rican nationalist who advocated for the independence of Puerto Rico beginning in the 1930s. Frederic Ribes Tovar, *Albizu Campos: Puerto Rican Revolutionary* (New York: Plus Ultra Educational, 1971).

51. Jiménez, interview by James; Jiménez, interview by author.

52. "Marcha en Honor al Doctor Don Pedro Albizu Campos," *Y.L.O.* 1, no. 5 (January 1970): 3.

53. Jiménez, interview by James; Jiménez, interview by author.

54. "Marcha en Honor al Doctor Don Pedro Albizu Campos," 3.

55. "Memorial Rally," September 10, 1969, box 301, folder 12, item 8-1, Red Squad Papers; *Rising Up Angry* 1, no. 3 (October 1969): 8; Jiménez, interview by author.

56. Edward McClelland, *Young Mr. Obama: Chicago and the Making of a Black President* (New York: Bloomsbury, 2010), 36–37.

57. Gary Rivlin, *Fire on the Prairie: Chicago's Harold Washington and the Politics of Race* (New York: Holt, 1992), 26–27; McClelland, *Young Mr. Obama*, 37.

58. Rivlin, *Fire on the Prairie*, 26.

59. Trevor Jensen, "Edward V. Hanrahan, 1921–2009: Political Career Ended by Black Panther Raid," *Chicago Tribune*, June 10, 2009; Jo Napolitano, "Edward Hanrahan, Prosecutor Tied to '69 Panthers Raid, Dies at 88," *New York Times*, June 12, 2009; Abdon M.

Pallasch, "Former State's Attorney Edward Hanrahan," *Chicago Sun-Times*, June 9, 2009; Patricia Sullivan, "Prosecutor Oversaw Fatal 1969 Raid of Black Panthers in Chicago," *Washington Post*, June 12, 2009.

60. "I Came Down from the Mountain to the Valley," *Y.L.O.* 1, no. 5 (January 1970): 14.

61. Ibid.

62. Jiménez, interview by author.

63. "Background Report: Jose Jiménez," September 9, 1974, box 304, folder 11, Red Squad Papers; "Jose Jiménez Statement of Candidacy," June 20, 1974, box 304, folder 11, items 33-1 and 33-2, Red Squad Papers; "Leader of Young Lords Is Candidate for Alderman," *Chicago Today*, June 21, 1974. A Red Squad observation report indicates that there were approximately a hundred people at the press conference consisting of "40% Caucasians, 40% Puerto Ricans, and 20% Negroes, of mixed gender, ranging in ages from 5 to 50 years of age." "Surveillance Report: Jose 'Cha-Cha' Jiménez," June 20, 1974, box 304, folder 11, items 30-1 and 30-2, Red Squad Papers.

64. Ellis Cose, "Why Latino Ex-Gang Leader Will Run for Alderman," *Chicago Sun-Times*, June 24, 1974.

65. Bridges, "Cha-Cha Jiménez," 1.

66. Ibid.

67. Ibid., 6.

68. Jiménez, interview by author; "Leader of Young Lords Is Candidate for Alderman"; Bridges, "Cha-Cha Jiménez," 6.

69. Bridges, "Cha-Cha Jiménez," 6.

70. Ibid., 1.

71. Jiménez, interview by author.

72. Ibid.

73. Ibid.; Rivlin, *Fire on the Prairie*, 55.

74. Robin D. G. Kelley, "Into the Fire: 1970 to the Present," in *To Make Our World Anew: A History of African Americans*, ed. Robin D. G. Kelley and Earl Lewis (Oxford: Oxford University Press, 2000), 580.

75. Monica Davey, "Chicago Divided over Proposal to Honor a Slain Black Panther," *New York Times*, March 5, 2006.

76. Robert (Bob) E. Lee III, interview by author, October 22, 2008.

77. Kelley, "Into the Fire," 580.

78. While traditional organizations such as the NAACP, the Chicago Urban League, and Jesse Jackson's Operation PUSH had for years tried to mobilize the city's black vote, the most significant participants represented grassroots community efforts within and outside of the black community. These groups and advocates were the Chicago Black United Community (headed by Lu Palmer), Citizens for Self-Determination (led by Mercedes Maulette), the activist Al Sampson, Concerned Young Adults, the Independent Grassroots Youth Organization, Vote Community (founded by Ed Gardner of Soft Sheen hair products and Tim Black), the African Community of Chicago, the People's

Movement for Voter Registration and Education, and the Political Action Committee of Illinois (headed by Sam Patch). Abdul Alkalimat and Doug Gills, *Harold Washington and the Crisis of Black Power in Chicago* (Chicago: Twenty-First Century, 1989), 40–41.

79. Ibid., 40–41, 64–65.

80. Harold Washington, "It's Our Turn" (1983), in *Let Nobody Turn Us Around: Voices of Resistance, Reform, and Renewal*, ed. Manning Marable and Leith Mullings (New York: Rowman and Littlefield, 2000), 535–36.

81. Jiménez, interview by author.

82. Browning, "From Rumble to Revolution," 19.

83. Denise Oliver-Velez, remarks delivered at the Young Lords and Black Panther Party Symposium, Sonja Haynes Stone Center for Black Culture and History, University of North Carolina, Chapel Hill, 2007, disc 1, 45:06–51:02.

84. Jakobi Williams, "The Original Rainbow Coalition: An Example of Universal Identity Politics," *Tikkun*, November 12, 2013, http://www.tikkun.org/nextgen/the-original-rainbow-coalition-an-example-of-universal-identity-politics (accessed November 12, 2013).

CHAPTER 7

"A Common Citizenship of Freedom"

What Black Power Taught Chicago's Puerto Rican Independentistas

DAN BERGER

Born in 1943 in the town of San Sebastian in northwestern Puerto Rico, Oscar López Rivera migrated to the United States with his family as a teenager. The López Rivera family joined thousands of other Puerto Ricans coming to Chicago during Operation Bootstrap, the U.S.-backed industrialization of the island. More than thirty-two thousand Puerto Ricans resided in the Windy City by 1960, and Chicago's Puerto Rican population doubled over the next decade. While this number is small compared with the almost nine hundred thousand Puerto Ricans living in New York City in 1960, it constituted a sizable demographic shift within Chicago. Most of these migrants settled either on the Near Northwest Side of the city or on the South Side.[1]

Arriving in the late 1950s, the López Riveras were not a nationalist family, preferring to keep their distance from the Puerto Rican Nationalist Party. Formed in 1922, the PRNP became a major political force on the island after the fiery *independentista* Pedro Albizu Campos—a Harvard-trained lawyer and engineer who fought in the U.S. Army in World War I and was influenced by the Irish struggle against British rule—became the party's leader in 1930. Albizu Campos took the party in a more working-class, more insurrectionary direction. When police in Puerto Rico killed four student demonstrators at a Nationalist Party rally in 1935, two nationalists responded by assassinating U.S. colonel Elisha Francis Riggs, the highest ranking military authority on the island, in 1936. The two assassins were arrested and executed without trial, and Albizu Campos, who had praised their actions, was convicted of seditious conspiracy (plotting to overthrow the U.S. government by force). He spent ten years in the federal penitentiary at Atlanta, which had previously housed anarchist Alexander Berkman, socialist Eugene Debs, and nationalist Marcus Garvey.

Albizu Campos was released in 1947 and resumed control of the Nationalist Party. Weakened by his exposure to radiation while imprisoned, Albizu Campos nonetheless continued to push the party toward mass revolt against U.S. rule. After the Puerto Rican Senate passed Law 53 in 1948—which, like the Smith Act did for communists in the United States, severely restricted the rights of independence organizations and the Nationalist Party—the PRNP began planning for an island-wide revolt. On October 30, 1950, nationalists attacked seven towns across the island and the governor's mansion. The United States declared martial law and crushed the revolt, jailing thousands of people; among them was Pedro Albizu Campos. He would spend most of the next fifteen years in prison before his death in 1965.[2]

While the Nationalist Party never represented the majority of the island, the massive repression following the October revolt (Grito de Jayuya) frightened many Puerto Ricans from even expressing sympathy with the party. A similar expression of fear took hold among Puerto Ricans in the United States after members of the Nationalist Party there shot at President Harry Truman on November 1, 1950, in protest of the martial law in Puerto Rico. In 1954, four nationalists led by Lolita Lebrón shot at the U.S. House of Representatives to draw attention to the ongoing U.S. colonization of the island. The United States responded to these attacks by raiding Puerto Rican Nationalist Party offices in Chicago, New York, and throughout Puerto Rico.[3]

While the Nationalist Party failed to gain much public support after the 1950 revolt and the 1954 attack on Congress, the idea of Puerto Rican nationalism began to gain more traction among the Puerto Rican diaspora in the late 1960s. Chicago had been home to a small, tightly knit Puerto Rican community for decades. As migration off the island continued, Chicago was the most popular destination after New York City. In response to the growing numbers of Puerto Ricans, the Windy City held its first Puerto Rican Day Parade on June 12, 1966. The parade—or, more specifically, its aftermath—would make the city's Puerto Rican population well known throughout the country.

At a celebration after the parade, police shot Aracelis Cruz at a bar on the corner of Damen and Division Streets in the Humboldt Park neighborhood. Police then beat people in the crowd who attempted to intervene, sparking two days of rioting in Humboldt Park that destroyed numerous businesses and led to sixteen injuries.[4] Some members of a youth gang called the Young

Lords fought with police during the Division Street riots. Two years later, the group reconstituted itself as a political organization (see chapter 6). Their battles against the city police during the riots showed the rising militancy of Chicago's Puerto Rican community, militancy that would extend well beyond the Young Lords.[5]

Oscar López Rivera was not a Young Lord. He was not even in Chicago in 1966. Like many young men of color in the 1960s, López Rivera became politicized while serving in Vietnam. Angered by the racism of U.S. troops against the Vietnamese people, he came back to the United States in 1967 committed to fighting racism in Chicago. He became a successful tenant organizer with the Northwest Community Organization, a grassroots group co-founded by Saul Alinsky and run by veteran organizer Shel Trapp. By 1976, he was on the FBI's Most Wanted list, accused of being the leader of a clandestine revolutionary group, the Fuerzas Armadas de Liberación Nacional (FALN; Armed Forces for National Liberation), which was bombing dozens of government and corporate buildings in protest of U.S. colonialism. He was arrested in 1981 and ultimately sentenced to seventy years in prison for seditious conspiracy. As of 2015 he remained in prison at the Federal Correctional Institute at Terre Haute. How López Rivera made the trip from apolitical migrant to revolutionary nationalist and Marxist guerrilla is the story of the 1970s revival of Puerto Rican nationalism in deindustrializing American cities, especially Chicago.[6] This was a political movement formed amid a carceral moment—a time of sweeping police repression and antiprison activism—that developed to fight against the rising power of the police and the increasing significance of prisons in the lives of working-class black and Latino communities.

In Chicago, Puerto Rican revolutionary nationalism emerged at the crossroads of heavily policed spatial segregation, racial militancy, and the Alinskyite model of local community organizing. Such conditions brought together the black, Chicano, and Puerto Rican residents of Chicago, even if political and spatial differences created a tendency toward separation. In the 1970s this combination of policing, pride, and politics joined the neighborhood and the nation as symbols of struggle. The specific neighborhoods Puerto Ricans called home were constantly shifting as a result of the changing patterns of development and disinvestment in the 1970s. In Humboldt Park and West Town, Puerto Rican migrants and their children discovered ethnic nationalism.[7]

Black Power provided the political foundation and ideological scaffolding on which this nationalism developed. Puerto Ricans had been, at different moments throughout the twentieth century, considered as auxiliary members of black communities. Yet in the shadow of Black Power's embrace of ethnic pride, cultural specificity achieved new prominence. In the coming years, Puerto Rican activists influenced by Black Power's combination of pride and protest would take their place at the forefront of militant antiracism.

In describing the relationships between black and Puerto Rican groups, scholars have focused often on the Young Lords, whose transformation into a Black Panther–like organization after leader José "Cha-Cha" Jiménez met Black Panther leader Fred Hampton while both men were briefly incarcerated in 1967 proved a considerable evolution for Puerto Rican activists. The two men, both political activists with connections to street organizations, believed they could put an end to the violence between black and Puerto Rican gangs on the South Side of Chicago. After they both were released, the pair brokered such a truce, and the Young Lords began organizing in the Puerto Rican barrios in southern Chicago using a style and framework borrowed from the Panthers.[8] Chicago was the site of the original Rainbow Coalition, a multiracial united front of progressive groups working together on a shared platform. The Chicago Young Lords and the original Rainbow Coalition of which it was a part were impressive but short-lived phenomena. The police murder in 1969 of Fred Hampton, the visionary behind the coalition, and the repression directed against the member organizations, including the Young Lords, ended the initial effort after two years.[9]

This chapter takes a somewhat different, if still related, look at Chicago's Puerto Rican activism in this period. Instead of examining the multiracial coalition building of the late 1960s, I focus on the internationalist nationalism of the mid-1970s. Black Power—especially through its experience with and understanding of state violence—influenced the contours of Puerto Rican militancy beyond any one coalition or immediate political campaign. I argue that the revival of Puerto Rican nationalism in Chicago joined the history of the island-based Nationalist Party with the era's black nationalist protest. Black Power's expansive notion of community provided a useful guide for Puerto Rican radicals. Building on deep legacies of black radicalism, Black Power offered an internationalist embrace of the Third World with a pointed critique of state violence in the form of policing and prisons. This combination labeled education, housing, and the criminal justice system as three institutions of racialization. Black activists forged their sense of racial identity in this crucible throughout the "Long Sixties," and Puerto Ricans did likewise in the 1970s. This chapter focuses especially, but not exclusively, on two groups: the Movimiento de Liberación Nacional (MLN; Movement for National Liberation) and the FALN. Both organizations espoused a Marxist-Leninist and Third World nationalist notion of Puerto Rican independence. The MLN was headquartered in Chicago and engaged in a variety of community organizing initiatives while the FALN was a clandestine guerrilla organization that claimed responsibility for more than a hundred bombings between 1974 and 1983.[10]

The experience of these militants points to the need to rethink scholarly and political assumptions about the nature of coalitions. Shared organizations and campaigns provide a vital dimension for understanding the political stakes, tensions, and possibilities in an increasingly multiracial United States. Some comparative studies have complicated this picture by pointing to the ways in which different groups battled similar issues differently as a result of their community's history, resources, or structural location. These works have shown both that the civil rights movement was always a multiracial movement and that there were steep barriers to multiracial *unity*. This scholarship has successfully demonstrated that different groups of people of color have often elected to "fight their own battles."[11]

Chicago's Puerto Rican militants, however, present another model of comparative political activism, one that can be understood through the performative theories of race and radicalism that urban anthropologists have advanced. Puerto Rican groups utilized similar tactics and strategies for similar reasons as black radicals even where the groups lacked strong organizational coalitions. Light-skinned Puerto Rican activists came to know themselves as politically and racially aligned with (the example set by) black radicalism.[12] While black and Puerto Rican activists in New York City forged alliances and joined each other's otherwise racially exclusive organizations with some ease—owing to the close proximity of black, Puerto Rican, and Dominican communities—patterns of segregation made such alliances more difficult in Chicago.[13] Yet there were alliances, both organizational and, as I am principally concerned with here, ideological and strategic.

The different natures of the alliances reflect different places and spaces, as well as different times. The historical arc to Puerto Rican activism differed from that of black activism. The black freedom struggle had, by the time Puerto Rican radical groups sprouted up, more than two decades of high-profile political struggle. The era after World War II, the post–Great Migration generation, witnessed the growth or expansion of a variety of black political organizations. While a diverse range of liberal and radical organizations had long coexisted, the mixture of legislative changes, urban crises, and martyred leaders, among other issues, resulted in a more radical representation of black activism in the public eye. The Black Panthers occupied center stage in 1970; even the director of the once pacifist and staunchly integrationist Congress of Racial Equality was preaching Black Power. A wide range of black artists, intellectuals, activists, and politicians gathered under the banner of "nation time."[14] These efforts were fraught and in many ways fleeting, but they nonetheless established the macrohistorical landscape of American racial formation.

Puerto Ricans therefore entered a political context that had, to a large extent, been established by the black freedom struggle. Chicago's Puerto Rican nationalists developed tactics, strategies, and ideologies by infusing their own ideas and histories into the context established by black radicalism. In particular, Puerto Rican radicals deployed a brand of nationalism that utilized community service programs and grew in tandem with its targeted opposition to state repression in the form of prisons.

Black Power influenced the racialized politicization of a wide range of Latino and Asian American groups during this time.[15] Black Power was at the center of what scholars Cynthia Young and Laura Pulido have called the U.S. Third World Left.[16] The influence of Black Power on other revolutionary organizations of people of color at this time can be found across a host of political platforms: the (Chinese) Red Guards, like the Black Panthers who tutored them, adopted a Ten Point Program, while the Young Lords had a Thirteen Point Program. Both platforms borrowed the language and discourse of the Panthers (which was building on the Nation of Islam and other earlier organizations), and both groups adopted a similar posture aesthetically and politically: the wearing of berets and leather jackets, and the development of community service programs. But as the Panthers weathered repression and acrimonious splits in the early 1970s, groups such as the Red Guards and the Young Lords changed their look and altered their work.[17]

As many black liberation groups shrunk or split in the 1970s, the influence of Black Power on Puerto Rican groups was less mimetic and more ideological. Since black and Puerto Rican people continued to share an increasingly policed urban condition backed by a diasporic history, they had overlapping notions of race and politics. Specifically, Puerto Rican militants took from Black Power a political program that, in Stokely Carmichael and Charles Hamilton's terms, sought to "redefine themselves," "reclaim their history, their culture," and "create their own sense of community and togetherness."[18] Political redefinition, cultural "reclamation," and collective self-determination: this is what Chicago's Puerto Rican *independentistas* learned from Black Power.

The theory of internal colonialism stitched together the Third World Left. This notion, long common to black radicalism, gained widespread popularity among a diverse range of black activists in the 1960s. It held that black people were a distinct nation held captive within the broader nation of the United States. Asian, Latino, and indigenous radicals all utilized some version of this theory in explaining their own oppression. This theory held special sway among Puerto Rican activists, who came from a formal and internationally recognized colony of the United States.[19]

Taking inspiration from the Black Panther Party and the Republic of New Afrika, among others, Puerto Rican militants in Chicago developed community service programs using a framework of anticolonial nationalism, embraced armed self-defense, and defined community control of the barrios as the necessary response to police brutality and educational inequity. Black Power helped Puerto Rican independence activists identify and develop a strategic orientation and political analysis in the United States. This framework sustained ideological affinities, a certain imagined community, between black and Puerto Rican radicals that made up for sparse organizational alliances. This group of Puerto Ricans began to understand themselves as politically and racially aligned with black communities, even if they were spatially and organizationally separate from them. It was a manifestation of Carmichael and Hamilton's notion of separate bases of power expressing solidarity by closing ranks. Writing from Marion prison, where he was incarcerated for his role in the 1954 attack on Congress, Rafael Cancel Miranda identified this connection as a "common citizenship of freedom."[20]

The Puerto Rican community in Chicago at this time, largely congregated on the Near Northwest Side with an additional enclave on the South Side, was mostly working class. Chicago—with its large industrial base and sprawling geography—had long been a destination for migrants, including some people who exemplified the colonial citizenship that has typified Puerto Ricans: black southerners headed to the city in droves throughout the first half of the twentieth century.[21] Black migrants of the early twentieth century, like Puerto Rican migrants in the middle of the century, arrived in a city controlled by an extensive political machine and a violent police force. Urban renewal and white hostility pushed Puerto Ricans into and out of different neighborhoods on the Near North Side and West Side throughout the 1940s and 1950s until many of these migrants settled in and around the Humboldt Park neighborhood by the 1960s. As historian Lilia Fernández reports, "Puerto Ricans experienced high rates of unemployment, upwards of 18%, widespread poverty, and overcrowded, substandard living conditions."[22] Dilapidated housing joined low-quality schools without a Latino-relevant curriculum, interracial strife with white and sometimes black neighbors, and the endemic problem of police brutality.

Puerto Rican nationalism in Chicago emerged in campaigns addressing schools, housing, and police brutality in the context of a growing Latino population in the Midwest. Because these issues involved the traditional building blocks of community—the ability to learn and live in an atmosphere of personal safety—they attracted progressive community organizations in the Alinsky tradition as well as Marxist radicals whose organizing was connected to their ideological world view. Several Puerto Ricans initially got involved in Alinskyite models out of a proto-nationalist fealty to their community and went on to become revolutionary nationalists. This rapid transformation from liberal reformers to Marxist revolutionaries points to the unique condition of the Puerto Rican 1970s. In a time when many New Left and Black Power groups were constricting, Puerto Rican radicalism was on the rise. There was so much activism that people went quickly from believing in the U.S. system to fighting for its overthrow. Indeed, the 1970s was arguably the most fertile and dynamic moment of Puerto Rican politics in the continental United States, shaped as well by the growing radicalism on the island against the U.S. military presence and for independence.

The many influences on Chicago's Puerto Rican movement included more than a decade of black organizing on the same issues of conscription and curriculum reform, urban renewal, and hyper-policing. The Black Panthers titled their community programs Survival Pending Revolution. The programs became a hallmark of the Panthers' success and of their threat to the established order.[23] Puerto Rican community organizers took notice. They set out to build their own survival programs that connected local community concerns with opposition to the carceral state—the punitive system of governance structured by policing, surveillance, and imprisonment[24]—and support of Puerto Rican independence. A nationalism inflected by Black Power and Puerto Rican history allowed them to join what might have otherwise been disparate issues into a program of communal self-reliance.

Issues surrounding education were an especially fertile ground for organizing. The lack of Puerto Rican or Latino histories in the curriculum became a cause for mobilizing high school and college students. The civil rights and Black Power movements had long organized around school curriculum, from the freedom schools that civil rights workers established as part of their desegregation efforts in the South to the campus takeovers of the late 1960s that gave rise to black studies. Study groups on and off campus formed the basis of black radical organizations such as the Revolutionary Action Movement and the Black Panther Party. These varied efforts pointed both to the absence of classes relevant to students of color and to institutional policies that either barred students of color from attending school or failed to retain them once they matriculated. Although the civil rights movement's freedom schools conducted classes for people of all ages, the Black Power movement targeted university campuses with its critique of curriculum and retention.[25]

Puerto Rican radicals, meanwhile, set their sights on local high schools. Student organizers argued that the lack of Latino history or bilingual education contributed to the low rates of admission and retention for Latino students. For instance, Edwin Cortés became an activist as a high school senior after his teacher informed him that there were no Puerto Rican history classes because "Puerto Rico had no history."[26]

As other Puerto Rican students faced similar obstacles, especially at Tuley High School in Humboldt Park, they collaborated with a few Puerto Rican guidance counselors, with college students who had been waging similar struggles at Northeastern Illinois University, and with local community organizers (including Oscar López Rivera) to establish an alternative high school oriented toward Puerto Rican students. While alternative education practices were common in 1960s protest, the creation of a lasting alternative institution was of a different order.[27] Founded in 1972 and now an awarding-winning charter school, the new high school opened in the basement of a small church with eleven students. Several of the founding members, both students and staff, later went on to be members of either the MLN or the FALN.

The school acquired its own building in 1973, and students named it Rafael Cancel Miranda High School, after one of the imprisoned nationalists. The five nationalists had been largely forgotten since their conviction in the 1950s. But with the resurgence of Puerto Rican nationalism came an outpouring of interest in the nationalist prisoners as symbols of Puerto Rican radical history. Cancel Miranda, one of the participants in the March 1954 shooting inside the U.S. Congress, was the most prolific author of the Puerto Rican political prisoners at the time. He was also the one most expressly interested in making connections between Puerto Rican activists and the North American Left. According to José López, one of the founders of the school and the younger brother of Oscar López Rivera, the adults involved wanted to name the school after Pedro Albizu Campos, the deceased former head of the Nationalist Party, who remained a vital symbol of the revolutionary aspirations of Puerto Rican nationalism. But the students insisted on naming it after Cancel Miranda, at least until he was freed. Some of them also began to correspond with Cancel Miranda. López Rivera remembers the students reading his letters aloud so that all could feel their connection with him. The school, then, was from its inception a part of the campaign to free the five nationalists.[28]

This high school was one of several means through which Puerto Rican militants in Chicago in the 1970s used service provision as a vehicle for political mobilization by making visible the histories and current struggles of Puerto Rican communities. At times these projects emerged out of long-standing networks; more often they developed out of the desire of young militants to ameliorate the conditions of poverty and racism in Puerto Rican communities. The effort, as José López described it, of "trying to understand the complexity of the national question from the perspective of the diaspora," of experimenting with the meanings of "independence" from within another country, compelled Puerto Rican militants to provide services in the context of political mobilization.[29] Service provision aimed to eradicate inequities in schooling, housing, garbage collection, and health care. Through combining Marxism, nationalism, and social work, such projects crafted a political biography of anticolonialism.[30]

Throughout the 1970s Chicago's Puerto Rican activists emphasized institution building under the banner of revolutionary nationalism. This community work provided the scaffolding of Puerto Rican nationalist sovereignty as it did for the Black Panther Party. The Panthers, as Donna Murch notes, imported southern values of education and community service to the nascent black communities of the urban West. The more than a dozen programs they created left a vital legacy of black political power in Oakland—and in Chicago, where Panther leader Fred Hampton instituted a free breakfast for children program alongside a host of grassroots social service initiatives.[31]

The subaltern studies scholar Partha Chatterjee argues that "anticolonial nationalism creates its own domain of sovereignty within colonial society well before it begins its political battle with the imperial power."[32] In the Panthers and in the Puerto Rican nationalists, however, this anticolonial nationalism created its own domain of sovereignty *alongside* its political battle with the imperial power. Puerto Rican militants developed institutions as part of their anticolonial nationalism—not in a direct bid for state power but to undermine its reach in their neighborhoods and to spread an ethos of anticolonialism. As the Panthers receded from the scene in Chicago, nationalistic Puerto Rican organizers stepped in. They materialized the metaphoric national community through neighborhood organizing and service provision. These institutions demonstrated sovereignty through highly localized expressions of the diaspora.[33]

Designed for the benefit of "the Puerto Rican people," such alternative institutions were fundamentally shaped by the streets of Humboldt Park and Lincoln Park. They created Puerto Rico within portions of Chicago. "Lincoln Park was our Puerto Rico," declared Young Lords co-founder José "Cha-Cha" Jiménez, speaking of the area in South Chicago where the Lords formed and began their political organizing. Luis Rosa, who served almost twenty years in prison on charges of belonging to the clandestine Fuerzas Armadas de Liberación Nacional, identified Chicago as an extension of Puerto Rico.[34] The nationalist investment in Puerto Rican Chicago interpreted land as the seeds of a new society. Projects like the Rafael Cancel Miranda High School and the Puerto Rican Cultural Center extended the territorial impulse of the black freedom struggle, South and North. As Malcolm X and the Black Panthers theorized, experiments with local control could lay the groundwork for more ambitious projects of collective self-management.[35] For the young *independentistas*, institution building in Chicago's barrios allowed them to imagine an independent Puerto Rico.

These community projects drew attention to the often desperate conditions of the barrios, highlighting them as expressions of colonialism akin to the control the United States maintained over the island of Puerto Rico. Black Power's critique of the police as an armed force of occupation helped Puerto Rican nationalists connect the barrios' conditions to current island realities as well as to the ongoing imprisonment of Puerto Rican nationalists. Indeed, the five prisoners were to Puerto Rican radicals in the mid-1970s what Huey Newton, George Jackson, and Angela Davis had been for black militants a few years earlier. In the context of Puerto Rican activism in the 1970s, *the prison* signified U.S. imperialism while *prisoners* epitomized political struggle. The prison represented racist repression while the prisoners offered a model of heroic resistance. The campaign to free them, which united disparate groups of *independentistas* in the mid-1970s throughout the United

States and Puerto Rico, provided a narrative and a symbolic lens through which to view the history of Puerto Rico and its fight for independence. Prisoners were the bridge connecting the spaces of Puerto Rican racial formation: the barrio and the colony, the United States and the island.[36]

Born and raised in Puerto Rico, the nationalists' presence in U.S. prisons connected their U.S.-based supporters to the island. Through the imprisoned nationalists, young Puerto Rican activists in the 1970s exposed themselves to the culture and politics of anticolonial nationalism. The prisoners became gateways for young Puerto Ricans to counteract what Frantz Fanon called the deadliest part of colonialism: its attack on the past.[37] In fact, Black Power provided a significant part of the analysis through which Puerto Rican nationalists learned the history of Western imperialism and Puerto Rican radicalism. A diverse range of black intellectuals—Fanon, Amilcar Cabral, Malcolm X, Stokely Carmichael, and Fred Hampton, among others—had, through writings and speeches, maintained that history was a battleground for anticolonial struggle. Their combined emphasis on erudition and cultural pride as the basis for social action provided a cornerstone of the Boricua nationalist education. Puerto Rican activists studied Black Power thinkers alongside the works of historic Puerto Rican nationalists like Pedro Albizu Campos and contemporary militants such as Juan Antonio Corretjer, a poet and the head of the Puerto Rican Socialist League.[38]

The work to free the nationalist prisoners engaged the history of the nationalist opposition to the U.S. presence in Puerto Rico. By organizing for the prisoners' release, young Puerto Ricans and others learned about the U.S. relationship to the island. In the 1950s, Puerto Rican nationalism rejected U.S. control over Puerto Rico but did not confront the founding myths of the country itself. So, for instance, pacifist supporters of Oscar Collazo—the surviving participant of the shooting at Blair House in 1950—likened him to George Washington and even called him an "American patriot" because they said his assault on President Truman had the goal of forcing the United States to better live up to its democratic ideals by freeing its colonial possessions.[39]

By the 1970s, few argued that Collazo and the other imprisoned nationalists were American patriots aiming to improve the U.S. image. Rather, their supporters argued that the nationalists had served enough time or that what they did was right—but never that they could be recuperated within an American identity. Puerto Rican nationalists celebrated the prisoners as national heroes for their attacks on the U.S. empire. Fueled by the fusion of Marxism and nationalism, activists in the 1970s rejected the United States as a global imperial power and positioned the five prisoners as forerunners to the decolonization movements sweeping the globe, whose closest domestic parallel was the black freedom struggle. In fighting to liberate Puerto Rico from a colonialism often described in carceral terms, many Puerto Rican activists increasingly described the imprisoned Puerto Ricans as "prisoners of war," not just political prisoners. This terminology borrowed directly from the use of the prison as a metaphor for black subjugation over the previous decade, voiced by diverse figures, including liberal psychologist Kenneth Clark, singers Johnny Cash and Bob Dylan, journalist Tom Wicker, and black nationalist and activist Audley "Queen Mother" Moore. A 1976 statement that served as a precursor to the founding of the MLN defined the five as "soldiers in a war of national liberation" and therefore as prisoners of war.[40]

The nationalists owed their initial prominence to the abiding interest in dissident prisoners, who had been made visible through the efforts of black radicals. Michael Deutsch, a white lawyer from the People's Law Office in Chicago, a collective of leftist attorneys involved in the prisoner rights movement, first met Rafael Cancel Miranda after the 1972 strike at the federal prison at Marion, Illinois, when prisoners protested new forms of indefinite isolation.[41] Deutsch had no prior knowledge of Puerto Rican history or its colonial status when he met Cancel Miranda at the suggestion of other prisoners he was representing in legal cases emanating from the Marion strike. Impressed by Cancel Miranda—his stature, eloquence, and the respect he received from other prisoners across racial lines—Deutsch began visiting the other nationalist prisoners. He soon became the attorney of record for all five of them in the hope that he could help "bring their case to the attention of the world."[42] Their refusal to accept U.S. authority included an unwillingness to file suit against the government directly and a rejection of parole as a possible option; they would accept nothing that would acknowledge the legitimacy of U.S. authority over them. Three of the other imprisoned Puerto Rican nationalists, Oscar Collazo, Irvin Flores, and Andres Cordero, were involved in strikes and organizing at Leavenworth prison that were led by black and Chicano dissident prisoners.[43]

The strikes and riots at men's prisons were the most dynamic and dramatic aspect of what the historian Alan Eladio Gómez called the prison rebellion years.[44] But there were other ways in which black and Puerto Rican political prisoners, among others, forged common bonds—especially in women's prisons, where resistance typically takes the form of relationship building more than violent disruptions.[45] In West Virginia, Lebrón was incarcerated briefly with convicted Black Liberation Army (BLA) member Assata Shakur and with Marilyn Buck, a white woman accused of aiding the BLA. Shakur was a former member of the Black Panther Party who had gone underground with the split of the party. Arrested in 1973, she was charged with a slew of BLA bank robberies and attacks on police officers. She was acquitted in all of her trials except one: she was convicted in the shooting death of a police officer on the night of her arrest, though records of the event strongly suggest her innocence. Buck, meanwhile, was a former member of Students for a Democratic Society who was serving time for having bought ammunition for the black underground. Lebrón got to know these women at Alderson, a federal women's prison. In her autobiography, Shakur wrote that she and Lebrón instantly embraced each other at their first meeting. Shakur said that meeting the Puerto Rican nationalist was "one of the greatest honors of my life." Shakur, an ardent socialist and atheist, also studied liberation theology as a result of her encounters with Lebrón, a devout Catholic.[46]

While the Puerto Rican nationalists were intransigent in their refusal to acknowledge U.S. authority by applying for parole, they gave Deutsch permission to file a lawsuit on behalf of their family members and political associates. Along with independence organizers from the United States and the island, Deutsch traveled around Puerto Rico enlisting friends and family members as plaintiffs in a class action suit on behalf of the prisoners. The lawsuit was a political, not juridical, move. It was an attempt to achieve recognition for the prisoners and draw attention to their case after so many years of relative obscurity. The lawsuit helped catalyze a coordinated political campaign by making the prisoners visible in the U.S. court system for the first time since their arrests. Deutsch recalls that he and others on the legal team became "a conduit of information," facilitating the nationalists' involvement in their campaign and in the independence movement more broadly, as well as their ability to speak with one another. The suit was short lived; a federal judge separated the cases, assigning them to the jurisdictions where each prisoner was held. By that point, Andres Cordero had become quite ill. Organizers concentrated their efforts on winning his humanitarian release, which occurred on October 6, 1977.[47]

Deutsch's serendipitous involvement with the five prisoners coincided with other (re)discoveries of the nationalists, including the Chicago-based activists who started the Rafael Cancel Miranda High School. The call to free the nationalists synthesized the demand for Puerto Rican independence and the militancy of the black-led prison movement. The visibility of the nationalists lent support to both struggles. Several years before the Rafael Cancel Miranda High School opened in northwestern Chicago, the Young Lords office in the southern part of the city featured a mural of the five nationalists. Similar artwork, portrait drawings of the five, adorned the offices and brochures of various groups in the United States supporting Puerto Rican independence and prisoners' rights. These drawings often featured a picture of Lebrón in the foreground, with the other four encircling her like planets around the sun.[48] Lebrón was the most visible of the group. Her name represented all five prisoners, much as the five were said to represent all of Puerto Rico.[49] Oscar López Rivera said he committed himself to working to free the nationalists, a commitment that led him to join the clandestine FALN after hearing a recording of the statement Lebrón had made denouncing U.S. imperialism after being arrested. She refused to apologize for the assault on Congress. "After I heard her voice I made a commitment to work for the freedom of the five," he reflected forty years later from his own prison cell.[50]

The connections between radical black and Puerto Rican activists in Chicago became tenuous in the 1980s. The arrests of eleven suspected FALN members on April 4, 1980, along with several more arrests over the next three years, threw the militants at the Puerto Rican Cultural Center and Pedro Albizu Campos High School into a panicked fray of supporting high-profile defendants who largely refused the court's legitimacy to try them.[51] And the MLN's position of boycotting the electoral process meant that its members rejected the multiracial coalition that made Harold Washington Chicago's first black mayor in 1983—a coalition that brought together many progressive black, Puerto Rican, Mexicano, and white community groups from across the city. (When the MLN disbanded in the early 1990s, many of the activists involved altered their anti–electoral politics position and began working with a multiracial group of supportive politicians—most famously Congressman Luis Gutiérrez.) Meanwhile, the hyper-incarceration of Chicago's historic black community on the South Side, combined with growing class rifts within the city's black population, left few radical organizations there. The significance of such rifts was magnified in Chicago where the intensity of spatial segregation rendered citywide neighborhood alliances difficult at best.[52]

Yet the strength of the connection between black and Puerto Rican radicalism in Chicago was never based primarily in shared coalitions or organizations. Rather it was rooted in ideas and strategies for action—especially when it came to challenging the police and the prison as institutions of racist political repression. Chicago's Puerto Rican independence movement followed the lead of black activists who defined the prison as an institution laden with metaphoric and material significance for understanding racial formation.[53] In their confrontations with the state, Puerto Rican militants came to understand themselves racially, historically, and politically not *as* black but as sharing in the Third World condition that in the United States black radicals had best articulated. As generations of black activists had done, Puerto Rican militants appealed to the diaspora in their organizing in the United States.

Although they, in some sense, learned about the prison system from the black freedom struggle, Puerto Rican activists have had more success in freeing their political prisoners than black social movements have had. Over the course of twenty years, Puerto Rican nationalists succeeded in freeing two different groups of prisoners, totaling more than twenty people, who were serving lengthy sentences and who had been suspected or accused of violent acts against the U.S. government. Yet several former Black Panthers remain incarcerated on lengthy sentences that also originated in the militant activism of that generation. Further, the two groups of Puerto Ricans were freed in eras marked by mass incarceration: the five nationalists were freed just as U.S. rates of incarceration increased dramatically and became more racially determined. The second group was freed shortly before the United States passed the ignominious milestone of incarcerating more than 2 million people, more than any other nation on the planet. The rates of Puerto Rican and overall Latino incarceration are disproportionate to their population in the United States, so I do not mean to suggest that these campaigns halted (or even attempted to halt) the sting of mass incarceration. While a full accounting of this situation is outside the scope of this chapter, it remains the case that Chicago's Puerto Rican nationalist community waged successful campaigns that dented the reach of mass incarceration in an era when black struggles against the prison system have been less popular and far less successful.

By targeting the state and being targeted by it, activists from the MLN and other nationalist-oriented independence groups forged coalitions with organizations such as the Republic of New Afrika and the American Indian Movement. These connections were further strengthened through the incarceration of more than a dozen people for refusing to testify in front of grand juries investigating the FALN and ultimately through the arrest and incarceration of a dozen FALN members.[54]

While these black/brown (and red) coalitions were imagined more than actualized, they revealed a political strategy as well as a pragmatic ambition.[55] Puerto Ricans built on the model of the black freedom struggle. Through resisting repression, by seeking to establish forms of sovereignty that transcended the authority of the United States, these *independentistas* embraced the ethos of the black radical tradition.[56] This shared ethos might refocus the attention of scholars to the multiplicity of comparative histories and coalitional politics, looking not just to shared space but to shared demonstrations of racial consciousness and political praxis. Chicago's Puerto Rican independence activists learned to think in racial terms as a result of state violence, U.S. imperialism, and the diasporic imagination. The black freedom dream of a world without the racial state nurtured a Puerto Rican belief in a "common citizenship of freedom." Nearly a half century later, this common citizenship, diasporic and democratic, might yet serve as the breeding ground for future generations of transformative alliances.

NOTES

1. Johanna L. del C. Fernández, "Radicals in the Late 1960s: A History of the Young Lords Party in New York City, 1969–1974" (PhD diss., Columbia University, 2004), 17, 19; Maura I. Toro-Morn, "Boricuas en Chicago: Gender and Class in the Migration and Settlement of Puerto Ricans," in *The Puerto Rican Diaspora: Historical Perspectives*, ed. Carmen Teresa Whalen and Victor Vázquez-Hernández (Philadelphia: Temple University Press, 2005), 134. On Puerto Ricans in Chicago more generally, see Gina M. Pérez, *The Near Northwest Side Story: Migration, Displacement, and Puerto Rican Families* (Berkeley: University of California Press, 2004); Andrew J. Diamond, *Mean Streets: Chicago Youths and the Everyday Struggle for Empowerment in the Multiracial City, 1908–1969* (Berkeley: University of California Press, 2009); Lilia Fernández, "Latina/o Migration and Community Formation in Postwar Chicago: Mexicans, Puerto Ricans, Gender, and Politics, 1945–1975" (PhD diss., University of California, San Diego, 2005); Ana Y. Ramos-Zayas, *National Performances: The Politics of Class, Race, and Space in Puerto Rican Chicago* (Chicago: University of Chicago Press, 2003). The population of Puerto Ricans in both cities and elsewhere in the United States continued to rise throughout the 1960s and beyond. In Chicago, for instance, the number of Puerto Ricans more than doubled between 1960 and 1970. For more on Operation Bootstrap, see Jorge Duany, *The Puerto Rican Nation on the Move: Identities on the Island and in the United States* (Chapel Hill: University of North Carolina Press, 2002); Carmen Theresa Whalen, *From Puerto Rico to Philadelphia: Puerto Rican Workers and Postwar Economies* (Philadelphia: Temple University Press, 2001).

2. Nelson A. Denis, *War against All Puerto Ricans* (New York: Nation Books, 2015).

3. See Dan Berger, "'We Are the Revolutionaries': Visibility, Protest, and Racial Formation in 1970s Prison Radicalism" (PhD diss., University of Pennsylvania, 2010); César J. Ayala and Rafael Bernabe, *Puerto Rico in the American Century: A History since*

1898 (Chapel Hill: University of North Carolina Press, 2007); Stephen Hunter and John Bainbridge Jr., *American Gunfight: The Plot to Kill President Truman—and the Shoot-Out That Stopped It* (New York: Simon and Schuster, 2005); author interviews with Lolita Lebrón, July 1, 2009, and Juan Mari Bras, July 2, 2009.

4. Mérida M. Rúa, *A Grounded Identidad: Places of Memory and Personhood in Chicago's Puerto Rican Neighborhoods* (Oxford: Oxford University Press, 2012); Studs Terkel, *Division Street, America* (New York: New Press, 1993); Pérez, *The Near Northwest Side Story*; Diamond, *Mean Streets*; Mervin Mendez, "A Community Fights Back: Recollections of the 1966 Division Street Riot," *Dialogo* 2 (1997), http://chicago.indymedia.org/newswire/display/72578/index.php (accessed July 26, 2012).

5. On the Young Lords, see Fernández, "Radicals in the Late 1960s"; Darrel Enck-Wanzer, "The Intersectional Rhetoric of the Young Lords: Social Movement Ideographs, Demand, and the Radical Democratic Imaginary" (PhD diss., Indiana University, 2007); Enck-Wanzer, ed., *The Young Lords Reader* (New York: New York University Press, 2010); Michael Abramson, *Palante! The Young Lords Party* (New York: McGraw Hill, 1971); Miguel Melendez, *We Took the Streets: Fighting for Latino Rights with the Young Lords* (New York: St. Martin's, 2003); Carmen Teresa Whalen, "Bridging Homeland and Barrio Politics: The Young Lords in Philadelphia," in *The Puerto Rican Movement: Voices from the Diaspora*, ed. Andrés Torres and José E. Velázquez (Philadelphia: Temple University Press 1998), 107–23; Pablo Guzman, "*La Vida Pura*: A Lord of the Barrio," in Torres and Velázquez, *The Puerto Rican Movement*, 155–72; Frank Browning, "From Rumble to Revolution: The Young Lords," in *The Puerto Rican Experience: A Sociological Sourcebook*, ed. Francesco Cordasco and Eugene Bucchioni (Totowa, N.J.: Rowman and Littlefield, 1973), 231–45.

6. This biography of López Rivera comes from my discussions with him, his family, and his attorney. Different iterations of it can be found online: http://denverabc.wordpress.com/political-prisoners-database/oscar-lopez-rivera/; http://artbyoscarlopez.org/?page_id=7; http://spectator.org/archives/2010/12/22/the-unrepentant-terrorist; http://boricuahumanrights.org/free-oscar-lopez-rivera/ (accessed January 6, 2013).

7. Fernández, "Latina/o Migration and Community Formation"; Lilia Fernández, *Brown in the Windy City: Mexicans and Puerto Ricans in Postwar Chicago* (Chicago: University of Chicago Press, 2012); Rúa, *A Grounded Identidad*; Terkel, *Division Street, America*; Pérez, *The Near Northwest Side Story*.

8. Johanna Fernandez, "Between Social Service Reform and Revolutionary Politics: The Young Lords, Late Sixties Radicalism, and Community Organizing in New York City," in *Freedom North: Black Freedom Struggles Outside the South, 1940–1980*, ed. Jeanne F. Theoharis and Komozi Woodard (New York: Palgrave Macmillan, 2003), 259–60; Jeffrey Haas, *The Assassination of Fred Hampton: How the FBI and the Chicago Police Murdered a Black Panther* (Chicago: Lawrence Hill, 2010), 44–45.

9. See, for instance, Amy Sonnie and James Tracy, *Hillbilly Nationalists, Urban Race Rebels, and Black Power* (Brooklyn, N.Y.: Melville House, 2011).

10. For more on the MLN and the FALN, see Berger, "We Are the Revolutionaries"; Ronald L. Fernandez, *Prisoners of Colonialism: The Struggle For Justice in Puerto Rico* (Monroe, Maine: Common Courage, 1994); MLN, *Program and Ideology of the MLN: First Congress of the Movimiento de Liberación Nacional Puertorriqueño* (Chicago: N.p., ca. 1987), in possession of author, courtesy of Matt Meyer; Michael González-Cruz, "Puerto Rican Revolutionary Nationalism (1956–2005): Immigration, Armed Struggle, Political Prisoners, and Prisoners of War" (PhD diss., SUNY, Binghamton, 2005). Several crucial documents from the 1990s campaign for the next generation of Puerto Rican political prisoners, including petitions by faith communities and other grassroots appeals, are collected in Matt Meyer, ed., *Let Freedom Ring: Documents from the Campaigns to Free U.S. Political Prisoners* (Oakland, Calif.: PM Press, 2008), esp. 311–61. See also Jan Susler, "Puerto Rican Political Prisoners in U.S. Prisons," in *Puerto Rico under Colonial Rule: Political Persecution and the Quest for Human Rights*, ed. Ramon Bosque-Pérez and Jose Javier Colón Morera (Albany: State University of New York Press, 2005), 119–38. For a scholarly account, see Yanira Reyes, "Law, Media and Political Dissent: The Case of the FALN" (PhD diss., Purdue University, 2002). The private papers of the Puerto Rican Cultural Center were also helpful in my understanding of the MLN.

11. Brian D. Behnken, *Fighting Their Own Battles: Mexican Americans, African Americans, and the Struggle for Civil Rights in Texas* (Chapel Hill: University of North Carolina Press, 2011). See also Nancy MacLean, *Freedom Is Not Enough: The Opening of the American Workplace* (Cambridge, Mass.: Harvard University Press, 2006); Mark Brilliant, *The Color of America Has Changed: How Racial Diversity Shaped Civil Rights Reform in California 1941–1978* (New York: Oxford University Press, 2010); Gordon Mantler, *Power to the Poor: Black-Brown Coalition and the Fight for Economic Justice, 1960–1974* (Chapel Hill: University of North Carolina Press, 2013).

12. Daryl J. Maeda, *Chains of Babylon: The Rise of Asian America* (Minneapolis: University of Minnesota Press, 2009), makes a similar argument for the Asian American movement that emerged in the San Francisco Bay area at this time. For more on the performative approach to race and politics, see John L. Jackson Jr., *Harlemworld: Doing Race and Class in Contemporary Black America* (Chicago: University of Chicago Press, 2001); Jackson, *Real Black: Adventures in Racial Sincerity* (Chicago: University of Chicago Press, 2005).

13. Johanna Fernandez, "Denise Oliver and the Young Lords Party: Stretching the Political Boundaries of Struggle," in *Want to Start a Revolution? Radical Women in the Black Freedom Struggle*, ed. Dayo F. Gore, Jeanne Theoharis, and Komozi Woodard (New York: New York University Press, 2010), 271–93. On Dominican activism in New York, see Jesse Hoffnung-Garskoff, *A Tale of Two Cities: Santo Domingo and New York after 1950* (Princeton, N.J.: Princeton University Press, 2010).

14. Peniel Joseph, *Waiting 'til the Midnight Hour: A Narrative History of Black Power* (New York: Holt, 2006); Cedric Johnson, *From Revolutionaries to Race Leaders: Black Power and the Making of African American Politics* (Minneapolis: University of Min-

nesota Press, 2007); Komozi Woodard, *A Nation within a Nation: Amiri Baraka (LeRoi Jones) and Black Power Politics* (Chapel Hill: University of North Carolina Press, 1999).

15. Maeda, *Chains of Babylon*; Lisa Lowe, *Immigrant Acts: On Asian American Cultural Politics* (Durham, N.C.: Duke University Press, 1996).

16. Cynthia A. Young, *Soul Power: Culture, Radicalism, and the Making of a U.S. Third World Left* (Durham, N.C.: Duke University Press, 2006); Laura Pulido, *Black, Brown, Yellow, and Left: Radical Activism in Los Angeles* (Berkeley: University of California Press, 2006). See also Dan Berger, *Outlaws of America: The Weather Underground and the Politics of Solidarity* (Oakland, Calif.: AK Press, 2006); Max Elbaum, *Revolution in the Air: Sixties Radicals Turn to Lenin, Che, and Mao* (New York: Verso, 2002).

17. The Red Guards and the New York branch of the Young Lords both became more traditionally Marxist: they backed away from displays of militancy, emphasized party building and organizing at the point of production, and debated the finer points of Marxist thought.

18. Stokely Carmichael and Charles V. Hamilton, *Black Power: The Politics of Liberation* (New York: Random House, 1967), 37, 11, 29–31, quoted in Maeda, *Chains of Babylon*, 78.

19. For explications of internal colonialism at the time, see Harold Cruse, *Rebellion or Revolution* (New York: Morrow, 1968); George Jackson, *Blood in My Eye* (1972; Baltimore, Md.: Black Classics, 1996); Robert Blauner, *Racial Oppression in America* (New York: Harper and Row, 1972). For more recent scholarly assessments, see Woodard, *A Nation within a Nation*; Young, *Soul Power*; Nikhil Pal Singh, *Black Is a Country: Race and the Unfinished Struggle for Democracy* (Cambridge, Mass.: Harvard University Press, 2003); Ramón A. Gutiérrez, "Internal Colonialism: An American Theory of Race," *Du Bois Review* 1 (2004): 281–95.

20. Rafael Cancel Miranda, undated open letter, 2, in Raúl R. Salinas Papers (hereafter RRS), box 5, folder 9, Green Library, Stanford University, Stanford, Calif.

21. Adam Green, *Selling the Race: Culture, Community and Black Chicago, 1940–1955* (Chicago: University of Chicago Press, 2006); Isabelle Wilkerson, *The Warmth of Other Suns: The Epic Story of America's Great Migration* (New York: Random House, 2010).

22. Fernández, "Latina/o Migration and Community Formation," 145; Pérez, *The Near Northwest Side Story*. For an early study of Puerto Rican politics in Chicago, see Felix Padilla, *Latino Ethnic Consciousness: The Case of Mexican Americans and Puerto Ricans in Chicago* (Notre Dame, Ind.: University of Notre Dame Press, 1985).

23. Donna Murch, *Living for the City: Migration, Education, and the Rise of the Black Panther Party in Oakland, California* (Chapel Hill: University of North Carolina Press, 2010); Paul Alkebulan, *Survival Pending Revolution: The History of the Black Panther Party* (Tuscaloosa: University of Alabama Press, 2007); Joshua Bloom and Waldo E. Martin Jr., *Black against Empire: The History and Politics of the Black Panther Party* (Berkeley: University of California Press, 2013).

24. See Dan Berger, *Captive Nation: Black Prison Organizing in the Civil Rights Era*

(Chapel Hill: University of North Carolina Press, 2014); Ruth Wilson Gilmore, *Golden Gulag: Prisons, Surplus, Crisis, and Opposition in Globalizing California* (Berkeley: University of California Press, 2007); Marie Gottschalk, *The Prison and the Gallows: The Politics of Mass Incarceration in America* (Cambridge: Cambridge University Press, 2006); Gottschalk, *Caught: The Prison State and the Lockdown of American Politics* (Princeton, N.J.: Princeton University Press, 2014); Naomi Murakawa, *The First Civil Right: How Liberals Built Prison America* (New York: Oxford University Press, 2014); Heather Ann Thompson, "Why Mass Incarceration Matters: Rethinking Crisis, Decline, and Transformation in Postwar American History," *Journal of American History* 97, no. 3 (2010): 703–34; Michelle Alexander, *The New Jim Crow: Mass Incarceration in an Age of Colorblindness* (New York: New Press, 2010); Loic Wacquant, *Punishing the Poor: The Neoliberal Governance of Insecurity* (Durham, N.C.: Duke University Press, 2009); Joy James, ed., *Warfare in the American Homeland: Policing and Prisons in a Penal Democracy* (Durham, N.C.: Duke University Press, 2007); Robert Perkinson, *Texas Tough: The Making of America's Prison Empire* (New York: Metropolitan, 2010).

25. Murch, *Living for the City*; Martha Biondi, *The Black Revolution on Campus* (Berkeley: University of California Press, 2012); Noliwe Rooks, *White Money/Black Power: The Surprising History of African American Studies and the Crisis of Race in Higher Education* (Boston: Beacon, 2006); Fabio Rojas, *From Black Power to Black Studies: How a Radical Social Movement Became an Academic Discipline* (Baltimore, Md.: Johns Hopkins University Press, 2010).

26. Quoted in González-Cruz, "Puerto Rican Revolutionary Nationalism," 207.

27. Chicano activists in the Southwest had tried a similar initiative, opening an alternative high school in Denver in 1970. The school was named Escuela Tlatelolco, after the plaza in Mexico City where army troops shot scores of protesters—the exact number is unknown—in 1968 prior to the summer Olympics. That school inspired the effort in Chicago. See Ernesto B. Vigil, *The Crusade for Justice: Chicano Militancy and the Government's War on Dissent* (Madison: University of Wisconsin Press, 1999); Rodolfo "Corky" Gonzales, *Message to Aztlán: Selected Writings* (Houston, Tex.: Arte Público, 2001). Oscar López Rivera acknowledged this inspiration in a September 1, 2009, letter to me. For discussion of similar efforts among Native Americans, see Elizabeth Castle, "The Original Gangster: The Life and Times of Madonna Thunder Hawk," in *The Hidden 1970s: Histories of Radicalism*, ed. Dan Berger (New Brunswick, N.J.: Rutgers University Press, 2010). For analyses of alternative modalities of education in black radicalism, see Charles M. Payne and Carol Sills Strickland, eds., *Teach Freedom: Education for Liberation in the African-American Tradition* (New York: Teachers College Press, 2008).

28. The school still exists as a charter school, located in the heart of Humboldt Park, a largely Puerto Rican neighborhood in northwestern Chicago. Not long after Cancel Miranda was released, the school was renamed the Pedro Albizu Campos High School. Its library is named after Andres Figueroa Cordero. My knowledge of the school's origin comes from my interviews with two of its founders: José López and Ricardo Jimenez. I

also relied on materials in the archives of the Puerto Rican Cultural Center; a September 1, 2009, letter from Oscar López Rivera; and Jan Susler, "Unreconstructed Revolutionaries," in *The Puerto Rican Movement: Voices from the Diaspora*, ed. Andrés Torres and José E. Velázquez (Philadelphia: Temple University Press, 1998), 144–53. Scholars of Puerto Rican Chicago have also been especially useful. See Pérez, *The Near Northwest Side Story*; Fernández, "Latino/a Migration and Community Formation."

29. José López, interview with author, May 24, 2009.

30. Cf. Melendez, *We Took the Streets*; Fernández, "Radicals in the Late 1960s"; Fernandez, "Between Social Service Reform and Revolutionary Politics"; Sonia Song-Ha Lee, *Building a Latino Civil Rights Movement: Puerto Ricans, African Americans, and the Pursuit of Racial Justice in New York City* (Chapel Hill: University of North Carolina Press, 2014); López, interviews with author, May 24, 27, and 29, 2009.

31. Murch, *Living for the City*; Haas, *The Assassination of Fred Hampton.*

32. Partha Chatterjee, *The Nation and Its Fragments: Colonial and Postcolonial Histories* (Princeton, N.J.: Princeton University Press, 1993), 6.

33. James Clifford, "Diasporas," *Cultural Anthropology* 9, no. 3 (August 1994): 302–8; Paul Gilroy, *There Ain't No Black in the Union Jack* (1987; London: Routledge, 2002).

34. Jiménez quoted in Karen Serwer Secrist, "'Construyendo Nuestro Pedacito de Patria': Space and Dis(place)ment in Puerto Rican Chicago" (PhD diss., Duke University, 2009), 63; Rosa quoted in González-Cruz, "Puerto Rican Revolutionary Nationalism," 199.

35. For a sophisticated overview of this use of sovereignty, see Singh, *Black Is a Country.*

36. On the significance of prisoners in the Puerto Rican independence movement, see Berger, "We Are the Revolutionaries," 330–439. For more on Newton, Jackson, and black prison organizing, see Berger, *Captive Nation.*

37. Frantz Fanon, *The Wretched of the Earth* (New York: Grove, 1966), 170. Fanon takes this theme up more centrally in *Black Faces, White Masks* (New York: Grove, 1967).

38. My conversations with José López and Oscar López Rivera helped me understand the confluence of theorists from the Black Power and Puerto Rican independence movements.

39. See unsigned and undated article "Plea for Oscar Collazo's Life," probably authored by Ralph Templin, in Ruth M. Reynolds Papers, Centro de Estudios Puertorriqueños, Hunter College (hereafter RMR), ser. IV, reel 2. Similar sentiments can be found in other printed matter from the Comité pro Vida de Oscar Collazo (Committee for the Life of Oscar Collazo, an organization that worked to prevent Collazo from receiving a death sentence), which can also be found in the Centro de Estudios Puertorriqueños.

40. March 1 Bloc, "Arguments and Proposals for the PRSC [Puerto Rico Solidarity Coalition] Conference," ca. 1976, Puerto Rican Cultural Center, private collection.

41. For more on the Marion events, see Alan Eladio Gómez, "Resisting Living Death

at Marion Federal Penitentiary, 1972," *Radical History Review* 96 (Fall 2006): 58–86; Raúl Salinas, *raúlrsalinas and the Jail Machine: My Weapon Is My Pen*, ed. Louis G. Mendoza (Austin: University of Texas Press, 2006).

42. Michael Deutsch, interview with author, May 26, 2009.

43. Prior to his time at Marion, Cancel Miranda did time at Alcatraz with Morton Sobell, a codefendant in the trial of Julius and Ethel Rosenberg and others. Sobell was released from prison in 1969 and published a memoir, *On Doing Time*, in 1974. He was a signatory to the founding of the U.S. Committee to Free the Nationalist Prisoners and was involved in the Puerto Rico Solidarity Committee. "U.S. Committee to Free the Five Puerto Rican Nationalists," September 15, 1977, RMR, ser. IV, reel 6. For Cancel Miranda's time in prison with Sobell, see Drew Morita, "Former Alcatraz Inmate Speaks about His Time," *Examiner*, October 9, 2009, http://www.examiner.com/x-25690-Alcatraz-Examiner~y2009m10d9-Former-Alcatraz-inmate-speaks-about-his-time (accessed May 3, 2010). See also Jonah Raskin, *Oscar Collazo: Portrait of a Puerto Rican Patriot* (New York: New York Committee to Free the Puerto Rican Nationalist Prisoners, 1978), and the unedited transcript of Raskin's interview with Collazo, both in possession of author, courtesy of Jonah Raskin; and Alan Eladio Gómez, "'Nuestras Vidas Corren Casi Paralelas': Chicanos, Independentistas, and the Prison Rebellions in Leavenworth, 1960–1972," in *Behind Bars: Latino/as and Prison in the United States*, ed. Suzanne Oboler (New York: Palgrave Macmillan, 2009), 67–96.

44. Gómez, "Resisting Living Death"; Gómez, "Nuestras Vidas Corren Casi Paralelas."

45. See Vikki Law, *Resistance behind Bars: The Struggles of Incarcerated Women*, 2nd ed. (Oakland, Calif.: PM Press, 2012).

46. My knowledge of Lebrón's time in prison comes from my interview with her on July 1, 2009; and Assata Shakur, *Assata: An Autobiography* (Chicago: Lawrence Hill, 1987), 255–56. For more on Marilyn Buck, see Dan Berger, "Marilyn Buck's Playlist," *Polygraph* 23–24 (2013): 111–25.

47. Michael Deutsch, interview with author, May 26, 2009; Associated Press, "Ailing Puerto Rican in 1954 Attack on Congress Is Freed by Carter," *New York Times*, October 7, 1977, 1. See also Raúl R. Salinas, letter to Michael Deutsch, September 16, 1972, RRS, box 6, folder 20; U.S. Committee to Free the Five Nationalist Prisoners, "President Carter: Human Rights Begin at Home: Free Andres Figueroa!," flyer, RMR, ser. IV, reel 6; Committee to Free the Five, "The Case of Andres Figueroa Cordero," flyer, RMR, ser. IV, reel 2.

48. Oscar López Rivera (letter to author, September 1, 2009) alerted me to the Young Lords mural. Artwork about the nationalists adorned many of the flyers for their release by organizations such as El Comité, the Movimiento de Liberación Nacional, the Puerto Rican Socialist Party, Puerto Rico Solidarity Committee, the U.S. Committee to Free the Five (or Four, after Cordero was released), and the Young Lords Party. Many such documents can be found at the Puerto Rican Cultural Center, private collection, and RMR,

ser. IV, esp. reels 2, 5, and 6. As the campaign grew in the 1970s, images of the nationalists were increasingly popular and could be seen in many places, including the back cover of a San Jose radical newspaper, *Sedition* 5, no. 3 (March 1976), in National Alliance against Racist and Political Repression (hereafter NAARPR) Records, box 1, folder: Committee on Public Safety, Schomburg Center for Research in Black Culture, New York Public Library.

49. For instance, in a section on current political prisoners in *If They Come in the Morning*, Angela Davis lists only Lebrón's name to introduce the section. The entry focuses disproportionately on her as well. See Angela Y. Davis et al., *If They Come in the Morning* (New York: Signet, 1971), 98. Similarly, the first major collection of Nuyorican poetry features a poem dedicated to Lebrón but makes no mention of the others in her case. See Lucky CienFuegos, "Lolita Lebrón, Recuerdos Te Mandamos (We Send You Our Love)," in *Nuyorican Poetry: An Anthology of Puerto Rican Words and Feelings*, ed. Miguel Algarín and Miguel Piñero (New York: Morrow, 1975), 59–60. Supporters published pamphlets with essays by and interviews with Collazo and Cancel Miranda. See, for example, Oscar Collazo, *Prisionero 70495*, and Rafael Cancel Miranda, *Lucha E Ideario de un Puertorriqueño*, both published by Editorial Coquí and archived in the Puerto Rican Cultural Center, private collection. Cancel Miranda published occasional poems in *Midnight Special* and, while he was in Leavenworth, in the Chicano prison newspaper there, *Aztlán*. Cordero published at least one poem in that newspaper as well. Copies of *Aztlán* can be found in RRS, box 7.

50. Oscar López Rivera, letter to author, September 1, 2009. Lebrón carried a note in her pursue that read: "Before God and the world my blood claims for the Independence of Puerto Rico. My life I give for the freedom of my country. This is a cry for victory in our struggle for independence, which for more than a half century has tried to conquer that land that belongs to Puerto Rico. I stated that the United States of America is betraying the sacred principles of mankind in their barbarous torture of our apostle of independence, Don Pedro Albizu Campos." Quoted in El Comité, "Nuestro Pueblo Se Respeta," *Unidad Latina* 1, no. 6 (May 26–June 9, 1971): 3, in New Left Collection, Hoover Institute, Stanford University, Stanford, Calif.

51. Fernandez, *Prisoners of Colonialism*; Reyes, "Law, Media and Political Dissent."

52. Probably the best source on Chicago's black community is Mary Patillo, *Black on the Block: The Politics of Race and Class in the City* (Chicago: University of Chicago Press, 2007).

53. For more on how black activists did so, see Berger, *Captive Nation*. See also Houston Baker, "Critical Memory and the Black Public Sphere," in *The Black Public Sphere: A Public Culture Book*, ed. Black Public Sphere Collective (Chicago: University of Chicago Press, 1995).

54. Berger, "We Are the Revolutionaries," 408–15.

55. I thank Craig Wilder for this formulation.

56. My sense of the black radical tradition is especially indebted to Cedric Robinson, *Black Marxism: The Making of the Black Radical Tradition* (Chapel Hill: University of North Carolina Press, 2000); Robin D. G. Kelley, *Freedom Dreams: The Black Radical Imagination* (Boston: Beacon, 2002); Fred Moten, *In the Break: The Aesthetics of the Black Radical Tradition* (Minneapolis: University of Minnesota Press, 2003).

CHAPTER 8

"Justice Now! ¡Justicia Ahora!"

African American–Puerto Rican Radicalism in Camden, New Jersey

LAURIE LAHEY

On the evening of July 30, 1971, in Camden, New Jersey, police officers Gary Miller and Warren Worrell stopped a forty-year-old Puerto Rican man for driving in "an erratic manner." The man, who would come to be known erroneously in the media as Camden resident Horatio Jimenez based on the driver's license found in his pocket, was actually Rafael Rodriguez Gonzales from nearby Penns Grove, New Jersey. According to eyewitness Carmen Villanueva, Rodriguez Gonzales was driving down Benson Street when he slowed to speak to a pedestrian, consequently stopping traffic. Police signaled for Rodriguez Gonzales to pull over. Miller asked for his license, and when Rodriguez Gonzales hesitated, probably because of the active traffic warrant pending against him, Miller told him to get out of the car. As Miller patted him down, Rodriguez Gonzales turned and asked, "What are you searching me for?" Villanueva, who was close enough to the incident to record the officers' badge numbers, said Miller responded by hitting Rodriguez Gonzales with his fist and then with his nightstick. Rodriguez Gonzales fell to the ground as both officers beat him with their nightsticks and kicked him in the abdomen.[1] Another witness, Elizabeth Rodriguez, remembered, "He was bleeding from his nose, his mouth, the blood was just dripping right out. . . . He had no chance . . . no chance at all, with the two police officers."[2] Villanueva "thought he was dead at the time."[3] The officers charged Rodriguez Gonzales with assaulting a police officer.[4]

Several bystanders, however, insisted it was the police who had assaulted Rodriguez Gonzales. According to the witnesses, Miller and Worrell—both twenty-five-year-old white men—not only clubbed Rodriguez Gonzales with their nightsticks, but also dragged him by his feet to their patrol car. The sole passenger in Rodriguez Gonzales's vehicle, seventeen-year-old Leslie Alan Whitesall, threatened to report the officers. When Whitesall asked for a pencil and paper to write down their badge and car numbers, Miller and Worrell cuffed him. By this time, fifty people had gathered to watch. Ominously, a man shouted: "You shouldn't have done that. . . . This is what can cause a riot."[5]

When the riot did come, it was different from any protests in the city's history. Although a direct response to a Puerto Rican man's encounter with police, the marching, sit-ins, and violence that ensued were steeped in a fusion of Black Power militancy and Puerto Rican nationalism. In the weeks that followed the beating, people draped their homes and businesses with red shirts, red towels, red dresses, red flags, and even red underwear to guard against the mayhem that engulfed the city, which a newspaper compared to the biblical Israelites protecting their firstborn children by painting their doorposts with blood. Signs reading "Puerto Rico Libre!" and "Black P.R." annotated the displays of red cloth. As North Camden resident Ida Robinson explained to a *Courier-Post* reporter, "If you have something red in your window, they won't touch your house. . . . It's a black power symbol."[6] The city's most influential Black Power leader, the chair of the militant Black People's Unity Movement (BPUM), Charles "Poppy" Sharp, publicly confirmed the alliance, announcing: "We have an awful lot in common. Blacks and Puerto Ricans must unite now under one cause—freedom."[7]

This interracial demonstration in Camden, a city of just 102,551 in 1970, provides a glimpse of black-Latino activism outside the better-documented arenas of larger cities like New York City and Chicago.[8] In Camden, there was no chapter of a national militant organization, such as the Black Panther Party or the Young Lords Organization. Indeed, there were no radical Puerto Rican organizations at all. While tenuous interracial coalitions had coalesced in Camden in the late 1960s, the bulk of the cooperation was among a cadre of African Americans, black and white Christian ministers, and suburban whites. Some Puerto Ricans had participated in that alliance, but not in the same public, radical manner as during the riot.

In considering how African American–Puerto Rican solidarity emerged in such an abrupt and forceful manner that summer, this chapter examines the circumstances surrounding what historian Daniel Sidorick has called "perhaps the most significant" Puerto Rican protest of the 1960s and 1970s.[9] This chapter argues that while the media and the few scholars who have considered this event characterized it as Latino, it was the product of interracial,

African American–Latino cooperation. This story is significant to the history of African American–Latino activism because it demonstrates how police violence in a secondary city united African Americans and Puerto Ricans in a way that no other social problems could. Their response included marches, sit-ins, meetings with local government officials, and, when these different forms of activism failed to produce the desired results, rioting. In this chapter I hope to provide insight into how Puerto Ricans in a city with no radical Latino organizations found common ground with black militants.

HISTORY OF AFRICAN AMERICAN–PUERTO RICAN RELATIONS IN CAMDEN

The 1971 riot was a dramatic finale to Camden's rapid post–World War II decline. Like so many cities, Camden had succumbed to the "urban crisis" that snaked its way across the North in the decades following the war.[10] While sections of downtown Camden remained stable, entire neighborhoods, particularly in North Camden and South Camden, where most African Americans and Puerto Ricans lived, were populated with decaying homes and closing businesses. As early as 1951 the *Baltimore Afro-American* reported that 70 percent of the housing in South Camden could be classified as "slums."[11] By the mid-1960s the city housing authority deemed that over half of all the housing in Camden was unfit for habitation, and, as late as 1966, the Federal Housing Administration had not granted a single mortgage within the city limits.[12]

In the late 1950s city planners had embarked on several projects to address Camden's housing issues and to draw businesses to the city. Like many urban renewal projects, these plans required leveling the areas marked as "slums." The city promised the community 500 town houses, at least three shopping centers, and a park on the cleared land. Yet, as the 1960s drew to a close, five thousand families had been displaced with no substantive assistance from the government. In that time, only 101 new low-income homes had been built, which were reserved exclusively for the elderly. The city anticipated that an additional three thousand residents would need to relocate by 1973.[13]

As the housing crisis grew more urgent, Camden's African American and Puerto Rican populations swelled. Between 1940 and 1960 Camden's white population decreased from 104,995 to 89,267 and its nonwhite population increased from 12,541 to 27,892.[14] Both African Americans and Puerto Ricans were drawn to the Camden area by the Campbell Soup Company, the city's most profitable industry and its first to hire minorities. The laborers served both the cannery, located in Camden, and the local farms that supported Campbell Soup. Both Puerto Ricans and African Americans found it difficult to find employment outside the cannery and agricultural industries. In 1954 no Puerto Rican had a white-collar job in Camden. Five years later, less than 1 percent of Puerto Ricans owned a business other than a few grocery stores. Both African Americans and Puerto Ricans had a difficult time joining unions.[15]

Several organizations and individuals had attempted to promote intraracial and interracial activism in Camden. In the 1930s radical labor leaders, typically Communist Party U.S.A. members, had some success crafting interracial labor strikes, although there is no evidence that this cooperation extended beyond the workplace. In the 1940s the Camden branch of the National Association for the Advancement of Colored People (NAACP) made some important gains in integrating elementary schools. In the 1950s the government-created Migration Division, which served as an official intermediary between Puerto Rican workers and U.S. employers, mediated workplace complaints and helped Puerto Ricans "assimilate" as they moved into Camden.[16] Still these efforts were limited, and African Americans and Puerto Ricans did not cooperate interracially in large numbers.

While much has been written about how African Americans and Puerto Ricans have interacted in major American cities, it is difficult to assess Camden's racial hierarchy in the 1940s–1960s because, aside from anecdotal remarks, there is not much evidence delineating how these groups related to each other or which group fared worse. While both African Americans and Puerto Ricans faced problems in housing, education, and employment, they were not always the same problems. Housing discrimination, for instance, was clearly antiblack: African Americans were excluded entirely from some places, while Puerto Ricans were evaluated on a case-by-case basis. The largest concentrations of Camden's Puerto Ricans were seasonal farm laborers, which created a host of unique issues for the Puerto Rican community. While African Americans and Puerto Ricans both sought equality in Camden's public schools, the major issue for Puerto Ricans was the language barrier.

In terms of how Camden's Puerto Ricans attempted to position themselves racially, some evidence suggests they were wary of being classified as "black," as many confronted the American racial binary for the first time. That none of the dozens of Puerto Rican social clubs in Camden used the term *puertorriqueño* despite its common vernacular usage could be read as a rejection of blackness. It was typical of Puerto Rican social clubs in the 1950s to claim "Hispanic" rather than "Puerto Rican" because of the former term's association with immigrants from Spain and, thus, "whiteness."[17] If, as Audrey Smedley and Brian D. Smedley argue, a defining characteristic of "race" is its rigidity, its permanence despite its social construction, Puerto Ricans had an advantage over African Americans. Puerto Ricans, like other ethnic groups in U.S. history, could hope to attain whiteness or, as some Camden Puerto Ricans did in the 1970s, they could reject it.[18]

Still, relationships among Camden's minorities seemed generally amicable. Most local Puerto Ricans would have spent time working closely with African Americans on nearby farms even before they settled in Camden. Moreover, unlike in large cities such as New York or Chicago, Camden Puerto Ricans typically occupied the same neighborhoods as African Americans, never developing a separate colonia in the city. While proximity does not guarantee friendship, if Camden African Americans and Puerto Ricans did not coexist in a relatively peaceful manner, one might expect to find reports or editorial commentaries in local newspapers of interracial disharmony. Additionally, neither the NAACP nor Migration Division records reveal any such animosity. While Puerto Ricans and African Americans often pursued divergent paths of social reform, perhaps the most likely reason there is limited evidence of Puerto Rican and African American activism at the height of the civil rights movement in Camden is that by the mid-1950s both of the city's major organizations, the NAACP and the Migration Division, promoted middle-class values in an increasingly working-class town. Neither of these organizations could ignite any real community activism, even among their own groups. From the late 1950s through the mid-1960s, there was no effective leadership and no grassroots organizing in Camden.[19]

An important shift occurred in 1964 when a white Episcopalian priest, Donald Griesmann, sensing the need for a more concerted approach to community organizing, formed the Camden Civil Rights Ministerium (CCRM), an interracial coalition of clergy, including African American Baptist minister Amos Johnson, white Presbyterian minister Samuel Appel, NAACP members, and some Puerto Rican community leaders, with the goal of involving the community more deeply in the quest for social justice. Initially, this organization too saw limited success; the sit-ins and marches it attempted were poorly attended. However, in 1967, acknowledging that these traditional, nonviolent methods of protest would not arouse Camden's citizens, the CCRM tested a new approach by bringing Black Power icon H. Rap Brown to Camden. While this move alienated less radical CCRM members, it did stimulate community activism: Brown headlined a rally in Camden, where he encouraged the several thousand in attendance to fight the establishment with violence.[20]

This rally inspired an ex-con and eighth-grade dropout named Charles "Poppy" Sharp to form the Black People's Unity Movement in Camden. While the BPUM was characterized by Black Power rhetoric and militancy, it came to work closely with black and white ministers, the white suburban Friends of the Black People's Unity Movement (FBPUM), and some members of the Puerto Rican community. For a few bright years, this unlikely coalition generated a unique synthesis of Black Power militancy and Christian nonviolence. Sharp, as the face of this coalition, became well known and highly respected in Camden's minority communities. In 1968 and 1969 alone, activists forced the city to close the Ben Franklin Bridge during a standoff with police, organized African Americans and whites in burning effigies of the city's mayor and police chief on the City Hall's steps to protest police brutality, and testified before the U.S. Congress about Camden's housing conditions.[21]

This activism proved difficult to sustain. By 1971, following the arrests of several key members on bogus charges brought by the city, the CCRM was virtually defunct.[22] The most egregious incident of police harassment occurred when police raided the BPUM headquarters in 1969 and arrested Poppy Sharp, claiming they found guns and forty-three packets of heroin. His arrest was a blow to social organizing in Camden. At Sharp's trial in 1970, the police admitted to planting evidence. After he was acquitted, Sharp remained the chair of the BPUM, but no longer maintained the same street presence. While Camden citizens may have considered the police department's actions reprehensible, it is likely they were not surprised. Minorities were regularly victims of police discrimination or violence. Sociologist Gregg Lee Carter has examined all the documented Hispanic riots of the 1960s and 1970s and found that 42 percent were in response to an instance of police brutality. The likelihood of a clash between a Puerto Rican or Mexican American and a police officer leading to a riot was significantly increased if the police force had recently become more aggressive and if the political response to the injustice was not swift. Both of these factors came into play in August 1971.[23]

The CCRM had kept track of the Camden Police Department's aggression toward minorities with the help of a black officer on the force. According to Donald Griesmann, "Police were a big problem. There was an African American police officer who dated [CCRM member] Carolyn Burton who was leaking things to her. . . . Hatred was being embroiled in the police about anything that was going on in the black movement. It was quite despicable. It took a long time for that to change."[24] In 1968 the *New York Times* confirmed these accusations, reporting that Chief of Police Harold Melleby, who had been "feuding" with the city's minorities, affixed a "confidential memo" to the police station's bulletin board, urging officers to "take the utmost precautions to safeguard their family, personal property, and police equipment from attack." The BPUM argued that this warning, which was unprovoked, would only "incite the police to irrational moves."[25]

In 1971 Camden's 328-person police force was mostly white. Approximately 20 percent of the officers were black, and four or five were Puerto Rican. Some of these minority officers, like Puerto Rican Clement Quieroz, thought the Camden Police Department fostered a hostile work environment: "I was called a 'spic.' I had to go in the back door. I was a lieutenant [but] . . . anytime I tried to discipline anyone, I was short circuited."[26] Following a falling out with the city's mayor, Joseph Nardi, Chief of Police Melleby was forced to cede some power to the director of public safety, William Yeager, whom Nardi appointed. Yeager had jurisdiction over both the police and fire departments. Soon after accepting the position, Yeager created the Strategic Relations Division (SRD) to combat crime in some of Camden's minority neighborhoods. Officers Miller and Worrell were both SRD members.[27]

African Americans and Puerto Ricans called the SRD "the Gestapo." People complained to Mayor Nardi about the unit as soon as it was founded. One resident asserted following the Rodriguez Gonzales incident: "We abhor the similarity of this squad [to] Hitler's obnoxious S.S., both in its abbreviations and intent."[28] In the police department, other officers were wary of the SRD and Miller and Worrell in particular. Black sergeant Richard Conrad Hailey, one of Miller's and Worrell's supervisors, had reviewed their arrest record in the summer of 1970 and found that more than 95 percent of the people they arrested were black or Puerto Rican. Many arrests started with a minor infraction, such as a traffic violation, and escalated to violence. Some black officers, represented by the Brotherhood for Unity and Progress, were so appalled by Miller's and Worrell's behavior in the Rodriguez Gonzales encounter that they placed an announcement in the *Courier-Post*, condemning the "recent acts of violence" and censuring "bullies who use their nightsticks as Nazi-like weapons for self-imposed law." The Brotherhood for Unity and Progress was "[especially] appalled when incidents fomented by police carry racial overtones."[29]

THE RIOT

Immediately following Rafael Rodriguez Gonzales's encounter with Officers Miller and Worrell, several witnesses went to the police station to complain, but were ignored. Concerned citizens began calling Joseph Rodriguez, one of the city's most prominent Puerto Rican leaders. Rodriguez's parents, Mario and Carmen, had arrived in Camden in 1930 and were the city's first Puerto Rican residents. The Rodriguez family became active in the community as the Puerto Rican population began to grow in the 1940s. In 1971 Joseph Rodriguez was a successful medical malpractice attorney and Camden's only Puerto Rican lawyer. His brother, Mario Jr., was a member of the State Commission on Civil Rights. Mario Rodriguez Jr. had been a councilman in Camden but left politics when he lost a bid for mayor in 1969. Through their own investigation, the brothers became convinced that the police had acted unethically in the Rodriguez Gonzales arrest. They were shocked when Mayor Joseph Nardi, a family friend, refused to take their calls. The longer the mayor ignored the community, the more restless it became.[30]

On August 12, almost two weeks after the beating, Camden citizens gathered their children and marched through the city, waving the Puerto Rican flag and the flag of the Puerto Rican Liberation Front, to protest police brutality. The protest was somewhat successful: Chief of Police Harold Melleby charged Miller and Worrell with atrocious assault and battery. However, the community sensed the move was insincere. Despite the new charges, the police department announced that it would not suspend the officers due to a lack of evidence. Later that same day, Puerto Rican leaders, including the Rodriguez brothers and Gualberto "Gil" Medina, a student at Rutgers University's Camden campus, presented a list of demands to the city's business administrator, Joseph Dorris, since Nardi still refused to meet with them. The group requested the suspensions of Miller and Worrell, a grand jury investigation to review the officers' conduct, an end to police brutality against Puerto Ricans, the creation of a supervisory panel to mediate differences between the police and the community, the hiring of more Puerto Rican police officers, interpreters and competent legal representation for Puerto Ricans charged with municipal offenses, the inclusion of representatives from the Puerto Rican community in any discussions on the course of the Rodriguez Gonzales case, and a complete report from Cooper Hospital on Rodriguez Gonzales's condition. Dorris rejected most of the requests. Medina recapped the meeting: "They answered most of our questions negatively. We are determined to prevent further assaults on Puerto Ricans."[31]

While witnesses turned to the Rodriguez brothers in the immediate aftermath of the Rafael Rodriguez Gonzales incident, their leadership style would prove insufficient. In the coming weeks Gil Medina, working under the tutelage of Poppy Sharp and the protection of BPUM bodyguards, emerged as the face of the movement. Medina had first become acquainted with Sharp in 1969 through his work with the interracial Black Students Unity Movement, a spinoff of the BPUM, at Rutgers University's Camden campus. While the Rodriguez brothers tried repeatedly and unsuccessfully to meet with Nardi, Medina organized a march to the mayor's office, where he planned to hold a sit-in until he got Nardi's attention. According to Medina, the Rodriguez brothers shared his goals, but used different tactics. Joseph and Mario Rodriguez believed in the political process, in working within the system to urge reform. Medina believed in confrontation.[32]

The philosophical chasm between the Rodriguez brothers and Gil Medina is representative of late 1960s and early 1970s shifts in Puerto Rican social organization. While the Rodriguez brothers were born in Camden in the 1930s and raised in a patriotic family, Medina migrated to Camden from Puerto Rico as an infant in 1954 and grew up in an ardently pro-independence household. Gil's father, Armando Medina, was an active member of the Puerto Rican Nationalist Party and worked to "indoctrinate" his children to be "nationalist, pro-independence," to the dismay of much of Camden's Puerto Rican population in the 1950s. By the time he was a teenager, Gil Medina was a self-described "fire-breathing, pro-independence radical" who fiercely admired Malcolm X, calling him a "John the Baptist" of social justice. For Medina, Poppy Sharp was Camden's Malcolm X.[33]

In 1971 Medina was a member of several leftist organizations, which were all either interracial or had friendly relationships with other racial and ethnic groups. Perhaps the most militant organization Medina joined was the Young Lords. Juan Gonzales, a New York activist, had moved to Philadelphia in 1970 to organize a Young Lords chapter there. Since there was no chapter in Camden, Medina traveled to Philadelphia for meetings, where he found like-minded young people:

> We were all somewhat naïve . . . maybe too idealistic, too radical sometimes, too prone to embrace confrontation. . . . They were espousing community control of our institutions . . . a form of democracy that would give Puerto

> Ricans, in communities where they lived, control of the key institutions that impacted their lives. It's a funny thing, because we were too prone to confrontation, but if you look at the agenda it wasn't that extraordinary or radical. It was the means that made them into a radical group. The Young Lords Party was largely not a violent group, although sometimes the group came off that way. It was largely a group that was into confrontation for the sake of raising issues and raising consciousness. At the same time we had really good relationships with the Black Panther Party.[34]

While not all Puerto Rican activists supported coalition building to the extent Gil Medina did, Medina's activism, much like Sharp's view that blacks and Puerto Ricans had "an awful lot in common," was indicative of a larger shift toward cooperation among radical African Americans and Puerto Ricans.[35]

While Puerto Rican activists had joined organizations like the Communist Party, the Student Nonviolent Coordinating Committee (SNCC), and the Congress of Racial Equality (CORE) in the 1960s, the widespread dissemination of Black Power politics in the late 1960s inspired a new sense of pride among people of color. Moreover, Black Power politics did not merely invite support for issues pertaining to African Americans. At the national level, important examples of black support of "Puerto Rican issues" abound, including SNCC chair Stokely Carmichael's 1967 visit to Puerto Rico, where African Americans and Puerto Ricans marched in support of Black Power and Puerto Rican independence, and H. Rap Brown's and Carmichael's attendance at a 1967 teach-in on Puerto Rico at Columbia University. Additionally, Puerto Ricans joined the Black Panthers, sometimes gaining notoriety for their actions. Jeffrey Ogbar points out that at least two members of the infamous Panther 21—the New York–based Panthers indicted in 1969 on charges of conspiring to blow up five department stores, a police station, railroad tracks, and the New York Botanical Garden—Raymond Quiñones and Albert Nieves, were Puerto Rican.[36]

An important ramification of this multifaceted, interracial organizing was that Puerto Ricans moved further away from identifying as "white," as they had tended to do in the 1940s and 1950s, and adopted a "brown" identity. Gil Medina recalls becoming aware of "race" when he was around seven years old, thinking of it "as a descriptive fact . . . not a differentiator."[37] As an adult, Medina considers himself and his relatives neither black nor white, but somewhere in between, depending on the shade of their skin. In Camden, the cooperation sprang from a generational shift, which saw younger radicalized

Puerto Ricans, who were less concerned with identifying with whiteness than their predecessors had been, actively standing in opposition to the increasingly aggressive police violence.

Frustrated by the lack of progress they were making through the political process, Gil Medina organized a demonstration at Roosevelt Plaza, a grassy space in front of City Hall, a week after the city's business administrator, Dorris, rejected the Puerto Rican list of demands. As the crowd grew, blacks, whites, and Puerto Ricans began chanting: "Justice Now! ¡Justicia Ahora!" Protesters carried signs demanding Miller's and Worrell's suspensions. People moved closer and closer to City Hall, encircling the building under former resident Walt Whitman's words, etched into the stone forty years earlier: "In a Dream I Saw a City Invincible." Gil Medina had commandeered a station wagon and outfitted it with speakers, fashioning a makeshift platform for speeches. Several BPUM members took turns speaking, consistently arguing that both Puerto Ricans and blacks were oppressed people who must unite to achieve political power. BPUM member Omar Davis argued that "only by unity can we lick this thing, together we are seventy-five percent of this city. Neither of us can do it by ourselves." Davis deferred to the Puerto Rican leaders, however, telling them, "whatever decision you make, we're going to be with you."[38] Poppy Sharp spoke to the crowd on behalf of the black community: "As a black man, and as a member of a suppressed minority, I know I speak for all blacks, including the silent ones because they know the next day it might be one of them whose rights are violated." Sharp announced, "All members of the black community will begin today wearing black armbands in support of the Puerto Rican community and will continue wearing them until unity, justice, and equality prevails. We support the Puerto Rican community because we too have been victims of police brutality. We must work together until justice becomes a part of the Camden community."[39]

Ruth Coleman, the head of the Camden County Office of Economic Opportunity, agreed with Sharp, affirming that he spoke for her as a member of the black community. The Camden County NAACP president, "Doc" John Robinson, shared Sharp's sentiments as well, stating that "the NAACP cannot speak for the Puerto Rican community, but they have our moral support. The police officers should have been suspended until a [legal] outcome. This would have given the communities [black and Puerto Rican] a feeling of equal justice." Robinson argued that the Rafael Rodriguez Gonzales incident was not simply a Puerto Rican problem: "It is an attitude of police towards the [minority] population in general."[40]

Two and a half hours into the demonstration, the crowd at Roosevelt Plaza approached eight hundred. The director of public safety, William Yeager, told the people that the mayor was not available to meet with them. Nardi remained at his home on Mitchell Street in the predominantly white East Camden. Joseph Rodriguez continued to urge Nardi, who had finally taken his call, to come to City Hall as the demonstration began to escalate. Rodriguez promised Nardi that the people in the plaza were not troublemakers, even noting that Rodriguez's own elderly parents were there. Still, Nardi would not budge. Meanwhile, Yeager ordered his men into riot gear and stationed them on Market and Federal Streets, flanking Roosevelt Plaza. At 3:30 p.m. a two-hour downpour commenced. Seeking cover, demonstrators ran into City Hall. City Hall employees and police felt "under siege" as shouts of "Justice Now!" and "¡Justicia Ahora!" rattled the building. Someone hung a Puerto Rican flag from a balcony overlooking the lobby. Still, the crowd remained peaceful. Yeager allowed the demonstrators to stay in the building, but stationed his men around the lobby, sealing the corridors.[41]

At 5:30 p.m. Nardi finally spoke with Medina by telephone. He agreed to meet with a delegation of six Puerto Ricans and four observers if the demonstrators would go home. By then, the crowd was difficult to control. Medina and the other leaders could not make the people leave immediately. The demonstrators finally exited the building shortly after 6:00 p.m., but many lingered in the plaza and on the front steps of City Hall. Nardi argued that the leaders did not keep their end of the deal: "These people are supposed to be leaders, yet they didn't disperse their people after we agreed to the meeting. I don't call creating a potential riot situation responsible leadership."[42] Around 8:00 p.m. Mayor Nardi finally agreed to go to City Hall.[43]

By the time Nardi arrived, the crowd in Roosevelt Plaza had reached twelve hundred. As Mario Rodriguez told the press later, "The longer you keep a crowd waiting, the harder it becomes to control." Explaining the restlessness, Hector Rodriguez charged, "you can only do so much with people in nine hours." In his seventeenth-floor office Nardi met with a delegation of Puerto Ricans, which included Gil Medina, Hector Rodriguez, Joseph Rodriguez, Mario Rodriguez, Angel Perez (the director of the Community Organization for Puerto Rican Affairs), and Luis Figueroa (the president of the Puerto Rican Action Committee). Joseph Rodriguez acted as the group's attorney. The men presented Nardi, Dorris, and Yeager with a list of demands, similar to the one they had given Dorris a week earlier. The Puerto Rican leaders' central demand was for Miller's and Worrell's suspensions, but Joseph

Rodriguez offered a concession: they could allow a county grand jury to decide.[44]

An hour into the meeting, as Nardi, Dorris, and Yeager discussed the seventeen demands privately, the crowd outside became alarmingly loud. Nardi panicked and told the Puerto Ricans there was violence in the streets. Yeager ordered the leaders to clear the crowd from City Hall: "You've got five minutes to clear it up . . . five minutes." By the time the leaders reached the street the demonstrators had begun throwing rocks, bricks, and trashcans at police. Again, the Puerto Rican leaders, with the help of the BPUM, urged the crowd to leave. The people refused.

Medina recalls it was around 9:30 p.m. "when a crowd numbering in the hundreds refused to disperse when it had gotten dark, in spite of my pleas for them to do so." Medina adds, "The police attacked men, women, children, and senior citizens." All hell broke loose, and bands of young men and women entered into running street battles with the police. Police moved in on the crowd, trapping about three hundred people with tear gas and dogs. Simultaneously, a fight at a nearby bar spilled into the street. Rioters torched several buildings—so many that firefighters lost count. For the next two nights rioters overturned police cars, destroyed and looted stores, and threw rocks at anyone who did not join them. Eighty-seven people reported injuries. Three people were shot. Camden's police force was soon supplemented by seventy-eight state troopers and seventy officers from suburban departments. By dawn after the first night of the riots, the violence had temporarily dissipated. But the tear gas used by the police lingered for days. One resident compared breathing the tear gas to electrocution: "It was like breathing in a jolt of electricity for adults." When her three-year-old daughter breathed the tear gas, she "convulsed with sobs."[45]

After the first night of rioting, the Puerto Rican leaders and, according to interviews reported in the *Courier-Post*, many other people in the community blamed the violence on Mayor Nardi for delaying the meeting. Camden business owners also had attempted to meet with Nardi, but were ignored. According to a fur store owner, Jerry Aronberg: "I firmly, one-thousand percent, believe Nardi should have stepped in sooner. . . . We blame everything on Nardi."[46] Puerto Rican leaders, including Gil Medina and the Rodriguez brothers, had spent the night strategizing in a home on Federal Street. Mario Rodriguez complained to the media that Nardi had riled the crowd by keeping them waiting: "He kept those people waiting for 10 hours. He kept them waiting in the heat and in the rain. He avoided sitting down with them."[47]

City Hall was an armed camp. Yeager released an incoherent and inflammatory statement, comparing himself to Franklin Roosevelt after the Japanese attack on Pearl Harbor: "On this morning of August 20, 1971, I feel just as . . . President Roosevelt must have felt on the morning of December 7, 1941." Yeager claimed the riot was premeditated and barbaric:

> Puerto Rican protesters situated in front of the city hall and city hall plaza secretly, quickly, and obviously pursuant to a well-planned method of operation effectively equipped a majority of the protesters with a huge quantity of deadly clubs and bludgeons. . . . The ruthless, despicable, cowardly and shameful conduct attributed to that animalistic group of rationless [*sic*] two-legged beasts could only be surpassed in nature and degree by the two-faced appalling action as represented by the representative negotiators busily disgracing their name and culture while their cohorts unleashed their fury against an unwilling police contingent situated at the scene.[48]

Both Puerto Rican and BPUM leaders were concerned about how Gil Medina would react to Yeager's statement; even the militant Poppy Sharp urged Medina to remain calm. Medina remained poised, but the community was outraged by Yeager's comments. As darkness fell on August 20, snipers began to fire at buildings around the city, including at Mayor Nardi's office. He began working by candlelight and required special clearance for any visitors. Police began using unmarked cars rented in Philadelphia because so many of their vehicles had been destroyed. The Puerto Rican and black community leaders worked to keep people off the streets and chastised the mayor for not imposing a curfew. The next day, an exasperated Hector Rodriguez reprimanded Nardi: "The chance of violence last night was pretty obvious to us. All the bars were open. He didn't insist on a curfew. We imposed our own curfew. If we hadn't, there would have been more people on the streets."[49]

The white, suburban-based Friends of the Black People's Unity Movement, which had worked closely with the BPUM since 1968 by raising money and participating in protests, supported the community through its Crisis Communication Network, which it had established in the summer of 1969. The FBPUM provided food, clothing, money, and other necessities to riot victims via a network of local churches. Internally, the FBPUM discussed developing a coalition with Gil Medina so that black leaders in the BPUM could become better informed about Puerto Rican concerns. It seems that the organization's attempts were successful: Angel Perez met with the group to discuss the riot and its aftermath. The FBPUM reported that it was pleased at the continued financial success of the BPUM Economic Development Corporation, which created black-owned businesses in Camden, and hoped to become connected with the Puerto Rican community in a more "structural" way.[50]

On August 21, Mayor Nardi finally declared a state of emergency, which included a curfew and several other regulations. Yet he knew he was beyond salvaging his reputation with the community, lamenting, "I ain't loved by nobody."[51] Both city and Puerto Rican leaders, realizing the situation was beyond their control, agreed to New Jersey governor William Cahill's suggestion to invite a professional mediator, Irwin Goldabor, to negotiate a truce. Goldabor had successfully mediated similar disturbances in Passaic and Asbury Park, New Jersey. At their meeting in nearby Cherry Hill, Goldabor recommended that the police department suspend Miller and Worrell. Nardi conceded. Just hours after the city announced the police officers' suspensions, the violence ended. When Rafael Rodriguez Gonzales died a couple of days later, three weeks after the assault, Miller and Worrell were charged with murder. However, when their case went to trial, the charges were downgraded to manslaughter. In 1973 Gary Miller and Warren Worrell were acquitted by a jury.[52]

CONCLUSION

Camden's 1971 protests and riot were a significant turning point in the city's history, leaving a lasting impact. Melvin "Randy" Primas, Camden's first black mayor and a former BPUM member, still felt the riot's influence on the city in the 1980s: "There was a mass exodus. As folks moved out, the folks coming in were of a lower economic level. There were more folks with needs."[53] Business owners blamed the riot for dwindling revenues. Just days after the protests, the Camden Business Improvement Association membership decreased from one hundred to thirty. Perhaps the association's members felt the way one shoe store proprietor did; on a Sunday morning in the midst of the riot, he explained to the *Courier-Post* why he refused to board up his store windows: "'I'm going to give it back to the city,' he said quietly. His windows had been smashed for the second time in two days of rioting on Saturday. . . . 'This just about finishes Camden as a businessman's city.'"[54]

African Americans' and Puerto Ricans' highly visible cooperation during the protests demonstrates a shift in how these groups perceived themselves both racially and politically, as well as how they understood their city's social hierarchy. While both African Americans and Puerto Ricans had faced numerous social inequities in previous decades, for the most part they had addressed them separately. By 1971 young Puerto Ricans in Camden, like Gualberto Medina, were inspired by radical activism throughout the nation and by the BPUM at home. No longer preoccupied with differentiating themselves from African Americans, as earlier generations had been, Camden's Puerto Rican youths found common ground with blacks. That summer African Americans and Puerto Ricans held sit-ins and marched through the streets together. African American and Puerto Rican community leaders gave speeches and met with government officials. Demonstrators drove around Camden waving Puerto Rican flags, gave Black Power salutes, and stormed City Hall. When they felt no one was listening, they rioted. In Camden, police brutality was not a "black problem" or a "Puerto Rican problem": it was a community problem that required interracial unity.

Ultimately Camden's minorities did not get the justice they sought. Police officers killed a Puerto Rican man and, despite the community's best efforts, they did not go to prison. However, for Gualberto Medina and maybe for the other African Americans, Puerto Ricans, and whites who joined his public rejection of the city's ambivalence, the community's united resistance was an accomplishment in itself. In reflecting on those four days in August, forty years later, Medina remembers one poignant moment more clearly than the rest:

> When [the riots] first broke out, a group of student leaders/organizers rushed to Broadway to attempt to stop the looting and attacks on merchants. One of the shops attacked belonged to Gypsies, today called Roma. I went in to apologize to the husband and wife proprietors. [The husband] stopped me from speaking, rolled up his sleeve and showed me the tattoos [that had been] engraved on his arm at Auschwitz. He gazed at me intently and said, "because we did not resist, millions of innocents died needlessly." A valuable lesson that all that is good in life—love, beauty, justice—sometimes comes at a price.[55]

Clearly the Holocaust, like African slavery or colonial Third World oppression, did not lack resistance from the dominated. Instead Medina's recollection—prone, of course, to time's depredation—emphasizes the framework in which black and Puerto Rican militants located their activism. Comparing their resistance to the struggles of those persecuted by the Third Reich, both in the shop owner story and through equating the Strategic Relations Division with the Gestapo, indicates that the 1971 riot was about more than Rafael Rodriguez Gonzales. Interracial cooperation in Camden was about more than local circumstances. Camden's story provides an additional layer to the larger story of black-Latino relations during the twentieth century by revealing how minorities framed their oppression in a secondary city and how, outside the influence of larger national organizations, that changed over time.

NOTES

1. "Five Charge Police Brutality in Arrest of Camden Man," *Courier-Post*, August 3, 1971.

2. Statement of Elizabeth Rodriguez, August 17, 1971, Camden Detective Bureau, Case No. 71-4708, in Prosecutor's File in *State of New Jersey v. Warren L. Worrell and Gary E. Miller*, Indictments Nos. 999-71 and 1000-71, Camden County Prosecutor's Office, Camden, N.J. (hereafter Prosecutor's File).

3. Grand jury testimony of Carmen D. Villanueva, February 17, 1972, Prosecutor's File.

4. "Five Charge Police Brutality."

5. Statement of Elizabeth Rodriguez, Prosecutor's File; "3 Say They Saw Police Beating Man Who Died," *Courier-Post*, January 31, 1973; "3 Testify to Seeing 2 Policemen Beat Gonzales on Camden Street," *Philadelphia Inquirer*, January 31, 1973; "Five Charge Police Brutality."

6. Barbara Irvin, interview with author, September 23, 2010; "Curfew Is Continued in Quiet but Riot-Torn Camden," *New York Times*, August 23, 1971; "Blood-Red Flag to Stay the Blood," *Courier-Post*, August 23, 1971.

7. "Two Patrolmen Charged in Beating of Motorist," *Courier-Post*, August 13, 1971.

8. *U.S. Census of Population and Housing, 1970* (Washington, D.C.: U.S. Government Printing Office, 1973).

9. Daniel Sidorick, *Condensed Capitalism: Campbell Soup and the Pursuit of Cheap Production in the Twentieth Century* (Ithaca, N.Y.: Cornell University Press, 2009), 165; Gregg Lee Carter, "Hispanic Rioting during the Civil Rights Era," *Sociological Forum* 7, no. 2 (June 1992): 301–22.

10. Thomas J. Sugrue, *The Origins of the Urban Crisis: Race and Inequality in Postwar Detroit* (Princeton, N.J.: Princeton University Press, 1996).

11. "Truman Okays Plan for Camden Low-Rent Project," *Baltimore Afro-American*, December 22, 1951.

12. Alex F. Schwartz, *Housing Policy in the United States: An Introduction* (New York: Routledge, 2002), 51.

13. Testimony of Donald Griesmann, in *Intergovernmental Cooperation Act of 1967 and Related Legislation Hearings, before Subcommittee on Intergovernmental Relations* (Washington D.C.: U.S. Government Printing Office, 1968); *Centerville Area in Need of*

Redevelopment Study (Camden, N.J.: Division of Planning, Department of Development and Planning, and Hopeworks, 2003).

14. *U.S. Census of Housing, 1960* (Washington, D.C.: U.S. Department of Commerce, Bureau of the Census, 1961).

15. Sidorick, *Condensed Capitalism*, 8; Thomas Bogia, "The Minority Group Worker in Camden County," in *A Report Prepared for the New Jersey Department of Education Division against Discrimination* (Newark: New Jersey Department of Education, Division against Discrimination, 1954), 6; Anthony Vega, letter to Eulalio Torres, March 7, 1960, in Migrant Farm Labor in N.Y. and N.J.: The Puerto Rican Experience, 1948–1993, Regional and Field Office Farm Labor Files, box 857, F8, Archives of the Puerto Rican Diaspora, Centro de Estudios Puertorriqueños, Hunter College, CUNY.

16. Carmen Teresa Whalen, *From Puerto Rico to Philadelphia: Puerto Rican Workers and Postwar Economies* (Philadelphia: Temple University Press, 2001), 80.

17. "Groups Hit Camden Renewal in Detailed Letter to Johnson," *Courier-Post*, February 16, 1967; "Camden Segregation: A Matter of Choice?," *Courier-Post*, June 8, 1966; Gwen Simon Gain, *Confessions of a Fair-Housing Agitator: How the Hahas Came to South Jersey* (Bloomington, Ind.: Xlibris, 2011); Ande Diaz and Sonia S. Lee, "'I Was the One Percenter': Manny Diaz and the Beginnings of a Black–Puerto Rican Coalition," *Journal of American Ethnic History* 26, no. 3 (Spring 2007): 52–80.

18. Audrey Smedley and Brian D. Smedley, *Race in North America: Origin and Evolution of a Worldview* (Boulder, Colo.: Westview, 2012), 31.

19. "What the Branches Are Doing," *Crisis* 66, no. 10 (1964): 687; Laura Briggs, *Reproducing Empire: Race, Sex, Science, and U.S. Imperialism in Puerto Rico* (Berkeley: University of California Press, 2002), 172; Camden Metropolitan Ministry (hereafter CMM) Notes, "Documentation of the Need for Community Organization in Camden, N.J.," October 1967, Gillette Collection, Camden County Historical Society, Camden, N.J. (hereafter CCHS).

20. CMM Notes, "Documentation of the Need for Community Organization"; Malik Chaka, interview with author, August 10, 2010; Donald Griesmann, interview with author, February 2, 2011; CMM Ad Council, minutes, February 23, 1967, box 1, Presbytery of West Jersey, CMM Records, 1964–1979, Presbyterian Historical Society, Philadelphia, Pa.; "Brown Rattles Sabres at Convention Hall Rally," *Courier-Post*, August 31, 1967.

21. "Camden Civil Rights Activist Looks Back," *Philadelphia Inquirer*, March 19, 1993; "Police, Protesters Clash at City Hall," *Courier-Post*, June 14, 1968; *Intergovernmental Cooperation Act of 1967 and Related Legislation Hearings*.

22. "An Addendum for the '70s," December 1969, CMM Records; Vic Jameson to Lawrence Black, William McGregor, Kenneth G. Neigh, Lawrence McMaster, and Charles Leber, 1969, CMM Records; Chaka, interview with author; Amos Johnson, interview with author, February 20, 2010; Griesmann, interview with author.

23. Howard Gillette, *Camden after the Fall: Decline and Renewal in a Post-Industrial*

City (Philadelphia: University of Pennsylvania Press, 2005), 83; Carter, "Hispanic Rioting."

24. Griesmann, interview with author.

25. "Police in Camden Warned by Chief," *New York Times*, July 9, 1968.

26. Clement Quieroz, interview with Deborah Velez, July 16, 1989, "Camden City" box, CCHS.

27. Statement of Sgt. Richard Conrad Hailet, August 18, 1971, Prosecutor's File; "A Policeman Prays—and Remembers," *Courier-Post*, March 12, 1974; "On His Way to Viet Nam: City Youth, 20, Bids Dad Goodbye at Hospital," *Courier-Post*, August 16, 1966.

28. "Yeager to Mario: 5 Minutes," *Courier-Post*, August 20, 1971.

29. Statement of Sgt. Richard Conrad Hailet; "A Policeman Prays—and Remembers"; "On His Way to Viet Nam"; "Black Police Lash Out at 'Nightstick Bullies' on Force," *Courier-Post*, August 14, 1971.

30. "Five Charge Police Brutality."

31. "20 Hurt, 40 Jailed in Camden Rioting," *Courier-Post*, August 20, 1971.

32. Gualberto Medina, interview with author, September 11, 2012.

33. Ibid.; Gualberto Medina, interview with author, September 9, 2010.

34. Medina, interview with author, September 9, 2010.

35. Whalen, *From Puerto Rico to Philadelphia*, 231.

36. Ibid., 151; Lorrin Thomas, *Puerto Rican Citizen: History and Political Identity in Twentieth Century New York City* (Chicago: University of Chicago Press, 2010), 345; Jeffrey Ogbar, "Puerto Rico en Mi Corazón: The Young Lords, Black Power, and Puerto Rican Nationalism in the U.S., 1966–1972," *Centro Journal* (Spring 2006): 151; Murray Kempton, *The Briar Patch: The Trial of the Panther 21* (Cambridge, Mass.: Da Capo, 1997).

37. Medina, interview with author, September 9, 2010.

38. "Both Sides Disclaim Riot Responsibility: The Protesters," *Courier-Post*, August 20, 1971.

39. "Yeager Hints Riot a Possible Plot," *Courier-Post*, August 20, 1971.

40. Ibid.

41. "20 Hurt, 40 Jailed"; Joseph Rodriguez, interview with Kevin Walker, October 3, 2006, "Camden City," box 1, CCHS; Joseph Rodriguez, interview with Howard Gillette, February 9, 1998, Gillette Collection, CCHS.

42. "Both Sides Disclaim Riot Responsibility."

43. Rodriguez, interview with Gillette.

44. "20 Hurt, 40 Jailed"; "Both Sides Disclaim Riot Responsibility."

45. "20 Hurt, 40 Jailed"; "Both Sides Disclaim Riot Responsibility"; "Businessmen Put Blame for Riots on Nardi," *Courier-Post*, August 23, 1971; Medina, interview with author, September 9, 2010; Gillette, *Camden after the Fall*, 85; "Rioting Deepened Camden's Divisions," *Courier-Post*, February 1, 2007; "Camden Put to the Torch, Can't Keep Count of Fires," *Courier-Post*, August 21, 1971; "18 Injured in Camden Violence during

Protest against Police," *New York Times*, August 21, 1971; "Baby Girl Can Only Cringe, Cry," *Courier-Post*, August 21, 1971.

46. "Businessmen Put Blame for Riots on Nardi."

47. "Both Sides Disclaim Riot Responsibility."

48. "Yeager Hints Riot a Possible Plot"; "20 Hurt, 40 Jailed."

49. Medina, interview with author, September 11, 2012; "New Riots Also Blamed on Nardi," *Courier-Post*, August 21, 1971; "Burning Camden: A Hell for Cops," ibid.; Rodriguez, interview with Gillette.

50. Administrative Council, CMM, memo to Committee on National Mission, Presbytery of West Jersey, n.d.; Phillip Kelly, "Letter to Richard Whitman," October 6, 1971; "The Crisis Communication Network: An Evaluation," n.d.; "Some Thoughts about Community Organization and Some Suggestions about Working with Spanish Speaking People," n.d.; CMM Ad Council, minutes, September 23, 1971, 2, all in CMM Records.

51. "Judge Joseph M. Nardi Jr. Dead at 71," *Courier-Post*, November 25, 2003.

52. "Proclamation," *Courier-Post*, August 21, 1971; "Both Sides Agree on Mediation," ibid.; "Rioting Deepened Camden's Divisions," ibid., February 1, 2007.

53. "Camden Still Struggles to Regain Lost Glory," *Courier-Post*, April 8, 2003.

54. "Businessmen Put Blame for Riots on Nardi."

55. Medina, interview with author, September 9, 2010.

CHAPTER 9

Forgotten Residents Fighting Back

The Ludlow Community Association and Neighborhood Improvement in Philadelphia

ALYSSA RIBEIRO

> The harmony that has been achieved by the Black and Spanish-speaking residents would not be present but for the efforts of Marvin Louis and his bilingual staff.
>
> "Philadelphia Urban Coalition: Service Roles"

In April 1966 a local television station, WFIL, shocked its audience with a provocative film documenting the ills of Ludlow, an inner-city neighborhood in North Philadelphia. *Assignment: 1747 Randolph Street* used the brutal gang rape of a black female crossing guard in 1965 as a narrative device to detail the area's dilapidated physical conditions and gang influence. Meanwhile, the film profiled local leaders pushing for change. During three months of research, news director Joe Phipps and cameraman Art Ciocco had found a "strange juxtaposition of hope and despair." Though the area was a "forgotten slum," its residents were "fighting back." The house at 1747 Randolph Street was razed during the filming, symbolizing both Ludlow's previous neglect and future possibilities.[1]

Assignment: 1747 Randolph Street immediately drew the city's attention to little-known Ludlow, an integrated area of black and Puerto Rican settlement. Airing just after an episode of the popular *Batman* television series and promoted heavily beforehand, the film reached an estimated audience of six hundred thousand. Hundreds of viewers wrote to the station about the film. Capitalizing on the publicity, a neighborhood organization called the Ludlow Community Association (LCA) actively pushed for local improvements from the mid-1960s through the 1970s, making significant progress in recreation and housing. In the process, the LCA created organizational, physical, and social spaces that brought black and Puerto Rican residents together.[2]

This chapter describes the LCA's organizational development and its efforts to improve life in Ludlow. A focus on one neighborhood organization tackling one area's problems brings researchers closer to street level, where countless day-to-day interactions took place between black and Puerto Rican residents. It also emphasizes the power of place in creating shared material conditions that might serve as the basis for integrated activism. The LCA consciously tried to reflect Ludlow's diversity and chose to concentrate on local resources in which residents of all colors had a stake. By effectively reaching a mixed population using place-based concerns, the LCA's efforts show the possibilities of united black and Puerto Rican activism at the neighborhood level.

Ludlow is not unique. It serves as another example of the harmonious black-Latino relations that historian Albert Camarillo describes as occurring "under the radar," where they fail to draw the outside attention or media coverage that conflict does. Studies of Compton and Chicago also suggest that grassroots connections based on shared neighborhood concerns can be particularly fruitful in areas where residents feel that their existing political representation is inadequate. Attention to the LCA's efforts in North Philadelphia bears out these observations. The LCA both benefited from and helped to foster relatively good daily relations between blacks and Puerto Ricans. At the same time, the LCA's activist stance made it an agent of change for black and Puerto Rican residents who could not effectively mobilize city resources on their own.[3]

BUILDING AN INTEGRATED COMMUNITY ORGANIZATION

Philadelphia's Ludlow neighborhood is located about a mile north of Center City. In the early twentieth century, the area had textile mills, factories, and warehouses surrounded by dense blocks of two- and three-story row houses. At one time home to Jewish, German, and Hungarian populations, Ludlow experienced rapid white flight and deindustrialization by the mid-twentieth century. As white homeowners left, many row houses were subdivided, the black population increased, and Puerto Rican migrants moved into the area. Uprooted by redevelopment in surrounding areas, some black and Puerto Rican residents relocated to Ludlow in search of affordable housing. By the late 1960s, Ludlow housed 12,500 residents in seventy-eight blocks. Railroad tracks running along Ludlow's west side left it relatively isolated from other parts of North Philadelphia. The Philadelphia Gas Works plant sat near the northern edge of the neighborhood, and a rapidly expanding Temple University was overtaking residential areas to the northwest. Ludlow's population at that time was about 45 percent black, 47 percent Puerto Rican, and 8 percent white or Asian.[4]

Assignment: 1747 Randolph Street found a bleak scene in Ludlow that would have looked familiar to countless inner-city residents. The majority of the housing stock was substandard, and 20 percent of the neighborhood's structures were vacant. Children played in trash-strewn alleys or vacant lots, and disabled vehicles sat at many a curb. Contentious relations with police made concerns about crime all the more vexing. The film's portrayal of long-standing neighborhood problems, however, elevated the leadership role of the LCA in pushing for change.

The Ludlow Civic Association, later renamed the Ludlow Community Association, was founded by Narcisa Cruz in 1960 as an outgrowth of the local home and school association. Cruz, originally from Guaynabo, Puerto Rico, had recently relocated to the area with her family after living in New York for thirteen years. The Cruzes lived just five blocks south of the address that would be featured in WFIL's film a few years later. Cruz quickly became involved in Ludlow, writing for the *Midtown Crier* newspaper. She organized the LCA because she felt "anxious to see all of the racially mixed residents of her part of North Philadelphia united in a common cause."[5] Cruz was also likely motivated by her own personal challenges. She and her husband, Ralph, continually struggled to provide for three orphans in addition to five children of their own. Ralph Cruz, a cabinetmaker, faced a seven-month stretch of unemployment in 1961 that was particularly hard on the family. The strain was ultimately too much for Narcisa Cruz, who took her own life in October 1961. Over 1,500 mourners attended her funeral, where she was called a "woman of greatness." At the time, observers described the LCA as one of the "first organizations . . . wherein Puerto Ricans might join together with people of other races and try to work as a group."[6]

After Cruz's death, LCA member Anne Colbert Louis helped convince her husband, Marvin Louis, to take over leadership of the organization. The couple had moved into a home on North Sixth Street in 1959, and Anne Louis, like Narcisa Cruz, quickly got involved in local organizations. Marvin Louis was at first reluctant to leave his job as a supervisor at Western Union to take on the low-paying and demanding presidency of the LCA, but he eventually agreed to try a six-month stint. The son of southern sharecroppers and a former welterweight boxer, Louis was determined and fearless as he set about "battling the system." The role stuck, and Louis went on to serve as the organization's public face and driving force for the next four decades. During those years, the LCA fostered a cooperative relationship between black and Puerto Rican residents and succeeded in obtaining concrete resources for the neighborhood, including a recreation center, better housing, and improved educational facilities.[7]

The LCA consciously strove for integrated involvement. At its second general meeting in 1961, the organization attracted an audience of three hundred and was commended by Mayor Richardson Dilworth for having a membership representative of "residents of the community of all races, religions, nationalities, political and social differences." When the group was considering goals and strategies later in the decade, Andrew Freeman of the Urban League urged the LCA to "make sure your membership continues to represent the total Ludlow community. There is room for all your residents. Negroes and Puerto Ricans—white and non-white." Maintaining integrated involvement was not always simple. When the LCA's Planning Committee held some meetings at Temple Presbyterian Church, no Puerto Ricans attended. When the committee moved the next meeting to the back room of a Puerto Rican restaurant, it drew substantial Puerto Rican attendance. A subsequent meeting at the church, though, again took place without any Puerto Ricans present. Committee members learned they would have to go "more than halfway" to get Puerto Ricans involved, possibly even carrying activities "to their doorsteps." The LCA circulated newsletters and flyers in both Spanish and English and drew on the translation abilities of bilingual volunteers.[8]

Promoting cultural exchange was another way that the organization sought to reach a diverse constituency. In the spring of 1968 the LCA joined with the Ludlow Home and School Association and the Singing City Choir to sponsor the Ludlow Folk Festival. The event drew "all kinds and colors of people" playing "folk songs, Latin songs, swingin' jazz songs, and spirituals," accompanied by a variety of dances. Emcee Leon Feliciano, who was active in the LCA's housing efforts, provided introductions in both English and Spanish. Feliciano told the crowd, "We need to get together like this more often. If we have good times together, we can get along like brothers."[9]

In the 1960s and 1970s, the basic needs and desires of Ludlow's black and Puerto Rican residents aligned, and the LCA played a strong role in uniting their efforts. Louis recalled that his Puerto Rican neighbors "wanted for their children and themselves the same as we did. We wanted a better community . . . because the housing was terrible as it could be . . . [and] kids would take to the streets. . . . Along with us, was the Puerto Ricans and blacks fighting together for the same cause." When asked about the issue of language, Louis explained, "Well, they didn't speak English . . . all that well, but you know everybody understood everybody, and . . . it was a language barrier but not to the extent where we couldn't work together and do things together and understand each other, no. In fact, it was a joint effort." Moments of tension and separation certainly occurred between Ludlow's black and Puerto Rican populations, but Louis recalled "no heavy buildup" between the groups, which remained focused on basic improvements.[10]

In the mid-1960s the LCA sought to further its goal of basic neighborhood improvement by getting involved in the War on Poverty and Model Cities programs. The organization ran a slate of candidates in the election for the neighborhood's Community Action Council, which would represent the interests of the local poor in the city's antipoverty efforts. The LCA's slate lost in a close contest to a slate with more white candidates led by Connie Galiczynski, which likely drew strong support from the adjacent neighborhood of Kensington. Frustrated by Galiczynski's ensuing reluctance to compromise, the LCA maintained tense relations with the local Community Action Council. The LCA and the Council of Black Youths eventually resorted to picketing the Philadelphia Antipoverty Action Commission's offices for more than a week. They claimed that Galiczynski was giving better services to residents on the east side of Fifth Street, which was a predominantly white area, compared to Ludlow and demanded her removal. The LCA's assertive posture did not preclude it from participating in the next round of antipoverty efforts. When the Model Cities program arrived in Philadelphia, the LCA was chosen as a "hub" location for distributing information and services to the neighborhood, reflecting its established reputation and reach.[11]

The LCA played a significant role in bringing *Assignment: 1747 Randolph Street* to fruition. The project arose after a social work student, David McDonald, who worked on local issues at the Friends Neighborhood Guild, grew frustrated with the excruciatingly slow pace of neighborhood improvement. McDonald approached WFIL-TV, where he piqued the interest of news director Joe Phipps and station manager George Koehler. Louis of the LCA and two representatives of the local Presbyterian church joined the second meeting with Phipps to give a two-hour account of Ludlow's condition. The film drew extensively on interviews with Louis and featured an LCA meeting. From the perspective of Koehler, "everybody had given up on the problem but the small group that formed the Ludlow Civic Association—and this group came to a television station and got results."[12]

By the summer of 1966, the film had further boosted LCA's profile, granting the organization greater leverage in its continuing negotiations with the city. The LCA became the prime point of local contact for city agencies and was asked to provide a comprehensive listing of vacant structures, abandoned vehicles, and poorly lit sites. City officials noted after a meeting with the LCA in May 1966 that residents were "quite active," producing "stepped-up interaction[s] between community groups." While turnout at earlier LCA meetings had been relatively low, over two hundred people were attending meetings in the wake of the film. The LCA had been "considerably strengthened" through the addition of new committees and greater resident involvement. With its membership tripled and a new sense of momentum, the LCA established an office at the Temple Presbyterian Parish House. It was also around this time that the organization changed its name, replacing "Civic" with "Community." The LCA explained that the new name better reflected "what we want to be—an association of, by, and for all the people of the Ludlow Community!"[13]

The LCA's larger profile not only helped it negotiate with the city, but also drew outside support. A predominantly white church in suburban Wayne soon partnered with the LCA to rehabilitate neighborhood housing. Building on its sponsorship of the film, the Philadelphia Gas Works helped fund other LCA efforts. As the LCA's influence and access to funding grew, it continued to use a mixture of political and protest strategies. According to Louis, the organization did "what most people do. We did protests, went down and fought with City Hall. And we also went to the state asking them and protesting."[14]

The LCA accepted external support while also striving to remain true to its grassroots origins; the balance was sometimes difficult to maintain. The group secured funding to hire a full-time community organizer in 1966. Helen Helfer, a white Bryn Mawr graduate who had worked previously with the Philadelphia Antipoverty Action Commission, filled the position. The LCA had high hopes for Helfer's efforts, envisioning her role as working to build relationships with neighborhood people and helping to foster unity. The top priority for her and a Spanish-speaking aide was "time, effort, and thought . . . given to organize Community people around issues that concern them." The LCA wanted Helfer to spend the majority of her time in the area "walking, observing, listening, talking to people in streets, homes, stores, barber shops, bars, etc.," with particular attention to residents who "were not normally attracted to 'respectable' social activities." In time, the LCA expected Helfer's role to be less prominent as indigenous leadership developed. Helfer, though, had a different conception of her job, once describing herself as "a lobbyist for the community." She attended meetings of numerous organizations in the area, but otherwise did not spend enough time with residents to please the LCA; she tended to focus on working through official channels. After two attempts to redirect Helfer's efforts, the LCA decided to fire her in August 1967.[15]

The split with Helfer reflected class tensions between her background and education and the life experiences of established LCA leaders. While the LCA wanted help in improving the neighborhood, it was reluctant to let an outsider exert too much control over those efforts. The organization had a similar falling out with a consultant hired to handle a massive rent strike in Ludlow in 1968. William R. Mimms, the executive director of the National Fair Housing Association, at first seemed like a good fit to manage the strike because of his expertise and leadership of tenants at the nearby Jefferson Manor Apartments. But the LCA became unsatisfied with Mimms's level of involvement in the neighborhood and criticized his continued overtures to tenants living outside of Ludlow. Ultimately, the organization terminated Mimms's role in the strike a month prior to the end of his contract.[16]

To further ensure grassroots involvement in the neighborhood's struggles, the LCA actively encouraged the organization of block clubs, featuring updates on these efforts in its newsletters. These clubs worked close to home to clean the streets and beautify the area. They also held social events and tried to find safe play areas and activities for youth. The actions of these groups had multiple benefits: residents gained a sense of accomplishment, built relationships with their neighbors, and even demonstrated to city officials that they were willing to work and were not to blame for poor conditions in the area.[17]

While balancing the goals of an integrated membership, grassroots relevancy, and tangible neighborhood changes, the LCA set about a broad campaign to improve Ludlow in the 1960s and 1970s. Improved recreation and housing were the LCA's top priorities, but the organization also made smaller contributions in a number of other areas. Like other community groups of the time, the LCA never viewed itself as a single-issue organization, but instead used an array of strategies to make Ludlow more livable.

CREATING SAFE PLACES TO PLAY

The LCA struggled for twelve years to secure a recreation center for the neighborhood. Inadequate play spaces had been a primary focus of the LCA ever since founder Narcisa Cruz wrote an article titled "The Boys on the Corner" for the *Midtown Crier* newspaper. As in other inner-city neighborhoods with comparatively young populations, safe recreation arose as a catchall solution to concerns about juvenile delinquency and fears of racial violence. Informal youth gathering sites like street corners and sidewalks posed a threat in the eyes of many adults, who supported the creation of more structured spaces where young people could congregate. Recreation programs were seen as a way to divert youth from street gangs, drug use, and other destructive behavior.[18]

Lacking safe play spaces, youths created their own stand-in recreation sites in ways that exacerbated concerns over neighborhood conditions. The LCA worked, for instance, to have the city tear down an abandoned industrial building at Marshall and Oxford Streets that had last been used by the Volunteers of America to bundle clothing donations. The city was slow to act on tearing the building down, and tragedy struck. A young girl drowned in a pit filled with rainwater after stopping to play in the structure on her way home from school. In a less severe case, a five-year-old boy was cut by falling glass while playing on the steps of an abandoned house on Oxford Street. Incidents like these raised community ire over the dangers of vacant buildings. In addition to safety hazards, abandoned structures also provided cover for youths drinking, using drugs, or sniffing glue. As Louis put it, kids had "nowhere to go" and were bound to "get into something if they ha[d] to roam the streets." Formal recreation sites, then, seemed to offer solutions to a number of urban problems.[19]

In the early 1960s the LCA made only halting progress on improving recreation facilities. The organization regularly approached City Hall, only to come away with empty promises. Even when City Councilman Gaetano Giordano promised the organization land for a recreation center in 1963, the funds dried up, and the LCA had to settle for a tot lot constructed in June 1964. Resenting a resource available only to small children, older youths vandalized the equipment and asked, "When are you going to get something for us?" The LCA continued to press for a recreation center.[20]

The long struggle for a recreation center had integrated community support. The LCA's leader, Marvin Louis, reflected, "[We were] in agreement that we needed the recreation on both sides, both Puerto Ricans and blacks . . . because the only place that they had to go was to the streets, and it wasn't working out well." In negotiating with the city for the construction of a comprehensive community center, the LCA used its diversity as an asset. Louis explained, "Our neighborhood is unique in that our population represents many racial and religious groups, and we strongly feel that a community facility will not only [enhance] our inter-group relationships [in] Ludlow, but will also draw from the surrounding areas, thus [enhancing] economic integration as well." Among the priorities for inclusion in the community center were a language lab intended to help Spanish speakers learn English, day care, and space for social services.[21]

Publicity generated by *Assignment: 1747 Randolph Street* helped push the city into taking action on a recreation center for Ludlow. The process had previously been hampered primarily by cost and location. The film inspired the city to look into federal funding, and officials soon secured a million-dollar development grant from the Department of Housing and Urban Development. As a stopgap measure during the lengthy planning process, the city installed pocket parks on some vacant Ludlow corners. With funding finally secured, site selection for the recreation center became a thorny issue. The density of structures in Ludlow meant that a block had to be cleared and repurposed. The recommended plot at Sixth and Master Streets was home to Vance Furniture Warehouse Company and Perry Equipment Company. Vance relocated to another portion of the city, but Perry presented more of a problem. The company employed a number of local residents and had recently expanded during a time when many other local enterprises were relocating or shutting down. The LCA was reluctant to lose local jobs in its pursuit of recreation, but felt the site was still the best option available, especially due to its close proximity to Ludlow Community School. In the end, Perry moved its operations to Puerto Rico, and construction of the recreation center proceeded, funded by the federal grant and matching money from the state.[22]

Ludlow's long-awaited recreation center was dedicated in the summer of 1973 with a crowd of two thousand in attendance. The center included a baseball field, basketball courts, a track, weightlifting facilities, and a small building for meetings and services. Use of the center was heavy. Columnist Rose DeWolf noted, "The recreation center at 6th and Master Sts was jumping the other night. It always is. There were dozens of kids on the playground, hundreds more watching a baseball game. Last summer, when the center was new, it was nothing for 2,000 people to be there in one night." The LCA was pleased to see the center become a reality, but the organization remained steadfast in its desire for a swimming pool, which would provide a respite from the summer heat and discourage residents from opening fire hydrants. Under continued pressure from the LCA, the city followed through and added the swimming pool a year later. With the center built, the LCA ran a youth program there called Ludlow Crusaders, involving children in sports, dance, and other activities to counter the appeal of gang activities. Louis pointed out that programs like the Crusaders not only kept youth busy, but "made the parents active, too." Eventually, to counter the damage caused by automobiles driving on the playing fields at night, the LCA successfully pressed the city to add a fence around the perimeter.[23]

In securing the recreation center, which would later be named after the LCA's founder, Narcisa Cruz, the LCA added a major resource to a relatively neglected area. The LCA's activism supplied black and Puerto Rican youth not only with safer places to play, but also with a shared space in which they could develop deeper social connections.

PROVIDING ADEQUATE HOUSING

In addition to pushing for a recreation center, the LCA crusaded for better housing. The organization attacked the problem at all levels, doing everything from distributing extra blankets in the winter to negotiating rehabilitation and new construction projects. One neighbor, Syreeta Broadnax, remembered, "If you had a problem with housing, [Marvin Louis] could get you whatever you needed—like that." From the 1960s forward, the LCA played a critical role in attending to Ludlow's housing needs.[24]

Black and Puerto Rican residents in areas like Ludlow shared an uphill struggle in improving their living conditions. Many row houses that originally housed one family had been subdivided to house multiple families, ensuring greater profits for property owners. Landlords further maximized their profits by neglecting basic maintenance and repairs, leaving their tenants to suffer the consequences or find a new address. Eventually, some owners simply abandoned their properties rather than deal with upkeep and tax obligations, and the number of vacant houses in North Philadelphia steadily increased from the 1950s through the 1980s. In the face of this property abandonment, the Philadelphia Housing Authority (PHA) became a prominent landlord in Ludlow, using rehabilitated row houses to house low-income tenants. But scattered-site public housing was vulnerable to vandalism, and it was not unusual, for instance, to find that electrical wiring had been ripped out. In one survey, the Department of Licenses and Inspections (L&I) found that 93 percent of Ludlow dwellings violated the housing code.[25]

The city lacked the financial and personnel resources to deal with the large number of deteriorating and abandoned houses. Responses to complaints were generally slow and unsatisfactory, assuming residents got any response at all. Even as the city surveyed problems in Ludlow, it had fifteen vacant positions on the sanitation staff, five rodent control crews had to serve ten health districts, and the existing staff was "overtaxed." City officials were also quick to point out that instead of simply blaming the government, community groups should criticize their neighbors for acts of vandalism. L&I representative David Valentine said, "I personally recognize that no one from [a wealthier area like] Chestnut Hill is coming into Ludlow to vandalize a building or to rip it down or to rip out the plumbing. I feel the community association would do itself and its community a great justice if it took hold of the people it represents and impressed the fact upon them that they too have an obligation to care for their community." City neglect was so routine that when officials made efforts to exterminate rats and clean up, residents worried that the sudden attention was a prelude to redevelopment that would push them out of the neighborhood.[26]

Absent a forceful city response, the LCA and Ludlow residents took matters into their own hands, employing a combination of strategies to improve North Philadelphia's housing landscape. Wielding financial leverage was one of their primary tactics. In November 1967 the LCA launched a large rent strike intended to take landlords to task for neglecting their properties. Because landlords often owned multiple properties, sometimes under different names, the group correlated ownership records using computerized assistance, an impressive feat for a small community organization at the time. Tenants took part in the strike by paying rent into an escrow account managed by the LCA. Rent monies were held for up to six months, and if the landlord did not bring the property into compliance, the LCA returned the funds to the tenant. Mr. and Mrs. Santiago Acevedo Elias joined the rent strike because of their landlord's delays in repairing a leaking roof. Showing a reporter around her home, Mrs. Elias commented, "Viva la rent strike." The LCA eventually filed suit against thirteen particularly egregious slumlords.[27]

Pennsylvania's rent withholding law helped tenants gain influence over delinquent landlords. But in order for tenants to qualify, their dwelling had to be declared unfit for habitation by L&I. Jesus Sierra, an L&I inspector who also served as the president of the Council of Spanish Speaking Organizations, explained that political pressure had changed inspection criteria, requiring more violations for a house to be declared unfit than in the past. Moreover, city fines were so low—$25 in the late 1960s—that landlords had little incentive to comply. By 1977 Louis was fed up with the process. Getting L&I approval was simply too slow, so the LCA decided to begin holding rent in escrow itself, even though this action skirted legal procedures. Louis stated, "Anyone who tries to evict people whose escrow is being held will have to fight us. We'll fight them legally first and then physically."[28]

In addition to withholding rent and pressing for more stringent code enforcement, the LCA fought for rent supplement appropriations for new apartments in order to keep Ludlow housing affordable. Louis, echoing the thoughts of many low-income residents, felt the city was "deliberately allowing certain neighborhoods to die and forcing area residents to flee so middle-class suburbanites can move in." This type of neighborhood "recycling" had already taken place in parts of nearby Spring Garden, and it seemed like Ludlow might be next on the list. City officials recognized the existence of a "general paranoid feeling in the community" about recycling. Throughout its housing efforts, the LCA tried to ensure that existing Ludlow residents could stay in the area.[29]

Meanwhile, the LCA pressed the city to address the dangers of vacant houses. Abandoned, decaying structures became havens for drug users and safety hazards for children. In one high-profile case, an elderly woman was raped and murdered after her assailants accessed her apartment through a vacant home. When boarding up the structures seemed insufficient, the LCA pushed for demolition. Razing was complicated, however, by the fact that most dwellings were row houses. Even when neighbors succeeded in having L&I tear down a dilapidated house, if its adjoining wall was not promptly patched, the adjacent house was exposed to weather and also deteriorated.[30]

The LCA also played a direct role in housing rehabilitation and construction projects. The organization's activism coalesced with the PHA's interest in pursuing scattered-site public housing and the city's nascent Urban Homesteading program. In one effort, the LCA partnered with members of the Central Baptist Church in suburban Wayne to transform old homes into new apartments. A major project undertaken by the LCA, North City Corporation, and the PHA sought to renovate four hundred homes and eventually provide affordable housing for nine hundred families. In reality, the renovation process was slow and rehabilitation results often fell short. One set of houses had locks installed that all used the same key, presenting a grave security risk to the occupants. In many of the rehabilitation efforts, a combination of overcrowding, shoddy workmanship, and vandalism gave the properties a short lifespan. The LCA's relationship with the PHA was often troubled. The organization could not dissuade the PHA from pursuing projects in areas impacted by a raucous bar and the drug trade. And Ludlow residents were displeased that the PHA placed so many families from outside the area in the rehabilitated units, claiming they did not mix well with the existing community. Meanwhile, the Urban Homesteading program, which should have allowed more individuals to rehabilitate vacant houses, drew sharp criticism for political favoritism in the distribution of properties.[31]

The LCA's housing successes were partial. Rehabilitation was no panacea, and much of the remaining housing stock deteriorated further over time. Yet the LCA's consistent, vocal efforts to wrest more housing resources from the city, often covered by the local newspapers, called more attention to code enforcement and spurred rehabilitation and construction. In the late 1990s Louis's efforts finally paid off in the first new construction of single-family homes in the neighborhood in a century.[32]

ATTENDING TO BASIC NEEDS

The LCA made numerous other contributions to the community's well-being by looking out for the basic needs of residents. Women affiliated with the organization, for instance, opened a thrift store to help clothe poor children in the neighborhood, drawing on volunteer labor and clothing donated by a white suburban church. On cold winter nights, Louis recalled, "we used to be out in the middle of the night with heaters and blankets, taking them door to door and giving them to people that really needed them."[33]

The LCA also pushed for educational improvements, working closely with Ludlow Elementary School, which served nine hundred students in kindergarten through sixth grade. In 1964 a limited arrangement at the school helped Puerto Rican students learn English with guidance in Spanish, while English-dominant students were gradually taught Spanish. School officials felt that the "integration of languages . . . helped with racial relations." When asked their thoughts on the program, a group of black mothers in Ludlow said they were pleased their children were learning Spanish, noting that they could now better relate to the Puerto Rican kids on the block. Yet bilingual programs could not overcome all the racial tensions at the school. A janitor

Manuel Perez and Chester Price install lights in the Ludlow Community Association's thrift shop in North Philadelphia in March 1968. Photograph from *Philadelphia Inquirer*, March 3, 1968. George D. McDowell Philadelphia Evening Bulletin Photographs Collection, Special Collections Research Center, Temple University Libraries, Philadelphia, Pa.

noted "many problems between the Negroes and the Puerto Ricans" in 1968, which he attributed mainly to the "disrespectful" and "negative attitude" displayed by the Puerto Rican boys.[34]

In 1966 Ludlow Elementary School became Ludlow Community School, one of four community schools started in the city at that time. *Assignment: 1747 Randolph Street* helped secure the school's spot in the program. Community schools were intended to be agents of neighborhood change, the center of a "constellation" of services and programs for old and young. In Ludlow, the school housed legal services and English language classes for Spanish-speaking adults and at times provided meeting space for the LCA. The school employed two community coordinators to help solve family problems; Anne Colbert Louis, the wife of LCA president Marvin Louis, held one of these positions. Maria Quiñones, who also worked at the school, noted the importance of her role in countering the alienation of Spanish-speaking families. When funding for the school's human services program was endangered, the LCA appealed to the school board and gained a reprieve. In addition, the LCA helped the school obtain a new addition and secured construction of a public library branch.[35]

The LCA also worked to protect Ludlow residents. In the early 1970s black and Puerto Rican students were encountering regular harassment on their way home from Penn Treaty Junior High School, located in a predominantly white area of Kensington that was fiercely resistant to residential integration. Louis recalled that when the school day ended, "they would have young men and all waiting outside the school and on Girard Avenue, and beating the kids, hitting them with chains, siccing dogs on them, and things like that." The LCA protested the situation, meeting with police, the school, and other community groups to find a way to protect black and Puerto Rican students. Their answer was a "safety corridor" that used buses to transport kids from Ludlow Community School to Penn Treaty and back. Some white residents resented the safety corridor's implementation, and Louis recalled one occasion when he and a few companions arrived to find three hundred protesters amassed outside of Penn Treaty. When the bus service was temporarily suspended in 1973, fourteen-year-old Julio Osorio drowned on the way home from school, possibly as a result of harassment by young white assailants. Amid community furor, Mayor Frank Rizzo reinstated the buses.[36]

Teenage violence, much of it gang related, was another pressing neighborhood issue. The brutal attack on the black woman working as a crossing guard recounted in *Assignment: 1747 Randolph Street* was only one vivid example. Dissatisfied with the inadequate police protection, the LCA took matters into its own hands, sending neighborhood men armed with clubs on nightly patrols. The scheme quickly drew the assignment of additional police to the area. Louis felt so strongly about community defense that he resigned from the board of the Friends Neighborhood Guild when the organization refused to purchase ax handles for citizen patrols.[37]

The LCA's activism encouraged others in the neighborhood to step forward and address the need for more responsive medical care. Three community residents pooled funds to donate a used ambulance to the neighborhood in an era before emergency medical services reached poorer, inner-city communities. Previously, local medical emergencies had to wait for police transport. The LCA planned to find volunteer drivers for the ambulance and keep it available around the clock. The organization also set up a blood drive with the Red Cross to ensure an adequate blood supply for Ludlow residents.[38]

Over time, the LCA also became involved with supporting prisoners from the area. Louis was originally called in 1970 to help in the case of a young boy from nearby Fishtown who had received an excessively long sentence. He began to make regular Saturday visits to Graterford, a state correctional facility located about thirty miles northwest of Philadelphia. Word got around, other inmates asked to see Louis, and a prison project emerged. Louis recalled, "That went on for years. . . . We had Hispanic prisoners up there, but at that time they didn't have anybody representing them. So what I would do, I would take one of my Spanish workers up there with me to translate whatever I had to have translated. And I worked with them, and like everybody else I went to commutation hearings and all. And eventually, [they] made me external president of a Latin prisoners' rights group that was incarcerated at Graterford." Louis regularly brought the families and friends of inmates along on his visits to the prison. Louis and the LCA protested when the state decided to relocate the dental training program for Graterford inmates, noting that it was one of the few transitional programs left in an era of budget slashing.[39]

By partnering with Ludlow Community School and attending to the safety and health of Ludlow residents, the LCA further cemented its role as the go-to organization in the neighborhood. It maintained an office for more than forty years, until the PHA-owned space that had housed the organization from the 1980s into the 2000s was leveled to make room for housing construction. Louis regretted the loss of the LCA's office, because he liked to store food and supplies there to be distributed as needed. Countless Ludlow residents benefited from the LCA's multilayered approach to activism, which remained cognizant of the community's short- and long-term needs.[40]

CONCLUSIONS

Beginning in the 1960s the LCA worked for the interests of both black and Puerto Rican residents. The organization learned to "push on city officials, threaten, wheedle, [and] cajole" in its quest for neighborhood improvement. Columnist Rose DeWolf wrote in the early 1970s that "whatever help Ludlow gets or has gotten in the past . . . can be largely credited to the efforts of Marvin Louis and the Ludlow Civic Association of which he is president. . . . Louis rallied the people and they began to demand some action." This activism continued in subsequent decades, and at the time of Louis's death in 2011, younger residents were hopeful that someone could fill his shoes in advocating for the neighborhood, although the organization he led no longer exists.[41]

The LCA's integrated nature and achievements benefited in part from timing. During the LCA's peak years of activity, the local Puerto Rican population was growing but still relatively small, and at the time no Puerto Rican organizations had developed within the boundaries of Ludlow. Louis explained, "At that time, yeah, we represented the Puerto Rican community. . . . We had . . . Hispanic members, a lot of them. But now they're well organized, and we don't have that much input in what they do." Moreover, in capitalizing on a film's publicity in 1966, the LCA benefited from funding that might not have been as forthcoming in subsequent years. As federal priorities changed and municipal budgets suffered, resources like recreation centers became even harder for neighborhoods to attain.[42]

Though progress was slow and incomplete, the LCA obtained an impressive number of physical enhancements in the neighborhood, including a recreation center, rehabilitated housing, an expanded community school, and an ambulance. Just as significantly, it provided spaces for residents to mix socially. The efforts of the LCA, then, show not only how blacks and Puerto Ricans could unite in neighborhood activism, but also how the results of that activism could encourage stronger ties between black and Puerto Rican neighbors. In 1979 an Urban Coalition report commented on the peaceful race relations in Ludlow: "The harmony that has been achieved by the Black and Spanish-speaking residents would not be present but for the efforts of Marvin Louis and his bilingual staff."[43] Long after *Assignment: 1747 Randolph Street* grabbed Philadelphia's attention, the LCA worked tirelessly to shift

Ludlow's balance of hope and despair by engineering physical improvements while encouraging social ties.

Ludlow offers several lessons about the broader landscape of black-Latino relations and activism. The LCA and similar organizations in integrated areas can form part of a feedback loop, in which they both arise out of and help to create harmonious intergroup relations. This happens in part because a manageable geographic area allows small organizations like the LCA to know many of their neighbors and bridge potential divides on an individual level. But it may still take strategic efforts to ensure diverse participation. A small organization's conscious use of bilingual staff and promotional materials can help reduce communication barriers, and varying meeting sites can draw different participants. Framing its goals as benefiting all residents in a given area, as the LCA did with recreation and housing, can help an organization reduce the potential for competition over resources. This strategy is particularly effective if organizations can build credibility among both local residents and policymakers. The savvy use of local media, as the LCA displayed with the documentary film and regular newspaper coverage, can help raise an organization's profile at all levels and make its goals more attainable. Overall, the LCA's efforts provide a model for local activism to improve not only neighborhood conditions but black-Latino relations as well.

NOTES

The epigraph is from "Philadelphia Urban Coalition: Service Roles, Six Months Ended November 30, 1979," 1979, 11, box 17, folder 4, MSS 114, Spanish Merchants Association, Historical Society of Pennsylvania, Philadelphia.

1. Joe K. Phipps and Art Ciocco, *Assignment: 1747 Randolph Street* (Philadelphia: WFIL-TV, 1966), filmstrip, Public Affairs Programming, WPVI-TV, Channel 6, Special Collections Research Center, Temple University Libraries, Philadelphia (hereafter SCRC); Joe K. Phipps, *"Assignment: 1747 Randolph St": A Call to Community Action* (Philadelphia: WFIL-TV, 1966), promotional materials, 1, 15A, bound volume, University of Pennsylvania Libraries, Philadelphia.

2. Phipps, *"Assignment: 1747 Randolph St"*, promotional materials, 4–5, 15, 17.

3. Albert M. Camarillo, "Cities of Color: The New Racial Frontier in California's Minority-Majority Cities," *Pacific Historical Review* 76, no. 1 (2007): 27; Camarillo, "Black and Brown in Compton: Demographic Change, Suburban Decline, and Intergroup Relations in a South Central Los Angeles Community, 1950–2000," in *Not Just Black and White: Historical and Contemporary Perspectives on Immigration, Race, and Ethnicity in the United States*, ed. Nancy Foner and George M. Fredrickson (New York:

Russell Sage Foundation, 2004), 372; John J. Betancur and Douglas C. Gills, "The African American and Latino Coalition Experience in Chicago under Mayor Harold Washington," in *The Collaborative City: Opportunities and Struggles for Blacks and Latinos in U.S. Cities*, ed. John J. Betancur and Douglas C. Gills (New York: Garland, 2000), 63.

4. Ludlow's rough boundaries were Montgomery Avenue and Girard Avenue on the north and south and Germantown Avenue and Ninth Street on the east and west. Phipps, *Assignment: 1747 Randolph Street*, preface; "3 Men Donate Ambulance to Serve Ludlow Area," *Philadelphia Evening Bulletin*, April 11, 1968, Ludlow Community Activities Center, Philadelphia Evening Bulletin Newspaper Clipping Collection (hereafter Bulletin Clippings), SCRC.

5. "First Ludlow Folk Festival Held," *Philadelphia Tribune*, June 25, 1968.

6. Nancy Giddens, "Hundreds Mourn the Death of Narcisa Cruz," *Philadelphia Tribune*, October 7, 1961.

7. Marvin Louis, interview by author, November 9, 2009, transcript, 15–16; Larry Copeland, "Ludlow's Urban Tiger Is Still Fighting after 30 Years of Activism," *Philadelphia Inquirer*, November 29, 1993; Cherri Gregg, "Ludlow: A Community Struggles to Find a New Leader," *Philadelphia Neighborhoods*, June 27, 2011, Multimedia Urban Reporting Lab, Temple University, http://philadelphianeighborhoods.com/2011/06/27/ludlow-a-community-struggles-to-find-a-new-leader/ (accessed January 25, 2014).

8. "Mayor Speaks at Meeting of Ludlow Group," *Philadelphia Tribune*, July 11, 1961; Andrew G. Freeman, "Community Goals: The Ludlow Civic Association," May 24, 1966, 4, 8, box 17, folder 174, URB 16, Urban League, SCRC; "Ludlow: Options for Action," August 1966, 15, box 17, folder 176, URB 16, Urban League, SCRC.

9. Betty L. Medsger, "Ludlow Residents Dance and Sing on a Parking Lot," *Philadelphia Evening Bulletin*, May 26, 1968, Ludlow—Phila. Section, Bulletin Clippings, SCRC.

10. Marvin Louis, interview by author, November 6, 2009, transcript, 3–4.

11. Galiczynski's name appears as "Valiczynski" in some sources. Samuel T. Swansen to Robert D. Abrahams, memo re: Location of Law Office of Community Legal Services, Inc., in Anti-Poverty Program Area E, May 26, 1966, box 3, folder: Ludlow Branch Correspondence 1966–1967, 1970, acc. 253, 259, Legal Aid Society, SCRC; Nicholas W. Stroh, "Few File Petitions Here for Poverty Elections," *Philadelphia Evening Bulletin*, June 25, 1966, Bowser, Charles W.—Poverty & Poverty Commission 1966, Bulletin Clippings, SCRC; "Pickets Demand Removal of Poverty Program Official," *Philadelphia Evening Bulletin*, August 13, 1968, Ludlow Community Activities Center, Bulletin Clippings, SCRC; "Proposed AWC [Area Wide Council] Hub Locations," box 47, folder 33, acc. 625, Nationalities Service Center, SCRC; Alvin E. Echols, "Report and Recommendations to the Area-Wide Council by the Temporary Committee on Hub Structure," April 1967, box 47, folder 33, acc. 625, Nationalities Service Center, SCRC.

12. "A Two-Man Documentary That Brought Action before Its Telecast," in Phipps, *Assignment: 1747 Randolph Street*, appendix G.

13. Robert J. McMullin to John J. O'Shea, memo re: Progress Report on Activity in Ludlow, July 20, 1966, 1, in Phipps, *Assignment: 1747 Randolph Street*, appendix I; Ludlow Community Association, "Have You Heard about the Ludlow Community Association?," bilingual flyer, 1966?, box 17, folder 175, URB 16, Urban League, SCRC.

14. Marvin Louis to Tina Weintraub, December 27, 1966, 1, box 17, folder 174, URB 16, Urban League, SCRC; Louis, interview by author, November 6, 2009, 2–3.

15. Ludlow Community Association Executive Board, "LCA Staff Responsibilities Beginning May 1, 1967," April 27, 1967, box 17, folder 175, URB 16, Urban League, SCRC; "Ludlow Group Confirms Ouster of Social Aide," *Philadelphia Inquirer*, August 31, 1967, Ludlow Community Association, Bulletin Clippings, SCRC; Helen H. Helfer to Ludlow Community Association Executive Board, memo re: List of Meetings—October 3rd–January 12, 1967, box 17, folder 177, URB 16, Urban League, SCRC; Ludlow Executive Board to Members and Friends of the Ludlow Community Association, memo re: Dismissal of Staff Worker Helen Helfer, n.d., box 17, folder 175, URB 16, Urban League, SCRC.

16. John E. Cooney, "Strike Director Fired in Midst of Drive by Ludlow Association," *Philadelphia Inquirer*, February 26, 1968, Ludlow Community Association, Bulletin Clippings, SCRC.

17. "Ludlow News," April 9, 1967, box 17, folder 178, URB 16, Urban League, SCRC; "Ludlow News," June 17, 1967, box 3, folder 19, acc. 980, Neighborhoods and Urban Renewal, SCRC.

18. Giddens, "Hundreds Mourn."

19. Louis, interview by author, November 6, 2009, 7; Fletcher Clarke, "Ludlow Group Blames City for Boy Cut by Falling Glass," *Philadelphia Evening Bulletin*, August 28, 1971, mounted clipping, box 113, Ludlow—Phila. Section, Bulletin Clippings, SCRC; Phipps, *Assignment: 1747 Randolph Street*, script, 68.

20. Phipps, *Assignment: 1747 Randolph Street*, script, 38–40.

21. Louis, interview by author, November 6, 2009, 2; Louis to Weintraub, 1–3.

22. Phipps, *"Assignment: 1747 Randolph St"*, promotional materials, 19–20; "Statement by the Ludlow Community Association Regarding the Proposed Recreation Site at 6th and Master Streets," December 29, 1966, box 17, folder 177, URB 16, Urban League, SCRC; Louis, interview by author, November 6, 2009, 5; "U.S. Grants $1.1 Million for Ludlow Play Area," *Philadelphia Evening Bulletin*, May 23, 1968, Ludlow Community Association, Bulletin Clippings, SCRC.

23. "U.S. Grants"; "$400,000 Rec Center for Ludlow 'Nothing' Minus Swimming Pool," *Philadelphia Tribune*, August 6, 1968; Rose DeWolf, "Making the City Notice," *Philadelphia Evening Bulletin*, May 27, 1974, Ludlow Community Association, Bulletin Clippings, SCRC; Louis, interview by author, November 9, 2009, 15–17.

24. Louis, interview by author, November 6, 2009, 2; Gregg, "Ludlow: A Community Struggles."

25. "Public Housing in Ludlow Hit by Vandals," *Philadelphia Evening Bulletin*, March 29,

1971, mounted clipping, box 113, Ludlow—Phila. Section, Bulletin Clippings, SCRC; Eugene L. Meyer, "93% of Ludlow Houses Found Violating City Codes," *Philadelphia Evening Bulletin*, June 4, 1967, Ludlow Community Association, Bulletin Clippings, SCRC.

26. "First Warnings Sent on Blighted Buildings," *Philadelphia Inquirer*, April 30, 1967, mounted clipping, box 108A, Kensington (Section) Renewal, Bulletin Clippings, SCRC; Meyer, "93% of Ludlow Houses"; Valentine quoted in Sam W. Pressley, "Owners Start Razing Vacant Building Where North Phila. Girl, 7, Died," *Philadelphia Evening Bulletin*, April 26, 1973, Ludlow Community Association, Bulletin Clippings, SCRC; Migration Division, "Puerto Ricans in Philadelphia," 1962?, 2, pamphlet no. 668-8, General Pamphlet Collection, SCRC.

27. "Ludlow Area Tenants Start Computer-Aided Rent Strike," *Philadelphia Evening Bulletin*, October 8, 1967, Ludlow Community Association, Bulletin Clippings, SCRC; Lawrence Geller, "Start Rent Strike in 90-Square Block North Philadelphia Area," *Philadelphia Tribune*, November 7, 1967; Cooney, "Strike Director Fired."

28. Nelson Diaz, "Ahora!," *Philadelphia Evening Bulletin*, April 29, 1973, Sierra, Jesus M.—Spanish Speaking Unit, Bulletin Clippings, SCRC; "Ludlow Area Tenants"; "11 Property-Owners Fined for Heating Violations," *Philadelphia Evening Bulletin*, March 28, 1967, Ludlow—Phila. Section, Bulletin Clippings, SCRC; Alfonso D. Brown Jr., "Tenants Vow Fight on Repairs," *Philadelphia Evening Bulletin*, October 2, 1977, Ludlow Community Association, Bulletin Clippings, SCRC.

29. Alfonso D. Brown Jr., "City Lets Ludlow Die, Activist Says," *Philadelphia Evening Bulletin*, January 21, 1979, mounted clipping, box 113, Ludlow Area Misc., Bulletin Clippings, SCRC.

30. "Ludlow Fears Vacant Houses," *Philadelphia Inquirer*, June 30, 1967, Ludlow—Phila. Section, Bulletin Clippings, SCRC; Fletcher J. Clarke, "Ludlow to Give City a List of 100 'Hazardous' Houses," *Philadelphia Evening Bulletin*, September 2, 1971, Ludlow Community Association, Bulletin Clippings, SCRC; DeWolf, "Making the City Notice."

31. "Main Line Church Seeks to Aid Ludlow Housing," *Philadelphia Evening Bulletin*, December 1, 1966, Ludlow Housing Improvement Association, Bulletin Clippings, SCRC; "Rebuilding Starts on Old Houses in Ludlow Area," *Philadelphia Evening Bulletin*, August 20, 1967, Ludlow Community Association, Bulletin Clippings, SCRC; John E. Cooney, "Same Key Fits All Rebuilt Ludlow Homes," *Philadelphia Inquirer*, March 19, 1968, Ludlow—Phila. Section, Bulletin Clippings, SCRC; Douglas Bedell, "Outlook Is Dim in Ludlow Area," *Philadelphia Evening Bulletin*, February 22, 1972, mounted clipping, box 113, Ludlow Area Misc., Bulletin Clippings, SCRC; "Ludlow Unit Claims PHA Creates Slum," *Philadelphia Evening Bulletin*, April 16, 1970, Ludlow—Phila. Section, Bulletin Clippings, SCRC; Linn Washington Jr., "Marvin Louis and the Dream of a Revitalized Ludlow," *Philadelphia Tribune*, June 17, 1997; Peter H. Binzen, "Ex-Boxer Trying to Hammer Together a Liveable Ludlow," *Philadelphia Evening Bulletin*, October 19, 1969, mounted clipping, box 113, Ludlow Area Misc., Bulletin Clippings, SCRC; Walter F. Naedele, "Klenk Sees 'Homesteading' Abuses," *Philadelphia Evening Bulletin*, June 23,

1978, Urban Homesteading—Phila. 1978 to [*sic*], Bulletin Clippings, SCRC; Ronald Goldwyn, "Phila '78 Smells Cronyism in Jannotti Homestead Plan," *Philadelphia Evening Bulletin*, April 27, 1978, Urban Homesteading—Phila. 1978 to [*sic*], Bulletin Clippings, SCRC.

32. Washington, "Marvin Louis."

33. "Ludlow Thrift Shop Is Helping Children," *Philadelphia Inquirer*, March 3, 1968, Ludlow Community Association, Bulletin Clippings, SCRC; Louis, interview by author, November 6, 2009, 5.

34. Francis Bosworth to Guild Board of Directors, memo re: Guild Cooperation and Involvement in the Community School Program of the School District of Philadelphia, July 11, 1966, 2, box 1, folder 5, URB 32, Friends Neighborhood Guild, SCRC; J. William Jones, "Two Exchange Teachers Help to Break Language Barrier for Puerto Ricans," *Philadelphia Evening Bulletin*, March 1, 1964, Puerto Ricans in Phila. 1964 and Prior, Bulletin Clippings, SCRC; Marianne Gabel, "El Programa de Educacion Bilingue," *Philadelphia Evening Bulletin*, June 16, 1971, Puerto Ricans in Phila. Bulletin Series 1971, Bulletin Clippings, SCRC; C. Garcia, "General Observations of My Visit to the Ludlow School," February 6, 1968, box 13, folder 1, acc. 625, Nationalities Service Center, SCRC.

35. Ludlow Community Association, bilingual flyer for meeting on May 4, 1967, box 17, folder 175, URB 16, Urban League, SCRC; Thomas B. Ridgely Jr. et al., notice to clients of Ludlow Branch of Legal Aid Society, January 10, 1967, box 3, folder: Ludlow Branch Correspondence 1966–1967, 1970, acc. 253, 259, Legal Aid Society, SCRC; Phipps, *Assignment: 1747 Randolph Street*, script, 46–49; "Ludlow Gets Reprieve," *Philadelphia Evening Bulletin*, July 30, 1968, Ludlow Community Association, Bulletin Clippings, SCRC; DeWolf, "Making the City Notice."

36. Louis, interview by author, November 6, 2009, 8–9; Jack Smyth, "Blacks, Whites, Puerto Ricans Propose Community Council," *Philadelphia Evening Bulletin*, May 26, 1971, mounted clipping, box 108A, Kensington (Section) Racial Demonstration, Bulletin Clippings, SCRC; Jack Smyth, "Safe Corridors Urged in Kensington Race Strife," *Philadelphia Evening Bulletin*, April 12, 1973, mounted clipping, box 108A, Kensington (Section) Racial Demonstration, Bulletin Clippings, SCRC; Charles F. Thomson and Alfonso D. Brown Jr., "15 Ask O'Neill to Press Probe of Boy's Drowning," *Philadelphia Evening Bulletin*, June 22, 1973, Puerto Ricans in Phila. Bulletin Series 1971, Bulletin Clippings, SCRC; Charles F. Thomson, "Rizzo Pledges Bus Service for Penn Treaty Pupils," *Philadelphia Evening Bulletin*, June 23, 1973, Puerto Ricans in Phila. Bulletin Series 1971, Bulletin Clippings, SCRC.

37. "Neighbors with Clubs Declare War on Hoods," *Philadelphia Inquirer*, April 2, 1968, mounted clipping, box 113, Ludlow Area Misc., Bulletin Clippings, SCRC; "More Policemen Promised Residents of Ludlow Area," *Philadelphia Evening Bulletin*, April 3, 1968, Ludlow Community Activities Center, Bulletin Clippings, SCRC; Copeland, "Ludlow's Urban Tiger."

38. "3 Men Donate Ambulance to Serve Ludlow"; "Self-Help at Ludlow," *Philadelphia Evening Bulletin*, April 13, 1968, mounted clipping, box 113, Ludlow Area Misc., Bulletin

Clippings, SCRC; "Ludlow Residents Set Up Blood Bank," *Philadelphia Evening Bulletin*, September 3, 1968, Ludlow Community Activities Center, Bulletin Clippings, SCRC.

39. Louis, interview by author, November 9, 2009, 1–2; A. W. Geiselman Jr., "Removal of Dental Training from Graterford Protested," *Philadelphia Evening Bulletin*, April 22, 1980, Ludlow Community Association, Bulletin Clippings, SCRC.

40. Louis, interview by author, November 9, 2009, 13.

41. DeWolf, "Making the City Notice."

42. Louis, interview by author, November 6, 2009, 8.

43. "Philadelphia Urban Coalition: Service Roles," 11.

CHAPTER 10

The Next Struggle

African American and Latino/a Collaborative Activism in the Post–Civil Rights Era

BRIAN D. BEHNKEN

In 1987 National Rainbow Coalition (NRC) leader Jesse Jackson appointed Mario Obledo as the chair of the organization's board of directors. Obledo, an important Mexican American activist and one of the founders of the Mexican American Legal Defense and Educational Fund (MALDEF), embraced the opportunity. He believed in the goals of the Rainbow Coalition, which had fought against poverty and for minority community empowerment for years. "Hispanic voters," Obledo argued, "can find much in common with the interests of Jesse Jackson and the nation's black majority."[1] He also welcomed the chance to extend the NRC's efforts to the Latino/a community and especially to Mexican Americans in the Southwest.[2] But soon after his appointment, Obledo realized his position was largely symbolic. He had no real power and ran up against constant opposition when he proposed new ideas and directions for the organization. He quit one year into his appointment.[3]

Never before in Mexican American or African American history had a major organization representing primarily one ethnic community appointed a person from another ethnic community to such a high post. This was an important accomplishment. But just as surely, the appointment of Obledo revealed some of the limits of interethnic cooperation: blacks were willing to give him a position, but only one with limited power. The late 1970s and 1980s were important years for black-Latino/a relations and set the stage for the types of activism(s) and race relations that can be seen today between these groups. As I have argued elsewhere, before the 1960s blacks and browns frequently had difficult racial and social relations. Jim Crow segregation pitted these groups against one another, and the racial dynamics of the late nineteenth century and early to mid-twentieth, which emphasized race as a binary of white and black, made cooperation across color lines often difficult. While there were many instances of collaboration during this period, cooperation was, I would suggest, not the norm.[4]

This chapter examines black-Latino/a interactions in the post–civil rights era, focusing specifically on points of cooperative activism and coalition building. I argue that in this period the ability of these groups to collaborate effectively was amplified since formal segregation had ended. Interethnic cooperation and coalition building became the next struggle, and there was considerable progress in black-brown civil rights activism. While there were—and always are—pitfalls to interethnic civil rights activism, those pitfalls were lessened in this period. I examine three areas of African American–Latino/a coalition building and cooperative civil rights activism in the late 1970s and early 1980s: the efforts of Mario Obledo and Jesse Jackson to build a united civil rights campaign through the Rainbow Coalition, especially a battle against the English-only movement; activism to end police brutality and harassment; and opposition to the reappearance of the Ku Klux Klan. These three instances of collaboration all demonstrate how black-brown activism worked at the local and national levels after the civil rights era.

COALITIONS, 1980S STYLE

Political coalition building among African American and Latino/a activists had occurred sporadically throughout the twentieth century. Well-known Mexican American political figures such as Edward Roybal in California and Henry B. Gonzalez in Texas had courted the African American vote in the 1940s and 1950s, while black politicians such as Barbara Jordan in Texas and Gilbert Lindsay in California had sought the Mexican American vote in the 1960s. Similarly, blacks and Latino/as had attempted to build political coalitions, such as the Democratic Coalition in Texas in 1963. But these coalitions frequently proved short-lived, not lasting beyond a particular election.[5] As the civil rights era ebbed, such coalitions became more common.

Mario Obledo's association with the Rainbow Coalition happened at a particularly auspicious moment. In 1983 Jesse Jackson was considering a presidential run, and it no doubt made sense to him that uniting with an important Latino/a figure would help in this regard. For his 1984 presidential bid, he and Obledo, who was then the president of the League of United Latin American Citizens (LULAC), worked closely to initiate a black-brown coalition.[6] At this point Jackson seemed concerned with appealing to Latino/as solely in order to pull support away from his challenger, Walter Mondale. Jackson, of course, failed in this effort. That failure taught him an important lesson, namely that he would have to do more to appeal to the Latino/a community. In 1987, on the eve of his second bid for president, he appointed Obledo to head the National Rainbow Coalition. Jackson's outreach to the Hispanic community began to differ from other leaders. While winning their votes was certainly important, Jackson appealed to Latino/as beyond the parameters of the campaign. He did not view Latino/as as foreigners, nor did he expect them to unquestioningly adhere to all the principles of the United States. Instead, Jackson seemed to view assimilation as a two-way street. He had asserted in 1984 that "when the black and Hispanic foundation comes together, everyone above has to adjust. We are not the bottom of this society, where things end up. We are the foundation, where everything begins."[7] Jackson certainly hoped Latino/as would adapt themselves to the United States, but he also hoped that Americans, and especially African Americans, would adapt themselves to the Latino/a community. With that in mind, he began in the mid-1980s to appoint an increasing number of Latino/as to the NRC board. As chair of the board, Obledo joined ten other Latino/as. Jackson also appealed to Latino/as by vocally opposing the English-only movement, a support that would crystallize years later in a call by the NRC for blacks to learn spoken Spanish as a novel solution to the language barrier between blacks and browns.[8]

In the mid- to late 1980s the English-only movement became increasingly popular. The English-only, or "English as the national language," debate touched on a number of important issues. It was primarily a right-wing response to two things: the increasing number of Latino/as in the United States and bilingual education. Some Americans disapproved of spoken Spanish and were offended to have to "press 1 for English, 2 for Spanish." Businesses with names that included words like *carnicería* or *taqueria* or *tortilleria* seemed a Latino/a "takeover" to white Americans. Spanish was viewed as a threat, Latino/as were taking over, and all of this was fueled by unchecked immigration.[9] Conservative Americans could not convince the federal government to respond to their desire to curtail immigration—and even when the government did revise the immigration statutes in 1986 with the Immigration Reform and Control Act, conservatives were dissatisfied. And so they channeled their anger into language restriction.[10]

The English-only movement was born in this climate of fear. The movement was led by a group called USEnglish, founded by John Tanton and Samuel I. Hayakawa in 1983. Tanton, the child of immigrants and an ophthalmologist by training, had reacted viscerally to the increasing immigration from Latin America and elsewhere around the globe. Hayakawa was a professor of English who had served as president of San Francisco State University from 1955 to 1968. In 1968 he earned his stripes with conservatives when he vocally opposed the formation of a black studies program at SFSU, and one time he pulled wires from a sound system to disrupt a Black Power rally on campus. He parlayed his developing popularity into a successful run for the U.S. Senate in the late 1970s. Hayakawa started USEnglish, and Tanton was the group's mouthpiece. Within about five years it had 250,000 members. The group took its inspiration from Canada after the province of Quebec passed a French-only law in the early 1980s. This move, which came to be called "Quebecking" in the United States, inspired the English-only movement.[11]

Both Hayakawa and Tanton engaged in some fairly rabid anti-Latino/a race baiting. Hayakawa sent out numerous flyers and surveys, for instance, in which he denounced "ethnic leaders" who proposed funding bilingual education programs in his home state of California. In his conception, bilingual education and spoken Spanish were part of a sinister plot to create a new Latino/a homeland, a reconquest of lost Mexican territory. "Some ethnic leaders seem to have a goal of creating several bilingual and bicultural states," Hayakawa declared, "[and] foremost among the states marked for bilingualism is California."[12] Where Hayakawa subtly appealed to Californians, and Americans more broadly, Tanton was more explicit in his racism. "Can *homo contraceptivus* ["man who uses contraceptives," i.e., white people] compete with *homo progenitiva* ["man who procreates," i.e., Latino/as] if borders aren't controlled? Or is advice to limit one's family simply advice to move over and let someone else with greater reproductive powers occupy the space?," Tanton wrote in a 1986 memo. He went on to add in an even more vociferous tone: "On the demographic point: perhaps this is the first instance in which those with their pants up are going to get caught by those with their pants down!" Here he tapped into the growing fear and largely presumptive white American understanding of Latino/a fecundity, suggesting that Latino/as would outbreed whites and thereby take over the country. He then asked, "What are the differences in educability between Hispanics (with their 50% dropout rate) and Asiatics (with their excellent school records and long tradition of scholarship)?" Like other English-only racists, Tanton saw in Latino/as a whole host of intelligence and educational deficiencies that warranted major immigration reform. It is no wonder that in the 1980s and 1990s he grew increasingly interested in the eugenics movement of the early twentieth century. And, to remind his readers of the central problem in his anti-Latino/a tirade, Tanton stated, "the whole bilingual education question needs to be mentioned."[13]

It was in this climate of fear and racism that Jesse Jackson and Mario Obledo came together under the auspices of the NRC. Since Jackson was interested in combatting all forms of racism, it is no wonder that he appealed to Obledo. For his part, Obledo saw collaborating with the Rainbow Coalition as an extension of his own activism, which went back to the 1960s. Obledo, of course, brought to the board a fluently bilingual leader who could ably oppose the racial dogma of the English-only groups.[14] Jackson began to forcefully speak out against the bigotry of the English-only movement in his 1988 presidential bid. "Give me your tired, your poor, your huddled masses . . . it didn't say English only," Jackson stated in a campaign speech in San Francisco.[15]

After his defeat in the 1988 Democratic primaries, Jackson continued to speak on black-brown cooperation and against the English-only movement. He asked, for example, in his speech at the 1988 Democratic National Convention, "What makes New York so special? It's the invitation of the Statue of Liberty—give me your tired, your poor, your huddled masses who yearn to breathe free. Not restricted to English only." He went on to assert, "Blacks and Hispanics, when we fight for civil rights, we are right—but our patch is not big enough." Jackson explained that the United States was like a quilt and only by expanding our collective "patches" could the nation move forward as a united entity.[16]

Eventually two forces came together to end the English-only movement in the 1980s and early 1990s. Jackson and Obledo both endorsed the concept of "English plus," which was reflected in an activist group of the same name. English Plus argued that the great value of the United States was its diversity and the equal protection under the laws of all people. "The 'English plus' concept holds that the national interest can best be served when all members of our society have full access to effective opportunities to acquire strong English language proficiency *plus* mastery of a second or multiple languages," the group explained in its statement of purpose. The English-only movement, English Plus leaders asserted, acted to the contrary. "'English Only' and other restrictionist language legislation," English Plus noted, "has the potential for abridging the citizen's right to vote [and fosters] governmental interference in private activity and free commerce."[17] English Plus was not just anti-USEnglish. Rather, the group offered an alternative program that not only aimed to educate non-English speakers in English, but also aimed to teach monolingual English speakers other languages. The concept was ingenious both in its program and in its rhetoric, which highlighted education in a foreign language as a positive national good. Soon states like New Mexico and Arizona had rejected their English-only propositions for English-plus propositions. The second factor that contributed to the decline in the English-only movement was the end of Republican rule in the White House. The election of Bill Clinton in 1992 ensured that English-only simply faded away. Indeed, the speed at which the English-only movement dissipated points clearly to the fact that this was a political issue engineered by the New Right, and nothing more.

Jesse Jackson and Mario Obledo eventually parted ways. Perhaps the diminishing of the English-only movement led to their separation. Obledo had seemed to recognize some of the hardship of black-brown cooperation going back to some of his first meetings with Jackson and his staff in 1983. He noted that in regard to black-brown alliances, "we've just been born, so to speak . . . and it's a long-term process."[18] Jackson had acknowledged in that same year that blacks and Latino/as "have a disorganized coalition."[19] But Obledo also found his role on the board of the NRC limiting. He had little direct power and was merely a symbolic leader. The institutional head of the Rainbow Coalition was Jesse Jackson, not Mario Obledo. As a leader who had helped found one major civil rights organization, MALDEF, and who had headed another, LULAC, Obledo expected a measure of control. When he did not get it, he resigned his position. But that did not stop Obledo's multiethnic coalition building. He served on the board of directors of the Martin Luther King Jr. Federal Holiday Commission, one of the few Mexican Americans to do so. He also pushed LULAC to adopt a resolution supporting the MLK holiday and criticizing Arizona for refusing to establish the holiday, a somewhat atypical stance by LULAC.[20]

Other Latino/a leaders also joined in other coalitions. For example, in late 1979 and into the early 1980s Ruben Bonilla, the president of LULAC, accepted an invitation to join Vernon Jordan, the director of the National Urban League, in a coalition campaign to fight for better housing conditions (a longtime Urban League goal) for all minorities, to hold a "national symposium" that would examine the possibility of developing "coalition politics," and to fight against police "use of force."[21]

POLICE VIOLENCE AND MULTIETHNIC COOPERATION

As many African American and Latino/a leaders understood, opposition to police brutality could be a potentially easy avenue for multiethnic collaboration. Shared grievances against shared injustices had indeed brought the two communities together throughout the civil rights era. Take, for instance, the police murder of Bobby Jo Phillips in San Antonio, Texas, in 1968.

The San Antonio police were called to the city's predominantly black east side after receiving reports about a knife-wielding individual in the area. According to eyewitnesses, the officers quickly disarmed this person, later identified as Bobby Jo Phillips. While allegedly intoxicated, Phillips offered little resistance to the two officers, who nonetheless proceeded to violently beat him. Phillips later died from these injuries. The officers were later indicted for killing Phillips, but in their subsequent trial, the jury found them not guilty.[22] African Americans and Mexican Americans rose up in protest over these events. The protests were assisted by the development of the San Antonio office of the Student Nonviolent Coordinating Committee (SNCC). The local SNCC office was led by activist Mario Salas, who self-identifies as an Afro-Mexican. The group focused purposefully on police harassment and the murder of blacks and browns. A year after the murder of Phillips, for example, San Antonio SNCC organized a protest to decry police violence. In April 1969 thousands of protesters descended on downtown San Antonio to block the parade route of the annual Fiesta San Antonio parade. While they successfully disrupted the parade, the activists encountered a massive police presence. Attacked and repulsed by the police, the activists retaliated by breaking into downtown stores. In at least one case they robbed a pawnshop of its guns and took the weapons to SNCC headquarters. Police then attacked the SNCC offices and arrested numerous activists.[23] While African Americans and Mexican Americans both demanded justice for Bobby Jo Phillips, they could not of course undo his murder nor the judgment of the local court. Instead, they protested. Those protests ultimately pushed the San Antonio police to adopt the concept of police-civilian review and to initiate the creation of an Internal Affairs Division.[24]

The events in San Antonio were mirrored by events in Houston almost a decade later. In May 1977 Houston police were called to a bar fight where they encountered an intoxicated Jose "Joe" Campos Torres. While he offered the officers no resistance, they nonetheless brought Torres to a secluded area and proceeded to beat him. They then took Torres to the city jail, but because of his battered condition the jail staff demanded that the officers escort him to the hospital. Instead, the officers returned to the secluded area, beat Torres some more, and then pushed him off a bridge into a local bayou. He drowned to death. Local Latino/a and black activists rose up in protest. These protests persisted for more than a year while the community awaited the outcome of the officers' trial. They were eventually found guilty of violating Torres's constitutional rights, but were sentenced only to five years of probation. At a demonstration decrying this light sentence in 1978, African American and Latino/a protesters clashed with police. As in San Antonio, the protests in Houston could not undo Torres's murder nor the light sentence the officers received, but they did force the police to create an Internal Affairs Department.[25]

Activists across the Southwest continued to confront police brutality and killings in the late 1970s and early 1980s. In Denver, the Crusade for Justice headed by Rodolfo "Corky" Gonzales boldly fought with police on a number of occasions in order to forestall police abuse. Denver police, however, responded by further hassling Crusade members, leading to several violent encounters. During one of these encounters, police officers attempted to arrest activist Luis "Junior" Martinez for jaywalking, a common type of harassment. Martinez fled down a blind alley and was killed by Denver police officer Stephen Snyder. Martinez's killing only further radicalized the Crusade for Justice.[26] The Crusade's activism also demonstrates some of the shared grievances and collaborative activities among militant groups of this period. For example, leaders in Houston wrote Corky Gonzales in June 1975 to praise the Crusade for Justice and offer support after the Martinez killing. "We know all too well the constant assault carried out by the police against the Chicano, black and poor white people," the Houston activists noted, concluding that "unidos venceremos" (united we will overcome) and "police terror will be ended forever."[27]

It should be noted that many radical groups during this period were perceived by the general public as anti-police. This perception most likely stems from the type of media attention given to groups such as the Black Panther Party. But many militant groups were not anti-police, and I would argue that the Panthers were also not anti-police, but rather they were anti–police brutality or anti–police murder. In one of Corky Gonzales's "messages to Aztlan," he asserted that police should "serve, protect and love and it can be reciprocated. Destroy, kill and treat our people with injustice and you might only receive the same in return."[28]

As in Colorado and Texas, people of color in Arizona also joined forces to battle police violence. Mexican American, African American, and Native American activists came together after a string of police raids on homes where the police made mistakes in street addresses. For instance, in August 1979 Tucson police raided the home of Margie Moraga. Moraga had just finished cleaning the house while her children listened to Walt Disney songs on the record player. Garbled yelling and pounding on the front door were followed by the door flying off its hinges as police rushed in. The police proceeded to search the Moraga home for drugs while Moraga cradled her young children. After finding no drugs, the officers seemed to realize they had raided the wrong home, and they left after explaining to Moraga how she could request reimbursement for her damaged front door.[29]

The Tucson police also erroneously disrupted a local birthday party. Police were called to investigate a fight at a nearby home, but they got the address wrong and instead wound up at the home of the Alberto Montenegro family. They mistook a birthday party at the Montenegro house for a fight and proceeded to accost and beat several members of the family and their guests. Police arrested six individuals, including Maria Montenegro, the matriarch of the family, who was also beaten by the police. Tucson police also beat and arrested Edward Montenegro, Maria's son, after he kicked at a police dog. Police knocked Xavier Montenegro unconscious and then allowed a police dog to bite him. Edward was tried for disorderly conduct. Maria was tried for hindering a police officer in the execution of his duties. A jury found her not guilty. Another brother, Jose, was found guilty of misdemeanor assault against a police officer.[30]

In a bold example of ethnoracial solidarity, Willie Lewis, the president of the local chapter of the National Association for the Advancement of Colored People (NAACP), noted, "What's going on here is typical in this community and common around the nation." And the local people involved were determined to stop it.[31] Lewis's statement serves as a reminder that blacks and Latinos share a common grievance around police brutality. Local Chicano leaders also vowed to support the Montenegros, and a legal aid committee was soon formed to advocate for them. Both blacks and Latino/as came together to assist the Montenegros.

The worst of the late 1970s encounters between minorities and police in

Arizona was in 1977 when Jose H. Sinohui Jr. was murdered by South Tucson police officer Christopher Dean. The reports of the events that led to Sinohui's death remain conflicting. According to most accounts, Sinohui had visited—or was driving by—a fast food restaurant when a large group of people began to fight. Police arrived to quell this disturbance. One account says that Dean ordered Sinohui to stop and exit his vehicle, which he did. Another account suggests (this is probably the correct version) that Sinohui was passing by the restaurant when Dean, who was escorting an arrested individual, walked out into the street and ordered Sinohui to stop so that he could cross the street. Sinohui evidently paused and then drove on. A third account states that Sinohui attempted to run over Dean while exiting the fast food restaurant—and in an extrapolation, the police said Sinohui attempted to run over Dean twice! The aftermath is easier to piece together: Dean shot at Sinohui's pickup truck, he fired at least eight times (including two illegal armor-piercing bullets), and one bullet struck Sinohui in the back. He died en route to a local hospital.[32]

The South Tucson Police Department suspended Officer Dean while an investigation took place. He was eventually tried for involuntary manslaughter and acquitted. The Mexican American and African American communities were outraged. As in other notorious shootings, justice seemed a hollow term for many minorities. Activists rallied around the Sinohuis. Chicano activists, with numerous black allies such as the NAACP's Lewis, raised money for a civil suit and put pressure on the federal government to prosecute Dean for violating Sinohui's constitutional rights. Their efforts resulted in a $5 million damage suit against Dean and the city of South Tucson. Filed by the parents of Jose Sinohui, the suit alleged that Dean had acted recklessly and had killed their son without provocation.[33]

After a prolonged trial, Judge Ben Birdsall agreed that Dean had violated Sinohui's rights by killing him without cause. He issued a bench judgment against the city and Dean. The city was forced to pay the Sinohuis $150,000, while Dean had to pay them $50,000. The judge noted that while Sinohui may have had his pickup truck in motion, Dean was never in danger nor in the path of the vehicle. Birdsall further declared that Dean either fired at the truck or directly at Sinohui, and in either case his actions were grossly negligent.[34]

While that trial took place, brown and black activists continued to protest. A group of fifty organized a demonstration that took the case to Washington, D.C. There, this group of activists picketed the Justice Department and demanded a federal inquiry into the case. President Jimmy Carter's Justice Department waffled. The activists, most of whom were affiliated with La Raza Legal Alliance, responded by asserting that the administration seemed unwilling to "seek justice where clear abuses and atrocities have been committed against the Latino community. They certainly do not reflect an aggressive civil rights policy that seeks to make equality under the law and human rights for all a reality."[35]

Further legal proceedings brought by Jose Sinohui's family slowly petered out. The case against Dean and the local government, while a strong one, was overshadowed by the more famous Hanigan case, which involved two white brothers who had captured and tortured three Mexican nationals on their ranch. Perhaps the sensational aspects of the Hanigan case distracted from the Sinohui case. The federal grand jury ultimately failed to indict Officer Dean for Sinohui's murder. Since he had already lost his home to the Sinohuis and the local case had long since closed, the grand jury seemed to feel Dean had suffered enough.[36] Chicano and African American activists, however, continued to push for a new trial. They got some encouraging news in late 1980 when authorities indicated they would reopen the case. Evidently the lower court had suppressed some key information, which only came to light after the grand jury had refused to pursue the case.[37] Activists continued to push for justice for Jose Sinohui. LULAC, for instance, dedicated its 1980 national convention to Sinohui and his family. The group also approved a resolution demanding that the Justice Department reopen the case.[38] But the Justice Department declined.[39]

African American and Latino/a individuals had for generations felt the sting of abusive law enforcement. While they had certainly challenged this treatment before and during the civil rights period, their activism only increased after the struggle. From rallies to legal cases to marches, blacks and browns united to halt police murder and harassment. The circumstances, of course, helped generate their activism and cooperation. Shared injustices and similar conditions made collaboration that much easier. The same could certainly be said for black and Latino/a opposition to the Ku Klux Klan.

ABAJO CON EL KLAN

Latino/as and blacks found it easy to unite to combat the racism and abuse of the Klan. While the KKK had seen its strength, membership, and influence diminish throughout the 1960s, the Klan once again reared its ugly head in the late 1970s, this time primarily in opposition to Latin American immigration and, in particular, Mexican immigrants. The Klan's reappearance coincided with immigration reform plans proposed by the U.S. Congress and supported by President Carter. Grand Dragon David Duke announced that not only would the KKK support these efforts, it would also begin patrolling the U.S.–Mexico border to apprehend undocumented border crossers. Its goal, according to Duke, was not racist but was instead designed to keep America "pure" and protect the United States from "foreign or alien influence or interest."[40]

Despite Duke's assertions to the contrary, the Klan utilized many of its tried and true racist tactics, this time aimed at Latino/as. These tactics included using cartoons to ridicule Mexican border-crossing men as fat and lazy and to portray all Mexican women as pregnant (all of whom in one cartoon rush to board a "Grease-hound" bus, which is a "lowered '44 Chevy"); and producing fake advertisements for "Instant Greaser" powder "for liberal, white 'Freedom Marchers,' race mixers and assorted 'Spic-Symps'" who desire "cultural enrichment" (simply sprinkle this powder on the ground, add water, and "hundreds of Chicanos spring up! Little greasers, big greasers, fat jew greasers, skinny greasers. Light greasers, charcoal brown greaser[s,] greasers here, greasers there; greasers, greasers everywhere!!"). The cartoon "White Power Comes to Midvale" featured a muscular white student who arrives at "Midvale High School" to save white students from blacks, Latino/as, and a clearly Jewish principal. Such depictions could easily have been applied to African Americans in previous generations.[41]

Exhortations containing racist viewpoints, statements that the Klan would support the government's efforts to reform the immigration system, and the KKK's patrols of the border pushed activists in southern California and around the nation to protest. For example, in October 1977 approximately two thousand to three thousand Chicanos, African Americans, Native Americans, and whites marched together against the Klan and the government's immigration reform proposals in San Ysidro, California. Activist groups and their leaders from around the country joined the protest. The Crusade for Justice's Corky Gonzales spoke at a rally after the march: "La Migra [the Immigration and Naturalization Service] is just as guilty, just as racist as the KKK. They are twins dressed in different uniforms who mistreat, terrorize and brutalize our people."[42] Other activists railed against Carter's immigration reform plans, which they saw as stimulating the Klan's border activities.[43]

Chicano and black activists assembled to prevent the Klan patrol missions.

They had several small skirmishes with Klan members.[44] But the activist groups mainly staged marches that resisted the KKK. The Klan patrols and apprehensions, which occurred primarily near San Ysidro, seemed reminiscent of the "night riders" of early Klan activity. An Immigration and Naturalization Service (INS) official, Allen Clayton, gave David Duke and Tom Metzger, the KKK grand dragon in California, a personal tour of the San Ysidro INS facility, which gave credence to black and Latino/a arguments that the Klan and the government were wedded over this issue.[45] Metzger had made himself known in southern California for his racist diatribes, which tended to merge antiblack and anti-Latino/a sentiments quite fluidly. Metzger, for instance, explained to a *Los Angeles Times* reporter his view that a "black hell" and "brown hordes" were simultaneously trying to overrun America and get him. The obvious response was Klan border patrols.[46] These patrols occurred sporadically and most often garnered the Klan bad press. In one of the most notorious incidents, four Klan members abducted an individual whom they perceived to be Mexican, who was hitchhiking near the San Diego–Tijuana border in April 1978. They delivered this person, later determined to be Juan Mendez-Ruiz, to the Border Patrol, which soon learned that Mendez-Ruiz was a legal immigrant. Evidently the Klansmen knew that as well: they had taken Mendez-Ruiz's immigration papers and discarded them along the side of Interstate 5. The Border Patrol soon found those documents and released Mendez-Ruiz. Local FBI agents conducted an investigation into the activities of the Klansmen, which resulted in two arrests and one conviction.[47]

The Mendez-Ruiz kidnapping garnered a significant response from activists in southern California. Local groups, such as the Committee on Chicano Rights founded by San Diego activist Herman Baca, the Crusade for Justice, the NAACP, the San Diego chapter of the National Urban League, and the Mexican American Political Association all took a keen interest in Mendez-Ruiz and similar cases. Baca noted that "meetings are being planned with organizational heads of the Black, Anglo, and Jewish communities to formulate strategies to insure that such incidents do not happen again."[48] These groups called upon local officials to investigate and prosecute the Klansmen involved. Baca wrote to INS officials; California state assemblyman Richard Alatorre; the acting U.S. attorney in the southern district of California, M. James Lorenz; and others to protest Mendez-Ruiz's treatment and to demand an investigation.[49] San Diego city councilman Jess D. Haro wrote personally to President Carter and U.S. attorney general Griffin Bell and argued that "individuals must not have their freedoms challenged because of their appearance."[50] Congressman Ed Roybal also wrote U.S. attorney Michael Walsh, demanding an investigation.[51]

Anti-Klan activities occurred in Texas also. There, black, brown, and white activists organized massive cross-racial coalitions to oppose the KKK. One of the first big protests occurred in Dallas. A group of activists had established an umbrella group called the Coalition for Human Dignity. In late 1979 the group conducted its first protest march against the Klan. Over two thousand African Americans, Latino/as, and whites marched, carrying signs that read "KKK—Scum of the Land" and "A People United Will Never be Defeated." The marchers drove away about fifty Klansmen who came out to oppose the rally.[52]

Similar protests developed in San Antonio. With its sizable Latino/a population and long history of civil rights activism, the city proved a perfect choice for anti-Klan activism. As in Dallas, San Antonians founded an umbrella organization, aptly titled the San Antonio Coalition against the KKK, to organize the protests. The San Antonio Coalition announced plans for a large rally in January 1980.[53] On January 19, 1980, approximately five hundred activists marched through downtown San Antonio. At a rally following the march, community organizer and longtime San Antonio activist Tommy "T.C." Calvert, who was then cochair of the Texas Black Caucus, stated unequivocally that "today we are putting the city and state officials on notice: the Klan is an illegal organization and we will not tolerate them." Jaime Martinez, another well-respected San Antonio activist and a union representative for the local Electrical Workers Union, was more succinct, calling the Klan "scum" and a "bunch of nobodies who wave the American flag while preaching racism."[54]

A few years later, in 1983, activists in Austin had several stressful encounters with members of the Klan. As in Dallas and San Antonio, the local Klan in Austin organized around the rallying cry of halting illegal immigration. The KKK had reappeared in Austin with some degree of fanfare. Local media ran several news stories depicting the Klan positively. Several illustrations in local papers showed Klansmen with high-powered automatic weapons, ready to protect the border. One Klan member allegedly told a newsperson: "[Latino/as]'re like niggers. . . . if you let one in, you have to let them all in."[55] When the KKK planned a major march in downtown Austin, the debate about allowing a parade permit aroused considerable controversy on the Austin City Council. Mayor Carole McClellan noted that she and others "deplore, abhor, and detest the Ku Klux Klan," but she quickly followed with a "however" that noted she supported freedom of speech more.[56]

Activists offered their own "howevers" by examining the racist history of the Klan and arguing forcefully that the new KKK was simply using the current anti-immigrant furor to mask its genocidal positions, which were just as fervently racist in the 1970s and 1980s as they had been in the 1870s and 1920s. For example, reading a statement from the Black Citizens Task Force, City Councilman Charles E. Urdy, the only African American on the council, noted that the Klan had always "advocate[d] and perpetuate[d] violence against black people and other minorities." Urdy hit at the irony of the Klan parade permit vote, stating that the freedom of speech issue was a false one: "it's an issue of white supremacy, terrorism, and violence." When Councilman John Treviño, the sole Latino on the council, voted in favor of granting the parade permit, the audience at the council meeting erupted in shouts of "no marcharan" (don't let them march). Adela Mancias, one of the leaders of the Chicano movement in Austin, chided Treviño for granting rights to a group that would deny those rights to Treviño and other Latino/as. Mancias further scolded Treviño and the council for authorizing a hate parade. Other local leaders took up this theme, asserting that "by granting the Klan's request this council will consciously refuse to recognize the true character of the Klan and accord it the so-called first amendment protection, which no terrorist organization ever obtained anywhere else in the world." The city council granted the parade permit.[57]

The local chapter of the Brown Berets, an activist Chicano organization that had developed in the late 1960s, had been founded in Austin in the early 1970s by Paul Hernandez, Adela Mancias, and others.[58] They were joined by the Black Citizens Task Force and the John Brown Anti-Klan League in protesting the Klan's activities. These groups planned a major counterdemonstration to oppose the Klan. As it turned out, the anti-Klan demonstration was larger than the Klan march itself. The approximately fifty Klan members, many of whom wore the traditional white robes and hoods, marched to the capitol grounds where they had a short rally. About a thousand anti-Klan protesters, which included Latino/as, blacks, and whites, lined the parade route the Klan took. Most of the Klan's opponents shouted, "We're fired up, won't take no more," "El pueblo unido jamás será vencido" (the united people will never be defeated), and "Hey hey, ho ho, the KKK has got to go" as the Klan members marched by.[59] Hernandez stated, "We're here to let the

Klan know and the police know and the city council know . . . that the KKK, even though they may be protected by all these people [he gestured to a large contingent of police] . . . that genocide is something we feel is directed at us [and] the KKK is out to do what they did to the blacks. . . . They want to do [the same thing] to the Mexican people now in this state, and we're not going to let them do it."[60]

Hernandez's words highlighted an aspect of the Klan/anti-Klan protests that a few minutes later spawned violence: the presence of numerous police officers. The Austin Police Department and the Texas Department of Public Safety had dispatched dozens of officers to protect the Klan members. After the Klan had passed, a number of Latino/a activist leaders, including Hernandez and Mancias, were attacked by the Austin police. Mancias believed the police singled them out for their role in planning the anti-Klan demonstration. She also noted that the officers had removed their name tags and badges so as to avoid identification. Hernandez was badly beaten, while Mancias and activist María Límon were bloodied but not seriously injured.[61]

"On February 19, 1983, at the Ku Klux Klan march, the Austin Police Department violently beat three Chicano activists," noted a flyer produced by the Brown Berets, the National Lawyers Guild, the UT Chicano Law Students Association, and the Comité para Justicia (Committee for Justice).[62] These activist groups soon developed a legal aid and redress committee under the auspices of the Comité para Justicia. Their goal was not only to free the activists jailed at the anti-Klan protest, but also to bring to light the unequal treatment meted out against the activists, since no Klan members were jailed during the protests. The committee saw the activists, correctly I would suggest, as political prisoners who had broken no laws yet remained in jail.[63] Moreover, the group understood that its success could only come from an activist coalition that included multiple ethnic groups and leaders. The activists ultimately succeeded in their goal: Mancias and Límon were acquitted of resisting arrest, while Hernandez was convicted of the same charge, appealed, and his conviction was overturned.

CONCLUSION

In the post–civil rights era, blacks and Latinos attempted to join forces on several important fronts. The next struggle involved each group discerning how they could unite to defeat the forces of racism in the 1970s, 1980s, and beyond. While there had been attempts at black-Latino coalition building for generations, those efforts had often foundered because of perceptions of racial difference; white repression; instances of rivalry and competition over power, jobs, and housing; and the divides generated by Jim Crow segregation. Once Jim Crow was officially outlawed, many activists rightly believed that the doors to cooperation were opened. The Black Power and Brown Power periods and the post–civil rights era thus witnessed considerable cooperation between blacks and browns.

Successful coalitions materialized around several particular moments in this period. Political activists and those concerned with the racist tenor of the English-only movement came together under the auspices of Jesse Jackson's National Rainbow Coalition. Mario Obledo's appointment to head the organization's board of directors clearly represented an important extension of the Rainbow Coalition's efforts to unite ethnic communities. When these two men and the NRC vocally opposed groups like USEnglish, they firmly communicated to activists, as well as to concerned citizens, that Latino/as and African Americans would no longer tolerate language racism nor racism of any other kind. While Obledo's role with the NRC proved short lived—and his departure tells us something about power sharing and some of the inherent difficulties in coalition building—his appointment nonetheless represented an important moment of unity.

Other examples of racist hostility during this period seemed almost tailor-made for generating cooperative civil rights activism. Police brutality affected blacks and browns in almost exactly the same way. Minorities had experienced police harassment and murder for generations, and while they had resisted this abuse for many years, the activism of Latino/as and African Americans increased in the 1960s, 1970s, and 1980s. Their activism was also combined, a unity that resulted in numerous protests, lawsuits, and the formation of internal affairs departments and police-civilian review boards in cities across the Southwest.

Perhaps no issue was better designed to generate ethnoracial unity and activism than the racism of the KKK. Certainly African Americans well understood the Klan and the need to oppose it. The KKK of the 1970s and 1980s focused its bigotry on Latin American immigrants, a group that, while perhaps a new target, experienced forms of abuse similar to those that black people had long suffered. Thus when Klansmen began capturing allegedly undocumented individuals (who later turned out to be documented), they aroused the anger of not only Latinos, but also blacks. Additionally, Klan racism became wedded to the issue of police abuse, which only further assisted the unification of blacks and Latinos. It is somewhat of a historical irony that police abuse and KKK racism, which seemed designed to generate discord and division, served to bring together Latino/as and blacks in a united campaign that ultimately pushed back the Klan and attempted to curb police abuse via a unified activist struggle. That example of unity continues to inform much of African American–Latino activism today.

NOTES

1. "Black, Hispanic Alliance Gains Momentum in California," *San Diego Union*, October 16, 1983.

2. In this chapter I use the terms "black" and "African American" to denote people of African heritage. For people of Latin American heritage, I use "Latina/o" and "Hispanic" and where more specificity is warranted "Mexican American," "Mexican descent," "Mexican origin," and "Chicana/o." I also occasionally refer to Latino/as as "brown." For people of European heritage, I use "white" and "Anglo."

3. "Obledo to Chair 'Rainbow Coalition,'" *El Hispano*, December 30, 1987.

4. See Brian D. Behnken, *Fighting Their Own Battles: Mexican Americans, African Americans, and the Struggle for Civil Rights in Texas* (Chapel Hill: University of North Carolina Press, 2011), esp. chaps. 1–4 for the difficulties of coalition building. See chaps. 5–7 for instances of cooperative efforts in the late civil rights period.

5. Ibid., 100.

6. "Latin Americans Urge Black-Hispanic Unity," *San Diego Union*, October 16, 1983; "Black, Hispanic Alliance Gains Momentum in California," ibid.; "Let's Resurrect Together," *Latino/a* (Winter 1984–1985).

7. "Jackson Bids for Black and Hispanic Cooperation," *New York Times*, April 17, 1984.

8. "Jesse Jackson Takes Unity Plea West," *Orange County Register*, August 23, 1987; "Jackson, Latino/a Activists Hope to Form 'Black-Brown Coalition,'" *Chicago Tribune*, April 5, 2008.

9. For an excellent analysis of this issue, see Leo R. Chavez, *The Latino Threat: Constructing Immigrants, Citizens, and the Nation* (Stanford, Calif.: Stanford University Press, 2008).

10. "The Perils of 'Quebecking,'" *Washington Post*, December 12, 1988.

11. Ibid.; "Say It in English," *Newsweek*, February 20, 1989.

12. Quoted in Daniel Wei HoSang, "Racial Propositions: 'Genteel Apartheid' in Postwar California" (PhD diss., University of Southern California, 2007), 322.

13. "WITAN Memo III," John Tanton to WITAN IV attendees, October 10, 1986, http://www.splcenter.org/get-informed/intelligence-report/browse-all-issues/2002/summer/the-puppeteer/witan-memo-iii#.UbIs7Gw059A (accessed June 7, 2013).

14. It is difficult to provide a clear picture of what Obledo did on the board. Board meetings occurred infrequently and took place behind closed doors.

15. "Jackson Woos Hispanics with New Amnesty Law Plan," *Mohave Daily Miner*, May 8, 1988. See also Associated Press, "Jackson Goes to Hollywood, Says He's 'Hot on the Heels' of Dukakis," May 6, 1988.

16. "The Democrats in Atlanta; Excerpts from Jackson's Speech: Pushing Party to Find Common Ground," *New York Times*, July 20, 1988, http://www.nytimes.com/1988/07/20/us/democrats-atlanta-excerpts-jackson-s-speech-pushing-party-find-common-ground.html?pagewanted=all&src=pm (accessed June 28, 2013).

17. "Statement of Purpose," *EPIC Events*, January–February 1989, Mario Obledo Papers, Special Collections, University of California, Davis (hereafter Obledo Papers).

18. "Hispanics and Blacks Try Again to Heal Rifts, Forge Voting Bloc," *Christian Science Monitor*, November 7, 1983, http://www.csmonitor.com/1983/1107/110769.html/(page)/2 (accessed June 28, 2013).

19. "Latin Americans Urge Black-Hispanic Unity," *San Diego Union*, October 16, 1983.

20. LULAC Resolution, June 27, 1987, Obledo Papers.

21. Ruben Bonilla to Vernon Jordan, November 14, 1979, William Bonilla Collection, Benson Latin American Collection, University of Texas, Austin.

22. "Black San Antonio III: They Call It Police Brutality," *San Antonio Express*, February 15, 1972; "Black San Antonio V: Political Inroads," ibid., February 17, 1972; "Bobby Jo Phillips Investigative File 1968," box 10, folder 4, Salas Papers, University of Texas, San Antonio (hereafter UTSA); Mario Salas, interview by author, November 20, 2009.

23. Salas, interview by author. See also "Student Nonviolent Coordinating Committee–S.A. (1 of 2), 1967–1975," box 8, folder 9, and "Student Nonviolent Coordinating Committee–S.A. (2 of 2), 1967–1975," box 9, folder 1, both in Salas Papers, UTSA.

24. Behnken, *Fighting Their Own Battles*, 167–68.

25. Brian D. Behnken, "'We Want Justice!': Police Murder, Mexican American Community Response, and the Chicano Movement," in *The Hidden 1970s: Histories of Radicalism*, ed. Dan Berger (New Brunswick, N.J.: Rutgers University Press, 2010), 200–208.

26. Ernesto B. Vigil, *The Crusade for Justice: Chicano Militancy and the Government's War on Dissent* (Madison: University of Wisconsin Press, 1999), esp. chap. 11; Jesús Salvador Treviño, *Eye Witness: A Filmmaker's Memoir of the Chicano Movement* (Houston, Tex.: Arte Público, 2001), 317; "Un Tributo a Luis 'Jr' Martinez," *El Gallo*, April–May 1976.

27. See "Telegrams of Support," *El Gallo*, May–June 1975.

28. "Message to Aztlan," *El Gallo*, October–November 1975.

29. "Violent Narcotics Raid Rattles Family but Net[s] No Drugs," *Tucson Citizen*, August 17, 1979.

30. See "Prosecutors Appealing Jury Trial for Montenegro," *Arizona Daily Star*, January 8, 1980; "Defense Case Pre-empted by Montenegro Mistrial," ibid., January 19, 1980; "Retrial of Montenegro Scheduled for Feb. 13," *Tucson Citizen*, January 23, 1980; "Sec-

ond Montenegro Is Found Not Guilty," ibid., February 14, 1980; "Jose Montenegro Convicted," ibid., February 22, 1980; "City Wins One, Loses One in Montenegro Litigation," ibid., February 26, 1980.

31. "Minorities Meet to Back Family in Police Complaint," *Tucson Citizen*, September 25, 1979.

32. "Opposing Views of Sinohui Killing Launch Trial in $5 Million Lawsuit," *Arizona Daily Star*, October 5, 1980; "Sinohuis 'Crippled,' Says Lawyer," *Tucson Citizen*, March 27, 1980.

33. "Sinohui's Parents File Civil Suit in Son's Death," *Tucson Citizen*, October 5, 1979; "Sinohui Case Reset for Judge, Not Jury," *Arizona Daily Star*, November 22, 1979; "Judge Will Make Decision in Suit over Sinohui Death," *Tucson Citizen*, November 23, 1979.

34. "Sinohuis Given $200,000 in Shooting Death of Son by Policeman," *Arizona Daily Star*, March 29, 1980. See also "Ex-Policeman Forfeits Home to Pay Off Suit," *Arizona Republic*, May 21, 1980.

35. "50 Hispanics Demand Prosecution in Slaying," *Arizona Republic*, April 18, 1980.

36. "Service Recalls 1977 'Hell' of Sinohui Death," *Arizona Daily Star*, July 12, 1979; "Hanigans, Sinohuis Lose in Court," *Tucson Citizen*, October 18, 1980; quotations are from "Sinohui Case Closed, Hanigans Lose Appeal," *Arizona Daily Star*, October 18, 1980.

37. "U.S. to Evaluate Any New Data in Sinohui Case," *Arizona Daily Star*, October 22, 1980; "Sinohui Probe May Be Revived," *Tucson Citizen*, October 22, 1980; "Sinohui Reprobe Is Urged," ibid., November 11, 1980.

38. "LULAC Recalls Sinohui," *Tucson Citizen*, June 27, 1980.

39. "Sinohui Case Closed, U.S. Won't Reopen Rights Probe," *Arizona Daily Star*, January 16, 1980.

40. "Strengthen America," Klan flyer, ca. 1977, Herman Baca Papers, Mandeville Special Collections Library, University of California, San Diego (hereafter UCSD); "KKK Racists to Begin Border Patrol," *El Gallo*, November 1977.

41. See "Grease-Hound Bus Lines, Inc.," "Instant Greaser," "White Power Comes to Midvale," and "White Man Wake Up!" (Klan advertisements and cartoons), ca. 1977, Baca Papers, UCSD.

42. "Community Unites in San Diego," CCR *Newsletter*, October 19, 1977.

43. "3000 Protest KKK," *El Gallo*, November 1977.

44. "From Night Riders to Border Patrolmen" and "Actions Kick Sheets Out of KKK," both in *The Worker*, n.d., Baca Papers, UCSD; "Secuestro de Chicanos por el KKK" [Seizure of Chicanos by the KKK], newspaper clipping, n.d., Baca Papers, UCSD.

45. "KKK—Enemigo del Pueblo" [KKK—Enemy of the People], *El Obrero*, n.d., Baca Papers, UCSD; "When the KKK and the INS Are on the Same Side," CCR *Newsletter*, October 29, 1977.

46. "On Guard against the Hordes, Klan Dragon Fears an Invasion," *Los Angeles Times*, April 16, 1978.

47. KGTV News, transcript, April 4, 1978; Charles C. Sava to Herman Baca, May 3,

1978; U.S. attorney Michael H. Walsh to Herman Baca, February 1, 1979; news release from U.S. attorney Michael Walsh, January 29,1979, all in Baca Papers, UCSD; "2 Men Indicted on Charges of Violating Alien's Rights," *San Diego Union*, November 4, 1978; "Mexicano Apprehended by KKK," *El Gallo*, May–June 1978. Walsh noted that Carl Shipton and Robert Cole were both indicted by the grand jury of southern California for interfering with the rights of a lawful resident alien. Shipton pled guilty; the case against Cole was dismissed due to lack of evidence.

48. "Mexicano Apprehended by KKK"; "La Raza against the KKK," *El Gallo*, May–June 1978.

49. Herman Baca to Michael Walsh, April 12, 1978 ; M. James Lorenz to Herman Baca, April 21, 1978; Richard Alatorre to Herman Baca, April 26, 1978, all in Baca Papers, UCSD.

50. Jess D. Haro to Attorney General Griffin Bell, April 19, 1978; Jess D. Haro to the Honorable Jimmy Carter, April 20, 1978, both in Baca Papers, UCSD.

51. Edward Roybal to Michael Walsh (Roybal's letter was cosigned by John Conyers, Don Edwards, and Elizabeth Holtzman), April 12, 1978, Baca Papers.

52. "Abajo con el KKK" [Down with the KKK], *El Pueblo*, December 1979.

53. "March against the Ku Klux Klan," *El Pueblo*, January 1980.

54. "El Pueblo Unido—the Fight against Racism," *El Pueblo*, February 1980; "500 Marchan contra el Racismo en S.A." [500 March against Racism in S.A.], ibid.

55. "No Marcharan!," Brown Berets Central Texas Region, flyer, February 3, 1983, http://renerenteria.files.wordpress.com/2013/04/austinbrownberets_march272013_19.jpg (accessed July 18, 2012).

56. *The Day the Klan Marched*, http://www.youtube.com/watch?v=FttayZRBcGE (accessed July 1, 2013).

57. Ibid.

58. On the Austin Brown Berets, who were not directly affiliated with the Los Angeles group, see Ernesto Chavez, *"¡Mi Raza Primero!": Nationalism, Identity, and Insurgency in the Chicano Movement in Los Angeles* (Berkeley: University of California Press, 2002); F. Arturo Rosales, *Chicano!: The History of the Mexican American Civil Rights Movement* (Houston, Tex.: Arte Público, 1996); "Brown Berets Allege Local Police Brutality," *Daily Texan*, November 14, 1977.

59. On the Klan march and anti-Klan demonstration, see Austin City Council minutes, February 24, 1983, 23, http://www.austintexas.gov/edims/document.cfm?id=16431 (accessed July 18, 2013).

60. For some commentaries on the Brown Berets' activism in Austin, see the interviews with René Rentería and Susana Almanza, http://renerenteria.wordpress.com/2013/04/09/austin-brown-berets-insights-reflections-and-discussion/#http://renerenteria.wordpress.com/2013/04/09/austin-brown-berets-insights-reflections-and-discussion/# (accessed July 18, 2013). See also *The Day the Klan Marched*.

61. "2000 Demonstrate against Klan in Austin," *Death to the Klan*, April–May 1983;

Virginia Marie Raymond, "Mexican Americans Write toward Justice in Texas, 1973–1982" (PhD diss., University of Texas, Austin, 2007), 131–32; "Austin's Rodney King," *Alternative Views* 475 (September 4, 1992), https://archive.org/details/AV_475-AUSTINS_RODNEY_KING (accessed January 15, 2014). See also "A '60s Voice Grows Quiet," *Austin American-Statesman*, April 5, 2008.

62. "Police Violence and Racism in Perspective: What the TV News Isn't Showing," flyer produced by the Brown Berets and the Comité para Justicia (Committee for Justice), April 18, 1983, file AF: Mexican Americans, Brown Berets, M4300 (4), Austin History Center, Austin Public Library (hereafter APL).

63. See the benefit flyer produced by the Comité para Justicia, the Brown Berets, and the Prison Coalition, ca. November 1983, file AF: Mexican Americans, Brown Berets, M4300 (4), APL; "Inquiry Set in Violence over Texas Klan Rally," *New York Times*, February 22, 1983. The police blamed the violence on the anti-Klan marchers: "Violence at Klan Rally Blamed on Hoodlums," *Victoria Advocate*, February 25, 1983; "Texas Police Chief Says Anti-Klan 'Hoodlums' Caused Rally Violence," *Lewiston Daily Sun*, February 25, 1983.

CHAPTER 11

Rainbow Reformers

Black-Brown Activism and the Election of Harold Washington

GORDON MANTLER

"When we started this campaign, we all said, 'We can win,'" Harold Washington told supporters just four days before the Chicago mayoral primary in 1983. "About ten days ago, I woke up and said, 'We have won!'" The crowd of two hundred black, white, and Latino supporters in a South Side campaign office exploded into a standing ovation.[1] They cheered and yelled encouragement as the sixty-year-old black congressman and one-time machine politician expressed supreme confidence that his campaign's vast grassroots effort would successfully beat Chicago's legendary Democratic political machine to elect him as the city's first African American mayor.[2] Washington was proven correct—although it would take longer than expected. Another month and a half passed, marked by white race-baiting during a surprisingly competitive general election, before Washington secured the mayoralty and made history.

But who is the "we" that Washington refers to? Who won exactly? In the context of this campaign rally, the multiracial crowd of supporters suggested a diverse electoral coalition of many races, backgrounds, and classes. Chicagoans interested in reform, in a rejection of machine politics, had triumphed. And those hungry for an alternative to the conservative federal policies of President Ronald Reagan were satiated briefly by the news from Chicago. Yet scholarly and journalistic accounts routinely offer far narrower interpretations. One analysis is purely biographical—the triumphant story of a former machine politician who showed his true colors by running as a reformer, freeing himself from the shackles of the party machinery.[3] As one biographer suggests, "It was the man more than the plan."[4] An overlapping narrative emphasizes the decline of the city's political machine since the death of Mayor Richard J. Daley in 1976 and the opening it provided not only to Washington, but also to his predecessor, Jane Byrne. And a third related narrative interprets Washington's "we" as the city's one million African Americans, who came out in record numbers to support the black candidate.[5] "Above all, it was the massive, unprecedented, and crusade-like folk movement led by charismatics and 'race' men that swept Washington into office," concluded Melvin Holli and Paul Green. "The base for Washington's victory was simply the overwhelming black vote."[6]

Indeed, African Americans in 1983 did buck the system in a way that had rarely been seen since the advent of the modern operation in 1931—at least partly in response to a machine under fire by a seasoned and charismatic black candidate. Blacks long had been taken for granted by an efficient, white-dominated political machinery that showered a few black community leaders, such as Congressmen Arthur Mitchell, William Dawson, and Ralph Metcalfe (until near the end of his career), with patronage and money in exchange for votes—as well as relative inaction and silence on civil rights.[7] This setup began to fail, however, as African Americans became more and more independent, especially in the 1970s, after several high-profile cases of police brutality. By 1983, a record number of black Chicagoans were registered to vote. And nearly 85 percent of black primary voters and an unheard-of 99 percent of black general election voters chose Washington as the city's first, and still only, African American mayor elected to office. It proved to be the culmination of a generation of rising black independent political power. Moreover, Washington's election and brief four-year tenure ushered in considerable black participation in the city's political process and governing. No longer were African Americans just cogs in a vast, corrupt system that favored a few.[8]

While such factors played an important role in the 1983 victory, the "we" that Washington employed that day in February 1983 suggested a broader truth of the campaign and the larger historical processes that made it possible. "This is the first time. Before, we were protesting," recalled José "Cha-Cha" Jiménez, the leader of the Young Lords, a one-time street gang, who spearheaded popular protests against the Daley machine in the 1960s and 1970s and then worked in primarily Latino precincts for Washington in 1983. That campaign "was a different feeling. . . . Now, we were winners. With the Harold Washington campaign, we felt like winners."[9] This feeling, even if fleeting for some, was widespread among the coalition members beyond the African Americans who voted and campaigned for Washington. Largely working-class Latinos provided most of the 46,250-vote margin Washington received to beat his Republican opponent in the general election in April 1983.[10] For many of them, Washington's triumph was as much theirs as it was African Americans'. And despite setbacks, rivalries, and miscommunications among the coalition partners—so often emphasized by journalists and scholars—the four years of the Washington administration demonstrated genuine empowerment for many Latinos.[11]

These achievements were made possible by painstaking community organizing well before the campaign of 1983. Working-class Latinos such as Cha-Cha Jiménez and Rudy Lozano and organizations like the CASA-HGT (Centro de Acción Social Autónomo–Hermandad General de Trabajadores, Center for Autonomous Social Action–General Brotherhood of Workers) and the Heart of Uptown Coalition built on neighborhood organizations and tentative black-brown coalitions in the 1970s and early 1980s. Immigration and migrant worker rights activism played a key role in building trust among African American and Latino workers—foreshadowing both the electoral coalition to come and Washington's own championing of immigration as a congressman, candidate, and mayor.

Thus, the coalition work that brought Harold Washington to power has implications well beyond the confines of Chicago and its unique political system. As I have argued was the case in the high-profile antipoverty activism of the late 1960s, black-brown coalitions were at best situational and contingent, full of real differences over ideology, strategy, and personality.[12] Sometimes these could be overcome, at least fleetingly. Electoral coalitions in Texas and opposition to state violence in Chicago and other places proved productive and were something activists could celebrate in the 1960s and 1970s. But unlike what the field's dominant interpretations routinely argue, most of these efforts at coalition building were neither great successes nor general failures.[13] Rather, they reflected a little of both. And Chicago in 1983 suggested those contingencies as well.

The broad multiracial coalition that supported Harold Washington for mayor also speaks to a more complicated narrative of the 1980s than scholars usually allow. Undoubtedly, federal retrenchment occurred in urban and racial policies after the late 1970s and the so-called Reagan revolution, including an expanded war on drugs, accelerated deindustrialization, and a revamped neoliberalism that plunged an already squeezed working class into further crisis. Yet historians of the era have exaggerated the top-down narratives of an "Age of Reagan" as the only worthwhile interpretation of the time.[14]

Rather, the 1980s also witnessed a muscular political alternative often led by black and Latino politicians and activists. Jesse Jackson's national campaigns deserve some credit, but the alternative politics of the 1980s mostly took shape at the local and regional levels—a politics rooted in neighborhood activism, shifting urban demographics, and broader national and transnational networks.[15]

In other words, the 1983 election of a black mayor and his subsequent administration in Chicago is not just a story of African American political power, the decline of the Daley machine, and one man's charisma. And it is not just a story of Latino political empowerment, multiracial coalition building, and neighborhood organizing in a city best known for disillusioning hardball politics often likened to hand-to-hand combat. Harold Washington's election is also a story of multiracial urban electoral activism offering the best answer—albeit a flawed and unsatisfactory one—to a declining working class and an ever more fleeting American dream.

* * *

During the reign of Richard J. Daley and his machine, Latinos had not played a substantial role in Chicago politics—and certainly not in coalition with African Americans. But this began to change in the mid-1970s, as the era's social movements and street actions gave way to more formal attempts to influence policy. Several Latinos ran for city council in 1975, including Jiménez, a Puerto Rican who translated the Young Lords' street protests against urban renewal into a viable campaign in the largely working-class communities of Lakeview and Uptown. Jiménez lost, but his effort signaled the potential of a multiracial coalition—black, Latino, white, and Native American—especially if the campaign emphasized voter registration. As political strategist Don Rose suggested, one route to independent success is "recognition of the burgeoning black and Latino population as the vehicle for social change" in the city.[16]

Across town in the largely Mexican American barrios of Pilsen and Little Village, the limits of the Chicano movement's cultural nationalism ushered in a more pragmatic politics of labor organizing and electoral coalition building.[17] The work of Pilsen activist Rudy Lozano epitomized this transition. A native of southern Texas, Lozano moved with his siblings and immigrant parents to Chicago in the 1950s and was raised in Pilsen as the neighborhood witnessed a dramatic shift from a mostly white ethnic enclave to a Mexican American one. Lozano attended Harrison High School, where he helped lead walkouts in 1969 as part of the national wave of Chicano school boycotts to protest discrimination against Spanish-speaking students. He continued his activism as a student at the University of Illinois Circle Campus, eventually quit school, and went to work with Legal Aid, which provided undocumented workers with legal assistance. In 1974 Lozano helped form a radical local chapter of the CASA-HGT, a Marxist-leaning organization founded in Los Angeles that "identified Mexican workers as crucial to the U.S. economy and integral to its work force," according to one Chicano scholar.[18] Originally a mutual aid society when it was formed in 1968, the CASA-HGT altered its mission when younger activists took over the leadership and pushed the organization into far more assertive labor organizing among Mexican immigrants. As the son of immigrants, Lozano viewed this fight as both personal and practical, especially amid the increasingly harsh rhetoric that scapegoated workers of Mexican descent—documented and undocumented—for the nation's rising unemployment and economic anxiety in the 1970s.[19]

The CASA-HGT in Chicago had deep roots in the area's community organizations, which led to a series of efforts to support Latino workers, especially the undocumented. Activists established student and community committees in defense of farmworkers, which organized produce boycotts and awareness campaigns, and a partnership with the Chicago-based Midwest Coalition for the Defense of Immigrants. Lozano eventually became a full-time organizer for Local 336 of the International Ladies' Garment Workers' Union (ILGWU), where he successfully organized immigrant workers in the city's notorious tortilla factories. Many days, his work consisted of simple gestures toward the workers, small amounts of assistance or mentoring. The factories' owners routinely threatened workers with federal immigration raids and deportation, but Lozano's painstaking work eventually led to three successful votes to recognize the ILGWU. His approach also created professional relationships he would make use of in the future.[20]

Early on, Lozano saw potential allies in the independent black politicians who emerged in the 1970s. While the CASA-HGT had an explicit campaign to build a durable Latino alliance, its ideological approach allowed the group to build partnerships with blacks. As a young Chicano activist, Lozano admired the accomplishments of African Americans during the civil rights struggle. The curricular reforms demanded by African Americans at Harrison and at the University of Illinois Circle Campus were models for his own arguments for Mexican American and Latino inclusion. In 1975 Lozano was a driving force behind the CASA-HGT's willingness to advocate for a black school superintendent rather than a Latino, which had been other activists' position, and the CASA-HGT's support produced valuable capital for the future. As a field organizer for the ILGWU, Lozano built ties with African American activists, such as Charles Hayes, Eloise Brown, and the Coalition of Labor Union Women's Johnnie Jackson, often advocating for both blacks and Latinos in the city's sweatshops. Blacks also lived along the edges of Pilsen and Little Village and thus made up part of the electorate in the otherwise Latino-centric ward. As Lozano began to translate his labor organizing into electoral work—including the Independent Political Organization (IPO), which he co-founded in 1981—African Americans became increasingly essential to his political ambitions.[21]

One key contact Lozano made was Harold Washington. Once a machine politician, Washington began to build a reputation for independence in the state legislature in the late 1960s and 1970s, and nearly lost his job because of it. Washington helped found the legislature's first black caucus and routinely championed civil rights in Springfield, limits on police power, and opposition to public aid for private schools (and thus white flight). He supported bilingual education efforts and minority business participation in government contracting in Illinois. And he sponsored legislation bolstering the state's fair employment regulations, including sharp penalties for discriminatory unions that held contracts with public entities. This addressed directly the concerns of black and Latino workers who found themselves excluded by conservative, white-dominated craft labor organizations connected to the machine. These independent political positions increasingly concerned Washington's machine supporters in Chicago.[22]

In 1977 Washington sealed his separation from the machine with a mayoral run against Mayor Michael Bilandic, who had been appointed after Daley's death in December 1976. Washington first declined to run, but he eventually made a late entry as a protest candidate. Washington won the endorsement of the Independent Voters of Illinois and a collection of progressive unions, yet he repeatedly refused to condemn the machine. Instead, he contended that it could work better and in a more democratic way. "I'm not anti-Machine," he told the *Chicago Reader*. "Obviously, you have to have an organization. My purpose is to reform the Democratic Party, not to dismantle it or destroy it." That position doomed his candidacy with independent good-government supporters, while most African Americans continued to back the favored and machine-backed Bilandic. Washington won an anemic 11 percent in the Democratic primary. Latinos remained aloof from the electoral process, voting in small numbers and mostly for the machine. Despite some inclusive rhetoric, Washington had not emphasized Latino outreach. Lozano did not endorse Washington, but he became intrigued by Washington's potential as a reformer and the progressive ties he cultivated. After Washington won reelection in 1978 to his state senate seat without machine support—albeit by only 206 votes—Lozano recognized the black politician as a potential ally in building a broader progressive coalition in the city.[23]

Despite his periodic success in labor organizing, Lozano in 1980 became increasingly convinced that electoral politics were essential to markedly improving the lives of the city's Latinos. After being part of the coalition that propelled Jane Byrne to a surprise mayoral victory over Bilandic in 1979, Latinos were quickly disillusioned with her leadership. Seemingly just days after defeating the machine's candidate, Byrne turned to the same Democratic Party machinery to govern the city, including the same kinds of divide-and-conquer tactics previous machine mayors had used against minorities. Yet the 1980 Census suggested that such a strategy might not continue to work as Chicago now boasted a much more robust Latino population—14 percent versus 3 percent of the city in 1970. In 1981 a group of Mexican Americans founded the Independent Political Organization on the Near West Side. The leadership consisted of some of Pilsen's and Little Village's most dynamic organizers, including Lozano; Jesus "Chuy" Garcia, a former Brown Beret, an officer of the CASA-HGT, and a future mayoral candidate (in 2015); Linda Coronado of Mujeres Latinas; and Art Vasquez of Pilsen's Casa Aztlán. The IPO's name echoed those of other anti-machine organizations, including the North Side's Independent Precinct Organization and the statewide Independent Voters of Illinois, and it promised to do similar work, especially in the Mexican American–majority Twenty-Second Ward.[24]

Unlike those organizations, however, the IPO had an explicit commitment to black-brown coalition—both a reflection of the Twenty-Second Ward's demographics and a larger citywide strategy. While the ward was roughly 74 percent Mexican American in 1980, it included substantial black-dominated precincts as well. Moreover, the IPO leaders decided that their "politics were going to be about change," recalled Chuy Garcia, "that they were going to be a vehicle for empowerment and enfranchisement, that we were going to work in coalition with other groups. In our situation, it was mandatory because we did not have the numbers by ourselves given the immigrant status of many people in the community, [so we decided] that we would work in alliance through a multi-racial approach to our politics."[25]

Local activist Jesus "Chuy" Garcia (*left*) and Cesar Chavez, the president of the United Farm Workers, flank Harold Washington after the mayor's announcement of support for a renewed grape boycott in 1985. Despite their differences at times, Mayor Washington maintained ties with both local and national Latino leaders throughout his administration. Chicago Public Library, Special Collections and Preservation Division, HWAC 1985-10-11.

This translated into a multipronged strategy of substantial voter registration efforts among Mexican Americans, the continued protection of and advocacy for undocumented workers of all nationalities, legal strategies to redraw the city council maps more favorably for Latinos, and the cultivation of black allies on the West Side and in community development networks across the city. Added to their earlier black labor connections were new allies, such as future alderman Danny Davis and activists Ronnell Mustin, Art Turner, and Pat Dickson. Black lawyers teamed up with Latino plaintiffs in crafting a legal challenge to the council's new machine-friendly maps. No tie, however, was more important than the one with the South Side's new congressman, Harold Washington.[26]

* * *

In 1980 the voters of the South Side elected Washington as their first truly independent congressman since the 1920s.[27] That same year, however, a conservative political tide swept through Illinois and the nation, electing the conservative Ronald Reagan as president and putting the U.S. Senate in Republican hands for the first time in more than thirty years. Thus, while Washington had achieved a lifelong dream of becoming a congressman, he entered a political climate that was remarkably hostile to his urban liberalism. Yet, soon after he arrived in 1981, he wielded influence far beyond his freshman status and became one of Reagan's most persistent critics, ranked by the *Congressional Quarterly* as the fifth most anti-administration member in the House. The congressman proposed a 20 percent cut in Reagan's inflated defense spending, arguing that the money could be better used in the nation's cities. He endorsed a nuclear freeze and became the floor leader for the renewal of the Voting Rights Act.[28]

Washington proved a particularly steadfast advocate of Latino concerns. "He did two things in Congress," said Nena Torres, who eventually worked in his administration. "One, he . . . supported immigration reform" by opposing the Simpson-Mazzoli Act, which made hiring an undocumented worker a federal offense and which critics argued would prompt workplace raids. Second, he "was one of the leading critics of the war in Central America." The Cold War proxy wars waged by Reagan in places like Nicaragua and Guatemala had become lightning rods for Latino criticism and even prompted a sanctuary movement for war refugees within the United States.[29] In his rhetoric, Washington routinely linked the violence in Latin America with racial lynchings at home, calling it "the international environment in which race hatred spreads."[30] Latinos also credited Washington for his work on the Voting Rights Act, in which he championed amendments to allow lawsuits challenging local at-large districts, which were designed to dilute minorities' voting influence. Latinos used these changes successfully to force localities to adopt single-member districts in Texas and to create more Latino-majority city council districts in Chicago in 1986. Overall, Washington continued to build a legislative and political record as a defender of the powerless. Of course, in Chicago that was not the usual path to City Hall.[31]

It took a confluence of factors in 1981 and 1982 to make Harold Washington's mayoral victory possible. As scholars have suggested, the campaign brought three distinct movements together, if ever so briefly: black nationalists, good-government reformers, and community development activists.[32] But whether nationalists like Lu Palmer, reformers such as Dick Simpson, or community development experts like Robert Mier, it has been middle-class professionals who have received the most credit for Washington's success. Left unstated has been the extent of working-class grassroots organizing at a critical juncture in the summer and fall of 1982. In the IPO, the Heart of Uptown Coalition, the Coalition of Black Trade Unionists, and many other organizations, working-class activists spearheaded the massive voter registration efforts and other coordination that persuaded Washington to run and believe he could win.

A series of community organizations and networks emerged to protest the city's development plans under Mayor Jane Byrne. The Community Workshop on Economic Development and the Chicago 1992 Committee joined older coalitions like the Rehab Network and the Chicago Association of Neighborhood Development Organizations—often with overlapping participants—in advocating for bottom-up, neighborhood-based influence on development, including affordable housing and commercial revitalization. These organizations often had professional spokespeople, but community activists generally drove their efforts. For instance, the Chicago 1992 Committee formed in the summer of 1982 to oppose the city's plan to host a world's fair ten years later. Arturo Vasquez, a veteran Pilsen community activist in the CASA-HGT and the IPO, was the committee's chair and viewed the world's fair development plan as one more effort by corporate leaders to gentrify an existing working-class neighborhood. In the 1960s it had been the Near West Side and then Lincoln Park; now, Pilsen could be overrun by new development. Vasquez was skeptical of the amount of city money to be spent on fair infrastructure, "given the problems of the city . . . steadily deteriorating housing stock, its deteriorating infrastructure, its neglected parks, its deteriorating schools—is this what we want to do with the little money that we've got?" Other community activists and organizations—ranging from former Black Panther and future congressman Bobby Rush to the League of Women Voters—had similar concerns and joined the coalition.[33]

At the end of the summer of 1982, an arguably more militant but overlapping coalition of activists aimed to turn such organizing toward larger electoral efforts in the rest of 1982 and in 1983. African American activists had been furious with Byrne ever since they helped put her in power in 1979 and she rewarded them with the replacement of black school board and Chicago Housing Authority members by inexperienced whites. She refused to negotiate with black-led unions and was generally insensitive to African American interests. Activists responded with a concerted effort to find a viable black candidate for mayor and a largely successful boycott of ChicagoFest, the city's annual summer street festival, which one writer deemed "Byrne's party." On the heels of the boycott, community organizations gathered in August to pass a "people's platform," which included an array of working-class demands. Delegates called for the election of Chicago school board members, the elimination of magnet schools (calling them "an elite educational system for the middle class" paid for by all city residents), citizen review boards to investigate cases of police brutality, strict enforcement of building codes, and an antispeculation tax.[34]

Expanding the voter base was one way for black and brown working-class activists to participate. In response to early entreaties to make another run for mayor, Harold Washington had told supporters to show him they were serious by registering 50,000 new voters. Some observers believed he chose an impossibly high number to have a ready-made reason to decline. Instead, activists responded. Forming POWER, the People's Organization for Welfare Economic Reform, an interracial coalition of community activists scoured the city for new voters. A record total of 94,882 were registered in the nine months before early October 1982, in time for the Illinois governor's race, and another 50,000 for the mayoral election the following February. Thanks to a lawsuit that led to expanded rules allowing voter registration in the city's public aid and unemployment lines and in libraries, POWER activists registered nearly 40,000 people in just four weeks—10,000 alone in front of such public offices.[35]

Much of the rest of the work was conducted in places less known for active citizenship, as organizer Modesto Rivera described. A Puerto Rican activist for the Heart of Uptown Coalition—part of POWER—Rivera had been interested in black politics since his days reading the Black Panther newspaper, which his father's store sold, the only one to do so in that part of the city. He recalled canvassing some of the roughest, most derelict apartment buildings in Chicago. "We were not afraid," said Rivera, although he carried a gun while doing voter work. "To us, everyone was a card-carrying voter. Prostitutes, junkies—what, they don't count? What you do for a living doesn't really concern us."[36] Paul Siegel, a white organizer who had campaigned for Cha-Cha Jiménez years earlier, said the same thing. The city's many rundown apartment buildings were electoral goldmines, if organizers were willing to spend time there. That was a strategy of Slim Coleman, who led the multiracial Uptown Coalition and was a leading voice in POWER. "Harold Washington would get a bigger white and Hispanic vote than the experts expect," he said. "A lot of people would say to us, 'I've been looking for a place to register.'"[37] Whites and Latinos in places like Uptown and Humboldt Park would be essential to Washington's victory. And so were black voters: 70 percent of those POWER registered in the fall of 1982 were African American.[38]

Harold Washington won reelection to Congress handily and promptly turned to the mayoral race, announcing his candidacy on November 10. While the room at the Hyde Park Hilton when he announced was full of black professionals—"black ministers, black lawyers, black doctors," as one reporter described it—what made the scene even more striking was the presence of whites and Latinos.[39] Standing on stage next to Jesse Jackson, Lu Palmer, and Renault Robinson were Slim Coleman; white independent politicians Bob Mann, Lawrence Bloom, and Barbara Flynn Currie; Rudy Lozano; and Puerto Rican pastor and community activist Jorge Morales. The rainbow coalition that many black leaders sought—whether it was supporting Fred Hampton in 1969 or Jesse Jackson in 1984—was in the room that cold November morning. And it was that coalition that Washington emphasized, alluding to the voter registration efforts: "The people of Chicago have announced their willingness to become involved, to unify and to act. . . . For if I am to be mayor, it will be as the spokesperson of this new movement—not the mayor of just a political faction—but mayor of all Chicago."[40] Going off script, he added, "We seek out the poor white who has been downtrodden. We reach out with open arms to the Latin community."[41]

Years of careful relationship building, a solid legislative record, and a progressive vision in line with the values of working-class black and brown neighborhoods culminated in Latino organizing and endorsements for his campaign that winter. Puerto Ricans were particularly supportive. "I believed in Harold Washington," recalled Cha-Cha Jiménez. "His whole theme of neighborhoods first was in line with what we believed in. . . . It fit right in with our philosophy. So I just started organizing."[42] The Reverend Jorge Morales agreed. The Puerto Rican founder of the West Town Coalition of Concerned Citizens and of an affiliated church dedicated to social justice and the poor, Morales viewed Washington as a key ally in the fight against infant mortality and other health concerns in his neighborhood.[43] Moreover, Washington's election would be "a means of self-determination for poor people in the city regardless of race, color, or religion," Morales said. "I understand the importance of self-determination and machine-free politics."[44] Jiménez saw allying with Washington as a continuation of the work he had started as a gang leader in the 1960s, when he fought police brutality, urban renewal, and the general displacement of the poor in Puerto Rican neighborhoods on the city's Near North Side. The issues were somewhat different, but related; for instance, hired arson ravaged areas like Lakeview and Humboldt Park because it was a way for developers to clear dilapidated buildings and collect the insurance. Jiménez recognized the Washington campaign as an opportunity to combat such practices but also to broaden the city's political discourse. "We wanted to raise the level of consciousness in the city," he recalled.[45]

While Puerto Ricans supported Washington in substantial numbers, demonstrating the common ground they often had with African Americans, other Latinos were a harder sell at first. The city's small Cuban American population was made up of disproportionately conservative business owners and professionals, while Mexican Americans and Central Americans were far less engaged with the political system and generally suspicious of a black politics shaped by the machine. But Rudy Lozano, Chuy Garcia, Linda Coronado, and others involved in the CASA-HGT, the IPO, and the ILGWU had worked to change that dynamic, registering voters, building ties with progressive black independents, and stressing the commonalities that Latinos and African Americans faced. Lozano used his IPO base to launch a challenge to a machine alderman, Frank Stemberk, who was rumored to not even live in the ward. Lozano openly campaigned on black-brown unity, alongside and for Washington, stressing its practical benefits. "Our ward is a community of ethnic neighborhoods rich in the history and cultures of Eastern European, Polish, Mexican, Latino, and Black people," one campaign flyer stated. "I believe in working together so that our community can grow and receive our fair share of services."[46] Both Lozano and Washington issued statements opposing the school board's closing of the mostly black and Latino Harrison High, and both showed up to protest the closing of a local Westinghouse Corporation plant. But while campaigning for Washington in the Twenty-Second Ward "could be pretty lonely," Nena Torres noted, Lozano nearly forced a runoff with Stemberk. He lost by only seventeen votes in a race with several other Latinos, most of whom had been machine plants designed to dilute the Latino vote.[47]

That same night Harold Washington made history in two ways. He became the first African American to win the Democratic primary for mayor—against Jane Byrne and political scion Richard M. Daley, the state's attorney, with 36 percent of the vote. Winning the primary usually was tantamount to victory in the heavily Democratic city. But in 1983, Washington's primary victory started seven more grueling weeks of campaigning since much of the Democratic Party machine tried to prevent the election of a black mayor and backed Republican Bernard Epton. The campaign featured considerable race baiting, including ominous calls to vote for Epton "before it's too late." Working-class people had been instrumental in Washington's primary win, especially the overwhelming number of African Americans voting for the congressman. They would turn out again in even larger numbers, but Latinos and poor whites were even more essential now.[48]

Washington's Latino campaign team, headed by Lozano and a young Puerto Rican, Peter Earle, pitched his candidacy along several lines: the improved services and input it would mean for neighborhoods like Pilsen, Little Village, and South Chicago; a new deputy mayor position held by a Latino, most likely Lozano; and a greater share of jobs and contracts going to Latinos. The Latino team also continued to stress Washington's track record on issues such as immigration, Central America, and sanctuary. But as Earle wrote in a memo soon after the primary victory, "The strategic issue is not whether or not Latinos that vote will support Washington, but rather how many Latinos will vote, period." Accordingly, Washington backed up his record with a heavy speaking schedule in the city's Latino communities, including a high-profile stroll through West Town with former New York congressman Herman Badillo. On Election Day, Lozano, Earle, Garcia, Torres, Coronado, and others mobilized to get every vote out. Latino turnout remained low, yet their votes were essential. In addition to the astounding 99 percent of African American votes, it took 75 percent of Latinos plus 12 percent of whites to win the general election, which Washington did, garnering 52 percent of the vote against Epton. In the election, "the degree of racial polarization [was] striking," noted political scientist Paul Kleppner. And so was the role of class. Large majorities of low-income Puerto Ricans and Mexican Americans backed Washington.[49]

* * *

As so many participants in electoral coalitions have learned, governing is much trickier than simply winning elections. Harold Washington's coalition proved no different. In the months after his election, machine-backed aldermen stonewalled nearly every policy and appointment Washington made, and Washington responded by vetoing the machine's more conservative legislation. A stalemate resulted. Moreover, Washington's reputation as a reformer and his campaign rhetoric of fairness translated into his signing the so-called Shakman decree, which greatly limited the number of patronage jobs available to the mayor in a city where power heavily relied on doling out public employment.[50] The practical result was that a high percentage of the city's limited patronage jobs went to those who had waited the longest—middle-class African Americans—and not to working-class blacks and Latinos. Take the example of Cha-Cha Jiménez. He could get in to speak with the mayor while others waited outside, but he did not receive a job. Jiménez, who had struggled with addiction throughout the 1970s, did not want to "embarrass the mayor. . . . After the campaign, I had no job. I didn't want a job with the city. Well, I wanted one with City Hall. But they couldn't do [that]." Instead, he left town.[51]

Months after they had made an electoral difference, frustrated Latinos started their own organization to monitor Latino affairs in the new administration. Rudy Lozano, the most obvious choice to become a high-ranking Latino official in City Hall, had been gunned down in his home in June 1983 under suspicious circumstances.[52] Others, such as Linda Coronado and Chuy Garcia, continued to work in their community groups, but could not land positions with the city. Frustrated with the Washington inner circle's unwillingness to integrate Latino issues and people into the agenda, a group of prominent Latinos, including many of the people who had "stuck their necks out" for Washington initially, made plans to announce the new organization. When it became clear that they were not going to back down from airing some dirty laundry, the mayor agreed to not only support a Latino affairs commission but also to give its members the freedom to hold the administration accountable.[53]

During the next four years, the Mayor's Advisory Commission on Latino Affairs became an influential advisory board, keeping tabs on everything from the slow hiring of Latinos to the administration's high-profile assistance of Central American political refugees and survivors of the 1985 Mexico City earthquake. Efforts to marginalize the commission failed, and it began to offer tough but realistic evaluations and recommendations by mid-1984, including letter grades for each agency on minority hiring and contracts. Nena Torres, an early Cuban American supporter of Washington and the commission's first executive director, was careful to point out that working with the mayor was "great," but as a longtime labor and civil rights progressive Washington "felt that [part of the coalition] was covered" by him. But during its four years advising Washington, the commission was an independent voice that did influence the mayor on key issues. The amount of Latino hiring and contracts improved each year, and commissioners held hearings and eventually swayed the mayor to abandon two initiatives: the 1992 world's fair and reforms to elect rather than appoint school board members (which commissioners believed risked diluting minority influence). The latter put them at odds with other members of the Washington coalition, who backed an elected school board. The commission also provided a good training ground for middle-class Latinos, including Miguel del Valle, who became an influential state senator, and Torres, who became a professor.[54]

The long-term legacies of the Washington coalition and his administration—in politics and policy—deserve their own extended treatment. He served just a little over four years, winning reelection in 1987 handily but then abruptly dying in office. Yet, from the remapping of city council districts and the election of two new Latino aldermen to the organizing lessons learned, ironically, by his opponents in the machine, the Washington era helped shape the city for a generation. His election certainly can be called a triumph and can be seen as the climax of black political power in Chicago—even more so than the election of Barack Obama as president of the United States twenty-five years later. It was also a turning point for Latino political empowerment in the city and, arguably, the nation. Washington would not have won without substantial Latino support—which was partly rooted in his expansive and sympathetic support for immigrants—and he eventually began to pay them back with greater roles in city government. In this sense, the Age of Reagan moniker for the 1980s misses the alternative politics of black-brown coalition building in the nation's cities. Unfortunately, these coalitions did not always deliver for those who worked the hardest to make them happen: working-class African Americans, Latinos, and poor whites. The alternative, progressive vision of Harold Washington and others like him slowed, but did not entirely stop, the long tide of deindustrialization and the corresponding despair that battered the nation's working class in the 1980s and beyond.

NOTES

1. While "African American" and "black" have become generally accepted, interchangeable terms for people of African descent in the United States, the terms used to identify Spanish-speaking people and their descendants are more contested. The term "Latino" is used for Spanish-speaking people of different nationalities in the United States, including Puerto Ricans and Cuban Americans. This contrasts with "Hispanic," a popular usage that privileges European heritage over indigenous and African influences in the Americas. When referring to people of Mexican descent, in this chapter I use "Mexican American" unless specifically referring to a recent immigrant from Mex-

ico (Mexican immigrant) or to a person of Mexican descent who identified as part of the Chicano movement of the late 1960s and 1970s (Chicano).

2. "'We Have Won,' Washington Declares," *Chicago Tribune*, February 19, 1983.

3. Gary Rivlin, *Fire on the Prairie: Chicago's Harold Washington and the Politics of Race* (New York: Holt, 1992); Rivlin, *Fire on the Prairie: Harold Washington, Chicago Politics, and the Roots of the Obama Presidency* (Philadelphia: Temple University Press, 2013); Florence Hamlish Levinsohn, *Harold Washington: A Political Biography* (Chicago: Chicago Review Press, 1983); Dempsey Travis, *Harold, the People's Mayor: An Authorized Biography of Mayor Harold Washington* (Chicago: Urban Research Press, 1988); Alton Miller, *Harold Washington: The Mayor, the Man* (New York: Bonus, 1989). Unless otherwise noted, this chapter cites the 2013 edition of Rivlin's book.

4. Rivlin, *Fire on the Prairie*, 103.

5. From the daily campaign and election coverage of the *Chicago Tribune* and *Sun-Times* to the most contextualized book-length accounts of Harold Washington's election and administration, analysis almost exclusively credits the interconnected rise of independent black political power and decline of the Democratic machine after Mayor Richard J. Daley's death. Even *Fire on the Prairie*, written by the *Chicago Reader*'s Gary Rivlin and considered by many to be the best of the Washington books, emphasizes these factors. Other accounts by journalists, sociologists, and political scientists—nearly all written in the 1980s or early 1990s—that frame Washington's campaign and administration similarly include William J. Grimshaw, *Bitter Fruit: Black Politics and the Chicago Machine, 1931–1991* (Chicago: University of Chicago Press, 1992); Paul Kleppner, *Chicago Divided: The Making of a Black Mayor* (DeKalb: Northern Illinois University Press, 1985); Melvin G. Holli and Paul M. Green, eds., *The Making of the Mayor, Chicago 1983* (Grand Rapids, Mich.: Eerdmans, 1984); Holli and Green, *Bashing Chicago Traditions: Harold Washington's Last Campaign, Chicago, 1987* (Grand Rapids, Mich.: Eerdmans, 1989); Abdul Alkalimat and Doug Gills, "Chicago—Black Power vs. Racism: Harold Washington Becomes Mayor," in *The New Black Vote: Politics and Power in Four American Cities*, ed. Roderick Bush (San Francisco: Synthesis, 1984), 53–179; Alkalimat and Gills, *Harold Washington and the Crisis of Black Power: Mass Protest* (Chicago: Twenty-First Century, 1989); Robert T. Starks and Michael B. Preston, "Harold Washington and the Politics of Reform in Chicago: 1983–1987," in *Racial Politics in American Cities*, ed. Rufus P. Browning, Dale Rogers Marshall, and David H. Tabb (New York: Longman, 1990), 88–107; Pierre Clavel and Wim Wiewel, eds., *Harold Washington and the Neighborhoods* (New Brunswick, N.J.: Rutgers University Press, 1991); Pierre Clavel, *Activists in City Hall: The Progressive Response to the Reagan Era in Boston and Chicago* (Ithaca, N.Y.: Cornell University Press, 2010), 96–145; Jeffrey Helgeson, *Crucibles of Black Empowerment: Chicago's Neighborhood Politics from the New Deal to Harold Washington* (Chicago: University of Chicago Press, 2014).

6. Holli and Green, *Bashing Chicago Traditions*, 17.

7. For more detailed—and generally sympathetic—accounts of how the machine

worked, see Milton Rakove, *Don't Make No Waves, Don't Back No Losers: An Insider's Analysis of the Daley Machine* (Bloomington: Indiana University Press, 1975); Rakove, *We Don't Want Nobody Nobody Sent: An Oral History of the Daley Years* (Bloomington: Indiana University Press, 1979); Mike Royko, *Boss: Richard J. Daley of Chicago* (New York: Plume, 1971).

8. Christopher Manning, *William L. Dawson and the Limits of Black Electoral Leadership* (DeKalb: Northern Illinois University Press, 2009); Rivlin, *Fire on the Prairie*, 51–53; Grimshaw, *Bitter Fruit*, 136–38; Clavel, *Activists in City Hall*, 118–52.

9. Jiménez, telephone interview by author, December 19, 2011.

10. Washington received 43,286 Latino votes. A few writers acknowledge this critical role but not in terms of class, and one of them—Doug Gills—credits progressive white support more. Rivlin, *Fire on the Prairie*, 124; Doug Gills, "Chicago Politics and Community Development: A Social Movement Perspective," in Clavel and Wiewel, *Harold Washington and the Neighborhoods*, 52; John Betancur and Douglas C. Gills, "The African American and Latino Coalition Experience in Chicago under Mayor Harold Washington," in *The Collaborative City: Opportunities and Struggles for Blacks and Latinos in U.S. Cities*, ed. John J. Betancur and Douglas C. Gills (New York: Garland, 2000), 59–87; Teresa Cordova, "Harold Washington and the Rise of Latino Electoral Politics," in *Chicano Politics and Society in the Late Twentieth Century*, ed. David Montejano (Austin: University of Texas Press, 1999), 31–57; María de los Angeles Torres, "Latino Politics in Chicago," in *Chicago's Future in a Time of Change*, 5th ed., ed. Dick Simpson (Champaign, Ill.: Stipes, 1993), 248–53.

11. A handful of scholars—all Latino—offer optimistic conclusions about Washington's impact on Latino politics, including John Betancur, a native Colombian. Betancur and Gills, "African American and Latino Coalition Experience"; Cordova, "Harold Washington and the Rise of Latino Electoral Politics"; María de los Angeles Torres, "In Search of Meaningful Voice and Place: The IPO and Latino Community Empowerment in Chicago," in *La Causa: Civil Rights, Social Justice and the Struggle for Equality in the Midwest*, ed. Gilberto Cardenas (Houston, Tex.: Arte Público, 2004), 81–106; Torres, "Latino Politics in Chicago," 248–53; Torres, "The Commission on Latino Affairs: A Case Study of Community Empowerment," in Clavel and Wiewel, *Harold Washington and the Neighborhoods*, 165–87.

12. Gordon K. Mantler, *Power to the Poor: Black-Brown Coalition and the Fight for Economic Justice, 1960–1974* (Chapel Hill: University of North Carolina Press, 2013).

13. On moments of success, see Jeffrey O. G. Ogbar, *Black Power: Radical Politics and African American Identity* (Baltimore, Md.: Johns Hopkins University Press, 2004), chap. 6; Laura Pulido, *Black, Brown, Yellow, and Left: Radical Activism in Los Angeles* (Berkeley: University of California Press, 2006); Shana Bernstein, *Bridges of Reform: Interracial Civil Rights Activism in Twentieth-Century Los Angeles* (New York: Oxford University Press, 2011); Lauren Araiza, *To March for Others: The Black Freedom Struggle and the United Farm Workers* (Philadelphia: University of Pennsylvania Press, 2013); George

Mariscal, *Brown-Eyed Children of the Sun: Lessons from the Chicano Movement* (Albuquerque: University of New Mexico Press, 2005), chaps. 5 and 6; Max Krochmal, "Labor, Civil Rights, and the Struggle for Democracy in Texas, 1935–1965"(PhD diss., Duke University, 2011). Of course, Carey McWilliams, *Brothers under the Skin* (Boston: Little, Brown, 1964), remains the classic study in this vein. On failure and the sometimes parallel nature of these struggles, see Behnken, *Fighting Their Own Battles*; Neil Foley, *Quest for Equality: The Failed Promise of Black-Brown Solidarity* (Cambridge, Mass.: Harvard University Press, 2010); Foley, "Partly Colored or Other White: Mexican Americans and Their Problem with the Color Line," in *Beyond Black and White: Race, Ethnicity, and Gender in the U.S. South and Southwest*, ed. Stephanie Cole and Alison M. Parker (College Station: Texas A&M University Press, 2004), 123–44; Foley, "Straddling the Color Line: The Legal Construction of Hispanic Identity in Texas," in *Not Just Black and White: Historical and Contemporary Perspectives on Immigration, Race, and Ethnicity in the United States*, ed. Nancy Foner and George M. Fredrickson (New York: Russell Sage Foundation, 2004), 341–54; Foley, "Becoming Hispanic: Mexican Americans and the Faustian Pact with Whiteness," in *Reflexiones: New Directions in Mexican American Studies*, ed. Neil Foley (Austin, Tex.: CMAS Books, 1997), 53–70; William S. Clayson, *Freedom Is Not Enough: The War on Poverty and the Civil Rights Movement in Texas* (Austin: University of Texas Press, 2010); Robert Bauman, *Race and the War on Poverty: From Watts to East L.A.* (Norman: University of Oklahoma Press, 2008); Matthew C. Whitaker, *Race Work: The Rise of Civil Rights in the Urban West* (Lincoln: University of Nebraska, 2005), chap. 6; Nicolás C. Vaca, *Presumed Alliance: The Unspoken Conflict between Latinos and Blacks and What It Means for America* (New York: Rayo, 2004); Bradford Luckingham, *Minorities in Phoenix: A Profile of Mexican American, Chinese American, and African American Communities, 1860–1992* (Tucson: University of Arizona Press, 1994); Peter Skerry, *Mexican Americans: The Ambivalent Minority* (New York: Free Press, 1993). Studies that fall in between these two interpretive poles include Mark Brilliant, *The Color of America Has Changed: How Racial Diversity Shaped Civil Rights Reform in California, 1941–1978* (New York: Oxford University Press, 2010); Brian D. Behnken, ed., *Struggle in Black and Brown: African American and Mexican American Relations during the Civil Rights Era* (Lincoln: University of Nebraska Press, 2012); Luis Alvarez, *The Power of the Zoot: Youth Culture and Resistance during World War II* (Berkeley: University of California Press, 2008); Sonia Song-Ha Lee, *Building a Latino Civil Rights Movement: Puerto Ricans, African Americans, and the Pursuit of Racial Justice in New York City* (Chapel Hill: University of North Carolina Press, 2014).

14. Sean Wilentz coined the term "Age of Reagan" and is one of several historians who ignore the alternative politics of the time. Wilentz, *The Age of Reagan: A History, 1974–2008* (New York: Harper, 2008); Gil Troy and Vincent J. Cannato, eds., Living in the Eighties (New York: Oxford University Press, 2009); Troy, *Morning in America: How Ronald Reagan Invented the 1980s* (Princeton, N.J.: Princeton University Press, 2005); John Ehrman, *The Eighties: America in the Age of Reagan* (New Haven, Conn.: Yale Uni-

versity Press, 2005); Steven F. Hayward, *The Age of Reagan, 1980–1989* (New York: Crown Forum, 2009); James T. Patterson, *Restless Giant: The United States from Watergate to Bush v. Gore* (New York: Oxford University Press, 2005); Philip Jenkins, *Decade of Nightmares: The End of the Sixties and the Making of Eighties America* (New York: Oxford University Press, 2005); Jefferson Cowie, *Stayin' Alive: The 1970s and the Last Days of the Working Class* (New York: New Press, 2010). One response to this interpretation also embraces the "Age of Reagan" moniker but offers a more complex take on the decade, including the responses observed in black politics and culture: Bradford Martin, *The Other Eighties: A Secret History of America in the Age of Reagan* (New York: Hill and Wang, 2011). Others who briefly acknowledge the alternative coalitions in the 1980s include Robert O. Self, *All in the Family: The Realignment of American Democracy since the 1960s* (New York: Hill and Wang, 2012); Thomas J. Sugrue, *Sweet Land of Liberty: The Forgotten Struggle for Civil Rights in the North* (New York: Random House, 2008).

15. My thinking here is influenced by several studies of black and Latino migration and the activism that often followed: Donna Jean Murch, *Living for the City: Migration, Education, and the Rise of the Black Panther Party in Oakland, California* (Chapel Hill: University of North Carolina Press, 2010); Marc Simon Rodriguez, *Tejano Diaspora: Mexican Americanism and Ethnic Politics in Texas and Wisconsin* (Chapel Hill: Published in association with the William P. Clements Center for Southwest Studies, Southern Methodist University, University of North Carolina Press, 2011); Lilia Fernández, *Brown in the Windy City: Mexicans and Puerto Ricans in Postwar Chicago* (Chicago: University of Chicago Press, 2012).

16. Don Rose, "The Independents—a Scenario for Success," *Chicago Tribune*, April 13, 1975.

17. Fernández, *Brown in the Windy City*, 210–11.

18. Juan Gómez-Quiñones, *Mexican-American Labor, 1790–1990* (Albuquerque: University of New Mexico Press, 1994), 225. For more on the CASA-HGT's origins and evolution from mutual aid society to Marxist-Leninist organization, see Laura Pulido, *Black, Brown, Yellow, and Left: Radical Activism in Los Angeles* (Berkeley: University of California Press, 2006), 117–20; Ernesto Chavez, *"¡Mi Raza Primero!": Nationalism, Identity, and Insurgency in the Chicano Movement in Los Angeles, 1966–1978* (Berkeley: University of California Press, 2002), 98–116.

19. Torres, "In Search of Meaningful Voice and Place," 89; Francisco Piña, "His Life," in *Rudy Lozano: His Life, His People* (Chicago: Taller de Estudios Communitarios, 1991), 53–56; Fernández, *Brown in the Windy City*, chap. 3; "Pilsen Celebrates a Victory," *Chicago Tribune*, September 17, 1975.

20. Rudy Lozano, "Notes from Labor Workshops," 1978, box 3, folder 21, and "Report and Daily Analysis of Daily Activities," 1980, box 3, folder 20, both in Rudy Lozano Papers, Special Collections and University Archives, University of Illinois, Chicago (hereafter RL); Robert Starks, interview in *Rudy Lozano*, 110; "'Larger in Death than in Life': Murder of Lozano Galvanizes Hispanics," *Chicago Tribune*, May 27, 1984.

21. CASA-HGT, "Local Report: Campaign of Resistance and Unity," 1977, box 3, folder 22, and "Report and Daily Analysis of Daily Activities," 1979–1980, box 3, folder 20, both in RL; "Jesse Charges Racism in Picking School Boss," July 20, 1975, "Blacks to Bypass Byrd Bypass," July 24, 1975, "Power Once More Eludes Powerless," July 25, 1975, "Climatic Effects on the Public Schools," July 30, 1975, all in *Chicago Tribune*; Starks, interview in *Rudy Lozano*, 113–14.

22. "House Gets Strong Bill on Job Bias," March 3, 1971, "Asks Appeal: House Unit Okays Stop, Frisk End," March 14, 1973, "Fight over State Employees' Pay Hikes Stalls Legislature," July 1, 1976, "Police Spying Curbs," June 15, 1977, and "Black Senators Seek Study of Alleged Property Tax Bias," April 20, 1979, all in *Chicago Tribune*; "An Interview with Harold Washington," *Chicago Reader*, March 4, 1977; Rivlin, *Fire on the Prairie*, 36–37; Robert Mier and Kari J. Moe, "Decentralized Development: From Theory to Practice," in Clavel and Wiewel, *Harold Washington and the Neighborhoods*, 72.

23. "Loses Promised Support: Washington Refuses Mayor Bid," January 22, 1977, "IVI Unit Picks Washington in Dem Mayor Bid," February 21, 1977, and "Union Group Backing Bid by Washington," March 17, 1977, all in *Chicago Tribune*; "An Interview with Harold Washington," *Chicago Reader*, March 4, 1977 (source of quote); IVI endorsement, March 31, 1977, and press releases, April 7 and 18, 1977, all in box 11, folder 3, Illinois State Senatorial Records, Harold Washington Archives and Collection, Chicago Public Library (hereafter HWAC); Grimshaw, *Bitter Fruit*, 150–51; Nena Torres, interview by author, June 27, 2012; Starks, interview in *Rudy Lozano*, 113–14.

24. Jorge Morales, interview by author, June 6, 2013; Torres, "In Search of Meaningful Voice and Place"; Carlos Arango, interview in *Rudy Lozano*, 122–23; U.S. Department of Commerce, *The 1980 Census of Population*, vol. 1: *Characteristics of the Population, Chapter B: General Population Statistics, Part 15, Illinois* (Washington, D.C.: U.S. Government Printing Office, 1982), 15–76.

25. Chuy Garcia, interview by John Betancur and Douglas Gills, box 1, folder 3, RL.

26. Torres, "In Search of Meaningful Voice and Place"; Garcia, interview by Betancur and Gills; Arango, interview in *Rudy Lozano*, 123; Cordova, "Harold Washington and the Rise of Latino Electoral Politics," 42.

27. The machine had chosen Bennett Stewart, a notoriously self-serving black alderman, to succeed Congressman Ralph Metcalfe after he died in 1978. Stewart served one term in Congress before losing handily to Washington. A mentor to Washington, the legendary Metcalfe had distanced himself from the machine over police brutality and the harassment of African American youth, famously saying "it's never too late to be black." Grimshaw, *Bitter Fruit*, 137, 153–54; Rivlin, *Fire on the Prairie*, 14.

28. "Washington Earned Reputation as Liberal: How They Voted," *Chicago Tribune*, April 3, 1983; Rivlin, *Fire on the Prairie*, 37–38; Wilentz, *Age of Reagan*, 141–44.

29. For the sanctuary movement in Chicago, see Robin Lorentzen, *Women in the Sanctuary Movement* (Philadelphia: Temple University Press, 1991). For more general accounts, see Susan Bibler Coutin, *The Culture of Protest: Religious Activism and the U.S.*

Sanctuary Movement (Boulder, Colo.: Westview, 1993); Miriam Davidson, *Convictions of the Heart: Jim Corbett and the Sanctuary Movement* (Tucson: University of Arizona Press, 1988).

30. "A Frightening Wave of Racial Violence," *Chicago Tribune*, January 9, 1981.

31. Nena Torres, interview by author; Modesto Rivera, interview by author, June 23, 2012; "Washington: A Thoughtful Legislator," February 24, 1983, and "Hispanics Use New Voting Rights Act to Reshape Texas Politics," April 25, 1983, both in *Washington Post*; "Illegal-Alien Plan Includes ID System," March 18, 1982, "U.S. Acts to Block Chicago Ward Remap," September 16, 1982, and "Benefits of Crackdown on Illegal Alien Worker Questioned," November 5, 1982, all in *Chicago Tribune*; *Ketchum v. Byrne*, 83-2044, 83-2065, 83-2126 U.S. (7th Cir. 1984); U.S. Senate, Subcommittee on the Constitution, Committee on the Judiciary, *Voting Rights Act*, pt. 1 (Washington, D.C.: U.S. Government Printing Office, 1982), 1646–50.

32. John Betancur and Doug Gills document this best; see their "African American and Latino Coalition Experience," 62.

33. "Neighborhoods Cry Foul over World's Fair," *Chicago Reader*, October 8, 1982; "Groups Seek Clearer Signals on World's Fair," September 17, 1982, "More Data Asked on World's Fair," March 1, 1983, and "Pilsen Coalition Says Fair Officials 'Shut Us Out,'" April 23, 1983, all in *Chicago Tribune*; Gills, "Chicago Politics and Community Development"; Mier and Moe, "Decentralized Development." See also Torres, "The Commission on Latino Affairs," 178–79; and the 1985 minutes of the Mayor's Advisory Commission on Latino Affairs, Chicago Historical Society.

34. "School Board Elections Aim of City 'Congress,'" August 23, 1982, and "Activist Groups Draft 'Platform' for City Races," August 30, 1982, both in *Chicago Tribune*; "The Washington Strategy," *Chicago Reader*, November 26, 1982; Rivlin, *Fire on the Prairie*, 47–49, 50–51; Kleppner, *Chicago Divided*, 136–43.

35. "Record Voter Sign-Up Here Relied on Blacks," October 3, 1982, and "City Report: Voter Sign-Ups May Hit Byrne," October 7, 1982, both in *Chicago Tribune*; Slim Coleman and George Jenkins, *Fair Share: The Struggle for the Rights of the People* (Chicago: Justice Graphics, 1989), 63–64.

36. Rivera, interview by author.

37. "Record Voter Sign-Up Here Relied on Blacks."

38. Paul Siegel, interview by author, June 7, 2013; "Record Voter Sign-Up Here Relied on Blacks."

39. "The Washington Strategy."

40. Statement of candidacy, November 10, 1982, box 45, folder 9, Mayoral Campaign Records, HWAC.

41. "Washington in Race for Mayor," *Chicago Tribune*, November 11, 1982; Jorge Morales, interview by author, June 6, 2013; "The Washington Strategy."

42. Cha-Cha Jiménez, telephone interview by author, January 20, 2012.

43. The West Town Coalition of Concerned Citizens operated out of the same store-

front in which Morales's small United Church of Christ congregation met. Social justice organizing and worship were interrelated and often put the organization at odds with the Byrne administration, which routinely tried to co-opt activists by offering city jobs and funding. Morales, interview by author.

44. *Chicago Defender*, March 19, 1983; Morales, interview by author.

45. Jiménez, interview by author; List of Latino Supporters, box 25, folder 17, Mayoral Campaign Records, HWAC. Other prominent Puerto Rican supporters were Peter Earle, who worked tirelessly for the Washington campaign, and a future congressman and alderman, Luis Gutiérrez. The latter cut his organizing teeth as a public housing activist but also worked as a cabbie to put himself through school. Gutiérrez, *Still Dreaming: My Journey from the Barrio to Capitol Hill* (New York: Norton, 2013).

46. Rudy Lozano for 22nd Ward alderman, flyer, 1983, box 4, folder 43, RL.

47. "CBUC Endorses Rudy Lozano," February 16, 1983, box 4, folder 46; Lozano campaign press release, February 16, 1983, box 4, folder 43; "The Residency Issue," *Chicago Sun-Times*, May 10, 1985, box 4, folder 44; and Lozano, press statement—Harrison High closing, January 12, 1983, box 5, folder 50, all in RL; "The Trouble with Harrison High," *Chicago Reader*, May 20, 1983; Torres, interview by author; Fernández, *Brown in the Windy City*, 263–68; Piña, "His Life," 65–67. The Chicago Black United Communities was Lu Palmer's organization, which rarely endorsed any nonblack candidates.

48. Kleppner, *Chicago Divided*, 208–11.

49. Peter Earle memo to Harold Washington, March 14, 1983, box 3, folder 4; Edwin Claudio, "Harold Washington's Program for Chicago's Latino Community," March 14, 1983, and Aida Giachello and Raul Hinojosa, "Proposal for a City of Chicago Commission on Latino Affairs," March 28, 1983, both in box 21, folder 3, and "En la Unidad Esta la Fuerza," 1983, box 4, folder 40, all in RL; Kleppner, *Chicago Divided*, 217–20.

50. "Mayor Gains Ground in Patronage Plea," May 24, 1983, "Judge Bars Mass Firings by Mayor," May 25, 1983, and "Mayor Writes to Appease Aides," June 2, 1983, all in *Chicago Tribune*. While reformist on its face, the Shakman decree meant that Washington "was stuck with" a lot of "political hacks of the opposition who now enjoyed the court's protection against political firing." Robert Brehm, "The City and the Neighborhoods: Was It Really a Two-Way Street?," in Clavel and Wiewel, *Harold Washington and the Neighborhoods*, 249; *Michael L. Shakman and Paul M. Lurie v. Democratic Organization of Cook County, et al.* 69 C2145 (N.D. Ill. 1972, 1983), http://www.shakmanmonitor.com/court_orders/1972_Consent_Decree.pdf and http://www.shakmanmonitor.com/court_orders/1983_Consent_Decree.pdf (both accessed November 1, 2013). The Shakman decree and monitor remain in effect.

51. Jiménez, interview by author.

52. Lozano's death produced an outpouring of grief from people across Chicago, including Harold Washington, who spoke briefly at his funeral. A multiracial procession, organized by veterans of the Washington campaign, marched down Eighteenth Street in Lozano's honor. His death remained in the news during the subsequent trial and con-

viction of gang member Gregory Escobar, which included accusations that Lozano had been assassinated for his antimachine and pro-union activities. "Washington Aide Lozano Is Killed," June 9, 1983, "Friends Claim Politics behind Lozano Killing," June 10, 1983, "Hispanics Mourn 'Son of the People,'" June 13, 1983, "Unity, Tears Mark Mass for Lozano," June 14, 1983, "Lozano Slaying Linked to Street Gang Rivalry," July 7, 1983, and "'Larger in Life than in Death': Lozano Murder Galvanizes Hispanics," May 27, 1984, all in *Chicago Tribune*; Jiménez and Torres, interviews by author; Gary Rivlin, "Who Killed Rudy Lozano?," *Chicago Reader*, 1985, box 4, folder 37, RL; "The Assassination," in *Rudy Lozano*.

53. Torres, interview by author. See also Torres, "The Commission on Latino Affairs," 165–87.

54. Torres, interview by author; "Latino Board Opposes World's Fair," *Sun-Times*, March 15, 1985; "Latino Blocks Elected School Board," March 16, 1985, and "Against World's Fair," March 20, 1985, both in *Chicago Defender*; MACLA, "The Proposed 1992 World's Fair: Consequences for Chicago's Latinos," 1985, box 1, folder 8, and MACLA meeting minutes, February 5, 1985, box 1, folder 3, both in Records of the Mayor's Advisory Commission on Latino Affairs, Chicago Historical Society.

CHAPTER 12

Southern Solidarities

U.S. Civil Rights and Latin American Social Movements in the Nuevo South

HANNAH GILL

In 2008, the summer that local police agencies throughout the Southeast started participating in the 287(g) immigration enforcement program, residents of Alamance County, North Carolina, noticed a brightly colored poster appearing on buildings. "Cuidado!!" (Caution!!), it warned, and then, in a font evocative of an old-time wanted poster, it continued in Spanish to describe why Hispanics should avoid the police "as if they were the devil": "Police are doing raids, traffic checks and deporting undocumented people. . . . be attentive and careful with these kidnappers." At the bottom of the broadside was a clue to its inspiration: instructions to view the web page of a museum exhibit of historical documents created during the times of slavery and abolition. It includes an advertisement from a Boston newspaper in 1851 warning escaped slaves of bounty hunters from the South. It reads, "Caution! Colored people of Boston . . . keep a sharp look-out for kidnappers and have a top eye open."[1]

Of course the poster's author, abolitionist Theodore Parker, did not realize that his message would resonate with communities more than 150 years later. Those communities were experiencing a different kind of persecution, but one that nevertheless involved identification by the color of their skin, arrest, and "repatriation" against their will. Indeed, the fears of the summer of 2008 anticipated more problems to come: in the next five years, deportations reached historic levels as thousands of immigrants were arrested in traffic checkpoints or for minor violations, and racial profiling lawsuits were filed across the nation.

The new immigration policies have complicated persistent problems that

Two Way Bridges | Puentes de Doble Via. Mural by artist Cornelio Campos (from Michoacán, Mexico) and others in Durham, N.C. Photo by Miguel Rojas Sotelo.

have long impacted communities of color in the United States. While slavery has been officially abolished in the United States for 150 years, the modern-day practices of racial profiling and mass incarceration continue to disproportionately affect African Americans, who make up nearly 1 million of the total 2.3 million incarcerated people in the United States. Criminal justice is one of many areas in which the struggles of migrants in new destination states resonate with the issues affecting other minorities. These issues are not just limited to law enforcement, but relate to many different historical and contemporary areas of shared struggle: poverty and unemployment, lack of political representation, voting disenfranchisement, and difficulties accessing education and health care. The legacy of slavery, the successes and ongoing struggles of U.S. civil rights movements, and the persistence of social and economic inequality provide the backdrop for the issues that immigrants in new destinations in the U.S. South face today. At the same time, Latin American immigrants—many of whom have been displaced for economic or political reasons—have brought their own histories of struggle to their new homes in the United States.[2] These experiences, both shared and distinct, form a strong foundation for new solidarities among human and civil rights activists in the U.S. South.

Scholars have written more about conflict than collaboration between Latino and African American communities, as Joel Alvarado and Charles Jaret note in their 2009 report, *Building Black-Brown Coalitions in the Southeast.*[3]

The few works on race relations in North Carolina reach similar conclusions. In her book examining immigration, race, and legal status in the eastern part of the state, Helen Marrow finds tensions between African American and Latino communities fueled by perceptions of job competition, anti-immigrant sentiment, and restrictive policies at local and state levels.[4] Paula McClain's study of the attitudes of Latino immigrants in a southern city found that they held negative stereotypical views of African Americans.[5] By contrast, this chapter examines the disparate historical struggles of subaltern groups in the United States and in Latin American countries and explores how they have come together in the contemporary transnational American South to advance shared agendas for social justice. Latinos have made important contributions to historical civil rights struggles in traditional destination states like California, New Mexico, Texas, and Florida, but are relatively new allies in states like North Carolina, where the demographic changes are comparatively recent. Using a transnational lens, I discuss interethnic cooperation and cross-racial civil rights organizing in the Nuevo South and demonstrate how activists from immigrant and native U.S. communities of color understand and articulate shared issues, exchange strategies and experiences to advance their work, and build coalitions. The legacy and ongoing work of the long U.S. civil rights movement has shaped immigrant integration efforts in service and advocacy organizations and in local governments.[6] Moreover, Latin American social movements have also helped black-brown solidarity efforts in North Carolina.

This chapter draws on twelve years of qualitative fieldwork in North Carolina communities. My fieldwork included the collection of 150 oral histories and interviews in 2007–2010 and 2013 with policymakers, activists, educators, business owners, and organizational leaders of immigrant and nonimmigrant origin across the state. The people I interviewed included individuals from Mexico, El Salvador, Guatemala, Colombia, the Dominican Republic, Haiti, Honduras, Costa Rica, and Ecuador. Participant observation was conducted in immigrant neighborhoods, schools, public and private universities, Latino-owned businesses, churches, sporting events, nonprofit organizations, courtrooms, and local government meetings. This chapter also draws from archival research in the New Roots oral histories, a collection of more than 150 digitized oral histories documenting immigrant perspectives in the Southeast, which were conducted by students and faculty at UNC, Chapel Hill.

DEMOGRAPHIC CHANGE IN THE SOUTHEASTERN UNITED STATES

The growth of Latino communities in the U.S. South since the 1980s is one of the most significant demographic changes in the recent history of the nation. Between 2000 and 2010 Latino populations doubled in seven southern states: Alabama, Arkansas, Kentucky, Mississippi, North Carolina, Tennessee, and South Carolina. In North Carolina, foreign-born populations grew at more than twice the national rate, while Latino populations increased by 111 percent to three-quarters of a million people.[7] While predominantly Mexican in origin, new Latino communities in the southern United States are made up of diverse peoples with ancestry in dozens of countries in the Caribbean, Central America, and South America. As migrants have put down roots in what scholars increasingly call the Nuevo South, they have opened a new and distinct chapter in the long history of Latin American migration to the United States, which has traditionally involved gateway regions in the Southwest, Florida, and the Northeast.[8] Latino migration is part of a larger demographic trend that includes people relocating from all parts of the United States to the Nuevo South, seeking to take advantage of the cheaper cost of living and economic opportunities, and the return of many African Americans to the South after the great twentieth-century migrations to northern and western cities.

North Carolina has figured prominently as a new destination for Latino migrants, and a growing body of literature has documented this phenomenon.[9] For three decades, Mexicans and Central Americans have been recruited to work in the construction, service, and agricultural industries—the historical work of African Americans. A smaller percentage of Latin Americans have arrived to work as high-skilled professionals or to study in the state's universities. Latinos are also permanently settling in the state. By 2017 there will be thirty thousand additional high school graduates in North Carolina, and twenty-two thousand of them will be Latino.[10] Demographers project that one in three children born in cities like Durham in the next ten years will be Latino.[11]

Some of these migrants have encountered significant obstacles to socioeconomic integration. The language barrier and a lack of legal status (3.5 percent of North Carolina's population was undocumented in 2010) have impaired immigrants' ability to earn livable wages, advocate for their rights, and access basic services and educational opportunities.[12] The work of migrants on farms in the eastern United States is among the most hazardous and lowest paid in the nation.[13] The North Carolina legislature, like many others across the country, passed successive laws in the 2000s to ban undocumented immigrants from obtaining driver's licenses and enrolling in the public university system as in-state students, effectively barring thousands of youth from college. The state also piloted 287(g) and Secure Communities, local-federal law enforcement partnership programs that facilitate deportations.[14]

Rather than achieving the mythical American dream that drove so many immigrants to the state, Latinos have experienced stagnant and even downward socioeconomic mobility in what scholars refer to as "segmented assimilation."[15] Latinos share many of the same challenges as African Americans and Native Americans: all three groups continue to face higher rates of poverty and unemployment and lower high school graduation and college entrance rates compared to whites and Asians in North Carolina. For example, in 2010 Latinos and African Americans earned $15,000 less on average than whites.[16] In 2012 the unemployment rate for African Americans was 17.3 percent, more than double the state's white rate, one of the greatest racial employment disparities in the nation.[17] Latinos and African Americans have the highest high school dropout rates statewide.[18] Poverty rates are also disproportionately high for African Americans and Latinos. Nearly 42.6 percent of Latino children and 40.2 percent of African American children lived in poverty in 2010 in North Carolina, while overall 33.9 percent of Latinos and 27.7 percent of African Americans lived in poverty, compared with 11.8 percent of whites.[19]

IMMIGRATION AND THE EXPANSION OF U.S. CIVIL RIGHTS AGENDAS

The U.S. civil rights movement has played an important role in shaping the modern U.S. immigration system and establishing structures to defend the rights of immigrants. Civil rights activists in the 1960s influenced the passage of the Immigration and Nationality Act of 1965, which abolished the national origins quota system, opening the door for Latin Americans and Asians to come to the United States in greater numbers.[20] Activists dismantled some of the last official forms of state-sponsored oppression with the passage of the Civil Rights Act of 1964 and the founding of the Equal Employment Opportunity Commission in 1965, and established a successful methodology for social change that has been influential in global social movements ever since.

In North Carolina, the organizations and enforcement structures born out of the U.S. civil rights movement have played an important role in immigrant advocacy and service provision. While hundreds of organizations and institutions have facilitated the economic and social integration of immigrants and their families since the early 1980s through direct service,[21] fewer organizations have engaged in policy advocacy because of widespread anti-immigrant sentiment and the antilobbying provisions governing nonprofit and public educational institutions.[22] Moreover, immigrant-serving organizations have been located primarily in urban centers, while rural parts of the state have had more limited basic service provision and less access to the activist networks in Raleigh, Chapel Hill, Durham, and Charlotte. (In the twenty-first century the landscape of immigrant advocacy in the state has shifted with the increased political activism of immigrant youth, who use social media to transcend geographical barriers across the state and nation.)[23] Organizations and institutions that have historically advocated for African American civil rights have alleviated some of these barriers to access by expanding their efforts to include immigrants. Some of the more established organizations with statewide reach are the N.C. Justice Center, the N.C. American Civil Liberties Union, the N.C. branch of the National Association for the Advancement of Colored People, the N.C. Council of Churches, the American Association of Retired Persons (AARP), the Manpower Development Corporation (MDC), and Self-Help, which have dedicated resources and staff for immigrant advocacy. Universities and colleges, another incubator of civil rights activism in the region, have expanded programs of study and research to focus on immigration and Latino studies.[24] Leaders in these and other organizations have been publicly active in articulating shared issues such as economic inequality, voting disenfranchisement, racial profiling and lack of access to health care. For example, when N.C. lawmakers introduced a voter ID bill (signed into law in August 2013) requiring residents to provide a photo ID when voting, the NAACP, the NC-ACLU, and other organizations launched a campaign to fight what they perceived as a major setback to African Americans and Latinos.[25]

In his "state of the state" address at the 2013 N.C. NAACP convention, the Reverend William Barber referred to shared issues when he told the audience that they were engaged in a new civil rights movement, and he described the many issues facing people of color, including Latinos. "With an upsurge in racism and hate crimes, criminalization of young black males, insensitivity to the poor, educational genocide, and the moral and economic cost of a war, we must stand together now like never before," he said.[26] The N.C. NAACP under Rev. Barber's tenure has also championed issues specific to immigration. The

NAACP's Fourteen Point People's Agenda includes demands to protect the rights of Latin Americans and provide immigrants with health care, education, workers' rights, and protection from discrimination. It also demands that all graduates of N.C. high schools be eligible for admission to state universities at in-state tuition rates; that federal lawmakers adopt comprehensive immigration reform; and that state and local law enforcement stop participating in the 287(g) program.[27] For the Reverend Elijah Freeman, a High Point native who was president of the N.C. NAACP in the 1990s, the inclusion of immigrant rights in the core activities of the organization is consistent with its long-held ideals. "Our basic mission," he noted, "is to address issues that affect people, period. African Americans happened to be the key target for the institution, but we have always reached beyond that premise. For every case that the NAACP wins or puts in front of the people, everyone benefits, not just the black folks."[28]

African American and Latino leaders in other organizations have also articulated their shared concerns at a number of events for black and brown unity. On October 3–4, 2008, the Beloved Community Center of Greensboro and partner organizations, including the Southern Anti-Racism Network, held a conference to explore "the interconnectedness of the cultures and struggles within African American and Latino communities." The Beloved Community Center, founded in 1991, identifies itself as an inheritor and steward of the historic civil rights organizing in the area, "drawing deeply from the life and work of movement leaders such as Dr. Martin Luther King, Jr. and Ella Baker."[29] The conference, attended by four hundred people, deepened the sponsoring organizations' relationships with "local and national organizations that also work to serve as community builders between African Americans and Latinos." The Beloved Community Center has subsequently addressed law enforcement profiling practices with its citizen police review board and continues to work with the Farm Labor Organizing Committee, an organization that negotiated a historic settlement in 2004 with the Mt. Olive Pickle Company to improve conditions and pay for migrant farmworkers.

Other events, such as the African American–Latino Unity Summit conference organized by the Charlotte-based Latin American Coalition in March 2009, have created space for discussions about "the treatment of workers, access to quality health care, and lack of political representation."[30] Similarly, the Black Immigration Network's national conference in 2012 in Atlanta, an event defined as "a united voice for racial justice and immigrant rights," brought together civil rights and immigrant advocates primarily from southern states.

At this event, Ajamu Dillahunt from the N.C. Justice Center, who is a founding member of Black Workers for Justice, framed issues across racial lines, drawing attention not only to contemporary structural inequalities, but also to shared histories of forced labor: "Labor and work—that's why we are here. [We have been] forced to do work, or forced to come here to do work. It's a thread that brings us all together."[31] This event was notable in its attempt to break down racial and ethnic dichotomies by discussing the shared racial identifications of African Americans and Latinos of African descent.

Moving beyond rhetoric, civil rights and immigrant rights leaders have worked together to engage thousands of native and new North Carolinians in social action and protest. For example, the NAACP's Moral Monday movement has mobilized tens of thousands of people since 2012; more than nine hundred have been arrested for civil disobedience. The Historic Thousands on Jones Street, an annual march in Raleigh that the NAACP and others started in 2007, has collaborated with immigrant rights organizations, such as the Association of Mexicans in North Carolina, El Pueblo, El Vínculo Hispano, the N.C. Dream Team, Reform Immigration for America, Student Action with Farmworkers, and El Kilombo. In Charlotte, the Latin American Coalition uses the strategies of lobbying and direct action advocated by Martin Luther King Jr. and other African American civil rights leaders. Other organizations have expanded their missions and devoted significant resources to legal advocacy. The N.C. Justice Center, one of the state's largest advocacy organizations for social justice, launched the Eastern Carolina Immigrants' Rights Project in 2007 and today has six dedicated staff members who provide legal services statewide. The ACLU fought to overturn the disenfranchisement of African Americans in the South in the 1920s, and today the N.C. branch dedicates resources and bilingual staff to the defense of immigrants, regardless of legal status.

LOCAL ACTIVISM AND COALITIONS

These examples illustrate how nonprofit, educational, and faith-based civil rights organizations have broadened their missions and actions to include immigrants. Until recently, few local governments, particularly in the South, have been part of efforts to promote equality and opportunity for immigrants. Local government plays an important role in residents' everyday lives, from the regulation of utilities, business permitting processes, emergency and law enforcement services, and housing to the opportunity for civic engagement through boards, commissions, and elected offices. The extent to which a city can communicate and engage with its diverse residents has important implications for economic development, public safety, and community relationships. While government bureaucrats have played a role in helping individual migrants, local governments in the South have made few formal efforts in these areas.[32] Rather, the nationwide trend for municipalities has been to restrict immigrants' rights in the twenty-first century.[33]

Since 2007, however, N.C. municipalities have started to engage with foreign-born communities to develop immigrant leadership capacity. Some municipalities have turned to their human relations commissions, structures within local governments originally created to enforce key legislation of the civil rights era, to devise solutions to improve the lives of immigrant residents. The High Point, Greenville, Orange, and Chatham counties' human relations commissions have engaged in substantive efforts to promote immigrant integration through communications and leadership development plans, cultural education, or by passing resolutions against restrictive programs like 287(g). In other parts of the United States where immigrants have joined the ranks of other minority groups facing multiple forms of persistent discrimination, human relations commissions have expanded their focus. In their historical review of human rights in the United States, Kenneth Saunders and Hyo Eun Bang noted a nationwide shift as Asian and Hispanic communities grew in the 1980s and 1990s: "The change in demographics and rising diversity called for changes in emphasis by human rights commissions."[34] In Los Angeles, the human relations commission has worked on immigration-related issues that include the treatment of undocumented individuals and securing affordable housing.[35] In Dayton, Ohio, the human relations commission has embraced a comprehensive plan to welcome immigrant newcomers.

Today, all states except for Alabama, Arkansas, and Mississippi have human rights and human relations commissions, which "share a common goal of preventing and eliminating discrimination through a diverse set of means, including enforcement of anti-discrimination laws, community outreach and awareness education, and training."[36] In North Carolina, local human relations commissions originated in a government body called the Good Neighbor Council, which was formed in 1963 by Governor Terry Sanford as an interracial committee charged with promoting nondiscriminatory employment practices in the private sector. Today there are fifty-seven local commissions that counties and cities call upon to deal with conflicts, provide diversity trainings, and investigate complaints of housing or employment discrimination.

In High Point and Greenville, cities with populations of around 100,000 people with more than 10 percent born in foreign countries, human relations commissions have embraced demographic change in constructive and inclusive ways. Both developed citywide comprehensive immigrant integration plans through a three-year planning process that engaged more than 350 foreign-born residents from more than twenty-five different countries.[37] High Point's immigrant integration action plan (approved in 2012) is comprehensive, involving all city agencies as well as multiple community institutions. Greenville's action plan (also approved in 2012) was designed around several priorities that included improving access to services and information, particularly about the city's public transit system and emergency services, which research revealed to be underutilized by foreign-born residents.[38]

Both municipalities adapted existing human relations programs and tools initially created to address the civil rights of minorities to make these programs more inclusive of immigrants. For example, High Point added educational content about the backgrounds of foreign-born residents to its Front Porch conversation series, a program designed to address social justice and diversity issues. The city reenvisioned an annual event as the Festival of Cultures and in May 2013 featured the performances of immigrant and refugee artists. It created a plan for the translation of the city website and utility bills into Spanish, Arabic, and Vietnamese. In its ongoing trainings for city agencies and community organizations on diversity and racial equity, the human relations commission now incorporates educational content about the cultural and religious backgrounds of its new residents. Greenville proposed the expansion of the city's free Lunch and Learn sessions to increase the cultural awareness of city staff.

The Reverend Elijah Freeman, who has served on the High Point Human Relations Commission since 1992, communicated his conviction that these commissions have an obligation to work with new immigrant communities: "Human relations needs to be a leader in develop[ing] a relationship between people of different backgrounds and origins."[39] Engaging and adapting existing structures and their own expertise in discussing community conflict and diversity, human relations staff and commissioners are well placed to address any tensions that may arise between African American and Latino communities. An expertise in housing discrimination issues, for example, enabled the

High Point Human Relations Commission's director, Al Heggins, to address fears among African Americans of being pushed out of low-income housing as landlords seek to attract what they may perceive as more upwardly mobile immigrant communities. "Have things improved for everyone? Or are we creating a new population of migrants, poor blacks and whites?" Heggins asked.[40] At the National Immigrant Integration Conference in Miami in November 2013, Heggins described how the human relations commission brings together Latino and African American community members in "trusted spaces" to engage in open dialogue about issues.[41]

Both municipalities also created permanent advisory structures to enhance immigrants' civic engagement and leadership opportunities. High Point established the Interfaith Affairs Committee (IFAC), a multiethnic/multiracial group designed to promote religious understanding by bringing people of diverse backgrounds together. High Point mayor Bernita Sims, a prominent African American leader in the state, issued a "welcoming proclamation" for High Point's immigrants in September 2013 that stated, "regardless of race, gender, creed, or country of origin, we are joined in the values of hard work and shared opportunity that define us as North Carolina's international city."[42] Rev. Freeman, who is the chairperson of the IFAC, noted the common factors that unify people with different backgrounds: "We are all here together as one. We are all America. . . . We've got to live together."[43]

Like the human relations commissions, new coalition groups have also worked to bring together different ethnic communities for a common purpose. The Durham-based North Carolina Latino Coalition (NCLC) has been effective in the twenty-first century at mobilizing thousands of people for immigrants' rights across the state by building strategic relationships with other underserved populations. The coalition, which is made up of church congregations, neighborhood associations, unions, and sports associations statewide, seeks to "strengthen the leadership, voice and participation of immigrants in local, statewide and federal issues."[44] Established in 2004 by Mauricio Castro, Ivan Parra, and other activists, the NCLC has worked closely with Durham CAN (Durham Congregations, Associations, and Neighborhoods), an organization that seeks to break down economic and racial divisions. The NCLC is also based in Durham, a city with a history of civil rights organizing, and works closely with African American church congregations. Focusing on common issues has led to robust multiracial participation rates; for example, at a meeting the coalition organized in October 2012 at the Union Baptist Church in Durham, a thousand delegates from grassroots community organizations across the state discussed the foreclosure crisis, veterans' issues, and immigration.[45]

The NCLC leaders use relational community organizing and direct action as their main strategies, drawing from their own activism in Latin America and from teachings of the Industrial Areas Foundation (IAF), a national organization established in 1940.[46] Today, the IAF trains leaders to develop relationships "that grow the voices of families and communities that have little power over decisions that impact their own lives."[47] The NCLC explicitly discusses the importance of IAF strategies on its website:

> Relational organizing requires developing relationships of trust among a diverse array of institutions and their leaders. Relationships develop through face-to-face conversations in which we share stories about our experiences and concerns. This is done through institution-based leadership development; the building of relationships within and between institutions; the identification of and research on issues of mutual self-interest; and disciplined, organized action.[48]

The IAF's emphasis on relationship building and networking resonated with the NCLC's current and founding directors, Mauricio Castro and Ivan Parra, who used similar strategies in their countries of origin in Latin America. Castro's organizing history, which is rooted in his native El Salvador, was influenced by liberation theology and its methods, which include grassroots organizing, mass demonstrations, and building coalitions across community sectors. Castro started organizing in the 1970s after learning about economic disparities—an issue that sparked civil wars throughout the region in the 1980s. In their work to create what he calls a "fair, honest, and just society where all have opportunity," Castro and his compatriots strategically form relationships with a diversity of people from all parts of the country.[49] They understand that issues have to be framed in ways that people from different socioeconomic and geographic backgrounds can care about.

Castro also gained important experience through his connections with other Latin Americans after he came to the United States in 1980 for political asylum. Arriving in Boston, he went to school for engineering and continued organizing among other Salvadoran and Latin American immigrants, with whom he shared ideas, strategies, and contacts. Many of these transnational activists continued fighting for social issues in their home countries by raising awareness in the United States about its foreign policy in Central America. Many also engaged in work to improve the abysmal conditions for Latinos in the United States, and they helped build a network of transnational human rights organizations across the United States to respond to the needs of the thousands of Central Americans fleeing wars and civil strife.[50]

After Castro moved to North Carolina in 1995, he played an important role in setting up many of the first institutions to provide services and advocacy for Latino migrants in the state, including El Centro Latino in Carrboro and the Latino Credit Union. In North Carolina, he found that among the predominantly Mexican immigrant population, Central Americans "were a different breed of Latinos."[51] He met Ivan Parra shortly after Parra emigrated from Colombia and was hired at the new El Centro Hispano in Durham. In 2004 they helped to start the N.C. Latino Coalition. When they heard about the IAF's organizational strategies through Durham CAN, Castro thought: "This sounds like what we did in El Salvador."[52]

Parra reflected on their work and its connection to the organizing strategies that built solidarity in Colombia: "We have lots of experience in organizing in Latin America through churches, communities of faith, the Catholic Church, attacking poverty. We rely on those same principles. . . . It's important to build intentional relationships, develop a good power analysis, and research before you start."[53] He underscored the importance of working with different groups around common issues, building solidarity. "We have worked with fourteen hundred immigrants, whites, and African Americans. We are not in the room by ourselves. We rely on the knowledge and wisdom and experience of others," he stated.[54] This philosophy is a cornerstone of the NCLC's structure, which engages its members through community meetings in which participants are encouraged to share testimonies of their own experiences. This tradition of *testimonios*, the telling and publicizing of firsthand accounts of violence, was a widespread strategy of Latin American solidarity movements in El Salvador, Honduras, and Guatemala in the last decades of the twentieth century.[55] Both Castro and Parra also stressed the importance of the legacy of U.S. civil rights organizing for contemporary immigrant rights movements. "A lot of the strategies we use come from African American movements of the 1960s," noted Parra at a gathering of the MDC (a civil rights organization) in Durham in November 2013.

An important asset in the work of the NCLC is its leaders' experience with divisive issues in their countries of origin, where violence and conflict became normalized reactions to dissent, particularly during the 1980s and 1990s. "Backlash is necessary for social change. . . . It's impossible to think about social change without controversy," said Parra.[56] Castro and Parra maintain that their work is long term and that social transformation can take generations or more. This perspective is useful considering that political and economic strife continues to be the primary motivation for Latin American migration to the United States. "We are invested in a long-term struggle," said Parra.[57] In this way, they have found common ground with veterans of the 1960s U.S. civil rights struggles, who are still working to improve conditions for North Carolina's communities of color.

WITNESS FOR PEACE

The example of the N.C. Latino Coalition illustrates how Latin American activists have influenced the immigrant rights movement in their new homes in North Carolina. But U.S. citizens have also been involved in Latin American social movements for many decades, participating as transnational activists in Central American solidarity movements and in educational exchanges, and they have adopted these organizing strategies and applied them to their work for immigrant rights in North Carolina. Witness for Peace is an example of an organization shaped by the experiences, strategies, and philosophies of Latin American social movements. The organization started in North Carolina in 1983 in response to the U.S.-backed guerrilla war against the Sandinista government in Nicaragua, and over the course of the decade it sparked a national movement as thousands of Americans traveled to Nicaragua to witness and report on the impacts of war. Following the resolution of that conflict, the organization broadened its mission to "support peace, justice, and sustainable economies in the Americas by changing U.S. policies and corporate practices that contribute to poverty and oppression in Latin America and the Caribbean."[58] Over the years, according to co-founder Gail Phares, Witness for Peace has taken fifteen thousand people to Latin American countries.

The movement, which has been described as a "joint effort of U.S. and Nicaraguan people of conscience," was based strongly on the tradition of *testimonios*. "Witness [for Peace] sought out the testimony of the victims and publicized their words as widely as possible," noted Ed Griffin-Nolan.[59] In his history of the organization, Griffin-Nolan described the influence of Latin American liberation theology on the many delegates from the United States: "Latin America had become an even more important place for those, particularly Christians, seeking to understand and live out an integral life joining religious belief and political commitment. North American Christians had become aware of . . . a theology that spoke of liberation and working toward the reign of God here and now."[60] This theology was compelling for social-minded individuals and congregations around the United States, which engaged in the political act of expressing solidarity with the Nicaraguan people.[61]

Also important in the organization's model was building relationships between U.S. and Nicaraguan citizens and an immersion in communities embroiled in conflict. Witness for Peace delegates stayed in villages under siege, and some were even kidnapped by militias of the U.S.-backed Contra rebels, as in the case of North Carolinian Richard Boren.[62] This deep engagement with individuals and communities in Latin America continues to be a cornerstone of its work, enabling the ongoing exchange of ideas, strategies, and experiences between Latin Americans and North Carolinians. In the twenty-first century Witness for Peace has organized delegations to Cuba, Mexico, Colombia, and Honduras that sought to better understand issues related to immigration, labor rights, and U.S. military aid in Latin America. What began as a movement to support the Nicaraguan people in the 1980s has shifted to address immigrants' rights in the United States today.

Witness for Peace's model of engagement has been used by many other organizations in North Carolina to educate people about the history of Latino migration to the state and to raise awareness about human rights issues. For example, the Center for International Understanding, the Worldview Program, the Office of Durham Regional Affairs, the CHICLE Language Institute, and universities and colleges across the state have used this model of education through direct engagement: "The goal is to provide educators and policy leaders with firsthand experiences in Mexico to help them reach informed solutions to local challenges that come with changing demographics."[63] These exchanges provide North Carolinians with the educational background and personal relationships to facilitate continued involvement and advocacy.

North Carolina's deepening connections to Latin America have compelled educational institutions to sponsor Latin American figures to visit the state, which has resulted in another important resource for the exchange of Latin American ideas, experiences, and strategies. Since the 1980s the University of North Carolina and Duke University have brought in hundreds of Latin American social activists, artists, politicians, and writers. Sergio Berenstein, Isabel Allende, Carlos Fuentes, Victor Montejo, and Nicario Jiménez Quispe are among the many Latin Americans who have traveled to North Carolina to talk about their work in Argentina, Chile, Mexico, Guatemala, and Peru as part of public events, ongoing conferences, film festivals, or university courses in which ideas are exchanged, debated, and further disseminated. These visits play an important role in educating the general public and future leaders, and they facilitate communication between native North Carolinians and Latin American immigrants. "With the wars there was tremendous interest in Central America, and with these stories, people looked at Latino immigrants in the state in a different light. For those involved, these visits were influential in getting the larger community to notice and care about new migrants," said Sharon Mújica, the outreach coordinator for the Duke-UNC Consortium of Latin American and Caribbean Studies from 1983 to 2009.[64]

CONCLUSION

In North Carolina, the civil and human rights struggles of the United States and Latin American countries have come together to inform social justice movements. U.S. civil rights organizations have deepened their institutional commitments to immigrant communities and adapted existing programs to move beyond black-brown collaborations. The examples in this chapter illustrate how contemporary immigrants' rights efforts, particularly in the Nuevo South, must be understood in the context of the historic U.S. civil rights movement, which paved the way for the migration of Latin Americans to the United States, established many of the nation's legal structures for the defense of immigrants' rights, and developed successful methodologies for social change.

At the same time in North Carolina, this U.S. civil rights framework has incorporated Latin American paradigms and experiences and has been influenced by Latin American leaders and organizations with strong roots in Central American solidarity movements and with connections to transnational networks of migration and educational exchange. This work not only has advanced immigrant rights agendas in the state in recent decades, but has been important for building solidarity with civil rights leaders and organizations in shared geographical spaces in North Carolina. Leaders from immigrant and native communities of color understand and articulate shared issues, exchange strategies and experiences to advance their work, and build coalitions. The practice of sharing the lessons learned from these disparate pasts will strengthen relationships across racial and ethnic lines as Latinos and other immigrant communities continue to join the ongoing civil rights movement in southern states. This approach calls attention to the many possibilities for transnational idea exchange, which may ultimately lead to social equity in the Nuevo South.

These collaborations have important implications for immigrants' rights activism across the region and the country. In addition to forming coalitions around specific issues in the fight for social and economic equity, leaders from U.S. and Latin American civil and human rights movements share a common temporal perspective of an ongoing struggle and a long track record of successes and failures. This shared view of social justice as a continual work in progress has steeled immigrant advocates to persist in their work even though the U.S. Congress has continually failed to pass comprehensive immigration reform. It has also buoyed immigrant rights activists' repeated attempts to pass in-state tuition bills in the N.C. General Assembly. This long-term perspective is particularly valuable for the Dreamers, the new generation of youth activists who form the most persuasive force in immigrant rights movements today. Through mass mobilization and personal revelations of their own "illegality," the Dreamers have exposed the dysfunction of U.S. immigration laws in a manner that echoes the civil disobedience of African Americans in defiance of Jim Crow laws in the 1960s. As activists face yet another legislative battle to reform the U.S. immigration system, the legacies of adversity and solidarity provide a foundation and continuing inspiration for the ongoing fight.

NOTES

1. Lost Museum website, http://chnm.gmu.edu/lostmuseum/lm/307/ (accessed November 1, 2013). This chapter uses the terms "Hispanic" and "Latino" interchangeably.

2. Many Central Americans fled civil wars in the late twentieth century, while a Mexican recession in the 1980s exacerbated poverty and motivated many to look for better economic opportunities in the United States. Latin Americans with African and indigenous roots have a history of enslavement and subjugation by European colonists.

3. Joel Alvarado and Charles Jaret, *Building Black-Brown Coalitions in the Southeast: Four Case Studies of African American–Latino Collaborations* (Atlanta, Ga.: Southern Regional Council, 2009).

4. Helen B. Marrow, *New Destination Dreaming: Immigration, Race, and Legal Status in the Rural American South* (Stanford, Calif.: Stanford University Press, 2011).

5. Paula D. McClain, "North Carolina's Response to Latino Immigrants and Immigration," in *Immigration's New Frontiers*, ed. G. Anrig and T. A. Wang (New York: Century Foundation Press, 2006), 7–32.

6. This chapter uses the framework of the "long civil rights movement" to acknowledge the ongoing struggles of many different groups since the 1960s, when African American activists and their allies fought to end racial segregation and discrimination and to enforce constitutional voting rights. See Jacquelyn Dowd Hall, "The Long Civil Rights Movement and the Political Uses of the Past," *Journal of American History* 91, no. 4 (March 2005): 1233–63. Although I focus on the continuation of economic and race-related issues relevant to African American and Latino communities, many of these issues are also relevant to the civil rights struggles of other ethnic and racial groups, women, and gays and lesbians. Using this framework, I refer to some entities in this chapter as "civil rights" organizations because they were active during the 1960s and 1970s or, in the case of more recently formed organizations, because of their commitment to these historic and ongoing struggles.

7. U.S. Census Bureau, 2000, http://www.census.gov/main/www/cen2000.htm (accessed November 1, 2013).

8. Jorge Durand, Douglas Massey, and F. Charvet, "The Changing Geography of Mexican Immigration to the United States, 1910–1996," *Social Science Quarterly* 81 (2000):1–15; Rubén Hernández-León and Victor Zúñiga, "Appalachia Meets Aztlan: Mexican Immigration and Intergroup Relations in Dalton, Georgia," in *New Destinations: Mexican Immigration in the United States*, ed. V. Zúñiga and R. Hernández-León (New York: Russell Sage Foundation, 2005), 244–73.

9. David Griffith, *Jones's Minimal: Low-Wage Labor in the United States* (Albany: SUNY Press, 1993); Hannah Gill, *The Latino Migration Experience in North Carolina: New Roots in the Old North State* (Chapel Hill, University of North Carolina Press, 2010); Paul Cuadros, *A Home on the Field: How One Championship Team Inspires Hope for the Revival of Small Town America* (New York: HarperCollins, 2006); Hernández-León and Zúñiga, "Appalachia Meets Aztlan," 244–73.

10. "UNC Tomorrow Commission Report," http://www.northcarolina.edu/ (accessed November 1, 2013).

11. *Durham's Immigrant Communities: Looking to the Future* (Chapel Hill: Latino Migration Project, University of North Carolina, 2012).

12. Jeffrey S. Passel and D'Vera Cohn, *Unauthorized Immigrant Population: National and State Trends, 2010* (Washington, D.C.: Pew Hispanic Center, 2011).

13. Melinda F. Wiggins, "Farm Labor and the Struggle for Justice in the Eastern United States," in *Latino Farmworkers in the Eastern United States*, ed. Thomas A. Arcury and Sara A. Quandt (New York: Springer 2009).

14. Mai Nguyen and Hannah Gill, *The 287(g) Program: The Costs and Consequences of Local Immigration Enforcement in North Carolina* (Chapel Hill: Latino Migration Project, University of North Carolina, 2009).

15. Alejandro Portes and Min Zhou, "The New Second Generation: Segmented Assimilation and Its Variants," *Annals of the American Academy of Political and Social Science* 530, no. 1 (1993): 74–96.

16. U.S. Census Bureau, 2010, http://www.census.gov/2010census/ (accessed November 1, 2013).

17. Mary Gable and Douglas Hall, "Unemployment Rate for African Americans Fourth in Nation, More than Double the State's White Rate," issue brief of the Economic Policy Institute, May 16, 2013, http://www.epi.org/publication/ongoing-joblessness-north-carolina-unemployment/ (accessed September 15, 2013).

18. N.C. Department of Public Instruction, "2011–2012 Grade 1–13 Dropouts by School, Gender, Race/Ethnicity," http://www.dpi.state.nc.us/docs/research/dropout/reports/2011-12/113countbylea.pdf (accessed November 15, 2013).

19. N.C. Budget and Tax Center, "Analysis of United States Census, American Community Survey, Five-Year Averages, 2006–2010," http://www.law.unc.edu/documents/poverty/events/factsheet_firstleg.pdf (accessed September 15, 2013).

20. Douglas Massey, Jorge Durand, and Nolan Malone, *Beyond Smoke and Mirrors: Mexican Immigration in an Era of Economic Integration* (New York: Russell Sage Foundation, 2002), 41.

21. Organizations across the state offer a multitude of services for immigrants: interpretation/translation, English-language classes, financial literacy, legal assistance, civic education around rights and responsibilities, medical care, professional development, crisis management, and cultural activities.

22. Most commonly, these efforts take place in nonprofit organizations with national, state and local ties; institutions of higher education, including community colleges and universities; K–12 public schools; religious organizations; and state- and locally funded social service agencies.

23. It is important to note that the vast majority of immigrants are not able to participate or engage directly with service or advocacy organizations, which are mostly located in areas with comparatively greater resources.

24. At UNC, Chapel Hill, there are more than fifteen student organizations dedicated to service or advocacy for Latino immigrants.

25. The U.S. Justice Department filed a lawsuit in October 2013 against the state of North Carolina over provisions of the bill that allegedly violate the Voting Rights Act.

26. Blog of Rev. Dr. William Barber II, http://jimbuie.blogs.com/barber/ (accessed December 1, 2013).

27. Website of the N.C. NAACP, http://www.naacpnc.org/14_point_agenda (accessed December 1, 2013).

28. Reverend Elijah Freeman, interview by author, April 27, 2013.

29. Website of the Beloved Community Center, http://www.belovedcommunitycenter.org/ (accessed December 1, 2013).

30. Alvarado and Jaret, *Building Black-Brown Coalitions in the Southeast.*

31. Video footage of the Black Immigration Network's 2012 national conference in Atlanta, Ga., http://www.youtube.com/watch?v=GszZ1u9lVtk (accessed August 1, 2013).

32. Marrow, *New Destination Dreaming*, 228.

33. National Conference on State Legislatures, "2007 Enacted State Legislation Related to Immigrants and Immigration," http://www.ncsl.org/research/immigration/2007-enacted-state-legislation-related-to-immigran.aspx (accessed December 1, 2013).

34. Kenneth Saunders and Hyo Eun Bang, "A Historical Perspective on U.S. Human Rights Commissions," Executive Session on Human Rights Commissions and Criminal Justice, Kennedy School of Government, Harvard University, June 2007, http://www.hks.harvard.edu/index.php/content/download/67465/1242670/version/1/file/nhri.pdf (accessed May 19, 2015).

35. Philip Ethington and Christopher West, "The Challenge of Intergroup Relations in Los Angeles: An Historical and Comparative Evaluation of the Los Angeles City Human Relations Commission, 1966–1998" (unpublished paper, 1998), Department of History and the Southern California Studies Center of the University of Southern California, http://www.usc.edu/dept/LAS/SC2/pdf/lachrc.pdf (accessed August 10, 2013).

36. Saunders and Bang, "A Historical Perspective on U.S. Human Rights Commissions."

37. These efforts were part of an initiative called Building Integrated Communities and were supported by the University of North Carolina, Chapel Hill, and the Z. Smith Reynolds Foundation.

38. Hannah Gill et al., *Building Integrated Communities in High Point, NC* (Chapel Hill: Latino Migration Project, University of North Carolina, 2014).

39. Freeman, interview by author.

40. CBS, "Hundreds of Immigrant Advocates Gather in Miami," November 18, 2013, http://miami.cbslocal.com/2013/11/18/hundreds-of-immigrant-advocates-gather-in-miami/ (accessed December 1, 2013).

41. Author's field notes from the National Immigrant Integration Conference, November 18, 2013, Miami, Fla.

42. Gill et al., *Building Integrated Communities in High Point, NC*, 61.

43. Freeman, interview by author.

44. Website of the N.C. Latino Coalition, http://latinocoalitionnc.org/ (accessed October 1, 2013).

45. Ibid.

46. Cesar Chavez and other Latino leaders worked with the IAF, using organizing principles they used with the United Farm Workers.

47. Website of the Industrial Areas Foundation, http://www.industrialareasfoundation.org/ (accessed October 1, 2013).

48. Website of the N.C. Latino Coalition, http://latinocoalitionnc.org/?page_id=29 (accessed June 2, 2015).

49. Mauricio Castro, interview by author, October 22, 2013.

50. Héctor Perla, "Central American Counterpublic Mobilization: Transnational Social Movement Opposition to Reagan's Foreign Policy toward Central America," *Latino Studies* 11 (2013): 167–89.

51. Castro, interview by author.

52. Ibid.

53. Author's field notes from a public presentation by Ivan Parra at the MDC in Durham, N.C., November 12, 2014.

54. Ibid.

55. Ed Griffin-Nolan, *Witness for Peace: A Story of Resistance* (Louisville, Ky.: Westminster/John Knox, 1991), 20.

56. Ibid.

57. Ibid.

58. Website of Witness for Peace, http://www.witnessforpeace.org/section.php?id=81 (accessed November 15, 2013).

59. Griffin-Nolan, *Witness for Peace*.

60. Ibid., 39.

61. Edward T. Brett, *The U.S. Catholic Press on Central America: From Cold War Anticommunism to Social Justice* (Notre Dame, Ind.: University of Notre Dame Press, 2003).

62. "American, 12 Others Reported Seized in Contra Raid," *Los Angeles Times*, March 5, 1988.

63. Website of the Center for International Understanding, http://ciu.northcarolina.edu/what-we-do/ (accessed October 1, 2013).

64. Sharon Mújica, pers. comm., December 11, 2013.

CONTRIBUTORS

BRIAN D. BEHNKEN is an associate professor in the Department of History and the U.S. Latino/a Studies Program at Iowa State University. He is the author of two monographs, *Fighting Their Own Battles: Mexican Americans, African Americans, and the Struggle for Civil Rights in Texas* (2011) and, with Gregory Smithers, *Racism in American Popular Media: From Aunt Jemima to the Frito Bandito* (2015), and he has edited two collections, *The Struggle in Black and Brown: African American and Mexican American Relations during the Civil Rights Era* (2012) and, with Simon Wendt, *Crossing Boundaries: Ethnicity, Race, and National Belonging in a Transnational World* (2013).

DAN BERGER is an assistant professor of comparative ethnic studies at the University of Washington at Bothell. His research focuses on critical race theory and U.S. social movements, with a particular emphasis on the carceral state. He has published and organized widely on these subjects. Berger is the author or editor of several books, including *Outlaws of America: The Weather Underground and the Politics of Solidarity* (2006), *The Struggle Within: Prisons, Political Prisoners, and Mass Movements in the United States* (2014), and *Captive Nation: Black Prison Organizing in the Civil Rights Era* (2014).

HANNAH GILL is the assistant director of the Institute for the Study of the Americas and a research associate at the Center for Global Initiatives at the University of North Carolina at Chapel Hill. She is the author of *The Latino Migration Experience in North Carolina: New Roots in the Old North State* (2010).

LAURIE LAHEY is an instructor in the Africana Studies Department at the University of South Florida, where she teaches courses on racism in American society and the African diaspora. She is currently working on a monograph, "'The Grassy Battleground': Race, Religion, and Activism in Camden's 'Wide' Civil Rights Movement," which considers interracial alliances in the civil rights movement in Camden, New Jersey.

KEVIN ALLEN LEONARD is a professor in the History Department at Western Washington University. He is the author of *The Battle for Los Angeles: Racial Ideology and World War II* (2006).

MARK MALISA is an assistant professor at the College of Saint Rose in Albany, New York. He is the author of *(Anti)Narcissisms and (Anti)Capitalisms: Human Nature and Education in the Works of Mahatma Gandhi, Malcolm X, Nelson Mandela and Jurgen Habermas* (2010) and "Songs for Freedom: Music and the Struggle against Apartheid," in *The Routledge History of Social Protest in Popular Music* (2013). His research interests include education and pan-Africanism.

GORDON MANTLER is an assistant professor of writing at the George Washington University. He is the author of *Power to the Poor: Black-Brown Coalition and the Fight for Economic Justice, 1960–1974* (2013).

ALYSSA RIBEIRO is a research scholar at the Center for the Study of Women at the University of California, Los Angeles. She specializes in late twentieth-century urban history, race, and ethnicity. She is currently revising a book manuscript titled "Making the City Brotherly: Black and Latino Community Activism in Philadelphia, 1960s to 1980s."

OLIVER A. ROSALES is an associate professor of history at Bakersfield College, Delano. He is currently revising his dissertation, "'Mississippi West': Race, Politics, and Civil Rights in California's Central Valley, 1947–1984," into a book manuscript.

CHANELLE NYREE ROSE is an associate professor in the Department of History at Rowan University. She is currently revising her dissertation, "Neither Southern nor Northern: Miami, Florida, and the Black Freedom Struggle in America's Tourist Paradise, 1896–1968," into a book manuscript.

JAKOBI WILLIAMS is an associate professor in the Department of African American and African Diaspora Studies and the Department of History at Indiana University. He is the author of *From the Bullet to the Ballot: The Illinois Chapter of the Black Panther Party and Racial Coalition Politics in Chicago* (2013).

INDEX